GOD UNIVERSE AND MAN

THE HOLY QURAN AND THE HEREAFTER

GOD UNIVERSE AND MAN

THE HOLY QURAN AND THE HEREAFTER

ENGR: FATEH ULLAH KHAN

KITAB BHAVAN
New Delhi -2 [India]

KITAB BHAVAN
Publishers, Distributors, Exporters & Importers
1784, Kalan Mahal, Darya Ganj
New Delhi-110002 [India]

Phones : (91-11) 3274686, 3277392, 3277393
E-Mail : nasri@nda.vsnl.net.in
Website : http://www.kitabbhavan.com
Fax : (91-11) 3263383

First Published in India 1999

ISBN 81-7151-261-5

Laser Typesetting at :
Laser Track
1784, Kalan Mahal, Darya Ganj
New Delhi-110002 [India]

Printed & Published in India by :
Nusrat Ali Nasri for Kitab Bhavan
1784, Kalan Mahal, Darya Ganj
New Delhi-110002 [India]

To my wife

SAEEDA FATEH

A Word to the Readers

The source of inspiration for writing this book is my wife who often used to ask me the explanation of the allegorial verses with arcane meanings specially those which describe the scientific matters about the physical universe and man while reading the Holy Quran. This motivated me to study and thoroughly ponder over the Holy Quranic verses, grasp the sense and the substance of the verses and tried to understand their meanings and sense in the context of the knowledge of the natural sciences of all living and non-living physical objects in the universe mentioned by the Holy Quran. As a result of thorough contemplation I have found to my utter surprise that there is a great similarity of the knowledge of all natural sciences describing the physical universe and man with the Quranic verses revealed 1400 years ago when there was absolutely no knowledge of the natural sciences and the people were ignorant. These facts directly lead man to logical conclusion (and also by inferences it is derived) that the Holy Quran is undoubtedly the Word of Allah and that the creation of the physical universe and all its objects and man himself are His portents and tokens so that man could derive wisdom out of the marvels of the creations of Allah. And that these tokens and the knowledge encompassed about them in the Holy verses 1400 years ago lead mankind to know that undoubtedly there is the Creator behind the creation Who is Allah and the Holy Quran in which these are described is His message to all mankind for guidance. The Holy Quran further informs man about the reality of the 'Hereafter', i.e. the absolute certainty of the life after death of mankind which is eternal.

I am grateful to my wife who became the source of inspiration for my humble piece of work. Because of this, I know more and more attributes of Allah as the Creator of man and the universe and of all things, and His Last Messenger Prophet Muhammad (PBUH) who revealed the Holy Quran, the message of God, for the guidance of all mankind which reveals the doctrines of Eschatology and tells about the life after death in the 'Hereafter'.

Description of Terms and Their Meanings

The description of some of the terms mentioned in the Holy Quran is given so as to facilitate the reader in understanding their meanings and the sense that they convey.

These are the following:-

Allah, Prophet Muhammad (PBUH), Revelation, the Holy Qurán, Islam, the Hereafter, the 'Doomsday', the Resurrection, the Accountability, the Day of Judgement, and the method of quotation of the Quranic Verses, their location by giving Chapter or (Surah) and verse number, (PBUH) and Eschatology.

Allah:

The Arabic word Allah (the stress is on the last syllable) is used for the word 'God'. There is no corresponding word in English for Allah. The word Allah has neither feminine nor plural and has never been applied to anything other than the 'Unimaginable Supreme Being'.

Allah is Unity The Creator, Sustainer and Restorer of the worlds. There is no God but Allah and Muhammad (PBUH) is His Last Prophet, on whom the Holy Quran was revealed by inspiration for the guidance of all mankind. Muhammad (PBUH) is the Last Prophet and the Holy Quran is the Last Heavenly Book in which all the previous heavenly Books are consummated.

Prophet Muhammad: (PBUH)
(570 - 632 A.D)

Muhammad, son of Abdullah, son of Abdul Muttalib of the tribe of Qureysh, was born at Mecca fifty three years before the

Hijrah, which corresponds to 570 A.D. His father died before he was born and his mother died when he was six years old. He was brought up by his grandfather, Abdul Muttalib. After the death of his grandfather, when Muhammad (PBUH) was eight years old, he was brought up by his uncle, Abu Talib. He travelled with his uncle in merchant's Caravan to Syria and some years afterwards made the same journey in the service of a wealthy widow named Khadijah. He faithfully conducted the widow's business and so excellent was the report of his behaviour that she requested him for marriage. He remained devoted to his wife for 26 years when she died. This marriage gave him rank among the notables of Mecca, while his conduct earned for him the surname Al-Amin, the 'Trustworthy'.

The First Revelation:

Prophet Muhammad (PBUH) was in the cave of Mount (Hira) near Mecca, when he heard a voice say: 'Read'! He said: 'I cannot read.' The voice again said : 'Read'. He said: 'I cannot read.' A third time the voice, more commanding said : 'Read'! He said, 'What can I read?' The voice said:

'Read: In the name of thy Lord Who createth, (XCIV:1) ·
'Createth man from a clot or something which clings.' (XCIV:2) ·
'Read: And it is thy Lord the Most Bountiful'. (XCIV:3) ·
'Who teacheth by pen.' (XCIV:4) ·
'Teacheth man that which he knew not'. (XCIV:5) ·

The words remained 'as if inscribed upon his heart'. He went out of the cave on to the hillside and heard the same awe inspiring voice say: 'O Muhammad! Thou art Allah's messenger, and I am Gabriel.' Then he raised his eyes and saw the angel, in the likeness of a man, standing in the sky above the horizon. And again the commanding voice said: 'O Muhammad! Thou art Allah's messenger and I am Gabriel'.

The Quran or 'Reading'

Literally, Quran means Reading.

The angel Gabriel on Mount Hira bade him 'Read'! insisting on 'Reading' though Prophet Muhammad (PBUH) was illiterate — the sacred Book is known as Al-Quran, 'The Reading', the Reading of the man who knew not how to read: Quran is the final, perfect revelation of the eternal Book, revealed by inspiration through angel Gabriel on Prophet Muhammad (PBUH) by Allah. It is an infallible divine Book and is the true word of God that was revealed on Prophet Muhammad (PBUH) and the revelations were collected in book form after his death.All the Surahs of the Holy Quran had been recorded in writing before the Prophet's death and many Muslims had committed the whole Quran to memory. Quran is a heavenly Book and teaches the absolute truth in all matters, legal, religious, scientific, economic, social and spiritual.

The Quran cannot be translated to choose befitting language and corresponding words, as the Glorious Quran is inimitable symphony. Translation into any language can never take the place of the Quran in Arabic.

Islam:

The Arabic term Islam, literally meaning Surrender' or submission to the Will of One Allah (God) and acceptance of His Commands as revealed in the Holy Quran. Islam stands for peace of mind as well as peace between individuals and peace among nations leading to stability, progress and prosperity and to adopt a iife devoid of excesses.

Hereafter:

The 'Hereafter' means 'Life after Death'. The Hereafter is an eternal world for mankind, when after death he is resurrected for accountability and judgement to stay immortal in the metaphysical world of the Hereafter.

Doomsday:

Doomsday means the Catastrophic Collapse of the universe, or the gravitational collapse of the universe, when all physical things in the universe shall be reduced to nothing.

Resurrection:

Resurrection means to come back to 'Life after Death', on the Day of Judgement in the Hereafter.

Accountability:

This means the accountability of the good and bad deeds and actions of mankind performed in the physical world or this universe, which are recorded and which shall be produced in the Hereafter on the 'Day of Judgement' for award of Paradise or Hell as the case may be.

Day of Judgement:

The 'Doomsday' shall be the Day of Judgement for all mankind when accountability of good and bad deeds and actions shall take place and award given, either Paradise or Hell.

Quotations:

Quotation of 'Verse' or Passage with its 'Surah' or Chapter from the Holy Quran is referred to or indicated as follows:-

(20:4) Or (XX:4) means Surah or Chapter No. 20 and the verse No. 4.

PBUH:

This is an abbreviation of Peace Be Upon Him.

Eschatology

This means death, resurrection, accountability, judgement and immortality.

(In the name of Allah, the Beneficent, the Merciful.)

Preface

THE MIRACULOUS SIMILARITY OF SCIENCE WITH THE HOLY QURAN ON THE CREATION OF UNIVERSE AND MAN PROVE THAT THE QURAN IS NOT MAN-MADE AND IS THE WORD OF GOD AND TEACHES MAN THE PURPOSE OF HIS CREATION AND REVEALS TO HIM THE 'LIFE AFTER DEATH' CR THE HEREAFTER

This book is addressed to the entire mankind, specially to the Scientists and Thinkers, the Religious Heads and the Heads of all Nations of the World who are cordially invited to read it with open mind and ponder over the absolute Truth, Wisdom, Knowledge, Informations and Guidance of the Glorious Quran, the divine Message of God from beyond the seven heavens, revealed on Prophet Muhammad (PBUH) for the mercy and guidance of mankind 1400 years ago. The Holy Quran reveals miracles of physical truths and scientific facts recently uncovered about the physical universe and man and reveals wonders of the 'Hereafter' or the Metaphysical truths beyond the comprehension and understanding of man. It is found that all established laws of science are in complete similarity with the Holy Quran describing the universe and man. The heavenly Quran gives its proof that it is not man-made and that it cannot be man-made. The Holy Quran reveals that there is the Creator Who is Allah, the One God and Lord of the Worlds and of mankind.

This presentation attempts to explain and analyse along scientific lines, the tremendous sense and wisdom contained in allegory in the verses of the Holy Quran in the context of modern knowledge of science at the level of Black holes, particle physics, singularity and zero volume, Molecular and Cell Biology, RNA DNA, Chromosomes, Genetics, Exo-biology and Eschatology. It is surprising to find miraculous similarity and congruity of science in all its disciplines and branches with the Holy Quran in respect of the creation, evolution and the 'Doomsday' of the universe or the Catastrophic Collapse of universe and on the origin of life and the first creation of man (Adam) in Paradise beyond the earth and then the divine broadcast of Adam and his race to earth where they are (sown) seeded on earth to grow as a growth from the earth by the process of reproduction and to undergo development through the process of the normal universal physical laws and the multiplication of Adam's race on earth which is fixed as the abode of man till an appointed period of the 'Doomsday' or the gravitational collapse of the universe to nothing.

In this book, the author (who is a Civil Engineer by profession) has analysed just a few Holy verses in the context of science as it is a colossal task for various teams of scientists and experts to work over long periods for the study and analysis of all such verses of the Holy Quran which specifically reveal the science of creation of universe and man either in allegory or in direct form and the purpose of the creation of man and the universe and reveal about the reality of life after death i.e. the Hereafter.

The book further explains the similarity of the science of Exobiology and the reality of the existence of extra-terrestrial life in the boundless and inviolable universe as is revealed in the Holy Quran. The Holy Quran reveals the existence of life in an absolutely different form and different environment created out of different substances. It reveals the reality of the existence of invisible creature, the jinn, an intelligent living creation parallel to man, but in absolutely different shape and life supporting zone. This is besides the existence of invisible Angels having two wings or dimensions or power, to multi-dimensional angels which freely move and cross the barriers of the physical and metaphysical universe by the Command of God. In addition to the above, the Quran reveals that there is extra-terrestrial life in the universe where different languages are spoken. However man is preferred above many of those whom God created with a marked preferment. God created man and perfected him with a soul and gave him the ability of thinking and intelligence and inspired him with conscience to choose the path of his conduct and to distinguish between the right and the wrong.

The book explains to the reader to know the Creator of the heavens and the earth (Allah) from His infinite attributes and from

His Infinite Creative and Obliterative Powers through sound knowledge of physical matter and other sciences and faith and through the study of the physical universe and its visible and invisible objects and of man himself, in the light of the revelations of the Holy Quran. The created objects and the creatures serve as the portents and marvels of the Creator, Allah. The Holy Quran is full of wisdom, knowledge, information and guidance and is a document full of miraculous revelations revealing the ultimate reality of the existence of Allah as the Creator of all creations. Allah is the Omnipresent, the Omniscient, the Omnipotent, the Omnificent, the Omnific, the Living, the Eternal, the One and the Doer of what He will.

The complete similarity of science in all its branches with the Holy Quran revealed 1400 years ago conspicuously and vividly indicates beyond all doubts that the Holy Quran is a divine message, the word of God for man and is not man-made and cannot be man-made. Science has hardly a beginning of less than 500 years and modern science less than one hundred years but miraculously all modern discoveries and inventions are already present in the Holy Quran either in allegory or in direct form.

The truthful Quran — the Message of God, further reveals and teaches man to have faith in the unseen and in the invisible which lie beyond the understanding capability of man — as man's knowledge is limited and he is created so and is a creature on earth where he is subjected to unlimited physical limitations and barriers in the inviolable universe. Man cannot encompass realities beyond his limited capacity and limited power of understanding and knowledge. The Creator has therefore revealed the Holy Quran for the knowledge, information and guidance of man to know his Creator and to know the physical universe and man and to know the metaphysical world of the 'Hereafter' and to know the purpose of man's creation on earth for an appointed period. Thus, absolute faith and belief in the revelation of the Holy Quran, which is the Word of God and the belief in the unseen and in the invisible of the Holy Quran are among the fundamental doctrines of Islam and are the teachings of the Holy Quran, which lead man to know Allah and to know His message and His Messenger and to know the purpose of man's creation and to know the doctrines of Eschatology. Man must have unflinching faith in these fundamental doctrines as revealed in the divine message.

Man's knowledge of physical sciences with his inspired conscience and faith all together are in consonance with the truth described by the Quran in respect of the mysterious physical universe and man and its mysterious objects like 'black holes' and 'DNA' etc. This clearly indicates and leads to the belief that the Quran is obviously a divine message from God to man for his guidance. The Quran guides and teaches about the nature of the physical universe and man and about life and death and about life after death'. The Quran spans the two worlds in knowledge and informs man about his Creator and the purpose of man's creation.

Similarly and also by inferences, the doctrines of Eschatology of the Quran i.e. (death, resurrection, accountability, judgement and immortality in the Hereafter) are true and are necessary for requital to complete the mission for the creation of man. Man's knowledge of sciences, his common sense and his inspired conscience in the light of the Quran develops his faith and lead man to believe in the reality of the doctrines of Eschatology. Life after death starts on the resurrection of man in the Hereafter. His accountability and trial as a requital for his deeds, shall take place and a judgement announced accordingly. Man shall become immortal in the Hereafter and shall stay there eternally.

The Hereafter is a wonderful world, very pleasing and a world of unimaginable happy state. The Holy Quran gives the concept, the certainty and the reality of 'life after death', i.e.of the Hereafter, an immortal world and a world of Eternity, happiness and a place of abundance where man will get all that for which his soul desires. The universe and man as such, are not created in play by the Creator.

ENGR. FATEHULLAH KHAN

Contents

CHAPTER 10

CHAPTER 11

Part IV

CHAPTER 12

Part I

THE CREATION OF PHYSICAL UNIVERSE IN THE LIGHT OF THE HOLY QURAN

CHAPTER I	Knowledge, Meditation and Faith, the sources to understand the allegorial sense and the substance of the Holy Quran.
CHAPTER II	The Holy Quran the source of knowing the Infinite Attributes of the 'Unimaginable Supreme Being' The Almighty God, the Eternal, the Alive, the Creator of man and of universe and of all things and the Lord of the worlds and of mankind and of the 'Hereafter'. The concept of time after sleep and death and on the resurrection of man. The spirit is not life but two different things.
CHAPTER III	Man's inspired conscience, his wisdom, knowledge of sciences and faith can seek guidance from the Holy Quran to know the physical realities of universe and man and metaphysical realities of the 'Hereafter'
CHAPTER IV	God's Revelations of the Holy Quran by Inspiration on Prophet Muhammad (PBUH) when physical laws yielded to pass the Divine Message to his heart.
CHAPTER V	The physical world and the metaphysical world as the two different creations of Allah for mankind.

CHAPTER VI AND CHAPTER VII	Science in similarity with the Holy Quran on the creation, evolution, the interaction of matter and energy and on the Doom of the Inviolable Universe and then its re-emergence. Hubble's Law of Expanding Universe and Einstein's Theory of Relativity and many other laws in similarity with the Holy Quran.

In the Name of Allah, the Beneficent, the Merciful

Chapter I

KNOWLEDGE OF SCIENCE, WISDOM AND FAITH, THE MEANS TO UNDERSTAND AND GRASP THE LIGHT OF WISDOM OF THE HOLY QURAN

UNDERSTANDING THE LIGHT OF WISDOM OF THE HOLY QURAN — THE DIVINE MESSAGE OF GOD FOR MANKIND

The study of the Holy Quran reveals that it is a divine Scripture, the Word of God and reveals absolute truth for the guidance of all mankind. It is not man-made and cannot be man-made. The proof of this lies in the verses of the Holy Quran itself and in the substance which each verse reveals and in the script of it. More than 850 verses of the Holy Quran concerning scientific matters amazingly reveal physical facts of science on the creation, evolution and the ultimate obliteration of the universe and man. The Holy verses reveal astounding realities as far back as 1400 years ago about many physical objects (living and non-living) in the universe and on earth recently discovered. Thorough contemplation of the Holy Quran reveals that its verses encompass wisdom, knowledge information and guidance either in allegory or in direct conclusive form. Each verse contains scientific concepts and fundamental principles of the basic sciences, physical laws and the forces governing all that which exist in the universe and on earth. Latest discoveries and inventions of science concerning the creation of the universe and man are already present in the Holy Quran and are mentioned esoterically in an allegorial form. All that is required, is wisdom, knowledge and faith for grasping and understanding the esoteric and allegorial substance of each verse in the context of modern knowledge of sciences. It is found that knowledge of science about the universe and man and the sense contained in the verses of the Holy Quran are in similarity to an amazing and astounding degree. The Creator has already revealed in allegory, the basic principles of creations for the knowledge and information of mankind about more than a thousand years before man made a beginning to know and study the universe and man through the basic physical sciences as the tokens or the signs from the Creator Allah. Science has hardly a beginning of 500 years but the Holy Quran containing all these physical realities of the universe and man were revealed to the unlettered Prophet Muhammad (PBUH) by inspiration 1400 years ago. The presence and the mention of such physical and metaphysical realities in the Holy Quran for more than a thousand years before the beginning of science, gives direct proof that the Holy Quran is a heavenly Book and is the Word of Allah for the guidance of all mankind. It is in fact, the greatest divine document full of miracles, wisdom and guidance for all times. Man learns through science which makes progress day by day and knows more and more about the physical realities of the universe. Man's knowledge is therefore limited and is merely confined to the physical objects in existence within the observable limits.

The Holy Quran reveals total realities i.e. the visible, the invisible, the unseen, the known and the hidden. It reveals realities which are invisible, unseen, hidden and metaphysical. Realities of such types are undetectable by man and science. These realities lie beyond the scope of science and are thus beyond the understanding capacity and perception power of man.

As explained above, it is an established fact that the Holy Quran contains absolute realities about the physical universe and man and about the living and non-living creation of the physical universe, and science is found to be in similarity with it. This similarity and its presence as back as 1400 years ago, shows a great significance and is a proof that the Holy Quran is a heavenly Book and the Word of God for mankind.

Similarly, the Holy Quran contains absolute realities about the invisible, the unseen, and metaphysical matters and events, but in this field science is helpless as it is beyond its scope to probe for anything which is metaphysical. So, faith and belief is the source and the built-in power of man to grasp and understand the substance of the Holy Quran in the context of verses encompassed with wisdom and knowledge. Man's senses and inspired conscience substitute for science and one is guided and inspired by conscience and by the divine 'spirit' or 'soul' in man to believe in the unseen and the invisible mentioned by the Holy Quran as the absolute truth. God has inspired man with conscience and created him as the best of creation. The gift of 'conscience' by nature is a great quality infused in man to believe in the Holy Quran as the Word of God and to believe in the physics and metaphysics of the Holy Quran and to believe in One God Who is Allah, the Creator of man and of all things including the 'Hereafter'.

The Holy Quran reveals:-

(1) *'And a soul and Him Who perfected it' (XCI:7).*

(2) *'And inspired it (with conscience of) what is wrong for it and (what is) right for it' (XCI:8).*

The author in this presentation explains from various angles in various chapters, how physical sciences are in similarity and congruity with the Quranic verses revealing the realities of the physical universe and man, and the metaphysical realities and events in the 'Hereafter'. Modern knowledge of physical sciences describing physical universe and man, is in similarity with the Holy Quranic verses. The similarity of science with the Holy Quran revealed 1400 years ago indicates that the Holy Quran is the divine Scripture, the Word of God and is not man-made and cannot be man-made. So, all that which is revealed by the Holy Quran is absolute truth and it is incumbent on all mankind to obey and follow the Word of God and completely submit to the Will of Allah, the Creator of mankind.

It is beyond all doubt that the Holy Quran is from Allah — the Lord of the Worlds whose portents are the creation of man himself and all things on earth and all things in the seven heavens including our heaven or the universe, which is the nearest. Allah is the Lord of the 'Hereafter', which is the eternal abode of mankind after the doom or the catastrophic collapse of the universe. The Holy Quran is the conclusive Word of Allah. It is for mankind to believe in it and obey and worship Allah.

The Holy Quran reveals:-

(1) *'The revelation of the Scripture is from Allah, the Mighty, the Knower'* (39:2), (40:2), (46:2) and (45:2).

(2) *'The revelation of the Scripture whereof there is no doubt is from the Lord of the Worlds'* (32:2).

(3) *'Lo! in the heavens and the earth are portents for believers'* (45:3).

(4) *'And in your creation and all the beasts that He scattereth in the earth, are portents for a folk whose faith is sure'* (45:8)

(5) *'These are the portents of Allah which We recite unto thee (Muhammad) with truth. Then in what fact, after Allah and His portents, will they believe'?* (45:6).

(6) *'Lord of the heavens and the earth and all that is between them, if ye would be sure'* (44:7).

(7) *'And We have made (this Scripture) easy in thy language only that they may heed'* (45:58).

(8) *'By the Scripture which maketh plain'* (43:2) and (44:2).

(9) *'Lo! this (Quran) is a conclusive word'* (86:13).

The above Quranic verses revealed 1400 years ago on Prophet Muhammad (PBUH) categorically state that the Holy Quran is the true and conclusive Word of Allah. All creations in the universe including man are the portents of Allah. It is therefore incumbent on mankind to understand the absolute wisdom of the Glorious Quran and be enlightened from the divine message of God to man on earth. Sound knowledge with faith is the key to understand the wisdom of the Quran, which is a guidance and a mercy for people who believe. Each word and every verse of the Holy Quran is encompassed with tremendous wisdom and knowledge and surprises man of knowledge to his utter astonishment. Efforts are made to grasp the sense in some of the Quranic verses in the light of the lasted knowledge of natural sciences and it is amazing to find that science is in great similarity with the Holy Quran.

Knowledge—The Source of Understanding the Holy Quran

Science is systematized knowledge derived from observation study and experimentation, so as to find the nature or principles of what is being studied and is in constant pursuit of finding the truth about the physical universe and the living man.

Science is constantly changed and enlarged and grows to embrace more of nature as man learns and yet there is no vision of an ideal system that might embrace the whole of nature. Thus, we speak of no absolute truth in science, as we cannot cross all frontiers of knowledge to know the absolute reality through physical laws. We only seek in our postulates 'agreement with observed facts'. We lurch after exactitude and every time it appears within our grasp, it takes another step away towards infinity.

Recently, Mr. Fitch and Mr. Cronin, the two Physicists have proved that the Laws of Symmetry are inviable and that the universe is asymmetrical. This turn of events is so profoundly disturbing that, a number of new Einsteins would be needed to explain what it means. The implicit message of Bohr's Quantum theory is that the universe is incomprehensible.

Thus, science in the process of study will go on changing and improving in an attempt to become true science but every time it will find itself to be nowhere near the true science.

Knowledge and faith are the sources to understand the meanings of the revelations made in the Holy Quran. In this respect the Holy Quran reveals:-

> *'He detaileth the revelations for people who have knowledge' (10:5).*

The Holy Quran needs no proof of perfection as Allah has revealed on His Prophet Muhammad (PBUH) the Holy Quran which is a perfect Book of absolute truth and guidance for all mankind. Science, (which is systematized knowledge derived from the study and observation of nature and its principles), for lack of knowledge and limitations shall continue to remain imperfect in the inviolable universe and that scientific theories will go on improving and changing with time and gradually become more accurate, whereas, the Words of Allah, (the Creator of the Universe and the earth and all that is in between), are immutable, eternal and perfect reality. Again, scientists who study the Holy Quran and ponder over its verses and have thorough knowledge of it, are capable of receiving motivation and inspiration from the Holy Quran. The Holy Quran is not a text-book of science, but it is a Holy Scripture, the Word of Allah, the absolute truth revealing wisdom and knowledge, guidance and information in the form of allegorial and symbolic hints to mankind who believe in the Unseen and the Invisible. Science and religion are not the two competing forces. Rather the

Holy Quran and the religion of Islam teach wisdom and knowledge to mankind for their guidance, which ultimately leads mankind to know Allah the Creator of all things. The physical sciences probe realities and help in the achievement of knowledge of the observable creations of Allah, which serve as His portents so that man knows Allah. Science is man's efforts to know physical things in the universe, whereas the Holy Quran is the Word of the Creator (Allah) Who created the physical and the metaphysical worlds which includes all things i.e. the visible, the invisible, the unseen and the hidden of physical and metaphysical in nature and including man and the design of his thinking capabilities for acquiring the knowledge of physical sciences.

The Holy Quran reveals:-

(1) *'Praise be to Allah, Lord of the Worlds' (2:1)*

(2) *'Verily We have brought them a Scripture which We expound with knowledge, a guidance and a mercy for people who believe' (7:52).*

(3) *'This is the Scripture whereof there is no doubt, a guidance unto those who ward off (evil)' (3:2).*

(4) *'Who believe in the Unseen and establish worship and spend of that We have bestowed upon them' (3:3).*

(5) *'And who believe in that which is revealed unto thee Muhammad and that which was revealed before thee and are certain of the Hereafter' (3:4).*

(6) *'As for the disbelievers, whether thou warn them or thou warn them not, it is all one for them; they believe not' (3:6).*

(7) *'Allah hath sealed their hearing and their hearts and on their eyes there is a covering. Theirs will be an awful doom' (3:7).*

(8) *'Deaf, dumb and blind and they return not' (2:18).*

(9) *'O! mankind! worship your Lord, Who hath created you so that ye may ward off (evil) (5:21).*

The Holy Quran contains numerous hair-raising, awe inspiring and mysterious realities which are interspersed through its verses.

Certainly, the Holy Quran is the Word of Allah and reveals the absolute truth, the Divine truth about the physical universe, the living man and about the unseen, the invisible, the hidden and about the 'Hereafter', as Allah is the Creator of the heavens and the earth and all that is in between, including life and death and life after death (77:2), (3:2) and (3:4). The Holy Quran is a guidance for those who believe in it. The metaphysics of Quran has a link with the physical universe and man, and invites attention of all mankind to life after death. This is a great contribution by Islam to civilize mankind so that he is ready for accountability of his deeds on Resurrection on the 'Day of Judgement' in the 'Hereafter'.

Science has no access to probe and know about the 'Hereafter' i.e. life after death, and about the 'spirit' of living man. Science is confined to the knowledge of the physical universe, therefore, it is permanently beyond the scope of science to throw light on that aspects of the absolute truth which is Divine in nature and is not perceptive to physical observations. For example, to know how 'energy' and 'matter' i.e. the substance, composing the physical universe was originated in the beginning out of 'naught' or 'nothing', and to know what 'life' is and how it was originated? To know, what is the jinn (the invisible living creature), and the Angels (the invisible living creation of superior nature bestowed with great power and capabilities in the physical and metaphysical worlds), and many other invisible, hidden and unseen matters of physical nature and of other type. Similarly, it is beyond the scope of science to explain the 'Hereafter' and all Divine matters which are to take place in the 'Hereafter'.

The Divine message of the Holy Quran reveals wisdom and knowledge to mankind and tells about the Creator Allah, and His creations of the physical universe and the creation of man himself which is bodily physical but is living due to Allah's infused 'spirit' and consciousness in him. The spirit in man is therefore divine in nature and is distinct from matter and is not physical. The 'Hereafter' is totally a different world and is unseen, but is certainly a great reality, which the Holy Quran reveals. Knowledge of Science and the perceptive power of man is only limited to the observable physical universe. Man can never probe metaphysical matters. Science of religion has no limits and goes beyond the physical universe. The Holy Quran is the only source to reveal the metaphysical matters and the 'Hereafter'.

The Holy Quran reveals:-

'Praise be to Allah, unto whom belongeth whatsoever is in the

heavens and whatsoever is in the earth. His is the praise in the Hereafter and He is the Wise, the Aware'. (34:1).

Science is the means to understand the physics of Quran and to understand the religion of Islam and its doctrines taught by the Holy Quran.

The fact is that true religion and true science ever lead to the same great end of knowing Allah, Who is the Creator of the universe and of the 'Hereafter', and is the Lord of the Worlds. The 'Hereafter' is a much better world and is eternal, whereas the physical universe is temporary and is subject to 'time', or period which in turn is appointed and limited and is destined for a gravitational collapse.

Most modern science is found to be in similarity with the Holy Quran on all fundamental matters of physical nature. This is explained in the various chapters of this book. The similarity is so great that it completely surprises man and leads man to believe that the Holy Quran is the Word of God. Science has a beginning of only about 500 years ago. Before that little was known to man and ignorance mostly prevailed. The Holy Quran reveals basic physical facts and events of the universe and man, more than 1400 years ago. The realities contained in the holy verses are described in allegory which is the style of the Holy Quran and men of learning can understand it if they ponder and study the Holy Quran word by word.

Chapter 2

QURANIC DESCRIPTION OF ALLAH AS THE ABSOLUTE, THE ETERNAL, THE ALIVE AND OF INFINITE ATTRIBUTES AND THE LORD OF THE WORLDS AND OF MANKIND

The concept of God (Allah) is beyond the comprehension of mankind. Allah is unimaginable. Allah is Able to do all things at His Simple Command: Be! and it is. Hence, the recourse is to allegorial verse in the Holy Quran, which gives description of Allah, but that is beyond human understanding. However, it indicates that Allah is the Alive, the Eternal and of Infinite attributes with each attribute to Infinity. He is the Knower and the Creator of All things.

Allah is the One and is the unimaginable Supreme Being. Allah is the Eternal and Infinite self-glowing Divine Power with All knowledge, All wisdom and All power and is Able to do All things. He creates All things the moment He wishes and obliterates All things the moment He wishes. Allah speaks to mankind in allegory for He is the Knower of all things and gives allegorial description of Himself in the Holy Quran in the verse (24:35) which is:

> *'Allah is the Light of the heavens and the earth. The similitude of His light is as a niche wherein is a lamp. The lamp is in a glass. The glass is as it were a shining star. (This lamp is) kindled from a blessed tree, an olive neither of the East nor of the West, whose oil would almost glow forth (of itself) though no fire touched it. Light upon light, Allah guideth unto His light whom He will. And Allah speaketh to mankind in allegories for Allah is the Knower of all things' (24:35).*

The above Holy verse (24:35) which gives the description of Allah is purely allegorial and it is impossible to imagine and understand and interpret the allegorial description of Allah as Allah is unimaginable and the Invisible. What is possible to conceive and grasp is the sense of Supreme Living, Eternal and Infinite self-glowing Divine power of Allah. It is therefore beyond man's power to be able to conceive the unimaginable allegorial description of Allah from the above Holy verse. What is possible to know is that He is Infinity upon Infinity in all things. He is the Creator and the Knower of all things. Allah only speaks to mankind in allegory and by inspiration through prophets and Prophet Muhammad (PBUH) is the Last of the Prophets on whom the Holy Quran was revealed. Man knows Allah from His Infinite attributes and from all His creations which are His portents and handicrafts and from the revelations and the teachings of the Holy Quran which is Allah's own inspired word.

Besides the allegorial description of Allah in the above holy verse, the Holy Quran reveals many direct attributes of Allah in many other Quranic verses. Some of the Holy verses on Allah's attributes are as follows which may be read with the above holy verse (24:35).

The Holy Quran reveals :

(1) *'Allah! There is no God save Him, the Alive, the Eternal' (45:255) and (53:3).*

(2) *'Your God is One God: There is no God save Him, the Beneficent, the Merciful' (26:163).*

(3) *'This is a clear message for mankind in order that they may be warned thereby and that they may know that He is Only one God and that men of understanding may take heed' (14:52).*

(4) *'He is Allah, than whom there is no other God, the Knower of the invisible and the visible. He is the Beneficent, the Merciful' (60:22).*

(5) *'Your God is one God'. (18:110) and (41:6).*

(6) *'Allah (Himself) is witness that there is no God save Him. And the angels and the me of learning (too are witnesses). Maintaining His creation in justice, there is no God save Him, the Almighty, the Wise' (III:18).*

(7) *'He it is Who fashioneth you in the wombs as pleaseth Him. There is no God save Him, the Almighty, the Wise' (II:6).*

(8) *'He is the Living One. There is no God save Him. So pray unto Him, making religion pure for Him (only). Praise be to Allah, the Lord of the worlds!' (40:65).*

(9) *'Allah is the Creator of all things, and He is Guardian over all things' (39:62).*

(10) *'His are the keys of the heavens and the earth and they who disbelieve the revelations of Allah — such are they who are the losers' (39:63).*

(11) *'He created you from one being, then from that (being) He made its mate; and he hath provided for you of cattle eight kinds. He created you in the wombs of your mothers, creation after creation, in a three-fold gloom. Such is Allah, your Lord. His is the Sovereignty. There is no God save Him. How then are ye turned away' (39:6).*

(12) *'Allah! There is no God save Him. In Allah, therefore, let believers put their trust' (65:13).*

(13) *'He is Allah, than Whom there is no other God, the Sovereign Lord, the Holy One, Peace, the Keeper of Faith, the Guardian, the Majestic, the Compeller, the Superb, Glorified be Allah from all that they ascribe as partner (unto Him)' (60:23).*

(14) *'He is Allah, the Creator, the Shaper out of naught, the Fashioner. His are the most beautiful names. All that is in the heavens and the earth glorifieth Him, and He is the Mighty, the Wise' (60:24).*

(15) *'And He it is Who in the heaven is God and in the earth God, He is the Wise the Knower' (43:84).*

(16) *'Say: He is Allah, the One! (CXII:1).*

(17) *'The King of mankind' (CXII:2).*

(18) *'The God of mankind' (CXII:3).*

(19) *'The Beneficent, the Merciful' (2:2).*

(20) *'Owner of the Day of Judgement' (2:3).*

(21) *'Vision comprehendeth Him not, but He comprehendeth (all) vision. He is the Subtile, the Aware' (6:104).*

The above verses of the Holy Quran reveal the attributes of Allah. It reveals that Allah is One God and that He is the Alive, the Subtile, the Aware, the Seer, the Eternal, the Beneficent, the Merciful, the Hearer, the Sublime, the Tremendous, the Knower of the invisible and the visible, the Almighty, the Wise, the Creator of all things, Guardian over all things, the Creator of mankind and all things, Sovereign Lord, the Holy One, Peace, the Keeper of Faith, the Majestic, the Compeller, the Superb, the Shaper out of naught, the Fashioner, the Forgiver, the Omniscient, the Omnipresent, the Omnipotent, the Omnific, the First and the Last and the Outward and the Inward and He is Knower of all things, the Mighty and the

Wise. His are the most beautiful names, and these names show His attributes. The Holy Quran is a complete apperception of God.

The Holy Quran further reveals more attributes and Power of Allah in the verses (39:42) and (39:67) about the souls of mankind at the time of their death and while they are asleep, and about the earth, the universe and the heavens on the Day of Resurrection. These verses reveal Infinite Power, Wisdom and Knowledge of Allah and His command over His creations of mankind and the heavens and the earth. Their creations and death is all in His hand and Allah is able to do all things and that is easy for Him. And Allah is Doer of What He Will. When He decreeth a thing, He saith unto it only, Be! and it is.

The Holy Quranic verses are :

(1) *'Allah receiveth (men's) souls at the time of their death and that (soul) which dieth not (yet) in its sleep. He kepth that (soul) for which He hath ordained death and dismisseth the rest till an appointed term. Lo! herein verily are portents for people who take thought'. (39:42).*

(2) *'And they esteem not Allah as He hath the right to be esteemed, when the whole earth is His handful on the Day of Resurrection, and the heavens are rolled in His right hand. Glorified is He and High Exalted from all that they ascribe as partner (unto Him). (39:67).*

The Concept of Time after Sleep and Death and on the Resurrection of Man

Men of understanding may take guidance from the Holy verses of the Quran to know the absolute reality of Allah. The above verse (39:42) reveals that on the death of man, his soul is received by Allah, the moment it leaves the body. The same is true in case of man who is in his sleep. This indicates that man in sleep and a man who is dead, both are in the same state in regard to the transmission of soul or spirit. But for the man whom Allah ordered death, his soul is kept by Allah and so he is a dead man. On the contrary, Allah rejects the soul of a man in sleep so he is a live man, till the appointed term. This indicates that till the 'Day of Resurrection', the dead man is like a man fast asleep. And this is a great portent and a conclusion if one thinks over it. Man is then unaware of the time factor whether it is one hour, one year, one million years or one billion years or any time lapse.

The following Holy Quranic verses throw more light on it:-

(1) *'And the Trumpet is blown and lo! from the graves they hie unto their Lord'. (36:51).*

(2) *'Crying! Woe upon us! who hath raised us from our place of sleep. This is that which the Beneficent did promise and the messenger spoke truth'. (36:52).*

(3) *'Say: The angel of death, who hath charge concerning you, will gather you and afterwards unto your Lord ye will be returned'. (32:11).*

The Spirit and Life in Man are two Different Things

The Spirit is not Life

The second great portent indicated by the Holy verse (39:42) is that 'life' in man is different than the 'soul' or the 'spirit' in man. This is indicated by the Holy verse (39:42), that 'life' and 'soul' in man are two different things and that 'life' is not 'soul' or 'spirit' and the two are separate things. Life is because of the spirit and is subordinate to it.

The Holy Quran reveals:-

(1) *'And a soul and Him who perfected it'. (XCI:7).*

(2) *'And inspired it (with conscience of) what is wrong for it and (what is) right for it'. (XCI:8).*

The above Holy verses further reveal that Allah perfected man with a 'soul'. In this Holy verse perfection of man with 'life' is not mentioned. The next verse is that Allah inspired man with 'conscience'. This indicates that 'Inspired Conscience' has something to do with the 'soul' and is because of the soul or the spirit in man. The conscience is not connected with life. It is connected with the 'soul' or the 'spirit'. The inspired conscience is a great quality in man which makes him superior to many other creatures created by Allah with a marked preferment. Man is created as the best of all creatures and is bestowed with inspired conscience.

We do not know and cannot know what spirit is! The spirit is not 'life' as is generally misunderstood, but is something very superior to life and commands life. Spirit is closely connected with man's life, but is different than life', though life itself is mysterious. But the spirit is something more than mysterious.

The Holy verse (39:42) clearly indicates that the 'soul of a dead man' and the 'soul of man in sleep' is received by Allah. The soul goes back to Allah in these two conditions or on two occasions. The man who is ordained death his soul is kept by Allah, whereas of others the soul is dismissed or sent back or rejected, so they remain alive till an appointed term. This means that the man 'in sleep' who is not ordained death, his soul also goes to Allah but at the same time he is very much alive in his sleep or during the condition of sleep and has life in him. These two conditions of sleep and death revealed by the Holy Quran clearly indicate that 'life' is separate and distinct from the 'soul' or the 'spirit' in man, as life stays back, while the soul of man in sleep goes to Allah, but at the same time life is very much linked with the spirit in man. It further indicates that soul or spirit is something which is indestructable and is beyond the power of imagination and the knowledge of man. The spirit inhibits in man but its seat and location is unknown. The spirit is not physical. It is unseen and is invisible and hidden but still it commands life in man and it helps to operate conscience and enables him to exercise his thinking power and puts to work his nervous system through the brain and through the skin and has the operative command over all things in man including his impulses, feelings and all that which is in his mind and even if it is not uttered in words. Still we do not know what spirit is and where it resides in man. It instantaneously goes and comes back while man is in sleep or is awake and is above all physical things and things like speed, time and space, etc. It is something which Allah has breathed into man and so the spirit is unconceivable by man and lies beyond his power of understanding and comprehension. Scientific data are unable to cast any light on spirit as it goes beyond human understanding.

The Holy Quran reveals:-

(1) *'They will ask thee concerning the spirit; say: The spirit is by command of my Lord and of knowledge ye have been vouchsafed but little'. (17:85).*

(2) *'When thy Lord said unto the angels: Lo! I am about to create a mortal out of mire'* (38:72).

(3) *'And when I have fashioned him and breathed into him of My spirit, then fall down before him prostrate'* (38:73).

(4) *'We verily created a man and We know what his soul whispereth to him and We are nearer to him than his jugular vein'* (50:16).

The Holy verse (17:85) makes it clear that the spirit is by the Command of Allah and the knowledge of spirit is not revealed to man except very little. And that little knowledge is that the spirit is not physical and is not life and that it is in man by the Command of Allah Who breathed into man and governs the life in man. The spirit breathed into man by Allah and the conscience inspired in man by Allah are something highly superior and is beyond man's understanding. This is also clear from the Holy verses when Allah asked the angels to prostrate before man after man was fashioned and after Allah breathed His Spirit into him.

Allah has Infinite Powers, Wisdom and Knowledge and on the day of Resurrection all dead shall be brought back to life and the whole earth, and all the heavens, shall lie at the mercy of Allah, but still, the unbelievers among the mankind do not esteem Allah and His Infinite Powers, though Allah has the right to be esteemed Allah is Glorified and High Exalted.

The Holy Quran reveals Allah's message and wonderfully guides mankind in the following verse which is full of sense and is self explanatory:-

> *'Lo! Ye are those who argue about that whereof ye have some knowledge. Why then argue ye concerning that whereof ye have no knowledge Allah knoweth. Ye know not'* (III:66).

The sense of the above verse (III:66) is very simple, direct and clear. It appeals to the mind and is full of logic, sense, wisdom and guidance.

The Holy Quran wisely guides mankind that it is useless to argue on matters of which you have absolutely no knowledge. This is a great hint full of logic for men of understanding. Because, arguments only count where man has at least some knowledge of the matter which he discusses When he has no knowledge about a matter, then why to argue or discuss things, as such a discussion would be irrelevant and meaningless. But Allah, Who is the Creator of all things knows everything, whereas man knows nothing.

Furthermore, the Quranic verse (111:7) clearly tells that those people who try to explain the meanings of the Quranic verses differently are obviously in disagreement with the allegorial substance of the Holy Quran. The Holy Quran lays great emphasis that no one knows or can explain the substance of the allegorial verses of the Holy Quran except Allah. The Quran reveals that those people who have sound knowledge and understanding and pay attention will have clear grasp and sense of the Quranic verses. Such people really believe in the Holy Quran as the true word of Allah. The Holy Quranic verse (111:7) reveals:-

> *'He it is Who hath revealed unto thee (Muhammad) the Scripture wherein are clear revelations. They are the substance of the Book — and others (which are) allegorial. But those in whose hearts is doubt pursue, forsooth, that which is allegorial seeking (to cause) dissension by seeking to explain it. None knoweth its explanation save Allah. And those who are of sound instruction say: We believe therein; the whole is from our Lord; but only men of understanding really heed'. (III:7).*

So, it is the sense and the grasp and understanding of the substance of the Holy verses, the wisdom and faith, the conscience and sound knowledge of man, which makes man to believe in Allah and in His Word, (the Holy Quran), and makes him to believe in the invisible, the unseen and in the 'Hereafter'.

Those people who doubt would try to explain the allegorial verses differently, but Allah knows its explanation and men of sound knowledge who pay heed believe in it. The clear revelations are understandable to all and are the substance of the Holy Quran. Those who have sound knowledge and understanding, they grasp the sense and believe in the revelations of Allah and believe that these are from the Lord of the Worlds.

Allah's Act of Creation

Allah brings into being the creation by His Simple Command

'Be! and it is'. Allah is present everywhere but does not inhere in anything. He is the sole Creator and Sustainer of the Universe, wherein every creature bears witness to His Unity and Lordship. Allah is Just and Merciful. His Justice ensures 'order' in His creation, in which nothing is out of place and His Mercy is unbounded and encompasses everything. His creating and ordering the universe is the act of prime mercy for which all things sing His glories. Allah is Majestic and Sovereign and is nearer to man than man's jugular vein, and whenever a person in need or distress calls Him, He responds. Similarly Allah is aware about man's evil mind and plans. Above all, Allah guides everything, particularly man, the right way, 'the straight path'. Allah is the One. He has no partner and no equal.

The Holy Quran reveals numerous verses on creation. Only a few are quoted:-

(1) *'The Originator of the heavens and the earth! When He decreeth a thing, He saith unto it only: Be! and it is' (II:117).*

(2) *'Glory be to Him: When He decreeth a thing, He saith unto it only, Be! and it is' (19:35).*

(3) *'But His Command, When He intendeth a thing, is only that He saith unto it: Be! and it is' (36:82).*

(4) *'It is He Who created all things and ordered them in due proportions' (25:27).*

(5) *'It is He Who created the heavens and the earth in true proportions' (39:5-6).*

(6) *'Who created seven heavens in harmony. Thou (Muhammad) can't see no fault in Beneficent One's creation; then look again: Can't thou see any rift (67:3).*

(7) *'He it is Who created the heavens and the earth in truth. In that day when He saith: Be! and it is' (6:73).*

(8) *'We verily created a man and We know what his soul whispereth to him and We are nearer to him than his jugular vein' (50:16).*

(9) *'He created man of clay like the potter's' (55:14).*

(10) *'And the jinn did He create of smokeless fire' (55:15).*

(11) *'Who hath created life and death and that He may try you, which of*

you is the best in conduct; and He is the Mighty, the Forgiving' (67:2).

(12) *He is Allah, the Creator, the Shaper out of naught, the Fashioner. His are the most beautiful names. All that is in the heavens and the earth glorifieth Him and He is the Mighty, the Wise' (60:24).*

The above Holy verses reveal that Allah's act of creation when He intends is only: Be! and it is. This indicates that Allah's power of creation of infinite things is Infinite. He creates all things in perfect order with 'due proportions' and 'true proportions'. He is the Creator, the Shaper out of naught and the Fashioner of all things, the visible and the invisible, the living and the non-living including man and the jinn.

The Universe

In order to prove that Allah is the One, the Heavenly Quran lays great emphasis on the design and celestial order in the universe, which the Quran mentions as the 'marvel' of Allah. There are no gaps and dislocations in nature (Quran). Order is explained by the fact that every created thing is endowed with a definite and defined nature whereby it falls into a pattern. This nature, though it allows every created thing to function in a whole, sets limits; and this idea of the limitedness of everything is one of the most fixed points in both the cosmology and theology of the Quran. Everything in the universe has been assigned its own inherent laws and physical behaviour. The patterns of the physical behaviour have been endowed by Allah and are strictly limited. 'Everything has been created by Us according to a measure'. (Quran). Though every creature is thus limited and 'measured out' and hence depends upon Allah, Allah alone, Who reigns unchallenged in the heavens and the earth, is Infinite, Independent, Self-sufficient and Infinite in Knowledge, Wisdom and Power and in all things.

The Creation of the physical universe, its structure and the laws which govern its working and as described by the sciences of Physics, Cosmology, Astrophysics, Astronomy and Chemistry, is briefly given below:-

The Universe and its Origin

In the vastness of the universe, the Earth, Sun and Planets are tiny dots. The Sun is a single star in a galaxy (Milky Way) comprising 100,000 million stars. At least as many thousands of millions of other galaxies, each with its own star system, extend as far as the largest optical and radio telescopes can reach. The most remote object detected in the universe are up to16,000 million light years away, so distant that their radiation started its journey before the earth — and perhaps even our galaxy — was born.

This shows the inviolability of the Universe as the Holy Quran reveals in the verse given below:

> *'Then He ordained them seven heavens in two days and inspired in each heaven its mandate: We decked the nether heaven with lamps and rendered it inviolable. This is the measuring of the Mighty, the Knower' (41:12).*

Dr. Hubble examined more distant galaxies in 1920's, he made an even more sensational discovery: the galaxies all seemed to be moving away from one another at speeds that increased with their distances. It seemed that the entire universe was expanding.

Hubble made his discovery of the expanding universe by comparing the RED SHIFT in light from galaxies — a lengthening in wavelength caused by their recession — with their distances as measured from the brightness of stars within them. The relationship between distance and red shift is known as HUBBLE's LAW and has been proved accurate to ever-increasing distances. The actual rate of expansion is known as Hubble's constant.

The Holy Quran revealed the expansion of the universe 1400 years ago in Holy verse (51:47) quoted below:

> *'We have built the universe with might and We it is Who make the vast extent (thereof)' (51:47).*

This means the universe which Allah built with energy or power or might, is expanding and extending vastly in all directions.

George Lamaitre pointed out in 1931 that if the outward movement of all the galaxies were traced backwards, then they would presumably meet in a single point. This large blob of matter, known as the primeval atom or cosmic egg, must have been all that existed of the universe in the distant past.

Lamaitre suggested that for some reason this giant blob of matter exploded, flinging material outwards like a bomb. This marked the creation of the universe. Lamaitre's idea became known as the Big Bang theory.

The Holy Quran reveals the origination of the universe as follows:-

> *'The originator of the heavens and the earth! When He decreeth a thing, He saith unto it only: Be! and it is (II:117).*

According to Hubble's constant, the Big Bang must have occurred 18,000 millions years ago. The galaxies visible today are fragments from this explosion. This was confirmed during 1950's as radio astronomers probed deep into the universe.

Where the Cosmic egg came from, or what existed before Big Bang, are questions that remained unresolved and are beyond the scope of sciences. The answers to these questions lie in the guidance of the Holy Quran and one must ponder and try to grasp and understand the sense contained in the allegorial verses of the Holy Quran, which reveals:-

(1) *'But His Command, when He intendeth a thing, is only that He saith unto it: Be! and it is' (36:82).*

(2) *'Then turned He to the heaven when it was smoke and said unto it and unto the earth: Come both of you, willing or loth. They said: We come, obedient' (41:11).*

The only source which can guide man when things are beyond the scope of science, is the Holy Quran. It is the Holy Quran which reveals the creation and the origination of the universe from 'naught'. (60:24). The concerned Holy verse is quoted below:-

> *'He is Allah, the Creator, the Shaper out of naught, the Fashioner. His are the most beautiful names. All that is in the heavens and the earth glorifieth Him, and He is the Mighty, the Wise' (60:24).*

The Holy Quran further reveals that the universe is built of might i.e. energy and matter and that it is expanding. (51:47). It also reveals that the universe is so vast that it is inviolable. (41:12). The Quranic verses revealing all these realities are discussed in the relevant Chapters of this book and physical sciences describing the universe are found to be in complete congruity with the sense allegorially contained in the Holy Quranic verses.

In the structure of the universe, the earth is merely one planet of one sun in a corner of one of countless millions of galaxies that spread to the ever-receding boundaries of an expanding universe.

With the aid of telescopes, radio astronomy, artificial satellites and space probes, scientists have learned how galaxies are born from spinning clouds of gas and dust and how the stars die in monstrous nuclear explosions. They even suspect that the cores left behind by these explosions may be so dense that they collapse in on themselves endlessly, sucking all neighbouring matter into a black hole — perhaps into another universe. The Holy Quran already contains hints in allegory about the existence of innumerable black holes in the universe. It is revealed in the Holy verse given below:-

'By the heaven full of path' (51:7).

Path, is simile for black hole, which indicates that these paths lead to the gateway of other universes.

Sun

The sun is a giant nuclear reactor that blazes at 15,000,000°C.Its diameter is more than 100 times the earth and its mass is 300,000 times more than that of our planet, even though it consists mainly of the lightest materials in the universe, hydrogen and helium.

The Supernova Bombshell'

Stars in the process of evolution become supernovas. The supernova is the brightest object in the universe. Its temperature is 3500,000,000°C. In a matter of minutes it collapses under the pull of its own gravity. This implosion triggers an enormous nuclear explosion, which throws off the star's outer layers into space at speeds of 6000 miles per second. Such a steller bombshell is known as a supernova outburst.

The Working of the Universe (Matter and Energy) as a Whole under Fundamental Forces

The Holy Quran frequently mentions about the celestial bodies, their design and celestial order in the universe. The Holy Quran reveals that the universe is decked with stars (41:12) and that there are mansions of stars in the universe (25:6), (85:1) and (15:16) and that the universe is so vast that it has been rendered inviolable (41:12). It mentions that all these stars, planets and galactic systems are raised up in the universe without visible support, i.e. by the force of gravity and other fundamental forces (13:2) and (55:7), and that all these bodies and forces are created by Allah in true proportions (6:73) and (39:5-6) and in due proportions (25:2) and that for all things Allah has set the measure (55:7). Of the four basic forces, gravitation is the weakest; although it plays a vital role in the over all structure of the universe. The other basic forces play vital role in the over all structure of the universe. The other basic forces play vital role within the structure of an atom. The Holy Quran reveals that Allah has created seven heavens or universes in harmony and with perfection. (41:12). The sun and the moon are punctual (55:5) and each float in an orbit (21:33) and are constant in their courses (14:33) and are constrained to be of service to mankind (16:12) and that all things in the universes and the earth entreat Allah Who everyday exercises universal power (55:29). Allah created man and every animal from water (25:54) and (24:45). He fashioned and proportioned man and created man in the womb as pleases Him (82:7) and (II:6).

> *'Glory be to Him, when He decreeth a thing, He saith unto it only, Be! and it is' (19:35).*

Man and the universe and all matter and energy including the physical forces, the radiation and light and the physical laws governing them are created by Allah in true proportion and with set measure. Their interaction is governed under set physical laws of Physics, Chemistry, Biology and Genetics etc., Physics and Chemistry are the keys to understanding how the universe behaves and we know about it within the scope and limits of the physical sciences. The reality which lies beyond that is only revealed by the Holy Quran for the guidance of mankind.

The physical sciences — Physics and Chemistry — represent man's most systematic attempt to understand the universe in the context of the verses of the Holy Quran describing the physical universe.

Physics and Chemistry are concerned with five basic topics. The first is matter, the stuff of which everything is made. The second is energy, without which nothing in the universe could happen, since everything that happens involves the exchange of energy between one piece of matter and another. The third is radiation — a form of energy—which includes visible light, radio waves and X-rays.

The fourth concern of the physical sciences is space, the framework within which matter exists. From the point of view of the physical sciences time is regarded not as something apart but as a space-like dimension. Finally, there is information, wherever radiation or material is organized into a meaningful pattern, it can be analyzed to find out what happened in the past.

Chemistry deals with the properties of chemical elements, the ways they combine to form compounds and the conditions necessary to make them do so. There is, however, no completely sharp distinction between Chemistry and Physics. Both may deal with the same phenomena and make use of the same fundamental body of knowledge.

Science as it is understood today is no more than 500 years old. The Holy Quran is revealed 1400 years ago and contains all fundamental principles of the creation of the universe, its evolution and of its catastrophic collapse including that of man.

Science is in similarity with the Holy Quran. Science explains the physical facts of the universe and of man which the Holy Quran already contains either in allegory or in direct form. This fact reveals that the Holy Quran is a heavenly Book and is not man-made. Science emphasizes the use of knowledge to manipulate the physical world in order to obtain further knowledge and it insists on certain rules of procedure. These rules, which lie at the heart of all modern scientific research, are the basis for what is known as the scientific, or experimental method. Science is, therefore, the means to understand and grasp the wisdom of the Holy Quran which reveals absolute truth as it is the word of Allah revealed by inspiration on Prophet Muhammad (PBUH) for the guidance and knowledge of mankind and for the good of mankind. Quran teaches man which he does not know.

Light

Light plays a unique part in universe. To begin with, it makes seeing possible and visual observation is one of the main ways of gathering information about the universe. In addition, the speed of light in free space is one of the fundamental physical constants of the universe. It is the same at all times for all people in all places; and unlike other speeds, it remains unaltered however fast the observer may be moving. This simple fact underlines the whole of modern physics, for it governs the way, the universe behaves.

The Holy Quran reveals:-

'And the sky He has uplifted; and He has set the measure' (55:7).

This means all fundamental , physical constants, i.e. the velocity of light, the amount of energy, the amount of matter, the speed and composition of electrons in the structure of an atom, are physical constants for which Allah has set the measure'.

The amount of energy in the universe is fixed. One form of energy can be transformed into another, but new energy cannot be created. Nor can the stock of energy ever be exhausted, though it can be dissipated into ever less and less useful forms. The speed of light in the universe is constant at 186,000 miles per second.

The physical sciences—Physics and Chemistry—are the keys to understanding the entire universe, from the smallest atomic particles to whole galaxies. Physics explains how one kind of energy can be transformed into another, and sets out the laws of motion that govern alike earthquakes and musical harmonies, the surge of the tides and the lift-off of a space rocket. Knowledge of nature is a major source of power to understand the universe and get benefited.

Chemistry, on the other hand, explains how particles combine to form the elements, how they are held together and split apart, and how man, by re-arranging them, can create new materials.

The invisible particles inside the atom are the basis of all matter. Matter is the stuff that the whole universe is made of it. It exists in four states — solid, liquid, gas or plasma — each of which can change into one of the others according to changes in temperature or pressure. But whatever the state matter is in at any moment, it is always made up of the same basic particles called atoms. Moreover, the protons, neutrons and electrons of anyone atom are the same as those of any other. It is the number of each that determines the nature of any atom. All matter that exists in the universe is made up of different combinations of a few basic substances — the chemical elements. Some 90 elements are found in nature, each consisting solely of atoms of the same type.

The Holy Quran reveals that everything is in a clear record with Him and that the movements of smaller particles than an atom i.e. the invisible sub-atomic particles in the structure of atom and in the luminous bodies and in matter and in the universe as a whole are in Allah's Notice, as the following Holy verse reveals:-

> *'(He is) the Knower of the Unseen. Not an atom's weight, or less than that or greater, escapeth Him in the heavens or in the earth, but it is in a clear record'* (34:3).

The above Holy verse gives indication of the Science of Particle Physics and makes it clear that Allah is the Knower of the unseen and that even an atom's weight or the weight of sub-atomic particles cannot escape the notice of Allah and that all things are in a clear record with Him.

Man

The Holy Quran reveals: God created two parallel species of creatures, man and jinn, the one from altered wet clay and the other from 'essential' or 'smokeless' fire. About the jinn, however, the Quran says little, although it is implied that the jinn are endowed with reason and responsibility but are more prone to evil than man.

The Holy Quran is centrally concerned with man and is a guide for human race. The Holy Quran reveals that man is the noblest of all creations. The Holy Quran reveals that all nature has been made subservient to man; nothing in all creation has been made without a purpose, and man himself has not been created 'in sport', his purpose being service and obedience to God's Will. Human race is raised up as the best community for mankind.

Despite this lofty station, however, the Holy Quran describes human nature as frail and faltering. Whereas, everything in the universe has a limited nature, and every creature recognizes its limitations and insufficiency. The Holy Quran reveals: Man is self destroyed and ungrateful and that he is 'rebellious','mischief-maker' and full of pride, arrogating to himself the attributes of self-sufficiency. Pride thus, is the cardinal sin of man, because by not recognizing in himself his essential creaturely limitations and becomes guilty of ascribing to himself partnership with Allah thus associating a creature with the Creator and of violating the Unity of Allah. True faith thus, consists of belief in the immaculate Divine Unity of Allah and in Islam which means One's submission to the Divine Will.

Satan, Sin and Repentance

Satan or Iblis, had previously occupied a high station but fell from divine grace by the act of disobedience in refusing to honour Adam when he along with other angels were ordered to do so. Since then, his work has been to beguile man into error and sin. Satan is, therefore, the contemporary of man and Satan's own act of disobedience is construed by the Quran as the sin of pride. Satan's machinations will cease only on the Last Day. Before that Satan will misguide man and when he becomes obdurate, his heart is sealed by Allah. Nevertheless, it is always possible for a sinner to repent and redeem himself by a genuine conversion to the truth. There is no point of no return, and Allah is always willing and ready to pardon. Genuine repentance has the effect of removing all sins and restoring a person to the state of sinlessness with which he started his life.

Chapter 3

MAN THROUGH HIS INSPIRED CONSCIENCE, WISDOM, SENSES, KNOWLEDGE OF SCIENCES AND FAITH CAN SEEK GUIDANCE FROM THE HOLY QURAN TO KNOW THE PHYSICAL AND METAPHYSICAL REALITIES

All matters which are of physical nature lie within the range of scientific investigations and can be explained to reveal their reality, whereas, divine matters and metaphysical events lie permanently beyond the scope of science and man's physical observations. But the Holy Quran spans all knowledge and reveals the truth about both i.e. the physical matters in the universe including man and the metaphysical matters. The Holy Quran teaches the doctrines of Islam and reveals the unseen and the invisible. It reveals the Oneness of Allah and Allah as the Source of all visible and invisible creations. The Holy Quran discloses its own revelation as the inspired word of Allah to Prophet Muhammad (PBUH), and about the spirit, or soul of mankind, and about the Doomsday, the Resurrection of mankind, the Accountability, the Day of Judgement and about the 'Hereafter', besides the unseen and the invisible creations in all the seven heavens and the earth and all that is in between them.

It is man's wisdom, his senses, conscience, faith, and sound knowledge about the physical world and man, which makes him to feel and know the absolute reality of the metaphysics of Quran.

The physical creation and the metaphysical creation, as revealed by the Holy Quran, clearly indicate that there exists a Creator of Infinite attributes who is Allah, the Living, the Eternal, the

Wise, the Aware, the Creator and the Shaper out of naught and the Fashioner of all things.

The Holy Quran contains information about the visible and the hidden universe behind the literal sense of the Quranic word and many modern scientific concepts are already present in the Holy Quran. The Holy Quran reveals basic concepts and is in similarity with physical sciences on the creation, evolution and on the ultimate fate of the universe and of man as is discussed throughout the book. Moreover, the Holy Quran is the Divine source to guide man for his conduct and behaviour and for his social, moral and economic set up. Quran is certain of the 'Hereafter' i.e. 'Life after death', and man will be treated according to his deeds, whatever the terms of reference of his performance remained in the physical universe. The reality of the 'Hereafter' which is of great consequence to man is revealed by the Holy Quran as the permanent abode of mankind. The knowledge of sciences, the wisdom, the senses and inspired conscience and faith shall lead mankind to find the reality in the message of Allah - (the Holy Quran). It is, therefore, for mankind to ponder carefully and read the Quranic verses, word by word. Every word and every verse of the Holy Quran convey sense which reveals the Reality, which it describes.

Islam perfected as a Religion by Allah and then chosen for Mankind to follow

The Holy Quran reveals in the verse (5:4) that Islam is perfected by Allah and is chosen as a religion for mankind. Islam means complete submission and obedience to the Will of One Allah and the acceptance of all of His Commands as revealed in the Holy Quran. Islam unites in itself both the spiritual and temporal aspects of life and regulates the individual's relationship to God through his inspired conscience and social setting. In Islam, the love of God serves as a self check against all sins and as a great deterrent in preventing and protecting man from committing crimes, social immoralities and sin. He is more afraid by following the voluntarily adopted God-fearing Divine guidance rather than that of man-made laws to regulate and govern his conduct and behaviour.

The Holy Quran reveals:-

> *'This day have I perfected your religion for you, completed My favour upon you and have chosen for you Islam, as your religion' (5:4).*

The Holy Quran reveals that Islam has been perfected as a religion for mankind by Allah and thus by doing so Allah has completed His favour on mankind and then chosen the religion of Islam for mankind to follow.

Allah has created man with inspired conscience and has gifted him the power to choose between the right path and the wrong path. Man is also favoured with senses, wisdom and intelligence and has given him the power of thinking to distinguish between good and evil. The Holy Quran further reveals that there is no compulsion in religion. After giving conscience and wisdom to man, and after revealing the Holy Quran, it is now for man to choose the path of his conduct in this world, as the requital for which is to be paid accordingly in the 'Hereafter', as the Holy Quran reveals.

Man's inspired conscience and wisdom are gifts from Allah and his faith in the Holy Quran is as the built-in power motivated by man's conscience to grasp and understand the doctrines of Eschatology of the religion of Islam and to believe in the physical and metaphysical matters of the Holy Quran, including the unimaginable, the invisible, the unseen and the hidden matters.

Knowledge of sciences, their unchanging fundamental principles and physical laws throughout time and space indicate beyond doubt that there is a Creator behind these mathematically set and perfectly accurate and precise physical principles and the laws governing the creation, evolution, sustenance and the ultimate end of the physical universe including man.

The Creator is Allah Who has set the measure for every creation and has created everything in due proportion and in true proportion as the Holy Quran reveals.

The scientists while achieving knowledge of physical sciences study only the physical objects and their properties in the universe. They must also keep in mind Who created these objects and why? If a scientist keeps in mind the creative aspect of an object along with his observation and research, he will surely know the creator behind the creation who set the measure for all things and has created all things in due proportions and in true proportions and has constructed the universe without visible support as the Holy Quran reveals. The Holy Quran encompasses all things in knowledge and it is man's faith and wisdom which can grasp its sense and substance to know the Creator Allah, Who created man and the heavens and the earth and all things in between them.

All this shows that Allah is the Creator, Who is the Shaper out of naught and is the Fashioner and Who created the inviolable universe and an intelligent living man from non-living matter and inspired him with conscience and senses to know the Creator from His attributes of His creative power. Man is created to obey and worship his Creator and the universe is created for the benefit of man and as the token or portent or the sign of the Creator Who is Allah, the One God, so that man knows his Creator from the marvels of His creations of the universe and all things that it contains.

Chapter 4

REVELATIONS OF THE HOLY QURAN BY INSPIRATION TO THE LAST PROPHET MUHAMMAD (PBUH), WHEN PHYSICAL LAWS YIELDED TO PASS THE DIVINE MESSAGE

Prophet Muhammad (PBUH) is the Last of the Prophets to whom the Holy Quran (the word of Allah) was revealed by inspiration for the guidance of mankind. The Holy Quran reveals all kinds of things about the physical universe and its events and about mankind and about all that which is to happen in the 'Hereafter'.

The Holy Quran reveals the following verses about the Last Prophet Muhammad (PBUH) and convey the message of Allah to mankind for their knowledge and information:-

(1) ***'Say: 'O men! I am sent unto you all, as the Apostle of Allah, to whom belongeth the dominion of the heavens and the earth: There is no god but He. It is He that giveth both life and death. So believe in Allah and His Apostle the unlettered Prophet, who believed in Allah** and His words: Follow him that (so) ye may be guided' (7:158).*

(2) *'This Quran hath been revealed to me by inspiration that I may warn you and all whom it reaches'. (6:19).*

(3) *'Verily this is no less than a message to (all) the World'. (82:27).*

(4) *'**We have not** sent thee but as a universal (messenger) to men, giving them glad tidings and warning them (against sin), but most men understand not'. (34:28).*

(5) *'This day have I perfected your religion for you, completed My favour upon you and have chosen for you Islam as your religion'. (5:4).*

(6) *'Muhammad is not the father of any of your men, but (he is) the Apostle of Allah and the last of the Prophets'.(33:40).*

(7) *'The believers are but a single Brotherhood'* (49:10)

(8) *'Even as We have sent unto you a messenger from among you, who reciteth unto you Our revelations and causeth you to grow and teacheth you the Scripture and Wisdom and teacheth you that which ye knew not'* (25:151).

Prophecy and Muhammad (PBUH) as the Last Prophet

Prophets are men specially chosen by Allah to be His Messengers. Prophethood is indivisible. There is no discrimination among the prophets. Everyone was assigned a special task. Yet they are not all equal. All prophets are human and never part of divinity. They are simply recipients of revelations from God. Allah never speaks directly to a human except through inspiration. He either sends an angel as a messenger to him or makes him hear a voice or inspires him. Abraham, Noah, Moses, Jesus, David and Solomon were great prophets. Muhammad (PBUH) is the Last Prophet and its greatest member, for through him all the messages of earlier prophets were consummated. Prophet Muhammad (PBUH) received the revelation of the Holy Quran, the like of which no human can produce.

Allah descended the Holy Quran through the Angel Gabriel to Prophet Muhammad's heart. The Prophet could sometimes see and hear Gabriel, a heavenly spirit. The Prophet's revelations occurred in a state of trance when his normal consciousness was in abeyance. This state was accompanied by heavy sweating. The Holy Quran itself makes it clear that the revelations brought with them a sense of extraordinary weight: 'If we were to send this Quran down on a mountain, you would see it split asunder out of fear of God' (Quran). The phenomenon at the same time was accompanied by an unshakable conviction that the message was from Allah and the Quran describes itself as the transcript of a heavenly 'Master Book' written on 'Preserved Tablet' (Lohe-Mahfooz). The Quran categorically states that it is a heavenly Book and is not from any earthly source, for in that case it would be liable to 'manifold' doubts and oscillations. The Quran further states that no human can produce the like thereof. The glorious Quran mentions those prophets who imparted divine knowledge: Adam, Noah, Abraham, Issac, Jacob, Moses, David, Solomon, Jesus and others. None of these revealed Allah's message in full i.e. to all mankind, since they were sent only to one nation. On the other hand, the message revealed to Muhammad (PBUH) was sent to all mankind and also to the jinn. The messages of the Prophets before Muhammad (PBUH) are believed to have been either forgotten or distorted, but Islam reveals that the Quran both correctly confirms the saying of the earlier Prophets and Muhammad (PBUH) is the seal of Prophets i.e. the end of Prophecy. All prophecies before Muhammad (PBUH) were incomplete and point to the coming of the final revelation.

Chapter 5

THE PHYSICAL WORLD AND THE METAPHYSICAL WORLD AS DIFFERENT CREATIONS OF ALLAH FOR MANKIND

As revealed by the Holy Quran, there are two types of worlds the physical world to which the laws of science apply and the metaphysical world which extends beyond the frontiers of the physical laws and is not governed by such laws. The physical world or the universe is created to function for an appointed period, after which it is destined to collapse gravitationally, whereas, the metaphysical world or the 'Hereafter' is Eternal. There are many things which the Holy Quran describes as the visible and the invisible, the unseen and the hidden in the physical and the metaphysical worlds. These are discussed later in the book. The Quran invites man's attention to know them as far as he can, so as to ascertain the absolute reality of the existence of the Creator Who created them and know Allah's Infinite Power Infinite Knowledge, Infinite Wisdom and His Ability to do All things and and make an estimation of His attributes in the creation of the inviolable physical universe and man. The mysterious physical creations and the inviolable universe serve as a guide and show the Infinite attributes of the Creator Allah. The inviolability of the universe serve as an estimation to know the marvels of the Creator, Allah. Matter, energy, time and space and the physical laws governining them are not without a Creator of Infinite Wisdom, Infinite Power and Infinite Knowledge and are not by itself, but these are created by the Command of Allah; Be! and it is'. All physical laws and forces governing the interaction of matter and energy in time and space give proof as well as indicate by inferences the existence of the One Creator Allah, Who is All-Powerful, All Wise, All Knowledgeable and is the Eternal and the Living and is the Creator of the physical universe in which we live. He is the Builder of atom with might and the Creator of the expanding universe decked with innumerable stars and galaxies.

Similarly, there is a metaphysical world to which mankind shall be transferred. This will happen on the 'Doomsday' as the Holy Quran reveals. The Doomsday is the catastrophic collapse of the physical universe, when the 'Hereafter' begins and the Resurrection of mankind shall take place. The Holy Quran mentions important events which are to take place in the 'Hereafter', like the 'Doomsday', the Resurrection, the Accountability, the Judgement and the award or punishment of Paradise or Hell. The 'Hereafter' is another type of world and is Eternal. It is unseen and is beyond the imagination of mankind to perceive it. The Holy Quran describes the 'Hereafter' as a better world, more lasting and the enduring home where man shall have everything for which he prays and for which his soul desires. So man should not be afraid of death in the physical world which is inevitable. Obedience to the Will of Allah and man's good deeds and actions in this world would pay him in the 'Hereafter' with the award which shall be eternal.

The Holy Quran reveals that man is created out of clay and water (wet clay), when Allah breathed into him His Spirit to make him live (15:28-29), (17:85) and (23:79). Now, the 'Spirit' is not physical and is a divine matter and is beyond the scope of science to explain. So, mankind is partly physical and partly spiritual or (not physical). In the universe, man lives and exists as physical being. Similarly, he will exist in the 'Hereafter'. May be that he is in a transfigure form. About this the Holy Quran reveals :

> *That We may transfigure you and make you what ye know not' (56:61).*

Further, the Holy Quran reveals that the substance of the physical universe, which is built with might (51:47) i.e. energy, or force and matter, was made in that Day when Allah said 'Be! and it is' (6:73), (II:117) and (51:47). The simple decree by Allah is the source of origination of matter and energy or power and of all the physical laws and the known fundamental forces governing them, which, in course of time assumed the present shape of the physical universe, comprising the innumerable systems of galaxies and stars (41:11-12). The Holy Quran reveals spiritual matters and events beyond the boundaries of the physical universe (25:2), (17:44) and (78:12). The Holy Quran reveals about the unseen and the invisible where science has no access. The Holy Quran reveals all about the future fate of man and the universe and all that which is going to happen after the death of mankind and of the gravitational or the catastrophic collapse of the universe i.e. the 'Doomsday' and of the 'Hereafter' (21:104). Allah has revealed the Holy Quran to Prophet Muhammad (PBUH) by inspiration which describes the events of the past, the present and of the future of mankind and of the universe in clear revelations as well as in allegories (30:58). The symbolic hints given in the Holy Quranic verses encompass tremendous wisdom and knowledge in capsule form which reveals about the creation of man, the jinn, the angels and of other living creatures in space, and of the universe and all things visible and invisible, known and hidden between the heavens and the earth and the 'Hereafter'. The Holy Quran further reveals that all physical things are created with a purpose and for an appointed period, i.e. for a certain time limit (51:57). There is a definite end to everything which is created in the physical universe.

This book attempts to explain the sense encompassed in some of the Holy Quranic revelations, specifically, the Holy verses which relate to the description of the physical universe and man, in the context of the known knowledge of modern sciences and it is found to great astonishment that modern concepts are already present in the Holy Quran. All that is required by man is an adequate and sound knowledge and wisdom to understand the substance of the Holy Quran. Science to the extent of the known knowledge about the physical universe and to its observable limits is in complete consonance with the Holy Quran, but beyond the physical universe and beyond the observable universe or the invisible or the unseen universe, science is of no help and of no consequence. The conscience and sense of mankind with the help of knowledge, and understanding and deep contemplation make man certainly believe in the Oneness of Allah and in the Holy Quran as His Word and in the 'Hereafter' i.e. (life after death) as an absolute reality.

The following Quranic verses which are from the heavenly Scripture giving wisdom and guidance reveal to mankind symbolically as well as directly, the Infinite Knowledge, the Infinite Power, the Infinite Wisdom and the Ability to do All things by Allah, the Creator of mankind and the heavens and the earth. Allah is the Eternal and is the Creator and the Knower of all things, Allah has made serviceable for mankind all things in the universe and has made revelations in the Quran for people who have knowledge. The Holy Quran advises men of knowledge and wisdom to ponder over the revelations and believe in them and act accordingly and obey and worship Allah according to the teachings of the Holy Quran. Allah is All Knowledgeable and is the Knower of all things.

The Holy verses are:-

(1) *'And if all the trees in the earth were pens and the sea with seven more seas to help it (were ink), the words of Allah could not be exhausted. Lo! Allah is Mighty, Wise' (31:27).*

(2) *'Allah it is Who hath created seven heavens, and of the earth the like thereof. The Commandment cometh down among them slowly, that ye may know that Allah is Able to do all things and that Allah surroundeth all things in knowledge' (66:12).*

(3) *'He is the first and the last; and the outward and the inward and He is Knower of all things' (59:3).*

(4) *'See ye not how Allah hath made serviceable unto you whatsoever is in heavens and whatsoever is in the earth and hath loaded you with His favours both without and within Yet of mankind is he who disputeth concerning Allah without knowledge or guidance or a Scripture giving light' (31:20).*

(5) *'He it is Who appointed the sun a splendour and the moon a light and measured for her stages, that ye might know the number of the years and the reckoning. Allah created not (all) that save in truth. He detaileth the revelations for people who have knowledge' (10:5).*

The above Holy verses reveal that Allah has Infinite Wisdom and Infinite Knowledge and that all His creation is surrounded with knowledge. Allah has favoured mankind by making serviceable to him all that is in the heavens and the earth, but still mankind disputes concerning Allah without knowledge and the guidance from the Holy Scripture the Quran, which gives mankind, the knowledge, the guidance and the light of wisdom to feel and know the absolute reality in the word of God.

Allah has built the physical universe with might which is governed by physical forces under the appointed laws for a fixed period. Man is created in the physical world out of matter but owns its existence due to 'spirit' which is something beyond matter and is divine in nature and belongs to the other world. Similarly, Allah has created an eternal world i.e. the World of the 'Hereafter', a metaphysical world or the world beyond physical. After the physical collapse of the universe and the earth, man is destined for the 'Hereafter' which is his permanent abode. May be that man is transfigured there and may not retain his worldly shape over there. We take guidance about all these matters from the Holy Quran which is the word of Allah for mankind. It is for all mankind to have firm faith in the Holy Quran.

Physical man cannot perceive things beyond the physical and things which are invisible and unseen for him, and things of the other world i.e. the 'Hereafter'. For example, man will never know about his own 'spirit' which he cannot see and which keeps him alive and is a vital part of him. The only source of knowledge of all these things is the Creator Allah Himself, Who guides mankind through prophets by inspiration. Therefore, Allah has given a message for mankind i.e. the message of the Holy Quran, the word of Allah, which is a guidance and information and the light of wisdom revealed on the Last Prophet Muhammad (PBUH) for the benefit of mankind so that man knows all about the temporary nature of the physical universe and its fate including the fate of mankind, and about the eternal world of the Hereafter. The doctrines and the teachings of the Holy Quran (the word of Allah) are to be followed which are a guidance for mankind. It is for mankind to achieve knowledge about the physical creations, then have the wisdom and faith to understand the substance of the Holy Quran which is encompassed with knowledge and act upon the teachings from Allah, obey these, and worship Allah, the Creator of man, the earth and Lord of all the Worlds i.e. the physical world and the unseen world of the 'Hereafter'.

Chapter 6

QURAN AND SCIENCE ON THE CREATION OF THE PHYSICAL UNIVERSE, ITS DOOM AND RE-EMERGENCE

The Holy Quran reveals :

'Assuredly the creation of the heavens and the earth is greater than the creation of mankind; but most of mankind know not' (40:57).

Allah reveals in the above Holy verse that the creation of the heavens and the earth is a much bigger affair than the creation of mankind, but most of mankind do not know and realize how inviolable and expanding is the universe alone which has billions of galaxies, each galaxy having billions of stars and billions of planetary systems, billions of light-years away, from earth and each other.

After carefully reading the Holy Quran, verse by verse, and word by word, one is surprised and excited to learn about the tremendous knowledge, wisdom and information, contained in the verses of the Holy Quran, as energy is packed in the nucleus of an atom. Enlightened by the Quranic reading and on deep contemplation of the verses, human feelings, common sense and the inspired conscience guide knowledgeable man to the concept that Allah created with His Divine Power, the substance of the physical universe, i.e. smoke like spinning cloud and dust substance or energy or matter or mass to be of inviolable expanse in nature, out of 'nothing' or out of 'naught'.

The Holy Quran says :-

(1) *'He is Allah, the Creator, the Shaper out of naught, the Fashioner,*

His are the most beautiful names. All that is in the heavens and the earth glorifieth Him, and He is the Mighty, the Wise' (60:24).

(2) *'The Originator of the heavens and the earth! When He decreeth a thing, He saith unto it only: 'Be! and it is' (II:117).*

(3) *'Then turned He to the heaven when it was smoke and said unto it and unto the earth: come both of you, willing or loth. They said: We come obedient' (41:11).*

Allah originated the universe out of naught i.e. from 'nothing' to a point with infinite density and pressure or might i.e. singularity and zero volume and then shaped it and fashioned it from smoke like substance into the universe with innumerable galactic systems, their innumerable stars and planets including the earth, after the primeval explosion and set it as the inviolable and as the expanding universe, expanding unilaterally and full of might, as is explained by Hubble's Law of Expanding Universe in the later part of the book.

The Holy Quran further reveals :-

'We have built the universe with might, and We it is Who make the vast extent (thereof)' (51:47).

The sense contained in the above Holy verse is directly understandable. It means that the universe is built with might and that it is expanding in all directions. The above Holy verse is of great consequences if man thoroughly ponders in the context of the knowledge of Physics, Cosmology, Astrophysics and Astronomy. Einstein's Theory of Relativity that $E = mc^2$ (Where E = Energy; m = Mass, and c = Velocity of light (i.e. 186,000 miles per second), is in similarity with the first part of the above Holy Quranic verse.

Allah has assigned a recorded and coded behaviour and 'has set the measure in true proportions and in due proportions' for the formation of the structure of the atom and for formation of the galactic systems and for all of the components of the expanding universe comprising of matter, energy and forces, including the four fundamental forces, (i.e. gravitation, electro-magnetism, nuclear force and weak force), now interconvert into three fundamental forces (as per Dr. Salam's theory) and appointed physical laws for governing their interactions and ordered them to acquire the given or assigned physical and chemical properties with possibilities of infinite development and decay, 'in true proportions and 'in due proportions', right from the 'Big Bang' (the moment of creation) till the 'Big Crunch' i.e. the ultimate catastrophic collapse or the Doom of the universe when again there will be 'nothing' left or all things shall be converted into 'nothing' or 'naught' as before.

The Holy Quran reveals :-

(1) *'It is He Who created the heavens and the earth in true proportions' (VI:73) and (39:5-6).*

(2) *'It is He Who created all things and ordered them in due proportions' (25:2).*

(3) *'And the sky He hath uplifted; and He hath set the measure' (LV:7).*

(4) *'Lo! We have created everything by measure' (54:49).*

(5) *'And Our Commandment is but one (Commandment), as the twinkling of an eye' (54:50).*

The above five Holy Quranic verses clearly reveal that Allah created all things with specific designs and set measures and proportions. After the Doom or Catastrophic collapse of the universe, Allah promises to repeat the process of creation of similar universe. In this respect the Holy Quran reveals that Allah is Able to create afresh the like of this universe, and the like of this earth, for which He has appointed an end whereof there is no doubt. Allah is All-Wise Creator and it is easy for Allah, the One, the Almighty to efface and establish anything as He wishes as with Him is Source of Ordinance. After the catastrophic collapse of the universe Allah has promised that He will repeat the creation of Universe and earth, the same way as He began the first creation. The re-emergent universe shall be like the present universe and the present earth, as is revealed in the following Holy verses :-

(1) *'The Day when We shall roll up the heavens as a recorder rolleth up a written scroll. As We began the first creation, We shall repeat it. (It is) a promise (binding) upon Us. Lo! We are to perform it' (21:104).*

(2) *'Have they not seen that Allah Who created the heavens and the earth is Able to create the like of them, and hath appointed for them an end whereof there is no doubt'. But the wrong doers refuse aught save*

disbelief'. (17:99).

(3) *'Is not He Who created the heavens and the earth Able to create the like of them? Aye, that He is! For He is All-wise Creator'. (36:81).*

(4) *'On the Day when the earth will be changed to other than this earth, and the heavens (also will be changed) and they will come forth unto Allah, The One, The Almighty' (14:48).*

(5) *'Allah effaceth what He Will, and establisheth (what He Will), and with Him is source of Ordinance' (13:39).*

(6) *'Hath thou not known that Allah Knoweth all that is in the heavens and the earth? Lo! it is in a record. Lo! that is easy for Allah' (22:70).*

(7) *'Have not those who disbelieve known that the heaven and the earth were one piece and then We parted them and We made every living thing of water? Will they not then believe?' (21:30).*

(8) *'He is the Knower of the invisible and the visible, the Great, the High Exalted' (13:9).*

(9) *'And unto Allah belongeth, the unseen of the heavens and the earth and the matter of the Hour (of Doom) is but as a twinkling of the eye, or it is nearer still. Lo! Allah is Able to do All things' (16:77).*

(10) *'Abiding there so long as the heavens and the earth endure save for that which thy Lord willeth Lo! thy Lord is Doer of what He Will' (11:107).*

(11) *'Man is made of haste. I shall show you My portents, but ask Me not to hasten' (21:37).*

The science of Cosmogony and Astrophysics is in complete agreement with the Holy Quran.

The sense contained in the above Holy verses are of tremendous significance and are very clear and directly understandable.

The above Quranic verses clearly reveal true events to happen millions and millions of years ahead or at any moment in the future and reveal truly the realities that happened billions of years in the past. The Holy Quran truly reveals the present realities, and man will know of more realities when his understanding power develops with the achievement of more knowledge. The contents of the revelations in the above Holy verses make it very clear that the universe shall catastrophically collapse. After the collapse or the Doom of the universe, the Holy Quran says that Allah will revive and create a similar universe and a similar earth again. Everything in all the seven Heavens and all things in the earth are in a clear Record with Allah, Who is the Knower of the invisible and the visible. Time is a creation of Allah. Allah is not concerned by time as He is above time and is the Eternal and the Living for ever. Being so, and acting according to His Own Will and Programme, Allah addresses mankind not to ask Him to hasten, as man himself is made of haste, but surely Allah shall show to mankind His portents according to His Own Will and the way He commands. It is for mankind to believe the inspired words of Allah which the Holy Quran reveals for all mankind. The Holy Quranic verse (21:30) clearly reveals a cosmological event of billions of years ago in the past, when the universe and the earth were one piece — all gaseous mass at high temperature and pressure and later on the earth parted. So, in the beginning, earth was part of the universe as one piece, as is shown by the chemical composition of the earth and the average cosmic composition which were nearly the same. Later on, the earth parted in the process of evolution of the universe and finally in the same process, chemical changes in the earth's composition took place and all living things or creatures on earth including man were made by Allah of Water. Scientists have established that in the protoplasm of man, the total concentration of water is between 85 to 90 per cent. The fluid medium of all protoplasm is water. Protoplasm is a living substance and the basis of all living matters in which water plays the most vital role. Biologically, it is the dominant constituent of living matter and this biological fact is in complete similarity with the Holy Quran.

The Holy Quran reveals :-

(1) *'And Allah hath created every animal of water'* (24:45).
(2) *'And He it is Who hath created man from water'* (25:54).
(3) *'We made every living thing of water. Will they not then believe?'* (21:30).

Modern sciences of Physics, Cosmology and Biology have recently revealed to mankind the facts about the evolution of the universe, the earth and the mankind on earth and of all the living creatures. But the Holy Quran allegorially revealed all these facts 1400 years ago, when man almost had no knowledge. The similarity between the revelations and the modern sciences is amazing. The revelations made by the Holy Quran is the word of God and it is beyond human power to reveal such realities pertaining to all times about the physical universe and man, 1400 years back. There is complete concordance between modern sciences and the verses of the Holy Quran with regard to the creation, evolution and the catastrophic collapse of the physical universe including man.

Facts of great similarity of science with the contents of the Holy Quranic verses on all the basic and vital aspects of the universe and man, are discussed in various chapters on different subject matters in this book.

The existence of such a similarity is simply exciting and astonishing and leads to the firm belief in the existence of the One Allah as the All-Wise Creator of all things and the Holy Quran as His Message to mankind revealed on Prophet Muhammad (PBUH).

Chapter 7

QURAN AND SCIENCE IN AGREEMENT ON THE CREATION, AND EVOLUTION OF THE INVIOLABLE PHYSICAL UNIVERSE AND ON THE INTERACTION OF MATTER AND ENERGY

The physical universe (which includes living organism) is composed entirely of matter and energy, which together are the basis of all objective phenomena. Man's present knowledge of the origin and evolution of the universe and of all things which it contains, as a whole is pitifully small.

The Holy Quran, which is the message of Allah to mankind, reveals numerous verses which amazingly and miraculously contain most modern concepts about all the natural sciences, in respect of the physical universe. All such concepts are miraculously encompassed and allegorially contained in the holy verses. The Holy Quran reveals knowledge and wisdom about the absolute realities of the origin and evolution of physical universe and man and their ultimate end and their future fate.

The Holy Quran reveals about the existence of jinn — a living intelligent creation existing before mankind and is a parallel creation to man. The Holy Quran further reveals the existence of other living creations in the inviolable universe. But these creations are not known to mankind and are not visible or detectable. May be that the shape, the form, the environments and the substance of these invisible living creations be never made known to mankind, because of the inviolability of the universe and the constancy in the speed of light.

Surprisingly, there exists an open invitation to mankind from Allah in the verse (55:33) of the Holy Quran which invites man to penetrate the regions in space and to get out of the earth's gravitational force. This is obviously to benefit mankind from the bounties of Allah beyond earth and to know more about God's creation and take more benefit out of it. The innumerable mysterious creations of Allah in the inviolable universe indicate the Infinite Power and the Infinite Knowledge of the Creator Allah.

The Holy Quran already contains hints about the fundamental and vital modern concepts of science, which later on appeared in the form of inventions and discoveries about nature. The Holy verse (51:47) miraculously reveals in symbolic form that the universe is built with might. This 'might' corresponds to the fact that the nucleus of an atom is packed or is built with might or power. The indication of this power with which the atom is built, is clear from Einstein's equation $E = mc^2$ Thus the entire universe is built with might. The sun and the innumerable stars in each galactic system and the innumerable galaxies and supernova, etc., are nothing else than might or power in the universe. Matter and energy and the forces present in the universe are all 'might' or 'power', in one form or the other. Einstein's Special Theory of Relativity; $E = mc^2$ gives an indication of this power with which the atom is built. Allah said: 'Be! and it is'. Thus Allah with His divine power built the universe with might.

The same verse further astonishes man in revealing yet another vital and basic fact which has now become a law of science, pertaining to Physics and Cosmology that Allah makes the vast extent of the physical universe, i.e. Allah expands the universe. The Holy verse clearly and directly indicates that the universe is expanding. This part of the Holy Quranic verse is in similarity with Edwin Hubbie's Law of Expanding Universe This means that science or knowledge of the physical universe recently discovered is found to be in complete congruity with the Holy Quran, revealed 1400 years ago. The Law of Expanding Universe expounded by Edwin Hubble states that the physical universe is expanding isotropically i.e. the same in all directions since its creation. The Law of Expanding Universe is discussed later on.

The importance and great emphasis which the Holy Quran has laid on science or knowledge of nature or the physical universe, may be noticed from the remarks of Muhammad Aijaz-ul- Khatibe

of Damascus University that :-

> **'In contrast to 250 verses which are legislative, some** 750 verses of the Holy Quran almost one-eighth of **it—exhort the believers to study nature to reflect, to make the best use of reason and to make the scientific** enterprises an integral part of the community's life'.

The verse (51:47)· of the Holy Quran revealing scientific informations about the physical universe as explained above is quoted below :-

> *'We have built the universe with might and We it is Who make the vast extent (thereof)" (51:47).*

The sense of this Holy verse has been explained in brief above. However, its detailed scientific explanation in the light of the divine revelations of the Holy Quran is as follows :-

The moment Allah said 'Be! and it is', (6:73), (II:11) and (51:47) the universe came into existence all built with might or **energy. The above verse clearly points to the creation of the universe by Allah 'with might' and this might is the 'packed energy' in the atom, which is a loose assembly of its nucleus and the electron circling it in a set order and in due proportions. In this respect the Holy Quran further reveals :-**

> *'It is He Who created all things and ordered them in due proportions' (25:2). (VI:73) and (39:5-6).*

The nucleus itself is a dense entity; indeed, its dense constitution contains 'packed energy' or might or power or force which is the repository of the formidable forces of nature as is revealed in the first part of the verse (51:47). Indeed, the whole scheme of Chemistry, Physics, Matter, Cosmology and the entire universe revolves round the conception of various phenomena which emanate from the form and function of the entities, within the nucleus of atom. The truth or reality is that the make-up of the entire physical universe dwells in the make-up of the atom and its nucleus, wherein, Allah has packed formidable energy or might in each atom, the Day when the universe was built or created. The atom's nucleus is held together by the 'strong force' which is one of the four basic

forces of the universe. Electro-magnetic force and weak force are in fact both aspects of what is now known as the electro weak force. The fourth basic universal force is the force of gravity. From all above, it is evident that the Holy Quran reveals knowledge at the level of particle physics.

Dr. Einstein's Special Theory of Relativity explains mathematically that the universe is built with might. The special theory of relativity is the equation $E = mc^2$; i.e. energy equals mass multiplied by the square of the velocity of light. This relation shows that mass or matter is a form of energy and that in view of the magnitude of the velocity of light there is enormous energy stored in the atom of matter. This equation forms the basis for the explanation not only of the source of energy of the sun and other stars but also of atomic energy and the atomic bomb.

The discovery by Einstein revealing the fact that the structure of atom is built with might ($E = mc^2$) is found to be in similarity with the verse (51:47) of the Holy Quran revealed 1400 years ago.

The first part of the Holy Quranic verse (51:47) clearly explains the building of the universe with might. The remaining part of the Holy Quranic verse is:-

'and We it is Who make the vast extent (thereof)' (51:47).

This part of the Holy verse reveals that the universe which is built of might, 'is expanding'.

Hubble's Law of Expanding Universe in consonance with the Holy Quran

Cosmology is a science of modern times which deals with the study of the origin and evolution of the universe as a whole. According to the great discovery of Edwin Hubble's Law of the Expanding Universe, the expansion of the universe is going on and this expansion is isotropic — that is, the same in all directions. The Physical Law of Expanding Universe discovered by Edwin Hubble is in consonance with the above verse of the Holy Quran. The Hubble's Law states that the recession of distant galaxies implies that the universe is expanding and that the velocity of expansion equals distance over T (V = distance T where 1 / T is called Hubble's Constant. T = Infinity). (Encyclopaedia Britannica Vol:18 on page 1007 refers). What a miraculous and a surprising similarity of the science of Cosmology and of the Hubble's Law of Expanding Universe is with the Holy Quranic verse revealed 1400 years ago!

Recently, it has been known that scientists have found giant galaxies which appear to be much larger than the Milky Way and are 10 billion light years away from earth. The galaxies have been identified for the first time and may help scientists determine whether the universe is expanding indefinitely or is ıated to collapse inward itself.

Numerous verses from the Holy Quran on the 'Doomsday' or the Catastrophic Collapse of the Universe, are discussed with its scientific explanation in Chapter 12 of this book, which reveal miraculous agreement and similarity with the Holy Quranic verses on the awe inspiring events approaching the 'Doomsday'.

Men of understanding and knowledge find surprisingly true that a single verse (51:47) of the Holy Quran encompasses basic principles of the origin, evolution and the power packed structural make-up and characteristics of the entire physical universe. Moreover, the Quranic verses (25:2), (VI:73) and (39:5-6) clearly reveal that Allah has created all things right from the atom to the galactic system and to the whole universe with all its components, in a definite order and in set measures and in true proportions, i.e. the mass, speed, force and all other properties and characteristics including their make-up, shape and colour and all other interactions and their resultant products,etc. are in true proportions and in due proportions and are with a set measure.

Allah has created a specific amount of the substance forming the universe in the shape of matter and energy. The amount of this substance i.e. matter and energy is then made as physically 'constant' or a fixed amount. Similarly, Allah created physical 'constancy' in the velocity of light and fixed its speed at 186 000 miles per second. Allah has built the universe with energy or might and all objects in the universe are composed of energy or might in one form or the other and their interaction also involve energy.

With the knowledge of nuclear force and nuclear reactions, Physicists and Cosmologists know how the sun pours out vast amounts of energy and what makes the stars shine. The Hydrogen in the sun is continuously converted by nuclear fusion to Helium; and star-dust is nothing but a high grade nuclear fuel. Thus the whole universe is constituted or built of might or packed energy or power and is expanding as the Holy verse (51:47) reveals.

Physics indeed tells the story of all the might or substance in the universe, its constitution, structural make-up, the interactions and the micro-particles and the forces controlling and acting upon them, their interaction and linkage with one another became the prime concern of the Physicists and modern Cosmologists. In fact, with emergence of the weak and strong nuclear forces, the obvious attempt to unify these with the forces of gravity and electro-magnetism became the dream and desire of all the Physicists. The new pattern had started emerging which would give us the clues to a grand unification of all the known forces, the four fundamental forces of nature (now combined into three as per Dr. Salam's Theory and can be combined into one by inter-conversion) which emanated by the Divine Will of Allah, when in the beginning Allah said:

'Be! and it is' (19:35).

And the universe was thus created with might and forces and the appointed laws governing them and which is expanding till an appointed period when it is destined to collapse, as is revealed by the Holy Quran.

Quran describes Our Near Universe decked with Stars as inviolable which is the Measuring of the Might and the Wisdom of Allah in the Creation of the Universe

Attention of scientists the world over and of all the wise men of knowledge is specially invited to ponder over the Holy Quran and on the Quranic verse (41:12), containing modern concepts of science in allegory regarding the evolution of the universe, its inviolability and then using the inviolability as a yardstick for knowing the Infinite attributes and wisdom of the Creator (Allah) Who is the Mighty, the Knower and Who created the universe as His inviolable creation. The relevant Quranic verses are quoted below for contemplation and guidance:-

(1) *Then He ordained them seven heavens in two days and inspired in each heaven its mandate: We decked the nether heaven with lamps*

and rendered it inviolable. This is the measuring of the Mighty, the Knower' (XLI:12).

(2) *And verily in the heaven We have set mansions of the stars and We have beautified it for beholders'. (15:16).*

(3) *'By the Heaven, holding mansions of the Stars' (85:1).*

(4) *'Lo! We have adorned the lowest heaven with an ornament, the planets' (37:6).*

(5) *Blessed be He Who hath placed in the heaven mansions of the stars and hath placed there in a great lamp and a moon giving light' (26:61).*

(6) *Allah it is Who raised up the heavens without visible supports, then mounted the Throne, and compelled the sun and the moon to be of service, each runneth unto an appointed term; He ordereth the course; He detaileth the revelations, that haply ye may be certain of the meeting with your Lord' (13:2).*

(7) *'And the sky He hath uplifted; and He hath set the measure'. (55:7).*

(8) *'Have they not then observed the sky above them, how We have constructed it and beautified it, and how there are no rifts therein!' (50:6)*

The following sense is derived from the interpretation of the above Quranic verse (41:12) in the context of known knowledge of Physics and Cosmology.

The original pervasive form of the chaotic matter of the universe created by Allah had to organize under the force of gravity into vast structures such as galaxies, stars and the solar system etc, long before other forces could come into play. The outstanding features of the force of gravity is that nothing can be shielded from it. The gravitational force is present in the universe not because it is strong, but because it is quite weak. This means weak forces give rise to large or massive structures i.e. galaxies, stars and solar systems and strong forces to small structures i.e. atoms. The formation of the cosmological bodies is mainly due to the force of gravity in the universe. Gravitation appears to be the only interaction of matter that affects the behaviour of the universe in the large.

The above Holy verses clearly reveal the creation of the four fundamental forces of nature for the formation of the structure of the physical universe and encompasses tremendous wisdom and knowledge. The Holy verse (41:12) alone contains eight different revelations of great significance. Each part of the verse reveals the creative and evolutionary features of the universe. The sense encompassed in the Holy verse (41:12) in the context of modern knowledge of sciences and common sense is explained as follows:-

The first part of the Holy verse reveals the 'creation of Seven heavens' or 'Seven universes'. The second is about the 'time' taken in their formation. The third part of the Holy verse is that each heaven or universe is given its own 'mandate', i.e. a system and an authoritative order or command for the orderly functioning of its formation. The fourth and the fifth combine part of the Holy verse is that the 'nearest heaven' i.e. our universe which is the nearest and which is expanding and is boundless, is 'decked with innumerable mansions of stars (lamps) and galaxies'. The sixth part is that these galaxies and stars are located so far apart in the universe and are so vast that our near heaven or universe (one out of the seven heavens) is rendered 'inviolable' due to vastness or boundlessness. It is highly surprising that the universe is inviolable even by 'light' (one of the universe's own physical component), and which is the fastest and the ultimate source of travel of discrete material particles, travelling at the velocity of 186,000 miles per second in the expanding universe. How amazingly the basic facts of science are in congruity with the above Quranic verses. The reality of creating the 'constancy' in the velocity of light i.e. fixed rate of velocity, is a vital fundamental fact discovered by science and is the basic principle created by Allah for the inviolability of the universe in terms of its vastness as is indicated in the above Holy verse. Light, which is composed of infinitesimally discrete material particles has the fastest velocity for travel in the universe and nothing can travel faster than it. It is the ultimate speed of a material particle in the universe. The seventh, again an objective and conclusive part of the Holy verse, is that if one wants to know by 'measure the might of Allah' or an indication of His Creative power, then better take a hint from the inviolability of only the near universe (i.e. at present the observable part of the near universe), which is only one of the seven heavens, where billions of galaxies each containing billions of stars and billions of planets are billions of light years apart. (One light year is equal to light that travels for one year at the rate of 186,000 miles per second). The distances between the stars in our galaxy are so great that even if the number of stars were increased a million times, our near galaxy (milky way) would not be crowded.

British Astronomer Sir James Jeans stated:-

> 'If there were only three wasps over the whole continent of Europe, Europe would be more crowded with wasps than space is with stars'. (Encyclopaedia Britannica, 1979).

The eighth and the last objective part of the Divine verse is that Allah is 'the Knower' of all things which implies that He is the Creator of all things in seven heavens including our inviolable universe and is able to do all things. It is observed that each word of the Holy verse contains great guidance giving light of wisdom to knowledgeable men who may ponder. The Holy verse conveys tremendous information about the physical features of the universe which are of great consequence in knowing Allah and in knowing His attributes and His Creative Power in creating the inviolable universe. All such verses of the Holy Quran describe the portents of Allah and teaches man to believe in Allah and to believe in Prophet Muhammad (PBUH), the Last Prophet of Allah to whom the Holy Quran was revealed, and to believe in the Holy Quran as the word of Allah and to believe in the Hereafter and in all that which the Holy Quran contains in its verses. The inviolability of the universe may be examined from the discovery of a quasar called PKS 2000 minus 300, by Australian and British Scientists which is 18 billion light years away from earth and is the most distant and luminous object in the universe, emitting the energy of 100 million million suns. The discovery has shattered a theory that the edge of the universe had already been discovered: Cosmologists caution that their science is hardly an exact one that conventional wisdom can be wrong—and that new discoveries can alter the picture entirely.

Quran on the Interaction of Matter and Energy

Scientists, researchers, intellectuals, religious scholars and wisemen may ponder over another Holy Quranic verse (36:80), revealing facts and the physical laws governing the interaction of matter and energy at the level of sub-atomic particles and containing modern concepts in allegory on the evolution of the universe and the interaction of matter and energy.

The Holy Quranic verses reveal:-

(1) *'Who hath appointed for you fire from the green tree, and behold! Ye kindle from it'. (36:80).*

(2) *Have ye observed the fire which ye strike out' (56:71).*

(3) *'He knoweth that which goes down into the earth and that which cometh forth from it, and that which descendeth from the heavens and that which ascendeth into it. He is the Merciful, the Forgiving' (34:2).*

(4) *'Those who disbelieve say: The hour will never come unto us. Say: Nay, by my Lord, but it is coming unto you surely. (He is) the Knower of the Unseen. Not an atom's weight or less than that or greater, escapeth Him in the heavens or in the earth, but it is in a clear record' (34:3).*

The understanding of the above allegorial Holy verses and the sense contained in them and the meaning derived out of them, in the context of scientific knowledge acquired from the study of Molecular Biology, Particle Physics, the General Theory of Relativity, the Einstein's Relation, the Laws of Conservation of Matter and Energy, the Quantum Theory, the process of annihilation and the process of electron-positron creation, the mutual conversion of matter and energy, Laws of Thermodynamics, the Law of Definite Proportion, the process of radio-activity and the process of nuclear fusion of hydrogen in the sun to helium, the process of conversion of solar energy into plant material through the process of photosynthesis and many other phenomena and modern concepts are miraculously encompassed and divinely indicated and exposed in the above quoted Quranic verse. (36:80). The three verses quoted above, in the context of modern knowledge of all the sciences, clearly reveal that not an atom's weight or less than that i.e. of the sub-atomic particles or sub-nuclear particle and of the weight of electron can escape Allah's notice and that everything is in a clear record with Him and their movements and interaction and work according to His set measure and design, are in His notice. The Holy Quran again reveals that:

'Those who have been given knowledge see that what is revealed unto them from thy Lord is the truth and leadeth into the Path of the Mighty, the Owner of Praise. (34:6).

This verse clearly indicates that those men who are given knowledge including the scientists see that what is revealed by the Holy Quran is the truth and leads to the path and to the faith to know God Who is the Owner of Praise.

Again, the first part of the symbolic Quranic verse (36:80) indicates that Allah has appointed for mankind, fire from the green tree. The Holy verse (36:80) conveys the meaning that in the context of the knowledge of Physics and Chemistry, the solar energy is converted and stored in the green tree, i.e. in plant life which ultimately converts into organic matter of the hydro carboh family, which is combustible material or is fire or fuel or energy and is mineral wealth. Thus the sense from the allegorial verse can be deduced that 'Allah has appointed fire from the green tree' for the service and benefit of mankind which they burn. Another allegorial Holy verse (34:2) quoted above also indicates that the light energy goes down into the earth which sustains life on earth and come forth from it in converted form. Moreover, some part of energy escapes from the earth back into the universe. Similar is the journeying of mankind to the 'Hereafter'. The second part of the Holy verse (36:80) quoted above is that 'behold: Ye kindle from it'. This means the stored solar radiation or light energy of the sun after conversion into plant material or matter is made available as fuel for the service and benefit of mankind. Man ignites and takes benefit out of the sun's energy in its various forms. Man including all the living creatures on earth and the green tree which includes forests and all green vegetation on earth, depend and owe their existence due to the solar energy from the sun. Actually man burns solar energy in various forms for sustaining life. Even the growth and subsequent evolution of life on the earth's bio-sphere began with the interaction of the solar energy broadcast by the sun and as is revealed by the Holy Quran in the verse. (23:79).

The Holy Quran reveals :-

> *'And He it is Who hath sown you broadcast in the earth and unto Him Ye will be gathered'* (23:79).

The above Holy Quranic verse (23:79) excites feelings of far reaching consequences. It indicates that it is one of the main physical cause for the creation of the building-blocks of man, the animal and plant life and their growth on earth besides playing many other vital and basic roles in the interaction of matter and energy in the entire universe, right from the micro-particles in the atom to the formidable galactic systems and the known four interacting fundamental forces in the universe. The Holy verses clearly indicate that the movements and the interactions of the micro-particles, the forces controlling and acting upon them, their interaction, conversion and linkage with one another, their structural make-up and constitution and the substance forming the physical universe and its contents as a whole is in the knowledge of Allah and is on record with Him of which He is the Creator.

More Holy Quranic verses besides above verse (36:80) are quoted to explain further, the 'substance' in the universe (matter and energy), their constituents, the micro-particles and the fundamental forces controlling and acting upon them, their interaction and linkage with one another right from the structure of atom to galactic systems, including the sun and the moon which float in fixed orbits for an appointed period of time (13:2) in the universes without visible support and maintaining a perfect celestial order. All these celestial bodies exist and function and stay in order by the Command of Allah and are for the service and benefit of mankind. The benefit is that energy is used and stored in earth and provisions are made to grow and sustain all kinds of life on earth and to know and watch the infinite marvels of Allah.

Allah the Creator, the Compeller and the Guardian of the Universe and the Man

Some of the Holy verses reveal the science of the physical universe and of man, which reveal the Infinite Power of Allah, the Creator of life and death, and of the universe, and the Creator of the Unseen and of the invisible and the visible and the Creator of the seven heavens in perfect harmony and the Creator of the universe without visible support and holding perfect celestial order through the force of gravity and without fault by the Creator Allah Who is Able to do all things, some of the Holy Quranic verses are quoted below :-

(1) *'Those who disbelieve say: The hour will never come unto us. Say: Nay, by my Lord, but it is coming unto you surely. (He is) the Knower of the Unseen. Not an atom's weight or less than that or*

greater escapeth Him in the heavens, or in the earth, but it is a clear Record' (34:3).

(2) *'It is He Who created the heavens and the earth in true proportions' (VI:73) and (39:5-6).*

(3) *'Allah it is Who raised up the heavens without visible support. Then mounted the Throne and compelled the sun and the moon to be of service, each runneth into an appointed term' (13:2).*

(4) *'And the Sky He hath uplifted; and He hath set the measure' (LV:7).*

(5) *'Glory be to Him: When He decreeth a thing. He saith unto it only, 'Be! and it is' (19:35).*

(6) *'It is He Who created all things and ordered them in due proportions' (25:2).*

(7) *'Then turned He to the heaven when it was smoke and said unto it and unto the earth, come both of you, willingly or loth. They said we come, obedient' (41:11).*

(8) *'And the earth have We laid out, how gracious was the Spreader (thereof)! (51:48).*

(9) *'Disbelieve Ye verily in Him Who created the earth in 2 Days' (41:9).*

(10) *'And We created not the heavens and the earth and all that is in between them, in play' (XLIV:38).*

(11) *'And verily We created the heavens and the earth and all between them, in six days, not of weariness touched us' (50:38).*

(12) *'Have they not then observed the sky above them, how We have constructed it and beautified it, and how there are no rifts therein' (50:6).*

(13) *'Who hath created seven heavens in harmony Thou (Muhammad) can't see no fault in Beneficent One's creation, then look again can't thou see any rift' (67:3).*

(14) *'Then look again and yet again, thy sight will return unto thee weakened and made dim' (67:4).*

(15) *'You will not see in the creation of all Merciful, an imperfection. Return thy gaze again and again and it will come back to you dazzled, weary' (50:6).*

(16) *'The sun and the moon are made punctual'. (55:5).*

(17) *'The stars and the trees adore' (55:6).*

(18) *'Is it not for the sun to overtake the moon, nor doth the night outstrip the day. They float each in an orbit' (36:40).*

(19) *'And He hath constrained the night and the day and the sun and the moon to be of service unto you and the stars are made subservient by*

His Command. Lo! herein indeed are portents for people who have sense' (16:12).

(20) *'He is Allah, the Creator, the Shaper out of naught, the Fashioner, His are the most beautiful names. All that is in the heavens and the earth glorifieth Him, and He is the Mighty, the Wise'* (60:24).

(21) *'Who hath created life and death that He may try you, which of you is the best in conduct, and He is the Mighty, the Forgiving'.* (67:2).

(22) *'And hath made the moon a light terrin and made the sun a lamp'* (71:16).

(23) *'And We have built above you seven strong heavens'* (77:12).

(24) *'Who created thee, then fashioned, then proportioned thee'* (82:7).

(25) *'And He it is Who hath created man from water and hath appointed for him kindered by blood and kindered by marriage; for thy Lord is ever Powerful'* (25:54).

(26) *'Allah has created every animal of water. Of them is (a kind) that goeth upon its belly and (a kind) that goeth upon two legs and (a kind) that goeth upon four. Allah createth what He Will. Lo! Allah is Able to do all things'.* (24:45).

(27) *'Glory be to Him Who created all the sexual pairs, of that which the earth growth and of themselves and of that which they know not'* (36:36).

(28) *'Have they not seen how We have created for them of our handiwork the cattle, so that they are their owners'?* (36:71).

(29) *'Have not those who disbelieve known that the heavens and the earth were one piece, then We parted them and We made every living thing of water? Will they not then believe'?* (21:30).

(30) *'And He it is Who created the night and the day, and the sun and the moon. They float each in an orbit'.* (21:33).

(31) *'And if thou wert to ask them: Who created the heavens and the earth, and constrained the sun and the moon (to their appointed work) they would say: Allah. How then are they turned away'?* (29:61).

It is clear from the above quoted Holy verses that even the movement of an electron anywhere in the universe cannot escape Allah's notice as it is in a clear record with Him, i.e. permanently noted and preserved or known to Him, and is under His Command and stay in perfect order. Allah has raised the seven heavens with His invisible might or force and placed above them, the Tremendous Throne. It is Allah Who has created the sun and the moon, revolving in assigned orbits, for a definite period of time and are created for the service of mankind. All things are created by Allah in due proportions and are in true proportions and with a set measure. Allah is the Creator, the Shaper out of naught and the Fashioner of all things and there is no imperfection in His creation. Allah is the Creator of life and death and He will try mankind for their conduct, after proper accountability and Judgement in the 'Hereafter'. The accountability and its record as the physical sciences indicate the sense, is in similarity with the Holy Quranic verses as is discussed in the chapter on accountability.

Some more Quranic verses on the creation of the physical universe and man and a perfect celestial order in cosmos are quoted. These Holy verses reveal wisdom and knowledge to mankind who ponder and pay heed. The Holy verses reveal that Allah is the Knower of the invisible and the visible and of all things in the heavens and the earth. He is the Creator, the High Exalted, Almighty, the Wise, the Alive and the Eternal and exercises power on all things.

Holy verses (10.90-92) make miraculous revelation. that Allah preserved the dead body of Pharaohs drowned in the river thousands of years back and recently discovered (a few decades back) which is lying in a museum to serve as a portent of Allah for men who pay heed. The Holy Quran revealed this event 1400 years ago. The event took place thousands of years before the revelation of the Holy Quran and was re-discovered about more than 1300 years after the revelation. What a miracle is this? The Holy Quran truly reveals events of the past and of the future. This indicates the portent or the token of Allah. So that man knows Allah and believe in Allah, and in His Book and in His Prophet on whom the Holy Book is revealed for the guidance of all mankind.

The Holy verses reveal:-

(1) *'And maketh the sun and the moon constant in their courses to be of service unto you and hath made of service unto you the night and the day' (14:33).*

(2) *'He it is Who appointed the sun a splendour and the moon a light, and measured for her stages, that ye might know the number of the years, and the reckoning Allah created not (all) that save in truth. He detaileth the revelations for people who have knowledge' (10:6).*

(3) *'Hath thou, not seen that Allah hath created the heavens and the earth with truth? If He will, He can remove you and bring (in) some new creation' (14:19).*

(4) *'And that is not great matter for Allah' (14:20).*

(5) *'Allah knoweth that which every female beareth and that which the wombs absorb and that which they grow. And everything with Him is measured' (13:8).*

(6) *'He is the Knower of the invisible and the visible, the Great, the High Exalted' (13:9).*

(7) *'Lo! Allah (it is) Who spliteth the grain of corn and the datestone (for sprouting). He bringeth forth the living from the dead and is the Bringer-forth of the dead from the living. Such is Allah. How then are ye perverted?' (6:96).*

(8) *'Allah (Himself) is witness that there is no God save Him. And the angels and the men of learning (too are witnesses). Maintaining His creation in justice, there is no God save Him, the Almighty, the Wise'. (III:18).*

(9) *'Allah! There is no God save Him, the Alive, the Eternal'. (II:2).*

(10) *'He it is Who fashioneth you in the wombs as pleaseth Him. There is no God save Him, the Almighty and the Wise' (II:6).*

(11) *'The fate of drowning overtook him (Pharaohs) he exclaimed: I believe that there is no God save Him and I am of those who surrender (unto Him)' (10:90).*

(12) *'But this day We save thee in thy body that thou mayest be a portent for those after thee. Lo! most of mankind are heedless of Our portents' (10:92).*

(13) *'All that are in the heavens and the earth entreat Him. Everyday He exerciseth (universal) power' (55:29).*

(14) *'And verily We have beautified the world's heaven with Lamps and We have made them missiles for the devils and for them We have prepared the doom of flame' (67:5).*

(15) *'Hast thou not known that Allah knoweth all that is in the heaven and the earth? Lo! it is in a record. Lo! that is easy for Allah' (22:70).*

(16) *'Praise be to Allah, the Creator of the heavens and the earth, which appointeth the angels as messengers having wings two, three and four. He multiplieth in certain what He will. Lo! Allah is Able to do all things' (35:1).*

The Holy verse (35:1) on angel messengers can be explained that Allah has at His Command the angels rank on rank incharge of all kinds of forces, having wings or dimensions of two, three, four and a multiple of these wings or dimensions or powers as He wishes, as Allah is Able to do all things. The angels are made incharge of all such powers who discharge their duties as Allah wishes. Allah has given wings or (dimensions) to the angels and due to such wings (dimensions) or powers the angels are made capable to perform their various functions and duties as assigned by Allah in the physical and metaphysical worlds. The angels can therefore, travel from metaphysical worlds to physical world freely.

All kinds of messages from Allah revealed in the Holy Quran are in similitudes and in allegories. But some allegorial meanings are not understandable. There are, however, clear and direct revelations which are understandable. The Quran beautifully argues in the verse (30:58) that :-

(1) *'Verily We have coined for mankind in the Quran all kinds of similitudes and indeed if thou comest unto them with a miracle, those who disbelieve would verily exclaim. Ye are but tricksters!' (30:58).*

(2) *'Have they not observed what is before them and what is behind them of the sky and the earth? If We will, we can make the earth swallow them, or cause obliteration from the sky to fall on them. Lo! herein surely is a portent for every slave who turneth (to Allah) repentant' (34:9).*

Scientists, religious scholars and men of knowledge the world over, may objectively study the allegorial and clear revelations made by Allah in the Holy Quran as the message of Islam, which already contains basic principles and modern concepts of science to indicate the truth in the physical reality as token for mankind and at the same time teaches submission and obedience to Allah, Who is the Creator of man and the physical universe and knowledge concerning them is truthfully described by Allah in the Holy Quran. The understanding of the Holy Quran and to grasp its meanings encompassed in each verse is wide open to wisdom and knowledge of people who ponder and pay heed and is not confined to the ruts and grooves of whimsical interpretation. Every word of the Holy Quran is full of wisdom and knowledge and stands as absolute reality for all time to come. The Holy Quran is eternal truth. Science is knowledge and knowledge with common sense and conscience is the means to understand the real substance of the Holy Quran which reveals absolute truth about the physical universe and man and about the Hereafter'

The Holy Quran reveals :-

> *Those who have been given knowledge see that what is revealed unto thee from thy Lord is the truth and leadeth into the Path of the Mighty, the Owner of Praise' (34:6).*

The above Quranic verse clearly reveals that men who are given knowledge see and feel the truth in the revelations and lead them into the path of the Creator Allah Who is Mighty and is the Owner of Praise in the universe and in the 'Hereafter'.

Part II

THE CREATION OF LIFE IN THE LIGHT OF THE HOLY QURAN

CHAPTER VIII

(i) The Creation of Adam as the First man—The Coming into being of life—And Adam as the father of human race.

(ii) The Seeds of Life.

(iii) Life Wafted in from space and human spores propelled by the pressure of Light and seeded on earth with micro-organism—`Theory of Panspermia".

(iv) From Whence We came.

(v) Darwin's Theory of Evolution.

(vi) First man (Adam) had fully human body and mind and soul and was created by Allah with the Best Stature, Good Shape, Perfected with Soul and Inspired with Conscience and raised up as the best Community for mankind and was preferred above many of those created with a marked preferment and placed as the Viceroy of God in the Earth.

(vii) The Evolution of Ape into Man an Abominable concept.

(viii) The transformation of Man into Ape by Allah as a curse for disobedience.

Chapter 8

THE CREATION OF ADAM AS THE FIRST MAN-THE COMING INTO BEING OF LIFE AND ADAM AS THE FATHER OF HUMAN RACE

THE CREATION OF LIFE, WHEN ALLAH SAID: BE! AND ADAM WAS CREATED

It is beyond the power of science to trace the origin of life and spirit and to know the origin of the creation of the first man and to know Who appointed the genetics in the spores of man other than Allah, Who is the Creator of man and Who recorded a million pages of instructions in the spiral tape of the DNA Molecule of the living cell. The Holy Quran reveals it is Allah Who has created life and death and Who created Adam, the first living man by breathing His Spirit into non-living clay to make a living man (Adam) and made him to dwell in the Garden (Paradise). He was expelled from there to earth and Allah made his seed and appointed the earth for a period as his habitat and has sown his seed broadcast in the earth to grow as a growth on earth i.e. to grow under the universal physical laws, and Allah carry mankind on the land and the sea with provisions of good things for sustenance on earth. All this was done by the Divine Creative Power of Allah when He said: Be! and Adam was created. So, the creation of man is a portent and a marvel of Allah and on thorough study and contemplation, living man is a miracle of creation and is a universe in miniature. It is true that the origin of life which arose on earth is from outer space and is such an improbable event that its occurrence is unlikely and rare and could happen only once during the history of the Cosmos. Crick, Simon and Schuster have expressed their ideas in 'Life Itself'. Also refer to Science81, October 1981 Issue.

Attention of all men of knowledge is invited to the heavenly message of God for the guidance of all mankind which reveals that Allah is the Lord of the Worlds and the Creator of man. Allah is the sustainer of man and it is Allah Who produces and reproduces man.

The following Holy verses from the Quran are quoted:-

(1) *"And when thy Lord said unto the angels: Lo! I am about to place a viceroy in the earth, they said: Wilt Thou place therein one who will do harm therein and will shed blood, while we, we hymn Thy praise and sanctify Thee? He said: surely I know that which ye know not" (11:30).*

(2) *"When Thy Lord said unto the angels: Lo! I am about to create a mortal out of mire" (38:71).*

(3) *"And He began the creation of man from clay" (32:7).*

(4) *"Verily We created man from a product of wet earth" (23:12).*

(5) *"And He it is Who hath created man from water and hath appointed for him kindered by blood and kindered by marriage; for Thy Lord is ever powerful" (25:54).*

(6) *"And a soul and Him Who perfected it" (XCI:7).*

(7) *"And inspired it (with conscience of) what is wrong for it and (what is) right for it" (XCI:8).*

(8) *"They will ask thee concerning the spirit: Say: The Spirit is by command of my Lord, and of knowledge Ye have been vouchsafed but little" (17:85).*

(9) *"And when, I have fashioned him and breathed into him of My Spirit, then fall down before him prostrate" (38:72) and (15:29).*

(10) *"The angels fell down prostrate everyone" (38:73).*

(11) *"Saving Iblis; he was scornful and became one of the disbelievers" (38:74).*

(12) *"And when We said unto the angels: Prostrate yourselves before Adam, they fell prostrate all save Iblis. He demurred through pride and so became a disbeliever" (II:34).*

(13) *"And when We said unto the angels: Fall prostrate before Adam, they fell prostrate all save Iblis; he refused" (20:116).*

(14) *"He said: O Iblis! What hindereth thee from falling prostrate before that which I have created with My hands Art thou too proud or art thou of the high exalted?" (38:75).*

(15) *"And He taught Adam all the names, then showed them to the angels, saying: Inform Me of the names of these, if ye are truthful" (11:31).*

(16) *"He said: O Adam! Inform them of their names, and when he had informed them of their names, He said: Did I not tell you that I know the secret of the heavens and the earth? And I know that which ye disclose and which ye hide" (11:33).*

(17) *"And We said: O Adam! Dwell thou and thy wife in the Garden and eat ye freely (of the fruits) thereof where ye will; but come not nigh this tree lest ye become wrongdoers" (II:35).*

(18) *"Therefore We said: O Adam! This is an enemy unto thee and unto thy wife, so let him not drive you both out of the Garden so that thou come to toil". (20:117).*

(19) *"It is (vouchsafed) unto thee that thou hungerest not therein nor art naked". (20:118).*

(20) *"And thou thirstest not therein nor art exposer to the sun's heat". (20:119).*

(21) *"But the Devil Whispered to him, saying: O Adam! Shall I show thee the tree of immortality and power that wasteth not away?". (20:120).*

(22) *"Then they twain ate thereof, so that their shame became apparent unto them and they began to hide by heaping on themselves some of the leaves of the Garden. And Adam disobeyed his Lord, so went astray" (20:121).*

(23) *"But Satan caused them to deflect therefrom and expelled them from the (happy) state in which they were; and we said: Fall down, one of you a foe unto the other! There shall be for you on earth a habitation and provision for a time" (II:36).*

(24) *"He said: Seest thou this (creature) whom thou hast honoured above me, if Thou give me grace until the Day of Resurrection I verily will seize his seed, save but a few" (17:62).*

(25) *"We said: Go down, all of you from hence, but verily there cometh unto you from Me a guidance; and whoso followeth My guidance, there shall no fear come upon them neither shall they grieve". (11:38).*

(26) *"He said: Go down hence, both of you, one of you a foe unto the other. But if there come unto you from Me a guidance, then whoso*

followeth My guidance, he will not go astray no come to grief" (20:123).

(27) *"We said: Go down, all of you from hence, but verily there cometh unto you from Me a guidance; and whoso followeth my guidance, there shall no fear come upon them neither shall they grieve". (11:38).*

(28) *"Then Adam received from his Lord words (of revelation) and He relented toward him. Lo! He is the Relenting, the Merciful" (II:37).*

(29) *"Then his Lord chose him and relented toward him and guided him" (20:122).*

(30) *"Then He made his seed from a draught of despised fluid" (32:8).*

(31) *"Then placed him as a drop (of seed) in a safe lodging" (23:13).*

(32) *"And He it is Who hath sown you broadcast in the earth and unto Him ye will be gathered" (23:79).*

(33) *"And Allah has caused you to grow as a growth from the earth. And afterward, He maketh you return thereto. And He will bring you forth once again" (71:17).*

(34) *"Allah it is Who appointed for you the earth for a dwelling-place and the sky for a canopy, and fashioned you and perfected your shapes and hath provided you with good things. Such is Allah, your Lord. Then blessed be Allah, the Lord of the Worlds!" (40:64).*

(35) *"And Allah hath made the earth a wide expanse for you'. (71:19).*

(36) *"Lo! He it is Who produceth, then reproduceth" (85:13).*

(37) *"Lo! the likeness of Jesus with Allah is as the likeness of Adam. He created him of dust, then He said unto him: Be! and he is" (III:59).*

(38) *"He created you from one being, then from that (being) He made its mate; and He hath provided for you of cattle eight kinds. He created you in the wombs of your mothers, creation after creation, in a threefold gloom. Such is Allah, your Lord. His is the sovereignty. There is no God save Him. How then are ye turned away" (39:6).*

(39) *"Verily We have honoured the children of Adam. We carry them on the land and the sea and have made provision of good things for them, and have preferred them above many of those whom We created with a marked preferment". (17:70).*

The Creation of Life when Allah said: Be! and Adam was created

The Holy Quran reveals the above verses on the creation of Life or the coming into being of life created out of mire and infused it with spirit to create Adam as the first living man in the Garden beyond the universe when Allah said: Be! and Adam was created. Allah created Adam in perfect human form and then from Adam, Allah made its mate. Eve was his mate created out of Adam's rib by the Creative divine power of Allah.

Then Allah made Adam's seed and the genetic code from a draught of despised fluid and has sown him broadcast in the earth and caused Adam's race to grow as a growth from the earth. Thus, it is Allah Who creates and then enables His creations to reproduce and appoints the earth as a dwelling-place for mankind and has made the earth a wide expanse for them. Thus, mankind only exist on earth and nowhere else in the universe.

The Creation of Man in the light of Quran

Allah is the Lord of the worlds. He is the Creator of Seven heavens and the earth. He is the Creator of the universe and man. He is the Creator of the visible, the invisible, the hidden and of the unseen. He is the Creator of life and death and he is the Creator of 'Life after death'. He is the Creator of the Paradise as wide as the Seven heavens. He is the Creator of the Hell. He is the Creator of the world of the Hereafter. Allah is the Creator of Mankind, jinn and of Angels and of all other living creatures on earth and in all the heavens.

Allah created Adam as the first man from non-living clay or wet earth or mire or mud or dust and water or plastic clay. Allah then fashioned man in due proportion and gifted him with heart, eyes, ears, skins, brain and all other things and perfected him by infusing His Spirit and inspired him with conscience of what is wrong and what is right for him. Allah created man with a lofty station and preferred man above many of those whom Allah created. Thus Allah has honoured the children of Adam.

The Creation of a Mortal

Allah said to the angels that He is about to create a mortal out of mire or mud or clay and is about to place him as a viceroy in the earth. So, Allah breathed His Spirit into Adam and said: Be! and Adam was created. Allah asked the angels to prostrate themselves before him. All the angels fell down prostrate except Iblis who said that as he is created out of fire and Adam is created out of clay so he is created as superior to Adam and he demurred through pride and Allah therefore caused the fall of Satan till the Day of Resurrection.

Allah said to Adam that he and his wife may live in the Garden (Paradise) and may eat freely of the fruits but forbade them not come near the particular tree otherwise they will become wrong-doers. But Satan whispered to Adam to eat the fruit of immortality from the tree. Adam and his wife deflected and ate the fruit and their shame became apparent to them and they began to hide by heaping on themselves with some of the leaves of the Garden. Adam disobeyed his Lord and went astray. Thus, Satan deflected them from the happy state in which they were and Allah expelled them from the happy state as they became the wrong-doers and Allah also ordered their fall down and the Satan as a foe to mankind and appointed earth as a habitation for Adam and his race and made provisions on earth for them for a fixed time. Allah then said to Adam and his race, go down all of you from hence and there on earth My guidance shall come to you and whoso follow My guidance they should not fear and they will not be grieved. Adam received revelation from Allah and he was pardoned. Allah is the Relenting, the Merciful.

Allah then made his seed, the genetic code (the seed of reproduction of Adam's race, the DNA, the complete coded genetic instructions from a draught of despised fluid and then placed the seed in a safe lodging for reproduction. Allah has sown Adam and Adam's seed broadcast in the earth and caused the same to grow as a growth from the earth through the process of the normal universal physical laws. Allah has appointed the earth as the dwelling-place for man to multiply and reproduce and the sky as canopy and Allah has provided man with all the good things on earth and on its land and on its seas. So Gracious is our Allah, the Lord of the worlds. Ultimately, on the appointed Day, man has to return to Allah and he will then be resurrected once again to the state of immortality. He will stay immortal and would go either to the Paradise or to the Hell with reference to the deeds of his performance in the physical world in the light of the Quranic revelations, teachings and guidance.

From the above Holy Quranic revelations what is conceived by the Author at the humble level of his understanding, is that Allah Who is the Lord of the Worlds and the Creator of All things and the One Who is Able to do All things intended to create a mortal out of mire, a man out of clay for placing him as viceroy in the earth for a fixed time. So, Allah said: Be! and Adam was created out of clay. Allah knows the secrets of the heavens and the earth as He is the Creator of all things. Allah asked Adam and his wife to eat freely in the Paradise but forbade them not to go near a particular tree, but on Satan's deflection they ate the fruit from the forbidden tree and became wrong doers.

Furthermore, what is understandable from the revelations in the Holy verse (11:38), is that Allah said to Adam and his race including his wife to Go down, all of them from hence. They were expelled from the Paradise and sent down to the earth which Allah appointed as the habitat for Adam's race i.e. for mankind for a fixed time. Verse (40:64).

The Holy verse (32:8) reveals that Allah made the seed of Adam's race from a draught of despised fluid. The Holy Quran hints towards the molecular biology a modern scientific discipline: Thus Allah created and appointed the genetics of human race i.e. the DNA, carrying the complete genetic message in the blue-print of life, and all the biological elements and the processes of the creation of the chromosomes and their movements, the creation of the sperm and ova and their movements and the production and reproduction of the same in a safe lodging (23:13). Thus, Allah has sown (human race) Adam's seed broadcast and beamed in the earth from the Garden (the Paradise) or the heaven through a divine source, the secret of which only Allah knows. Allah as such has caused human race to grow as a growth from the earth under His appointed universal physical laws through the natural process of growth under the specially created favourable environments on earth.

The first creation of life originated out of non-living clay when "Allah said: Be! and Adam was created" and then his spouse was created out of his rib all by the divine Creative Power of Allah. After that Allah made the seed of Adam's race from fluid with perfection for production and reproduction and then Allah has sown Adam and his seed in the earth by divine broadcast and caused it to grow as a growth from the earth under the natural processes and the environment on earth. Allah did all this with His divine Creative Power and then left it to His set universal physical laws created for the purpose with assigned functions to grow and develop and multiply till the appointed Doomsday, when all mankind shall be resurrected by the divine command to become immortal in the Hereafter. On resurrection man is answerable and accountable for his deeds and actions on earth in the light of Allah's guidance as revealed on Prophet Muhammad (PBUH) in the Holy message of the Quran. The doctrines of Eschatology are described in Chapter 14 of this book.

The Creation of man as Scientists perceive so closely but miss the Quranic Guidance to know the absolute reality of Creation of the First Man and His Seed which were then broadcast to earth to grow as a growth from the Earth

Life wafted in from space and human spores propelled by the pressure of light and seeded on earth with Micro-Organsim-Theory of Panspermia by Physicists and Biologists

The Seeds of Life

An article by Francis Crick, a Biologist, entitled **'The Seeds of Life'**, appeared in the October, 1981 issue of the 'DISCOVER'. It theorized that life on Earth originated with micro-organisms sent by rocket from another planet in our galaxy. Crick along with other biologists called this act of delibrate seeding or 'Directed Panspermia'.

Crick and other scientists would know the absolute reality, if they read the Holy Quran for their guidance and shall find answers to the questions as Who created the first human and Who created the human spores and Who chose the earth as the habitat for mankind and Who directed the human seed to earth and has sown it to grow as a growth on earth. The light of wisdom on the creation of life and the knowledge about its Creator is revealed and is encompassed in the Holy Quran which gives guidance and information to people who read and ponder over the Holy Quran.

Crick explains that the energy pouring down from the stars—sun-light, in our case—on to the surface of the planet will cause the synthesis of numerous small organic compounds, thus turning the ocean into a thin, warm soup. These chemicals will, eventually, join on to each other and interact to produce a self-reproducing system, a primitive form of life. These simple living things will multiply, evolve by natural selection, and became more complicated until active, thinking creatures eventually emerge. Civilization, science and technology will follow and before long they will have mastered the entire environment of their planet. Then yearning for fresh worlds to conquer, they will learn to travel to neighbouring planets and then planets of nearby stars, choosing for their colonization those with favourable environments. They chose a beautiful place as our earth with favourable environments'.

The Holy Quran reveals that Allah has appointed the earth as a dwelling—place of man and fashioned and perfected man's shape and made provisions of good things on earth for him in the land and the sea (40:64) (27:61). Thus, Earth is the abode of man from the time he is sown in the earth and sown in the warm soup of the seas on earth and allowed to grow, develop and multiply by natural process and laws as assigned by Allah on earth till the appointed Doomsday.

Another scientist, a physicist Arrhencus is of the view that life did not originate on earth. It is wafted in from space. Astronomer, Sir, Fred Hoyle, Astronomer Chandra Wickramasinghe and Astrophysicist Armond Delsemme believe that life originated in far out space and that it is inherently unknowable. However, none of the scientists know or will ever know how the spores of life have safely been delivered through space on earth and that what is the source and origin of these spores and who seeded them in space and beamed them to earth. The creation of life is a divine phenomenon and its wafting and development on earth is also a divine phenomenon. The Holy Quran clearly indicates the wafting of life to earth through space from heaven garden and directed it to grow and develop in earth through the biological process of growth under the universal physical laws of nature. The Quran has revealed it 1400 years ago, when man was totally ignorant.

The following Quranic verses are quoted in support :-

(1) *'And He it is Who hath sown you broadcast in the earth and unto Him Ye will be gathered' (23:79).*

(2) *'And Allah has caused you to grow as a growth from the earth. And afterwards, He maketh you return thereto. And He will bring you forth once again' (71:17).*

The Francis Crick's article further explains as follows :-

The Swedish Physicist Arrhencus proposed that life did not start here by itself but was seeded by micro-organisms wafted in from space, primitive spores gently propelled by the pressure of the light falling on them. He called this idea panspermia, meaning 'seeds everywhere'.

But how could viable spores have arrived here, after such a long journey in space, undamaged by radiation'?

Crick and Leslie Orgel suggested that to avoid damages, the micro-organisms travelled in the head of an unmanned rocket sent to Earth by a higher civilization that had developed elsewhere some billions of years ago. The rocket was unmanned so that its range would be as great as possible. Life started here when these organisms were dropped into the primitive ocean and began to multiply'. We called our idea 'Directed Panspermia'.

The Holy Quran indicates and reveals in the verses (20:119-120) that Adam was created outside the solar system and outside the galaxy and outside this universe and at a place where universal laws are not applicable i.e. in the Garden or the heaven beyond the universe and that his seed was sown broadcast in the earth (verse 23:79) which means wafted through space by the divine power of Allah and that Allah caused man to grow as a growth from the earth. (Verse: 71:17) and that Allah appointed for man the earth for a dwelling-place (40:64) and (27:81) and Allah made the earth a wide expanse for man (71:19) where man's reproduction continues under the universal physical laws for human growth.

The Holy Quran reveals :

(1) *'All that are in the heavens and the earth entreat him. EverydayHe exerciseth Universal Power' (55:29).*

(2) *'And Allah has made the earth a wide expanse for you' (71:19).*

(3) *'And the earth have We laid out, how gracious was the Spreader (thereof) ' (51:48)'.*

The religion of Islam is a perfect religion and the Holy Quran is a true and perfect guide for all mankind. If Crick and other biologists take guidance from the Holy Quran, they will find the right answer to Crick's theory of 'Directed Panspermia' which states that the roots of our form of life go back to another place in the universe, almost certainly to another planet; that it had reached a very advanced form there before anything much had started here and that life here was seeded by micro-organisms, sent on some form of rocket'.

Crick's concept of the unmanned rocket part of his theory for communicating the micro-organisms from some place in the universe in an unmanned rocket to earth through the hostile space in the inviolable universe stinks with pure imagination and fiction. It is indicated by the Holy Quran that human spores or the micro-organisms or the seed of life are wafted in or beamed or broadcast from beyond the universe i.e. from the (Garden) to earth by the divine will of Allah, the Creator of Adam and his race for whom life supporting environments are created on earth so that human race grows, develops and multiply on earth which is placed in a life supporting zone from the sun in the solar system.

Crick and other Biologists shall find tremendous guidance from the Holy Quran if they study and ponder over the verses of the Holy Quran and bear in mind that there is a Creator Who also created the civilization in other planets which Crick considers had sent unmanned rocket to earth loaded with 'Directed Panspermia'?

The Holy Quran in the verse (17:70) clearly reveals that Allah carries the children of Adam on the land sea and on earth. Adam's seed and its growth on earth is indicated.

Have Crick and other Biologists ever thought who recorded the intelligent instructions and coded it in the tape of DNA molecule with genetic informations running into a million pages? The chemical DNA is the basic matter of life, the molecule that tells cells how to function and how they should reproduce.

Have these biologists ever thought who created the spirit or the soul or the vital force and 'Life' — the cause of a living matter or living man or living creature?

The Holy Quran reveals :-

(1) 'Allah made every living thing of water' (21:30).

(2) 'And Allah hath created every animal of water' (21:30).

(3) 'And He it is Who hath created man from water' (25:54).

The above Holy verses indicate that in spite of millions of varieties of species of the living creatures on earth and of the great variety of molecules and chemical reactions produced by evolution, the basic and major constituent is water and that all living things are made of water and other chemical elements into the cell, the fundamental unit of life. In spite of the differences, there is great similarity between the cells of animals and plants. Every living thing starts life as a single cell and that one single molecule, DNA is the controlling force of all forms of life and is the genetic code, but not the life itself.

The so-called idea of 'Directed Panspermia' by superior civilization elsewhere or in the Galaxy, in the light of the Holy Quran is totally refuted. Man himself is the most superior creature and his origin is from Adam when Allah breathed His Spirit into him and thus created the first living man in perfect human form and with conscience who is preferred above many of those creations whom Allah created with a marked preferment and gave him the best stature and good shape and was asked to eat freely in the Garden (Paradise). Regarding the higher status of man among the creatures that Allah created, the Holy Quran reveals :-

> *'Verily We have honoured the children of Adam. We carry them on the land and the sea and have made provisions of good things for them and have preferred them above many of those whom We created with a marked preferment'* (17:70).

The above Holy verse reveals that Adam's race (mankind) has been honoured by Allah and is placed above those who are created with a marked preferment. Man is, therefore, given a high station and the earth is appointed for him as his dwelling-place as pre-programmed.

It was by the Divine command that Allah sent down from the Garden Adam and his race in perfect human form and with conscience and sown the seed of Adam's race into the earth and caused it to grow as a growth from the earth under the Universal Laws of Physics, Chemistry, Biology and Genetics to take effect.

He is the Creator Himself and not an imaginary advanced creation which has sent the spores of (Adam's seed) into the earth. Earth is the only planet in the universe which is the dwelling-place of mankind. No other place has the life like mankind. Life in other places would be somewhat different to mankind.

The Panspermia, is therefore, not at all 'man-directed' or directed by any superior creation from elsehwere. The seed of

Adam's race is directed by the Creator Himself Who is Able to deliver it safely through space from the Garden to the earth against the most unimaginable hostile environments of space created by Allah. Allah is Able to do all things and that is easy for Him. It must be understood in simple words that the task of creation of 'life', the creation of its seed and the broadcast or wafting it to earth through space is simply Divine Act of God. The first creation of man is purely Divine and the making of his seed and fixing his genetics is also Divine. The seeding of man to earth is also Divine. However, the reproduction and multiplication of man on earth is placed to be governed by the ordinary universal laws of nature as appointed by Allah. But the spirit in man and 'life' in man are again Divine matters and are Divine Secrets. The abode of mankind is fixed on earth and man himself is the superior creature. The question of the existence of man on a planet other than the Earth (which is appointed and pre-programmed by Allah as the dwelling-place for Adam's race) does not arise. Life does exist in the universe at many places and many languages are spoken over there but we do not know what type of life and in which form and under what life supporting zone such life or living creatures exist.

Allah created the universe as inviolable. It is inviolable even for the speed of light. The universe is therefore boundless and Allah knows the visible, the invisible, the hidden and the unseen of the universe as it is His Creation. There are billions of galaxies in the observable part of the universe and life may exist at innumerable places, but Allah gave marked preference to man above many of Allah's preferred creations.

The Holy Quran reveals :-

> *'Verily We have honoured the Children of Adam We carry them on the land and the sea, and have made provision of good things for them and have preferred them above many of those whom We created with a marked preferment' (17:70).*

Modern sciences in all fields are in great similarity with the Holy Quran the Divine Document, which reveals the absolute reality of the Creator and all of His creations. The only thing lacking with the scientists is the ignorance of the divine knowledge of the Quran which is the vital message from the Creator of the worlds to all mankind and is full of wisdom and guidance. The Holy Quran is the word of God, the Creator of man and it is obligatory on man to pay heed to the word of his Creator. The Quran is not at all incompatible with science. Rather, the Holy Quran helps science and is in concordance with its realities and guides man to seek sound knowledge to know the realities of the wonderful, the mysterious, and the boundless creations in the universe so that man knows the attributes of the Creator and then from such attributes of the Creative power, knowledgeable man should be able to know the Creator Allah Who created man and the universe and all things in the seven heavens.

The religion of Islam perfected by Allah and then chosen for mankind can never be outmoded or superseded as the Holy Quran teaches. Science and the religion of Islam are not in competition. Rather, science is the means of knowing the Holy Quran which teaches the religion of Islam. The Holy Quran reveals perfect and absolute truth whereas science is an effort on the part of man or an attempt towards the search for truth and is just a peep into the infinite. The message of God taught by Prophet Moses and Prophet Jesus were absolute truth but were subsequently changed and manipulated by man. The message of God through the Holy Quran revealed on the Last Prophet Muhammad (PBUH) consummates all the previous messages of God to man and the Holy Quran is in perfect original form and is absolutely free from manipulation errors or changes. The religion of Islam is not an amalgam of arcane beliefs as alleged and as grossly mis-stated. The Holy Quran and Islam rather disclose the divine doctrines and the absolute realities about the working of the physical universe as a whole and about man and about the metaphysical world which is beyond the perception of science. The Holy Quran reveals all about them either in direct form or in allegory or sometimes in an arcane manner so that men of sound knowledge who ponder and who pay heed may be able to understand the wisdom and knowledge encompassed in the Holy Quran. Man is not yet able to encompass in knowledge some of the Holy verses as interpretation (in events) has not yet come to mankind. Man's knowledge of science has not yet developed to fully grasp and understand some of these Holy verses.

Science is not an alternative to religion if it is a reference to Islam as Francis Crick sees. However, science is the means of knowing the religion of Islam, which explains and develops man's understanding of the physical truths as revealed by the Holy Quran. The Holy Quran reveals metaphysical realities beyond the comprehension of man. Scientific data are unable to cast any light on a subject that goes beyond human understanding.

Attention of Scientists is invited to ponder over the following questions :-

(1) Has knowledgeable man ever thought Who created the inviolable universe and how perfectly it is constructed? For an answer refer to verses No. (41:12), (37:6), (67:43) and (50:6) in Chapter 7 of this book.

(2) Has knowledgeable man ever thought who decked the inviolable universe with billions of galaxies and billions of stars in each galaxy and with billions of planets system in each galaxy, and the placing of the earth in a 'life supporting zone' from the sun for creating in it the 'Life Supporting Environments'?

(3) Who placed the sun and the moon at specific distances from the earth and fixed the rotation of the earth around the sun at specific speed for the creation of day and night of specific duration and the rotation of earth along its own axis at a specific angle for the creation of seasons on earth, so as to make it a habitat for man? For answers refer to verse No. (40:64).

(4) Has knowledgeable man ever thought Who created matter and energy and made its quantity constant in the universe with infinite possibilities for interaction with each other and also made the velocity of light constant at the speed of 186,000 miles per second? (For answers refer to verses No. (19:35), (55:7), (25:7), (6:73) and (39:5-6) (in Chapter 7).

It is now for knowledgeable man (Scientist) to know about the creations of Allah as to What it is and How it is created? The Holy Quran guides and teaches man that Allah is the Creator of all things. The scientists must know and have firm faith that Allah is the Creator, and then the Scientists must work hard on the creations of Allah to know What it is and How it is created by the Creator and for What purpose it is created. The Answer to 'WHO CREATED' the Universe and man and WHO arranged all this, is revealed by the Holy Quran and the Answer is the Creator Allah.

The Originator of the universe with its substance (matter and energy), the Creator of man and the Creator of the 'Soul' or 'Spirit' and 'Life' is Allah, the Almighty. How are they created? The Answer is, it is only Allah Who knows how He created the universe and man and all things.

How things are created by Allah, in this respect the Holy Quran reveals :-

(1) *'Glory be to Him: When He decreeth a thing He saith unto it only, Be! and it is' (6:73) and (39:5-6).*

(2) *'The Originator of the heavens and the earth When He decreeth a thing, He saith unto it only: Be! and it is' (II:117).*

(3) *'But His Command, When He intendeth a thing, is only that He saith into it: Be! and it is' (36:82).*

(4) *'He it is Who created the heavens and the earth in truth. In that day when He said: Be! and it is' (6:73).*

(5) *'He is Allah, the Creator, the Shaper out of naught, the Fashioner. His are the most beautiful names. All that is in the heavens and the earth glorifieth Him and He is the Mighty, the Wise' (60:24).*

(6) *'The Doer of What He will' (85:16).*

(7) *'Allah is Able to do All things' (24:25).*

(8) *'That is easy for Allah' (64:7).*

Who could it be He other than Allah, Who created the inviolable and the infinite creations so perfectly and so truthfully as we see and as we ourselves are? It is only Allah and Allah alone, the Lord of the worlds! So, believe in Him and in His Messenger and in His Message to mankind.

The Holy Quran reveals :-

'I convey unto you the messages of my Lord and I am for you a true advisor' (7:68).

Besides the Holy Quranic verses on the Creation of man, life, the earth and the universe, man's attention is invited to the Holy verses on obliteration of the universe and man on the Doomsday. These are:-

(1) *'The Day when We shall roll up the heavens as a recorder rolleth up a written scroll. As We began the first creation, We shall repeat it (it is) a promise (binding) upon us. Lo! We are to perform it' (21:104).*

(2) *'Allah effaceth what He will and establish (what He will) and with Him is source of Ordinance' (13:39).*

(3) *'Have they not seen that Allah Who created the heavens and the earth is Able to create the like of them and hath appointed for them an end whereof there is no doubt? But the wrong-doers refuse aught save disbelief' (17:99).*

(4) *'On the day when the earth will be changed to other than this earth, and the heavens (also will be changed) and they will comeforth unto Allah the One, the Almighty' (14:48).*

(5) *'Man is made of haste. I shall show you My portents, but ask Me not to hasten' (21:37).*

Darwin's Theory of Evolution

An abstract from an article written by Barbara Krasnoff under the title 'From Whence We Came'—Creationists versus Evolutionists published in 'Future Life' Magazine September, 1981 Issue is partly discussed.

From Whence We Came

There are two groups of scientists and biologists, the ones who advocate Darwin's Theory of Evolution are called the evolutionists. Evolution means development by continuing natural processes. The other group advocate the 'Creation Science' and are called the Creationists. They advocate that life was produced in its present form several thousands of years ago by 'an un-named supernatural force'. Creation has to do with completed natural process.

Darwin's Theory of Evolution hypothesizes the natural and gradual development of current life from more primitive forms, and states that life evolved slowly over billions of years and through pure chance and that man in his present form, had originally became converted from an Ape like animal.

However, recently there has been a growing and very vocal movement of people who advocate what is known as 'Creation Science' which states that life did not evolve slowly over billions of years but was produced in its present form several thousand years ago by 'an un-named Supernatural Force

The Creationists or those who believe in the 'Creation Science' and are the challengers of the Darwin's Theory of Evolution and it seems that the tables are turning over the evolutionists.

A creationist believes that the basic systems of the universe have to be accounted for in terms of a supernatural creation that took place in the past; whereas an evolutionist would say that you could explain everything in terms of a natural processes that are still going on.

The Creationists argue :-

> In other words, the first man had a fully human body and mind and soul, and did not develop by natural processes from something like an ape or some primate form'.

The Creationists, with the help of such research institutions as the Creation Research Society and the Creation — Science Research Centre, have marshalled some impressive arguments tc support their position. These include:-

(1) The complexity of even a single living cell is so involved that it could not have possibly evolved through pure chance; but rather, must have had some sort of intelligence directing its creation.

(2) Evolution violates the second law of thermodynamics. (The second law of thermodynamics, in the words of Associate Professor of Linguistics Catherine A. Callaghan) — Who is not a creationist — states that "all the free energy of a closed system can be converted into heat, but not all the heat can be converted back to free energy. The biological analogue would be that closed systems change from a more organized to a less organized state through time'. Therefore, evolution, which states that complex life develop from more simple forms, cannot be correct.

(3) The fossil record which is used to illustrate the workings of evolution is incomplete and in fact actually supports the theory of a sudden and non-evolving creation. 'It supports creationism in the sense that there are no intermediate forms in the fossil', explains Dr. Moris. The Creation Model says that there would be many varieties, including may-be some extinct varieties such as Neanderthal Man, but these were men and there were no intermediate forms'.

(4) Many 'non-Creationist' Scientists are now tacitly conceding the legitimacy of creation science by admitting that there are too many gaps in the fossil record to support evolutionism.

(5) There is no way you can prove or disprove creation — because these have to do with things that happened in the past, and we cannot get in a time machine and go back and see what happened.

There is no way to disprove creation. We maintain that the creation model does the best job of co-relating and predicting data. Jerry Resnick, Biologist says about Creationism'. 'It's true, I can't go back to the very beginning and show what happened at that point'. That's why they talk about it as a theory. But we can show, for example, chemical evolution. In terms of the chemical evolution of amino-acids, Stanley Miller was able to show that, given the precursors of the organic materials that are present here today, he was able to create amino acids and scientists have gone to the extent of being able to create proteins through the conditions that were there for evolution.

Creationism is not a Science', Resnick says, 'In my opinion, Creationism really masquerades in the name of science, but basically its roots are fundamentalism, which deals in terms of religion.

On August 22, 1980, the Presidential Candidate Ronald Reagan addressed a meeting of an Evangelical Christian Organization during his electioneering campaign. When asked if he evolution should be taught in public schools, he is quoted as saying, 'Well, it is a theory. It is a scientific theory only. And it has, in recent years, been challenged in the world of science and is not believed in the scientific community to be as infallible as it once was believed. I would think that also the biblical theory of creation — which is not theory, but the biblical story of creation — should also be taught'.

One cannot talk about creation without there somewhere being a Creator and a Creator is an inherently religious belief. And 'it's hard to deny the religious roots that support the creationist arguments.

'People who are intelligent enough see that, call it what you will, scientific creationism smacks of religion, asserts Jerry Resnick.

'Supernatural External Force — those are the key words'.

However, our present activities, even expanded, will not be enough. A repudiation of evolutionary humanism, and a return to true belief in God as Creator and Sovereign of the universe is pre-requisite to any real solution of human problems, whether these problems are, personal, social or transnational in scope'.

There is a form of evolution called theistic evolution', says Dr. Miller, 'Which says that God in effect is an evolutionist; that He established the evolutionary process, and that as things evolve, actually somewhere behind all that God is supervising in some way. So that many people who are evolutionists also believe in God and their belief would be theistic evolution.

Evolution means development by continuing natural processes; creation has to do with completed natural processes!

However, the world was created by an unexplainable, unexplorable 'supernatural force' is religious.

Dr. Wayne Moyer, Executive Director of the National Association of Biology Teachers, at their National Convention on October 25, 1980 has expressed:-

To be complete humans, we need both science and religion'. The synthesis of the two has to be performed by each individual trusting his or her own good judgement.

To understand the problem of humanism and all other problems in the universe, the author of this book advocates that it is a pre-requisite to understand the Creator and all His attributes for which knowledge, wisdom and faith in the Holy Quran, the word of God are the essential pre-requisites. Faith, knowledge and wisdom would lead man to know the ultimate reality of the Creator Who is Sovereign Lord of the worlds and Who is Able to do all things. He is the Creator of life and death and He is the Creator of life after death. And the Doer of what He will. And that is easy for Him. The Creator has created man in perfect human form to know God and to submit to the will of God which is worship to Him. His message is revealed by inspiration on the Holy Prophet Muhammad, the Messenger of God, for the guidance of all mankind. So, it is for mankind to acquire knowledge all round to know the attributes of God and to study the work (physical creation of the universe and man) of God in the light of His revelations in the Holy Quran revealed on Prophet Muhammad (PBUH). On reading the Holy Quran, man will know that the word of God is the Absolute Truth and reveals the visible and the invisible, the hidden and the unseen realities of the universe, man, the beasts on earth and of the metaphysical world of the Hereafter. So, faith in the Creator and in His Messenger and Message and the sound knowledge of man are the pre-requisites to know the absolute reality and to know what man wants to know within human limitations.

First Man (Adam) had fully human body and mind and soul and was created by Allah with the best stature, Good Shape, perfected with soul and inspired with conscience and raised up as the best community for mankind and was preferred above many of those created with a marked preferment and placed as the viceroy of God on the Earth.

From all that which is said above by the creationists and the evolutionists through the 'Creation Science' or through the 'Science of Evolution', both the groups are advocating the way man was created. However, the views of creationists are more near to Religion of Islam, whereas the views of evolutionists are quite opposite to Religion of Islam. The living creatures on earth are of numerous types and forms and are created in different types of environments. Out of all creatures — human beings are the best of creatures, with the best stature and shape and are inspired with conscience, intelligence, wisdom, besides instinct and can distinguish between right and wrong as they are given thinking power to see, hear, feel, know, judge, decide and choose independently what is right. Human being is the only living creature created with such faculties by the All-Wise Creator.

However, there is another form of creation, which is non-living i.e. in form of "matter and energy"? This creation is created in a constant and fixed quantity by the Creator, Who is also the Shaper and Fashioner of matter and energy either in one form or the other. The non-living creation may be in any form but its behaviour, its functioning and its evolution and creation from one form to the other or its interaction is controlled and is governed through certain physical laws and the fundamental forces with perfection and in complete obedience to the All-Knowing, All-Powerful, All-Wise, the Sustainer and the Creator of all things. One cannot talk about such a perfect order in infinite matters and infinite creations without there somewhere being a Creator.

Matter, energy, forces and laws are not living creations and are not thinking creations but they are kept in perfect order and are made the means for living creations. These are governed by a Supreme Power — Allah, Who created them and Who maintains perfect order in all things and maintains perfect celestial mechanic in the universe and in all living and non-living matter and energy.

So, the 'Creation Science' or the 'Science of Evolution' and the process of creation itself whether in case of living or non-living creations, whether it may be thinking and intelligent living creation or living creation by instinct are all creations. The question how they are created is totally different and is immaterial whether we know it or not. The real question to know is who created them and what is that 'Supreme External Power' of the Creator Who actually created 'with His Creative Power', the creation of seven heavens and the earth and all the creatures on earth which modern man knows from his intelligence and his knowledge of the physical science about universe and man and about the wild life. The Holy Quran reveals that the 'Supreme Eternal Power' is of Allah, Who is the Creator of all things by design and not by chance and He is theCreator of man, when He simply said: Be! and man was created. And He is the Originator of the heavens and the earth! when He decreeth a thing, He saith unto it only: Be! and it is. Allah created the universe and man out of His Prime Mercy. Allah created man so that he might worship Him and know Him and His attributes. So, man has a purpose to perform before his Lord.

The Holy Quran reveals :-

> *'I created the Jinn and the Mankind only that they might worship Me' (21:57).*

Modern knowledge of physical sciences has established that infinite intelligence, infinite knowledge and infinite power is involved in the infinite interactions of matter and energy of the boundless and the inviolable universe. The Creator Who created all this and Who runs all this with perfection must be the Creator with Infinite attributes and perfection and the entire universe with its matter and energy both in living and non-living form are the marvel and tokens or signs or portents of the Creator. One can only know the Creator and His power from His attributes of the 'Creative Energy' or the Command. The Creator Himself is 'Unimaginable Supreme Being! It is beyond the power of the creature to know the Creator, as He has not revealed such things to man, nor man (the mortal) is given the capability and the imagination to know what is unknowable for him.

To be complete humans, we need both science and the Religion of Islam. One only knows the religion of Islam through faith, science, and sound knowledge as the Holy Quran itself teaches. The religion of Islam reveals the Absolute truth as it is the word of the Creator whereas science (the knowledge about physical things) is an attempt on the part of man (creature) to know the marvels of His creations. Science in its attempt and specifically when it becomes perfect science is therefore a very vital link to understand the religion of Islam and to understand the word of God — (The Holy Quran) and to know the physical creation of universe and man and to understand the unseen, the invisible, the hidden and the metaphysical creations revealed by the Quran and then believe in them and have faith that there is a Creator Who created them and have faith in the Message of God and in the Messenger of God on whom the Holy Quran was revealed for the guidance of man.

Look to the creation of man, who is a universe in miniature. Look to the marvels of the 60 trillion cells (60^{12}) in the body of the human baby and that the characteristics of each one are determined by that incredible, DNA, the genetic code containing genetic instructions which the Creator has coded in the DNA of each man and also of other living creatures.

The Evolution of Ape into Man an Abominable Concept

The basic question is, Who tapped or recorded all these intelligent and life forming information in the DNA? The only answer is that it is the 'Unimaginable Supreme Being' of Infinite Wisdom, Infinite Knowledge and Infinite Power, Who has done it, and Who is directing its creation with a specific design and in minutest and in greatest details at the sub-atomic, atomic and molecular level. It is not a matter of chance as the evolutionists say. It was pre-planned and a thing ordained to happen and is a creation of the Creator with a purpose to perform. The Creator knew He was creating a man from clay or mire and not an ape. And He created man very specifically.

There is therefore no fun for the Creator, to create an animal first, something like an ape, a lower form of creation, and then convert the ape into a human being or superior form of creation through the process of evolution over millions or billions of years. The Creator is Able to do all things and that is easy for Him, so it was not necessary to have created an animal (ape) first and then by changing mind and through the process of evolution and as a second thought have then started converting the ape into a man. The Creator knew very well what is He going to create and He created man (Adam) as a preferred creation with human body, shape, mind and soul and placed him above all whom He created with a marked preferment. The Creator has thus honoured man (Adam) and has given him a high station and has not created man in the lower category of an animal. Man is created with inspired spirit and conscience from the very moment of creation and with the inborn capability, intelligence and thinking power to choose the path of his conduct and to decide independently what is wrong and what is right for him. He is created in a handsome shape and with best stature and with all the human faculties and not as a tailed and four legged animal with humiliating stature. Man's first forefather was Adam and he was a human in perfect form, body and shape and was inspired with conscience and was specially created by Allah and was declared prior to his creation by Allah before the other creations of Allah having a very high station.

It is a divine truth that living man was created in its present form with all the faculties in a human body in perfect shape and stature as his inborn, preplanned and ordered characteristics. The same way his reproduction is duly designed, proportioned, shaped, fashioned like an intelligent man and not like an ape. No ape has ever been converted into a man. Man is a dignified, honoured, intelligent and responsible creation with conscience and with beautiful shape. He is created with a good stature and shape and the rest of living creations are placed in a subordinate position to man due to their built-in characteristics.

The creation of man, in the basic systems of the universe is therefore of prime importance. He is not a by-product of some creation and a victim of chance and evolution. He is created with a purpose and capability to know the Creator and as such, he is gifted with conscience, intelligence, wisdom and choice to know and to understand the Creator Allah. This is the reason that man is created with such superior faculties in his present human form and shape and was perfected by the Creator the moment he was infused with spirit and was made a living man from non-living matter and was inspired with conscience. The spirit, life, and the conscience and the good shape and stature and the faculty of intelligence and senses are the inborn qualities of man which make man superior to other creatures or creations and these qualities enable him to know the

Creator Who created him, and gifted the sense to appreciate the rest of physical creations in universe and on earth. The ape and other creatures have no such qualities. The ape is an animal and shall remain an animal and has no conscience and has no good shape, stature and is unaware of his Creator and has no power of speech and has no power of wisdom. He is a pure animal and no more than that.

Darwin's Theory is merely a theory and shall die as a theory. Darwin's Theory is against the religious beliefs of Islam and Christianity. It is also denounced and challenged in the world of science and is not believed any longer by Scientists.

Animals live only by instinct and have no spirit and conscience like man. Their purpose of life is only to defend themselves and to feed themselves and to mate and multiply their own breed by reproduction. The Power of 'instinct' is fundamentally different from the faculty of 'Conscience'. 'Instinct' of animals cannot develop by evolution into 'Conscience' as no animal in the world is found with conscience and wisdom or have developed intelligent power of speech. The instinct and the conscience are the two inherently different characteristics. The instinct is the quality in animals and insects whereas human being has the qualities of conscience and instinct both. Man is therefore highly intelligent and superior creature. The DNA of animal (ape) and man have different coded instructions to follow and all this is done by the Creator. One cannot talk about creation or creature without there somewhere being a Creator of Infinite attributes.

A repudiation of evolutionary humanism and a return to true belief in God as Creator and Sovereign of the universe is prerequisite to any real solution of human problems, whether these problems are personal, social or trans-national in scope.

The Creator is an inherently religious belief and it is hard to deny the religious roots that support the creationist arguments. No one has ever seen or could prove that apes are transfigured in human beings. It is a fundamental truth that the first man had fully human body, mind and soul and did not develop by natural processes from something like an ape or some primate form. It is true that life was produced in its present form by the Creator Allah. The Holy Quran is always there to guide man when man's knowledge of physical sciences and his power of conception about many things fail to guide him truthfully. The Holy Quran is not a text book of science but it is the word of the Creator and the Absolute truth and is revealed on Prophet Muhammad (PBUH)for the guidance and teaching of all mankind and the revelations are sometimes allegorial and hint towards many things for man's guidance and for his knowledge as it is the divine Book of wisdom for which sound knowledge is an absolute necessity.

The Holy Quran reveals :-

(1) *'He detaileth the revelations for people who have knowledge' (10:5).*

(2) *'Verily We have brought them a Scripture which We expound with knowledge, a guidance and a mercy for a people who believe' (7:52).*

(3) *'Those who have been given knowledge see that what is revealed unto thee from thy Lord is the truth and leadeth into the Path of the Mighty, the Owner of Praise' (34:6).*

(4) *'(This is) a Scripture that We have revealed unto thee full of blessing that they may ponder its revelations and that men of understanding may reflect' (38:29).*

(5) *'Say: Believe therein or believe not, Lo! those who were given knowledge before it, fall down postrate on the faces, adoring' (17:107).*

(6) *'Allah it is Who hath created seven heavens and of the earth the like thereof. The commandment cometh down among them slowly, that ye may know that Allah surroundeth all things in knowledge' (66:12).*

The Holy Quran reveals that man is created to be placed as a Viceroy on earth by Allah. Man is therefore chosen as God's Assistant and His Servant on earth. He is therefore created as an intelligent being and as among the best of creations and was created in a form as he is today. The Holy Quran revealed the first creation of man (Adam), and it revealed the making of his seed, then his broadcast to earth to grow as a growth from the earth and his multiplication and reproduction in the womb of his mother, then the development as child in the womb of his mother according to His design, measurements, proportion, shape, stature and faculties of intelligence and senses and as male and female. Allah created man and perfected him with His Spirit and inspired him with conscience and is placed higher and above the preferred creations of God. The concept of man developed from an ape is abominable, hideous and shocking, besides being against many religious beliefs and heavenly revelations. It is of great despisement for man and rather serves as warning to man against fault.

The Transformation of Man into Ape by Allah as a Curse for Disobedience

On the contrary the Holy Quran reveals and guides mankind about many things in a wonderful manner with miraculous revelations and in this case it is clearly revealed that those men who disobeyed the orders of Allah conveyed to them through their prophet and who broke the Sabbath, then Allah cursed those men and out of despisement and hate 'Allah said to them: Be ye apes so that you become example to your own men and to the succeeding generations and serve as an admonition to the God-fearing mankind'. It is therefore absolutely wrong to conceive that through evolution ape developed into man.

The revelations of the Holy Quran, in a case where God's instructions were defied by those men are quite opposite to what Darwin's theory hypothesizes. Man is created as man and in his own best human form and as superior human being. The Holy Quran clearly indicates that man is not developed from the animal (ape) by the process of evolution as the evolutionists suggest. Animal is created as animal and as such ape was created as an ape. The Holy Quran reveals that Allah created all the sexual pairs of all the species of animals, insects and all that which the earth grows and of the human being themselves and of all that which men do not know.

The Holy Quran reveals that men who broke Allah's commandment were turned by His Command into apes out of sheer despise and as punishment so that they be an example for the succeeding generations of mankind and to serve as an example before the God-fearing men. As a consequence of divine disobedience those men were punished, cursed and were transformed into apes, by the divine Command. The ape, in ape form, is a lesson for man and teaches man's subsequent generations the consequences of sin and disobedience to Allah, Who is the Creator of all things and is the Lord of the worlds and Lord of mankind.

Some of the Holy verses revealing the first creation of man (Adam), in good human form and shape and his superior status among God's creations, and about the great quality of inspired conscience due to which man is made independent so as to distinguish between right and wrong and then choose what he likes for him and about making earth as his dwelling-place where man is appointed viceroy, are quoted below. The Holy verses also reveal about the orderof descendentsof human race right from the first man (Adam) to Noah, and the family of Abraham and the family of Imran whom Allah placed above (all His) Creatures. Adam, Noah, Abraham, Imran were all descendents one of another of the human race and are traced down to man's known and recent history.

Moreover, a few Holy verses clearly reveal the transformation of sinful and disobedient men who broke Allah's order, into apes as a matter of punishment, cursed and despised and as admonition to the God-fearing.

The Holy verses on the creation of (Adam) human being and his high station are :-

(1) *'Lo! the likeness of Jesus with Allah is as the Likeness of Adam, He created him of dust then He said unto Him: Be! and he is' (61:59).*

(2) *'Allah it is Who appointed for you the earth for a dwelling place and the sky for a canopy and fashioned you and perfected your shapes and hath provided you with good things. Such is Allah, Your Lord. Then blessed be Allah, the Lord of the Worlds!' (40:64).*

(3) *'And when thy Lord said unto the angels: Lo! I am about to place a Viceroy in the earth, they said; Wilt Thou place therein one who will do harm therein and will shed blood, While we, we hymn Thy praise and sanctify Thee? He said: Surely I know that which ye know not' (11:30).*

(4) *'He created the heavens and the earth with truth and He shaped you and made good your shapes and unto Him is the journeying' (64:3).*

(5) *'He began the creation of man from clay' (32:7).*

(6) *'And He it is Who hath created man from water' (25:54).*

(7) *'Then He fashioned him and breathed into him of His spirit and appointed for you hearing and sight and hearts, small thanks give ye! (32:9).*

(8) *'And when I have fashioned him and breathed into him of My spirit. then fall down before him prostrate'. (38:72) and (15:29).*

(9) *'He said: O Iblis! What hindereth thee from falling prostrate before that which I have created with My hands Art Thou too proud or art thou of the high exalted?' (38:75).*

(10) *'Who created thee, then fashioned, then proportioned thee?' (82:7).*

(11) *'Surely We created man of the best stature' (XCV:4).*

(12) *'And a soul and Him Who perfected it' (XCI:7).*

(13) *'And inspired it (with conscience of) What is wrong for it and (what is) right for it' (XCI:8).*

(14) *'And We said: O Adam! Dwell thou and thy wife in the Garden and*

eat ye freely (of the fruits) thereof where Ye will; but come not nigh this tree lest ye become wrong doers' (II:35).

(15) *'Then He made his seed from a draught of despised fluid' (32:8).*

(16) *'And He it is Who hath sown you broadcast in the earth and unto Him ye will be gathered' (23:79).*

(17) *'And Allah has caused you to grow as a growth from the earth. And afterwards, He maketh you return thereto. And He will bring you forth once again' (71:17).*

(18) *'I created the jinn and the mankind only that they might worship Me' (21:57).*

(19) *'Glory be to Him Who created all the sexual pairs of that which the earth groweth and of themselves and of that which they know not!' (36:36).*

(20) *'And of His signs is the Creation of the heavens and the earth, and the difference of your languages and colours. Lo! herein indeed are portents for men of knowledge' (30:22).*

(21) *'Ye are the best community that hath been raised up for mankind. Ye enjoin right conduct and forbid indecency; and ye believe in Allah' (68:110).*

(22) *'Verily We have honoured the Children of Adam, We carry them on the land and the sea and have made provisions of good things for them and have preferred above many of those whom We created with a marked preferment' (17:70).*

The Holy Quran reveals verses on the order of descendency of the first human (Adam) and his race and traces it down to the period of man's known history.

The Holy verses are :-

(1) *Lo! Allah preferred Adam and Noah and the Family of Abraham and the Family of Imran above (all His) creatures' (III:33).*

(2) *They were descendents one of another. Allah is Hearer, Knower (III:34).*

The Holy Quran reveals the following verses on the transformation of those men into apes who disobeyed and violated His orders and Who broke the Sabbath. Allah cursed them with such punishment so that it should be example to them and should also serve as example to the succeeding generations of mankind and as a matter of an admonition to the God-fearing'.

Science in agreement with the Holy-Quran on reproduction of human life. Creation of Adam as the first human being and his spores sown broadcast in the earth

The Holy verses are :-

(1) *'And Ye know of those of you who broke the Sabbath, how We said unto them: Be ye apes, despised and hated!' (II:65).*

(2) *'And We made it an example to their own and to succeeding generations and an admonition to the God-fearing' (II:66).*

Man is a special creation of Allah. Allah says He created man with His own hands which means a lot. The above holy verses make it clear that the first man (Adam) was created with a fully human body and with a best stature and shape and with conscience and a high station. The creation of man is no matter for Allah. Allah is Able to do all things and He is the Doer of What He will. If man ponders over the creation of seven heavens and the earth and all that is in between, he will find that God is the Creator of infinite things and that the creation of man is no match in comparison to the rest of the creation.

The Holy Quran reveals :-

(1) *'Assuredly the creation of the heavens and the earth is greater than the creation of mankind; but most of mankind know not' (40:57).*

(2) *'Lo! Ye are those who argue about that whereof ye have some knowledge. Why then argue ye concerning that whereof ye have no knowledge? Allah knoweth. Ye know not' (111:66).*

(3) *'We verily created the man and We know what his soul whispereth to him and We are nearer to him than his jugular vein' (50:16).*

(4) *'Even as We have sent unto you a Messenger from among you, who receiteth unto you Our revelations and causeth you to grow and teacheth you the Scripture and wisdom and teacheth you that which ye knew not' (25:151).*

Science on the Origin of Life in Congruity with Quranic Revelations on Man's Creation and Reproduction

Hypotheses of Origin of Life on Earth

The most fundamental and the least understood biological problem is the origin of life. It is central to many scientific and philosophical problems and to any consideration of extra-terrestrial life. Most of the hypotheses of the origin of life fall into one of the four categories:-

(1) The origin of life is a result of a supernatural event; that is, one permanently beyond the descriptive powers of Physics and Chemistry.

(2) Life — particularly simple forms — spontaneously and readily arises from non-living matter in short periods of time, today as in the past.

(3) Life is co-eternal with matter and has no beginning, life arrived on earth at the time of the origin of the earth or shortly thereafter.

(4) Life arose on the early earth by a series of progressive chemical reactions. Such reactions may have been likely or may have required one or more highly improbable chemical events.

The above hypotheses are the most important and are very much consistent with the theology of the Holy Quran. The following Quranic verses are in similarity with the above hypotheses which state that the origin of life is a result of a supernatural event or a divine act and that life arises from non-living matter i.e. clay and water or wet earth. And that life arrived on earth thereafter and that physical, chemical and biological reactions and events took place on earth and created all the sexual pairs and caused them to grow as a growth from the earth's biosphere. The above hypotheses are in similarity with the following Holy verses:-

The Holy Quran reveals:-

(1) *'Lo! the likeness of Jesus with Allah is as the Likeness of Adam, He created him of dust then He said unto him: Be! and he is' (61:59).*

(2) *'And when, I have fashioned him and breathed into him of My Spirit, then fall down before him postrate' (38:72) (15:29).*

(3) *'They will ask thee concerning the spirit. Say: The spirit is by command of my Lord, and of knowledge Ye have been vouchsafed but little' (17:85).*

(4) *'Lo! I am about to create a mortal out of mire' (38:71) (15:28).*

(5) *'And He began the creation of man from clay' (32:7).*

(6) *'Verily We created man from a product of wet earth.' (23:12).*

(7) *'And He it is Who hath sown you broadcast in the earth and unto*

Him ye will be gathered.' (23:79).

(8) *'And Allah hath caused you to grow as a growth from the earth.' (71:17).*

(9) *'Glory be to Him Who created all the sexual pairs, of that which the earth groweth, and of themselves, and of that which they know not!' (36:35).*

(10) *'And of His portents is the creation of the heavens and the earth and of whatever beasts He hath dispersed therein. And He is Able to gather them when He will' (42:29).*

(11) *'Have not those who disbelieve known that the heavens and the earth were one piece, then We parted them and We made every thing of water. Will they not then believe?' (21:30).*

The above verses clearly reveal that the creation of life on earth is a 'divine act' and that life is created from non-living matter (wet earth). There is no accepted definition of life in science. In the use of the word protoplasm there is occasionally an implication that life cannot be explained solely by Physics and Chemistry, that some mysterious 'vital force' must be invoked. A living cell is a marvel of detailed and complete architecture. Seen through microscope there is an appearance of almost frantic activity.

Indeed, there is nothing debasing in the thought that man is made of atoms alone; it means he is intimately connected with matter that comprises the inanimate universe. What a wonder that atoms can be put together in so complex a pattern as to produce man. Man is a tribute to the subtlety of matter. A human being is an extraordinarily improbable object, but he is a reality. He is the handicraft of Allah made out of wet earth.

Ninety-nine per cent, both of the universe and of life, is made of the six types of atoms: Hydrogen (H), Helium (He), Carbon (C), Nitrogen (N), Oxygen (O) and Neon (Ne.). Can it be that life on earth arose when the chemical composition of the earth was much closer to the average cosmic composition and that some subsequent events have changed the gross chemical composition of the earth? The Holy Quranic verse (21:30) quoted above, beautifully supports the scientific concept that the chemical composition of the earth and the average cosmic composition are nearly the same i.e. the earth and the universe were one piece and that in subsequent events when earth parted, chemical changes took place in the composition of the earth and then life began on earth and all living creatures were made of water. Will mankind not then believe?

It has been shown that all the essential building-blocks for life and their polymers may have been produced in some fair concentration on the primitive earth. This possibility is certainly relevant to the origin of life, but it is not the same thing as the origin of life.

The origin of human life is due to the infused Spirit of Allah. The knowledge of spirit is not given to mankind. Earth was part of the universe when it was all in spinning gaseous form. Allah formed the earth out of the universe when it was all one mass of spinning clouds of gases and separated it and then created all living things of water i.e. of the protoplasm which is about 85 to 90 per cent water. And water is the combination of Hydrogen (H) and Oxygen (O). The portents or the tokens or handicraft of Allah is the creation of the heaven and the earth i.e. the universe, and of áll the beasts which are dispersed all over the earth, as revealed in the Holy verses (42:29) and (21:30) quoted above. This means the creation of matter and energy, in the form of heaven and the earth i.e. the universe and then creation of 'Life' out of non-living matter on earth are all the portents of the Creator Allah. Living man is a tribute to the subtlety of matter and it shows the handicraft or portent of the Creator Allah, Who created living things out of the non-living. Similarly, the living jinn is a tribute to the subtlety of 'fire' or energy and it shows another handicraft or portent of Allah but is invisible to man. The structure of jinn could be in a different atomic formation beyond the perceptive power of man and beyond all other physical detective methods. The Holy Quran clearly reveals that there are two types of different and distinct creations, created out of absolutely different 'substance'. The one is a living mankind created out of 'wet earth', the non-living matter, and the other is the living jinn created out of 'smokeless fire' or 'essential fire' which is non-living energy. The Holy Quran indicates that living creation in the universe and in the rest of the six heavens could be in various unimaginable forms created out of different non-living substances i.e. matter, energy, light etc., which are known and of other substances which are unknown to mankind. All such things can be classed as the invisibles of the heavens. The inviolable universe is full of mysteries and we have hardly made a beginning to uncover it.

Earth the Birth Place of Mankind

Allah created the earth and appointed it as the abode for

mankind and then created man (Adam) out of dust and water, thus created a mortal out of mire and breathed into him His 'spirit' to make him living man with conscience and with good shape and anatomy. And then created in him the capability of reproduction to multiply from the pairs made by Allah.

The Holy Quran reveals:-

(1) *'Allah it is Who appointed for you the earth for a dwelling-place and the sky for a canopy and fashioned you and perfected your shapes and hath provided you with good things. Such is Allah, Your Lord. Then blessed be Allah, the Lord of the Worlds!' (40:64).*

(2) *'He it is Who created you from dust, then from a drop (of seed) then from a clot (something which clings), then bringeth you forth as a child, then (ordaineth) that Ye attain full strength and afterward that Ye become old men — though some among you die before — and that Ye reach an appointed term, that haply ye may understand' (40:67).*

(3) *'He created the heavens and the earth with truth and He shaped you and made good your shapes and unto Him is the journeying' (64:3).*

Quranic Revelations on Man's Creation

The Holy Quran has revealed in numerous of the Holy verses in various forms that 'man is created of potter's clay of black mud altered' and that he is 'a product of wet earth' and that 'every living thing is made of water' and that man is sown broadcast in the earth' by Allah and 'have breathed into him His spirit', of knowledge man is vouchsafed but little. Modern knowledge of the science of Biology and Genetics is found to be in total congruity with the verses of the Holy Quran on the creation of man and on the reproduction of man.

Following are a few of the Holy Quranic verses in different forms on the creation of man by Allah from a product of wet earth :-

(1) *I created the jinn and the mankind only that they might worship Me' (21:57).*

(2) *'When thy Lord said unto the angels: Lo! I am about to create a mortal out of mire' (38:71) and (15:28).*

(3) *'And When I have fashioned him and breathed into him of My Spirit, then fall down before him prostrate' (38:72) and (15:29).*

(4) *'And He it is Who hath sown you broadcast in the earth and unto Him you will be gathered' (23:79).*

(5) *'And Allah has caused you to grow as a growth from the earth. And afterward, He maketh you return thereto. And He will bring you forth once again' (71:17).*

(6) *'Who made all things good which He created, and He began the creation of man from clay' (32:7).*

(7) *'We made every living thing of water' (21:30).*

(8) *'Verily We created man from a product of wet earth' (23:12).*

(9) *'So, when I have made him and have breathed into him of My Spirit, do Ye fall down, prostrating yourselves untoHim' (15:29).*

(10) *'Verily We created man of potter's clay of black mud altered' (15:26) and (15:28).*

(11) *'They will ask thee concerning the spirit. Say: The spirit is by Command of my Lord, and of knowledge ye have been vouchsafed but little' (17:85).*

(12) *'Is not He (best) who produceth creation, then reproduceth it?' (27:64).*

(13) *'Surely We created man of the best stature' (XCIV:4).*

(14) *'He bringeth forth the living from the dead, and He bringeth forth the dead from the living and He reviveth the earth after death. And even so Ye will be brought forth' (30:19).*

(15) *'And a soul and Him Who perfected it' (XCI:7).*

(16) *'And inspired it (with conscience of) what is wrong for it and (what is) right for it' (XCI:8).*

(17) *'Lo! the likeness of Jesus with Allah is as the Likeness of Adam, He created him of dust, then He said unto him: Be! and he is'. (61:59).*

(18) *'Then ask them (O: Mohammad): Are they stronger as a creation, or those (others) whom We have created? Lo! We created them of plastic clay' (37:11).*

(19) *'Then He made his seed from a draught of despised fluid'. (32:8).*

(20) *'Then He fashioned him and breathed into him of His Spirit, and appointed for you hearing and sight and hearts. Small thanks give ye!' (32:9).*

(21) *'Allah knoweth that which every female beareth and that which they grow. And everything with Him is measured' (13:8).*

(22) *'He hath created man' (55:3).*

(23) *'And in the earth are portents for those whose faith is sure' (51:20).*

(24) *'And (also) in yourselves, Can ye then not see' (51:21).*

(25) *'And He it is Who hath created man from water, and hath appointed for him kindered by blood and kindered by marriage, for thy Lord is*

ever powerful' (25:54).

(26) *'We verily created a man and We know what his soul whispereth to him and We are nearer to him than his jugular vein' (50:16).*

(27) *'The Creator of the heavens and the earth. He hath made for you pairs of yourselves, and of the cattle also pairs, whereby He multiplieth you. Naught is as His likeness; He is the Hearer, the Seer' (42:11).*

(28) *'Unto Allah belongeth the sovereignty of the heavens and the earth. He createth what He Will. He bestoweth female (off-spring) upon whom He will, and bestoweth male (off-spring) upon whom He will' (42:49).*

(29) *'Or He mingleth them, males and females and He maketh barren whom He will. Lo! He is Knower, Powerful' (42:50).*

(30) *'Allah created you from dust, then from a little fluid, then He made your pairs (the male and female). No female beareth or bringeth forth save with His knowledge. And no one groweth old who groweth old, nor is aught lessened of his life, but it is recorded in a Book. Lo! That is easy for Allah' (35:11).*

(31) *'Unto Him is referred (all) knowledge of the Hour. And no fruits burst forth from their sheaths and no female carrieth or bringeth forth but with His knowledge. And on the day when He calleth unto them: Where are now My partners? They will say: We confess unto Thee, not one of us is a witness (for them)' (41:47).*

(32) *'He created you from one being, then from that (being) He made its mate; and he hath provided for you of cattle eight kinds. He created you in the wombs of your mothers, creation after creation, in a three fold gloom. Such is Allah, your Lord! He is the Sovereignty. There is no God save Him. How then are ye turned away' (39:6).*

Science on the origin of life on earth is in full concord with the Holy Quran. Each verse of the Holy Quran on the creation of life on earth from non-living matter encompasses tremendous knowledge and leads to the conclusion and to the unflinching faith that there exists the Creator of mankind Who is Allah, the One, the Merciful, the Beneficent, Who created man from wet earth, clay, black mud altered, mire, plastic clay, dust and water.

The Holy Quran reveals :-

(1) *'Say: He is Allah, the One!' (CXII:1).*

(2) *'The King of mankind' (CXII:2).*

(3) *'The God of mankind' (CXII:3).*

(4) *'The Beneficent, the Merciful'* (2:2).
(5) *'Owner of the Day of Judgement'* (2:3).

The Holy verses quoted above clearly reveal that on the earth there are portents of Allah and those whose faith is sure they know these are the tokens or the signs of Allah for man to know the attributes of creative powers of Allah and then believe in the existence of Allah. The Holy Quran further reveals that the creation of man itself is a portent of Allah and that man must ponder over this reality and see how perfectly he is created and how marvellously he exists and functions as an intelligent, self-thinking living man created out of non-living clay and water.

Quran on the Reproduction of Man

How Human Life Begins?

The Reader's attention is invited to the Holy Quranic verses on the first creation of human life and about 32 verses are quoted above. Similarly on the reproduction of man (how human life begins?), about 25 verses are quoted on page107.These Holy verses be thoroughly read and contemplated upon. Furthermore, the following amazing verses from the Holy Quran reveal as how human life begins or is reproduced.

The Holy Quranic verses are :-

(1) *'Did We not create you from a base fluid?'* (77:20).
(2) *'Which We laid up in a safe abode'* (77:21).
(3) *'For a Known term'* (77:22).
(4) *'Thus We arranged, How excellent is our arranging'* (77:23).
(5) *'Lo! We create man from a drop of thickened fluid to test him, so We make him hearing, knowing'* (76:27).
(6) *'When He created you by (diverse) stages'* (71:14).
(7) *'Then placed him as a drop (of seed) in a safe lodging'* (23:13).
(8) *'Then fashioned We the drop a clot or (something which clings), then fashioned We the clot a little lump, then clothed the bones with flesh and then produced it as another creation. So blessed be Allah, the Best of Creators'* (23:14).

Science in agreement with the Holy Quran on reproduction of human life. Creation of Adam as the first human being and his spores sown broadcast in the earth

The Holy Quran reveals that God created man from a product of wet earth (23:12) and then perfected him with a soul (XCI:7), and inspired him with conscience (XCI:8). How human life begins is a miracle for biologists who are now trying to find the molecular processes to explain how billions of nerve cells in human embryo make connections that infuse mere matter (wet earth) with consciousness. The cells swarming out of nascent spinal cord to colonize far reaches of the embryo helping to form face, head and glands, and all other organs.

The Holy Quran reveals :-

(1) *'From a drop of seed, He created him and proportioned him' (80:19).*

(2) *'......................So We make him hearing, knowing'. (76:27).*

The explosion of such complexity and order----a heart that beats, legs that run and a brain powerful enough to contemplate its own organs --- seems like a miracle. The Holy Quran reveals :-

'Thus We arranged, How excellent is Our arranging'. (77:23).

Molecular biology seeks to interpret biological phenomenon in terms of molecules within the cell. The discipline has developed out of genetics and bio-chemistry as the technological advances of the 20th century.

Biologists face profound challenge about the mystery of embryonic development. The Holy Quran reveals :-

'When He created you by diverse stages' (71:14).

The Holy Quran reveals that God created man in various stages during the process of reproduction in the womb of mother. The various stages of creation is at molecular level and includes fertilization 'from a drop (of seed) of thickened fluid', 'in a safe lodging', by 'diverse stages'. This includes the constituents of the fertilized liquid, the implantation of the fertilized egg and the evolution of the embryo which develops and passes through various stages and then becomes fetus, the human-to-be and prepares for life outside the womb.

Scientists today are far more sophisticated, but some of their theories sound no less preposterous. They believe that an embryo develops parts and assumes form where neither existed before — an assertion that dares biologists to explain how it could happen. 'You have a bunch of cells that are all alike', says Harry Mac William of the University of Massachusetts Medical School. 'There are no external forces acting on them, yet the cells become different. It appears to violate all principles of determinism'.

The Holy Quran reveals :-

> *'He it is Who fashioned you in the womb as pleaseth Him. There is no God save Him, the Almighty, the Wise' (53:6).*

The biological development of the child in the womb of his mother passing through all the embryonic and fetus stages grows and develops at a molecular level 'in due proportions and in true proportions', in the womb of mother as God wishes. The fashioning of the drop (of seed) the sperm with the Ova becomes (something which clings) then it develops and goes to the stages of lump, then the lump is provided bones with flesh and in final stage it is produced in a creation and in this way human life begins.

That seeming paradox has made embryology the next frontier of biology. Incorporating genetics (the study of heredity), cell biology and molecular biology, it is emerging as the grand synthesis of the life sciences. Slowly, Scientists are finding precise molecular explanations for what yesterday's researchers could only describe.

A developing baby is known as embryo during its first eight weeks of gestation. The process starts at the moment of conception. Reference to the various Holy Quranic verses quoted hereafter may be made. These are: (80:19), (77:21-22-23), (76:38), (76:27), (71:14), (23:13-14), (13:8), (53:6) and many others,

Out of the hundreds of millions of sperm that swim to the waiting egg, only one manages to penetrate. It releases digestive enzymes, eating its way into the egg and alters the egg's surface so that no other sperm can follow. Then the sperm merges its genes with the eggs. Somehow — scientists do not know exactly how — that union creates a new life, and raises the scientifically unanswerable questions of just when that life became human. In this respect reference may be made to the Holy Quranic verses at

(38:72), (15:29), (17:85), (27:64) quoted in respect of man's creation.

In the first week the dividing cells form a hollow ball, within which is a bulging cell mass that will become the embryo cell of the mass that face into the cavity develop into inner organs including the liver, pancreas and lungs, outer cells form skin, mouth and central nervous system; middle cells are destined to make blood, muscle and skeleton. In the beginning, the cells of each layer are virtually indistinguishable, but invisible chemical changes have already begun to take place. For while the cells are all descendants of the same fertilized egg, and contain the same genes, some develop into heart cells and some become kidney, some round into blood cells and other branch into nerves, depending on which of their genes switch on or remain inactive.

In the next six weeks almost all of the internal organs are in place and the embryo, scarcely an inch long, looks like a tiny person. During the remaining 30 weeks the human to-be (now designate a fetus) grows and matures to prepare for life outside the womb.

The embryos carry the chemical blueprints of life, and every living cell contains all the genetic instructions needed to make a complete human being.

James Watson of the University of Oregon believes that as cells encounter different molecules, `they receive signals from these molecules that direct them down a particular path of development". `We believe that cells talk to each other", says biologist Laurie Iten of Purdue University. `They are not dumb"

Scientists also need to learn how genes recognize and react to the signals; how they guide — even if they do not determine — an embryo's progress.

The reader would find that there is a tremendous similarity of the Science of Biology in all its disciplines at the level of molecule with the Holy Quranic verses revealed 1400 years ago. This similarity is a token or portent or a sign for knowledgeable man, proving that the Holy Quran revealed on Prophet Muhammad (PBUH) is the Word of God and leads one to the absolute conclusion that there exists One Allah Who is the Creator of man and Who infuses mere matter with consciousness. The act of creation is the result of Infinite Power, Infinite Knowledge and infinite Wisdom and is ordered by the Command of Allah when He says: Be! and it is.

Following are a few of the Holy Quranic verses on the reproduction of man. These verses indicate that the basic principles of human sciences: i.e. the science of embryology, cell biology and molicular biology and genetics (the study of heredity), the DNA, thechromosomes and their interaction and all the events involved in the process of reproduction right from the embryo in the womb, the first stage, to the final stage of fetus (human-to-be) are in absolute consonance and similarity with what the Holy Quran reveals. What an embryo can and cannot become depends at the most basic level, on its genes. They carry the chemical blueprint of life, and every living cell contains all the genetic instructions needed to make a complete human being.

The Holy Quranic verses are :-

(1) *'Lo! He it is Who produceth, then reproduceth' (85:13).*
(2) *'So, Let man consider from what he is created' (86:5).*
(3) *'He is created from a gushing fluid' (86:6).*
(4) *'Createth man from a clot or something which clings' (XCIV:2).*
(5) *'Who created thee, then fashioned, then proportioned thee?' (82:7).*
(6) *'From what thing doth He created him' (80:18).*
(7) *'From a drop of seed: He created Him and proportioned him' (80:19).*
(8) *'Did We not create you from a base fluid?' (77:20).*
(9) *'Which We laid up in a safe abode' (77:21).*
(10) *'For a known term' (77:22).*
(11) *'Thus We arranged, How excellent is Our arranging! (77:23).*
(12) *'Lo! We create man from a drop of thickened fluid to test him, so We make him hearing, knowing' (76:27).*
(13) *'Was he not a drop of fluid which gushed forth?' (76:37).*
(14) *'Then he became a clot, (something which clings) then (Allah) shaped and fashioned' (76:38).*
(15) *'And made of him a pair, the male and female'. (76:39).*
(16) *'When He created you by (divers) stages?' (71:14).*
(17) *'Nay, verily. Lo! We created them from what they know'. (70:39).*
(18) *'Have you seen that which Ye emit?' (56:58).*
(19) *'And that He createth the two spouses, the male and the female' (53:45).*
(20) *'From a drop (of seed) when it is poured forth' (53:46).*

Science in agreement with the Holy Quran on reproduction of human life. Creation of Adam as the first human being and his spores sown broadcast in the earth

(21) *'Verily We created man from a product of wet earth' (23:12).*

(22) *'Then placed him as a drop (of seed) in a safe lodging' (23:13).*

(23) *'Then fashioned We the drop a clot (or something which clings), then fashioned We the clot a little lump, then clothed the bones with flesh, and then produced it as another creation. So blessed be Allah, the Best of Creators' (23:14).*

(24) *'Allah knoweth that which every female beareth and that which the wombs absorb and that which they grow. And everything with Him is measured' (13:8).*

(25) *'He it is Who fashioneth you in the wombs as pleaseth Him. There is no God save Him, the Almighty, the Wise' (53:6).*

The above Holy verses clearly reveal that the phenomenon of reproduction of man in the womb of mother takes place at the level of Molecular Biology, Cell Biology, DNA, Genetic Engineering and at the level of chromosomes.

If one scientifically studies and thoroughly contemplates over the Quranic verses on the creation and reproduction of man, it will be found that the Holy Quran clearly reveals that Allah began the first creation of a live man from clay and water or product of wet earth and that Allah has sown or seeded man broadcast in the earth and caused him to grow as a growth from the earth. The development and reproduction of life has been caused to grow out of the composition of the bio-sphere on the surface of earth, which is activated by the sun's energy to produce chemical and physical actions in the bio-sphere so as to provide building blocks, the fuel and the directions for the creation of life. God is the (best) Who produces creations then reproduces it. Allah has thus sown or seeded man broadcast and has caused life to grow as a growth from the non-living matter of the earth's bio-sphere.

The sense that one can grasp and understand from the above holy verses is that the spores of Adam's race are beamed and sown for reproduction and development in the earth out of bio-sphere (clay and water) and the sun's energy, when Allah infuses His spirit to make life or a living man. The 'spirit' in man is divine and is therefore beyond the knowledge of physical sciences. Allah has not revealed the knowledge of spirit to man, as spirit is not physical matter. This is clear in the verse (17:85) as quoted above. Moreover, man's body contains traces of such elements which were once in stars and then on the explosion of stars such elements were scattered widely in space and thus man's body contains such elements in traces which are broadcast in the earth from space.

The Nature and Origin of Life on Earth

On the total scale of creation, life seems to be an extremely rare phenomenon. There are at least 100,000 million galaxies in the universe, each composed of perhaps 100,000 millions stars and an unknown number of planets. Some scientists feel that life must exist in many places within the vast expanse, but there is proof of life only on earth.

Unlike the other planets in the solar system, the earth has a wet surface, and it is this surface that supports life. Water is the vital medium in which occur all the processes that are characteristic of living things growth, feeding, reproduction and response to stimuli. If life can exist at all without water, it must take a very different form from that of the plants and animals that share the earth.

All these organisms depend on water to dissolve the substances they feed on. Their entire METABOLISM the network of internal chemical processes that are unique to life-takes place among substances dissolved in water. And water is the common carrier in a living organism, transporting food, oxygen and other requirements to its various parts, removing waste materials and dispersing the heat produced by metabolic processes.

The Holy Quran revealed 1400 years ago that Allah made every living thing of water, when there was no knowledge worth the name. Science has hardly a beginning of 500 years ago and modern science less than one hundred years. The similarity of modern knowledge and the recently discovered facts of science with the Holy Quran are the miracles and the marvels of the Holy Quran, clearly indicating that Quran is the word of Allah and that man is the creation of Allah and is the portent of Allah on earth.

The Holy Quran reveals :-

(1) *'And He it is Who hath created man from water'* (25:54).
(2) *'Allah made every living thing of water'* (21:30)
(3) *'And Allah hath created every animal of water'* (24:45).
(4) *'And He began the creation of man from clay'* (32:7).
(5) *'Verily We created man from a product of wet earth'* (23:12).

Biologically, water is the dominant constituent of living matter and is the vital medium of all living things created on earth.

This basically includes mankind, animals and all other creatures and plants. The Zone occupied by life i.e. the bio-sphere is like a thin film enveloping the earth. This zone extends over those parts of the globe where water can exist in a liquid state.

Life however exists without water but that is in a very different form from that of man, animals and plants that share the earth.

The Holy Quran reveals this different form of life which is created out of 'fire' and is parallel to mankind and is called as jinn. They have absolutely different form, life pattern and mechanism and live in entirely a different environment and have a separate life support zone. Jinn is a tribute to the subtlety of energy.

The boundless universe may therefore have many different forms and patterns of life, created out of water or fire or some different substances to live in, different life support zones and in various zones of temperature, pressure and in other environments in space which is severely hostile to man.

About the jinn, the Holy Quran reveals :-

> *'I created the jinn and the mankind only that they might worship Me'. (21:57).*

The Holy Quran, thus reveals the creation of another pattern of living and intelligent creation, which is invisible to man, because of its form and because of its different life support zone. The existence of jinn as a creation is an absolute reality, but to perceive it is beyond the capability and scope of mankind, as man's normal senses are not designed to observe him. Moreover, there are many other barriers in nature which make the meeting of the two creations impossible, unless it is with the Will of Allah, Who is the Creator of all things.

There is a great diversity and unity in the living world on earth. From a few basic elements, more than $1\frac{1}{2}$ million species of living organisms have so far been catalogued.

So, life's diversity ranges from single-celled organisms such as bacteria, which are invisible to the unaided human eye, to gigantic whales of 150 tonnes; and to the wormlike creatures called pogonophorans living in the deep sea ooze.

There are some $1\frac{1}{2}$ millions species of living organisms so far detected on earth. About 10,000 new animals and 5,000 new plant species are added to the official lists every year.

Although life takes many extremely diverse forms, there lies behind that diversity an essential unity. For the complexities of the living world are built up from a handful of basic materials.

From about 90 elements that occur naturally, about 20 are used in the bio-chemical make-up of all plants and animals. The most abundant are: hydrogen, oxygen, carbon and nitrogen, which by weight account for 95 per cent of all living matter. Elements such as phosphorus, sulphur and calcium are needed in much smaller amounts; a number of others, though essential to life processes, are present only in the tiniest quantities.

The Fundamental Cell

The chemical elements are built up into a vast number of different compounds, many of them immensely complex. But the most important fall into a few major groups, such as the carbohydrates, fats, proteins and nucleic acids. These materials are built, in turn, into the cells, the fundamental units of which all living things are made. Cells exhibit every basic property that characterises life.

In spite of the differences, the similarities between all cells plants and animals are far more numerous and fundamental. It is these similarities that best express the unity of life, reinforcing the belief that life forms have a common origin in the primitive single-celled organism of 3,500 million years ago.

Every living thing starts life as a single cell, and converts the energy of the sun and the elements found on earth into fuel to power the ceaseless activity by which it develops and perpetuates its kind. In the 20th century science has dramatically confirmed the unity of the living world by discovering that one single molecule, DNA, is the controlling force of all forms of life, but not the life itself.

So far nothing is known as to what is 'life' and spirit and as such, there is no scientific explanation for life and spirit. The phenomenon of the creation of life is therefore permanently beyond the scope of science. (Encyclopaedia Britannica Volume - 10, Page 900).

The only explanation for the origin of living man created out of wet earth is due to a Divine command when Allah said unto him (man): Be! and he is. (61:59). And the creation of life is one permanently beyond the descriptive powers of Physics and

Chemistry. (Encyclopaedia Britannica Volume - 10, page 894). The composition of the bio-sphere on the surface of earth is distinctive; its chief constituents are compounds of Carbon Hydrogen and Oxygen, although it includes other chemical elements as well. The constituents are fixed in pattern peculiar to the bio-sphere form part of living organisms.

Life arises from non-living matter, i.e. out of wet earth from the earth's bio-sphere in which vital elements are: Carbon, Hydrogen, Nitrogen, Oxygen, Phosphorus and Sulphur. Water is a major predisposing factor, for all life depends on it. Biologically, water is the dominant constituent of living matter as already explained. Here again the Holy Quran reveals in verses (25:12), (VI:73) and (39:5-6), on creation of all things in the universe to be 'in due proportions', equally applies to living man. The scientific reality of man's composition out of the substance as of the earth's bio-sphere is in consonance with the above-mentioned Quranic verses including the one that:

(1) *'We make every living thing of water' (21:30).*
(2) *'And He it is Who hath created man from water' (25:54).*
(3) *'And Allah hath created every animal of water' (24:45).*

Structurally, life on earth is based on carbon and utilizes water as interaction medium. The sun's energy has activated chemical and physical actions in the bio-sphere in all these elements to combine them as proteins, lipids, carbohydrates and nucleic acid. The formation of these substances have provided the building-blocks, the fuel and the directions for the creation of life when God infuses. His 'spirit' or electron or atom of Divine force or vital force or soul to create life. The Holy Quran reveals only this much about the spirit which is the source of man's life :-

The Holy Quran reveals :-

> *'They will ask thee concerning the spirit, Say: The spirit is in command of my Lord and of knowledge ye have been vouchsafed but little, (17:85).*

The sense contained in this verse is clear and is understandable that Allah has not revealed the knowledge as to what spirit is? The Holy verse reveals only that the spirit is created by the command of Allah, which indirectly means that only Allah knows about the spirit and its knowledge is not given to man more than what is revealed in the above Holy verse. The only form of matter having 'vital force' is the living man which cannot be explained by Physics and Chemistry, that some mysterious 'vital force' must be invoked. There are many other hidden and spiritual matters in the Holy Quran, besides the spirit of man, such as, the creation of jinn and the angels, the creation of matter and energy, the creation of the Hereafter, the Resurrection etc., etc., which science cannot explain as these are beyond man's comprehension but are realities as man is a living reality. Man is a living reality because of the spirit, which is invisible, unimaginable and unexplainable. Modern science of physics and chemistry could explain little about the origin of life on earth. The creation of spirit and life are by the Command of Allah and as such Allah has not granted to mankind the knowledge of the spirit except little to the extent that it is from Allah and keeps mankind alive and conscious. This means spirit is metaphysical and as such is permanently beyond the scope of physical science to perceive it.

The Holy Quran reveals :-

> *'And of His signs is the creation of the heavens and the earth, and the difference of your languages and colours. Lo! herein indeed are portents for men of knowledge'* (30:22).

The Holy verse reveals that the heavens and the earth including our universe and the various spoken languages of mankind and their different colours serve as clear signs of the act of creation by the Creator and these creations are indeed portents for men of knowledge i.e. portents for Scientists and Scholars to ponder over the marvellous creations of Allah, including man, so as to know the Creator Allah.

From the verses of the Holy Quran on the creation of man and on the reproduction of man, it is revealed that man is created from wet clay and seeded and sown broadcast to earth to grow from the earth's bio-sphere with the activating power of the sun and with elements contribution in traces from the exploding stars. This means the sustenance and growth of man is from earth. Science of Biology, Cosmology and Physics are in great similarity with the Holy Quran on the creation and reproduction of man. Allah has created man from non-living matter basically out of wet earth. Then Allah infused His spirit to make man a living matter and created male and female among them, thus Allah gave the power of reproduction to mankind. The Holy Quran reveals numerous verses, describing the process of creation of man, and the process of the reproduction of mankind, which are in similarity with the science of Biology, Anatomy and Genetics. The Holy Quran in the verse (39:6) gives allegorial and symbolic description of the womb while revealing the reproduction of man. Allah has mentioned all these realities in the Holy Quran as portents for mankind and revealed it through Prophet Muhammad (PBUH) 1400 years ago when there was no scientific knowledge worth the name, as science at the most has a beginning of 500 years ago and modern science about one hundred years ago. The revelations are divine and absolute truth and every verse and each word is a miracle showing the existence of Allah as the Creator of mankind and of all things in the universe. The revelations by the Holy Quran regarding the creation and reproduction of man and the Science of Biology, Anatomy, Genetics, Embryology on the creation of man and his reproduction growth and sustenance are in great consonance. This leads to the conclusion that the Holy Quran is the Word of God and is not man-made.

Similarity of the Science of Anatomy of Womb with Quranic Verse describing the Reproduction of Man in the Womb of Mother

The congruity between the anatomical description of the womb where child grows and the description of the Holy Quranic verse on the creation of child in the womb of his mother 'in a threefold gloom' is a miracle revealing a scientific fact of anatomy while giving the Biological process of creation of man 1400 years ago by the Holy Quran.

The Holy Verse is :-

> *'He created you from one being, then from that (being) He made its mate; and he hath provided for you of cattle eight kinds. He created you in the wombs of your mothers, creation after creation, in a threefold gloom. Such is Allah, Your Lord. His is the Sovereignty. There is no God Save Him. How then are ye turned away'. (39:6).*

The Holy verse reveals that 'Allah created man in the womb of his mother, creation after creation, in a three-fold gloom'.

Here the Holy Quranic verse clearly mentions and hints to the anatomical description of the womb where man develops in three-fold gloom or darkness i.e. the three layered embryonic membranes in the womb of his mother. The verse objectively hints to the creation and evolution of man in the womb beginning with the implantation and establishment of the embryo within the uterus of the mother. And the differentiation of the uterine lining into a specialized decidual membrane, the development of placenta and the fetal-maternal association throughout pregnancy.

The Holy verse points towards the creation of the various stages of man's development and evolution in the womb. It describes the anatomy of the womb and its various embryonic and fetal stages in the process of creation and human development in the womb. The creation of man in a three-fold gloom means in three concealed or covered places or darkness or three dark places one over the other. The three glooms or dark places, are the three layered membranes of human embryo in the womb one over the other. These compartments or membranes or sacs in the womb are:-

(1) Amnion.

(2) Chorion.

(3) The Uterine Wall (lining) or the Uterus or the Womb.

Amnion

The amnion is the inner most membrane of the sac enclosing the embryo and it is filled with clear watery amniotic fluid. Human embryo and then fetus is enclosed in the amnion. The amniotic fluid performs several mechanical functions, it serves as a protective water cushion which absorbs jolts, equalizes pressures, prevents adherence of the amnion, and permits change of fetal posture.

Chorion

Chorion sac or capsule is the outer most of the two membranes that completely envelopes a fetus. The chorion is related to its increasing association with the lining of the uterus and acts in the function of nutritionm respiration and excretion.

Uterus or Womb

Uterus or womb is a hollow muscular organ of female in which the ovum is deposited and embryo and fetus are developed. The creation of human being develops in three-fold glooms or three fold sacs one enclosing the other. The amnion sac is enclosed by the chorion sac and these two sacs in turn are enclosed within the uterine wall or by the uterus or womb itself which acts as the third sac. The Holy Quran in the above verse invites attention of man towards the biological process in the creation of man and points in allegory towards the anatomical structure of the womb in the process of various stages of man's creation and human development in the womb of mother. Quran gives hints in allegory and clearly indicates the anatomical description of the structure of the womb, where child develops and grows while narrating the anatomy of the uterus in the biological process of creation. The similarity of Quranic verse revealed 1400 years ago describing the facts of Science of Biology and Anatomy of the womb is a Quranic miracle and leads to the firm belief of the existence of Allah as the Creator of mankind and the Quran as His inspired word revealed on Prophet Muhammad (PBUH).

The Quran then draws the attention of mankind in the same Holy verse that such is your Lord, Allah — the Creator of mankind, the Sovereign and the One God. Then, how it is that you turn away from your Allah in spite of all this that He is your Creator.

In the above verse, the Holy Quran indicates that Allah created man in the womb of his mother in a three-fold gloom, 'for a known term', which Allah laid up in a safe abode (77:22) giving protection, providing nutrition, enabling respiration, arranging excretion and ensuring overall safety to the child which grows from a microscopic clot (something which clings) to a full-fledged breathing live child in the womb of his mother in a three-fold gloom or three embryonic membranes.

In continuation of the above quoted verse (39:6), a few more verses are quoted again wherein the Holy Quran reveals that man is created from a drop of seed or a base fluid which is laid up in a safe place (mother's womb) for a known period where he is shaped, fashioned, proportioned and is given the power of hearing and knowing and has appointed in him sight and hearts. So watch how excellent is the arrangement of Allah when man is created from a drop of thickened fluid. Allah has created man so that He may test him. The verses clearly reveal the whole biological cycle in the creation and reproduction of man. The Science of Human Biology on reproduction is completely in consonance with the sense and wisdom contained in the Holy verses mentioned below:-

The Holy verses are :-

(1) *'From a drop of seed, He created him and proportioned him' (80:19).*

(2) *'Did We not create you from a base fluid?' (77:20).*

(3) *'Which We laid up in a safe abode' (77:21).*

(4) *'For a known term' (77:22).*

(5) *'Thus We arranged, How excellent is our arranging!' (77:23).*

(6) *'Who created thee, then fashioned, then proportioned thee?' (82:7).*

(7) *'Lo! We create man from a drop of thickened fluid to test him, so We make him hearing, knowing'. (76:27).*

(8) *'When He created you by (diverse) stages?' (71:14).*

(9) *'Then he became a clot, (something which clings) then (Allah) shaped and fashioned' (76:38).*

(10) *'Is not He (best) Who produceth it' (27:64).*

(11) *'And in the earth are portents for those whose faith is sure' (51:20).*

(12) *'And (also) in yourselves. Can ye then not see?' (51:21).*

(13) *'Surely We created man of the best stature' (XCIV:4).*

(14) *'Then placed him as a drop (of seed) in a safe lodging' (23:13).*

(15) *'Then fashioned We the drop a clot, (something which clings) then fashioned We the clot a little lump, then fashioned We the little lump bones, then clothed the bones with flesh, and then produced it as another creation. So blessed be Allah the Best of Creators!' (23:14).*

The Will of Allah Prevails in the Creation of Male or Female Child and the Science of Genetics in similarity with the Holy Quranic Verses

Man is advised to ponder over the following Quranic verses to grasp how Allah's Will prevails in the creation of male and female child and to know how science of genetics is in similarity with the Holy verses of the Holy Quran.

The Holy Quran reveals :-

(1) *'Unto Allah belongeth the sovereignty of the heavens and the earth.*

He createth what He will. He bestoweth female (offspring) upon whom, He will, and bestoweth male (offspring) upon whom He will' (42:49).

(2) *'Or He mingleth them, males and females and He maketh barren whom He Will. Lo! He is Knower, Powerful' (42:50).*

(3) *'Allah knoweth that which every female beareth and that which they grow. And everything with Him is measured' (13:8).*

(4) *'The Creator of the Heavens and the Earth. He hath made for you pairs of yourselves and of the cattles also pairs whereby He multiplieth you. Naught is as His likeness: He is the Hearer, the Seer' (42:11).*

The above Holy verses are explained in the context of the relevant sciences as follows :

The arrangement by nature for the fixation of sex whether male or female is according to the 'Will of Allah', and according to His set measure and is explained by the Science of Genetics as follows :

The genetic code i.e. the order in which four chemical constituents are arranged in huge molecules of DNA: these molecules are assumed to transmit genetic information to the cells by synthesizing ribonucleic acid in a corresponding order. Human body is made up of 60 to 75 trillion cells and that the characteristics of each one are determined by the incredible substance, DNA.

Each cell has a nucleus. The nucleus of each living creation has a definite number of chromosomes. The human cell has 46 chromosomes arranged in 23 pairs. The Holy Quran reveals in the verse (42:11) that 'He hath made for you pairs of yourselves and of the cattles also pairs, whereby He multiplieth you'.

In human beings, male as well as female, both have 22 pairs of the same type of chromosomes called autosomes. One of the pair, out of the 23 pairs, is different and is called sex chromosome. In female the sex chromosomes are of the same type i.e. X X Chromosomes. Thus, female has two X-Chromosomes. Whereas, in males, the pair of sex chromosome is somewhat different to female. In male the sex chromosome is XY.

The sex chromosomes are of two types, which are designated X and Y, and the pair of sex chromosomes may consist of two X chromosomes or of an X and Y paired together. The cells of males contain an X Y Pair and the cells of females contain an X X pair. Human beings, have cells with 22 pairs of non-sexual chromosomes or autosomes, together with an XX pair or an XY pair. The female has a total of 46 functional chromosomes. The Male has 45 plus a Y, which is mainly inert. Sex formation thus becomes a matter of balance. With one X chromosome plus the 44 autosomes in every cell, the whole course of development of primary and secondary sexual characteristics is towards the male; with two X chromosomes plus the autosomes in every cell the whole system is swung over to the female. All this is measured with Allah and the mechanism of movement of X or Y chromosomes and the matter of balance for sex formation lie in His will for the creation of male or female child. Similarly, Allah has fixed different number of chromosomes pairs for different types of animals and cattles.

The manipulation of this control system is readily accomplished during the special process of cell division that takes place in the gonads to produce sperm and eggs and their subsequent union at fertilization. In mammals, for example, since all cells in the female contain two X chromosome, all the eggs will receive single X chromosome when they are formed. All eggs are accordingly the same in this respect. In contrast, all cells in the male have the XY constitution, and therefore, when the double set of chromosomes is reduced to a single set during the formation of the spermatozoa, half of the spermatozoa will receive an X and half will receive a Y. Consequently, when an egg is fertilized by a sperm, the chances are about equal that the sperm carry an X or will carry a Y, since the two types are inevitably produced in equal numbers. If it carries an X, the XX female constitution results; if a Y, then the XY male constitution results.

Genes in Action

The genetic message in the fertilized egg determines the characteristics of the offspring, but every individual has two sets of genes one from each parent. The body has to decide by Allah's will, for each pair of genes, whether it is going to obey the instructions of the maternal or of the paternal gene.

The following sketch explains the process.

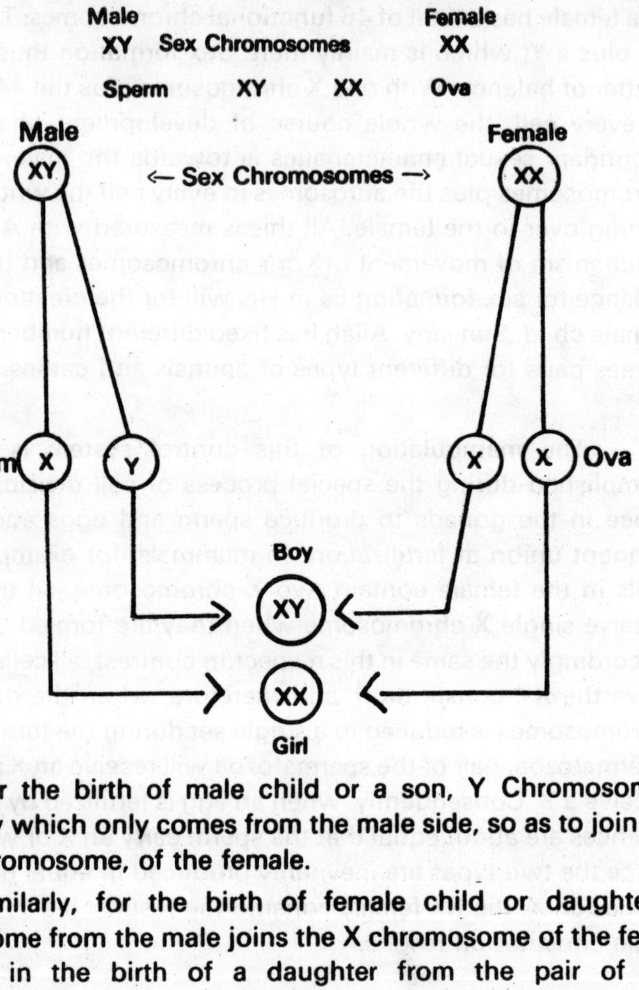

For the birth of male child or a son, Y Chromosome is necessary which only comes from the male side, so as to join with the X-chromosome, of the female.

Similarly, for the birth of female child or daughter, X chromosome from the male joins the X chromosome of the female resulting in the birth of a daughter from the pair of X X chromosomes.

It is impossible to predict which sperm from the male is going to join the ova of the female, therefore, it is beyond human power to specifically manipulate the birth of a male (son) or female (daughter).

It is only the nature, the will of Allah, which arranges a boy or a girl and the Will of Allah, Who is the Creator prevails in this phenomenon. The number and types of chromosomes are fixed and are thus measured by Allah for all species. The joining of XY-Chromosomes or XX Chromosomes creates male or female. Allah makes some people barren whom He will. Allah knows what the

wombs absorb with all the arrangement and movements of chromosomes as everything with Him is measured at molecular level and beyond that. Every female bears child with the knowledge of Allah Who is Powerful Creator and is the Knower of it. So, it is the pleasure of Allah, the way He fashions to be a male creation or a female in the womb of his/her mother. The same way the chemicals, the chromosomes, and the tendency for a male or female child **develops as the will of Allah directs at the molecular level.**

The following Quranic verses reveal the creation of male or female (offspring) and hint towards the similarity of the basic principles of genetics of human beings and the Science of Biology and Embriology dealing with the formation and development of embryos:-

(1) *'Allah knoweth that which every female beareth and that which the wombs absorb and that which they grow. And everything with Him is measured' (13:8).*

(2) *'Glory be to Him Who created all the sexual pairs of that which the earth growth and of themselves and of that which they know not' (36:6).*

(3) *'Unto Allah belongeth the sovereignty of the heavens and the earth. He createth what He Will. He bestoweth female (offspring) upon whom. He will and bestoweth male (offspring) upon whom He will' (42:49).*

(4) *'Or He mingleth them, males and females and He maketh barren whom He Will. Lo! He is Knower, Powerful'. (42:50).*

(5) *'Allah created you from dust, then from a little fluid, then He made your pairs (the male and female). No female beareth or bringeth forth save with His knowledge. And no one groweth old who groweth old, nor is aught lessened of his life, but it is recorded in a Book. Lo! that is easy for Allah' (35:11).*

(6) *'Unto Him is referred (all) knowledge of the Hour. And no fruit burst forth from their Sheaths and no female carrieth or bringeth forth but with His knowledge. And on the day when He calleth unto them: Where are my partners? They will say: We confess unto Thee, not one of us is a witness (for them)' (41:47).*

(7) *'The Creator of the heavens and the earth, He hath made for you pairs of yourselves and of the cattle also pairs, whereby He multiplieth you. Naught is as His likeness; He is the Hearer, the Seer' (42:11).*

(8) *'Lo! He it is Who produceth, then reproduceth'. (85:13).*

(9) *'Is not He (best) Who produceth creation, then reproduceth it, and Who provideth for you from the heaven and the earth? Is there any God besides Allah? Say: Bring your proof, if ye are truthful!'. (27:64).*

(10) *'And that He createth the two spouses, the male and the female' (53:45).*

(11) *'Then placed him as a drop (of seed) in a safe lodging' (23:13).*

(12) *'Then fashioned We the drop a clot, (something which clings) then fashioned We the clot a little lump, then fashioned We the little lump bones, then clothed the bones with flesh, and then produced it as another creation. So blessed be Allah, the Best of Creators' (23:14).*

(13) *'He it is Who fashioneth you in the wombs as pleaseth Him. There is no God save Him, the Almighty, the Wise' (53:6).*

The above Quranic verses describe the whole process of reproduction of mankind and its development as male and female in the wombs as pleases Allah.

The Holy Quran reveals the fundamental principles of the Science of Biology, Molecular Biology, Cell Biology, Chromosomes Embryology and Genetics. It reveals the principles and the process of the creation of human beings and cattles (animals) and all living things. It reveals that the number of chromosomes and their pairs are fixed and measured by Allah for every type of living creation. It also reveals that the creation of a male or female child is a matter of measure with Him and the balance lie in His Will, whether the process of creation of child is going to obey the instructions of the maternal or of the paternal gene. It is the Will of Allah which prevails which way to proceed in the creation of male or female child. So, the creation of male or female, boy or girl is according to the Will of Allah and He fashions boy or girl in the womb of mother as He pleases.

The possible misuse of discovery and development of new ideas and the biologist's manipulation of genes to direct further evolutionary development concerning hereditary mechanism, genetic engineering, by which human traits are made to order after selection for a change, many become a reality as scientists predict. In cases of genetic deficiencies and disease, the desirability of the change is obvious, but the possibilities for social misuse, are so numerous that they may far outweigh the benefits. Such misuse could result in freak development and may be that one day 'speaking animal' is created on earth.

The Holy Quran reveals :-

> *'And when the Word is fulfilled concerning them, We shall bring forth a beast of the earth to speak unto them because mankind had not faith in Our revelations' (27:82).*

The meaning of the above Holy verse is of tremendous consequence. Its complete sense is difficult to grasp and understand but what is partly understandable is that one day Allah will create a beast on earth who will speak to mankind. This will happen because mankind did not believe in the revelations of Allah and had no faith in it. So they will face an animal speaking to them to cause utter surprise, bewilderment and shock. Such token from Allah will cause them astonishment and then they will believe in Allah as the Creator of all things.

The Will of God behind the Subtlety of the Genetic Mechanism

According to the knowledge of biochemists, the most subtle forms of female choice and the most difficult to demonstrate, are those that may take place inside the female reproductive tract. John Hartung has suggested that the 'Ultimate female choice' may be some mechanism by which an egg selects among the millions of tiny, wiggling sperms struggling to penetrate its membrane. Whether this actually happens is highly theoretical, but evidence that some female insects are choosing among competing sperm has come in.

According to biochemist William Walker of Dalhousie University Nova Scotia, 'Female often actively regulate sperm movements within their reproductive tracts'.

The movements and mechanism by which an egg selects among the millions of sperms and penetrate its membrane is Regulated by the Will of Allah within the reproductive tracts of female at molecular level under a programmed system. This is clearly indicated by the following Holy Quranic verses :-

(1) *'He it is Who fashioneth you in the wombs as pleaseth Him. There is no God save Him, the Almighty, the Wise' (53:6).*

(2) *'Allah knoweth that which every female beareth and that which they grow. And everything with Him is measured' (13:8).*
(3) *'Who created thee, then fashioned, then proportioned thee?' (82:7).*
(4) *'He is Allah, the Creator, the Shaper out of naught, the Fashioner' (60:24).*

All this explains that modern scientific concepts and facts in all the diversified fields are in complete agreement with the Holy Quran and that the Religion of Islam teaches man perfect Science symbolically, allegorially and in direct conclusive form, hinting the fundamental principles and the basic concepts about the creation of life and the creation of Adam in perfect human form and universe and their working and their ultimate fate.

This book reveals amazing facts that every Scientist, Doctor, Engineer, Mathematician, Scholar, Intellectual and Religious man whether Muslim, Christian, Jew, Hindu, Buddhist, Agnostic or Atheist should know to understand the Holy Quran and the Religion of Islam intelligently.

Supergene Indicates that Man is Genetically Programmed by Allah

The Concept of Genetic Destiny in Agreement with the Holy Quran

Socio-biologists promote a theory of genetic destiny, which indicates that man is genetically programmed. This concept is in agreement with the Holy Quran.

Who will live long and who will die young? The answer seems tied to a complicated DNA cluster called the 'SUPERGENE', as is observed by Richard Canniff.

The Holy Quran reveals that :

'Everything have We recorded in a Book' (78:29).

The 'Book' in the Holy verse is a simili and points towards the DNA and the genetic destiny of man. It has the Record of life and death.

The Holy Quran further reveals :-

> *'Who hath created life and death and that **He may try you**, which of you is the best in conduct; and He is the **Mighty, the Forgiving**' (67:2).*

The eventful and circumstantial destiny of man which becomes his fate and luck is governed by the Will of Allah and is programmed accordingly. Allah has inspired man with conscience to choose the path of conduct and this quality makes him superior to the preferred creations of Allah. Allah programmes the complete destiny of man and that everything is on record with Him. The conduct of man has bearing on his destiny which is programmed by Allah at molecular and sub-atomic level and far beyond.

Within each of the 60 trillion or so cells that make-up the human body in a tiny cluster of genetic material so complex and extraordinary that scientists refer to it flatly as a 'SUPERGENE' Researchers almost daily turn new evidence of the supergene's influence on a remarkable range of biological process. It may determine how long people live, how well they fight out disease, even which diseases they will eventually succumb to. A recent study also suggests that differences in the SUPERGENE may be the reason some people suffer dental cavaties, while others go through life with almost perfect teeth. The supergene controls everything including the tip of your nose.

* It plays a major role in the immune system.
* It influences our susceptibility to certain cancers.
* The supergene appears to predispose certain people to more than 50 non-malignant disorders from arthiritis and diabetes to depression.
* Products of the Supergene on surface of every cell seem to act as an 'Identity Card for the Organism' and may determine the ability of one friendly cell to recognize and adhere to another.
* The supergene may influence chemical communication and mating behaviour between members of a species.
* It codes for the production of enzymes necessary in the synthesis of important steroid hormones, including cortisone and testosterone.

* The supergene may help determine the rate at which people age.

The above characteristic of the Supergene, its functioning, its trend for further change and development, its coding the DNA and its working at molecular and sub-atomic level and beyond very clearly indicates that man is genetically programmed by the Supreme Unimaginable Being Who is the Creator of man and is Allah the One God. Besides the genetic programming of man, his fate otherwise is also regulated and connected to follow a destined programme depending on many things including his conduct and the use of his conscience which are in clear notice of Allah as Allah is the Creator and the Knower of all things. He is the Shaper, the Fashioner and the Compeller of all things.

Life Span or Life Term of each Man is Appointed and is Pre-programmed by Allah in the Genetic Script (DNA) at Birth as Genetic Destiny.

Science of Genetics Regarding Senescence and Death in Similarity with the Holy Quran.

Whether the aging is programmed in the brain when at a set time the pituitary gland releases a "death" harmone or the existence of an "aging" gene, maintaining that senescence is written into the genetic script at birth as part of the normal developmental programme. The aging gene, or genes, "switch on" at a preprogrammed time. Once activated, the genes act to slow down or halt manufacturing processes crucial to the life of the cell. The genetic machinery—the DNA and its associated protein-making apparatus centres at the cellular level. What-ever be the cause of aging, the maximum age of each person is preprogrammed by Allah and the time, the Day, the Hour and the moment of death is fixed and appointed by Allah, as is revealed by the Holy Quran.

The Holy Quranic verses are:-

(1) *'No soul can ever die except by Allah's leave and at a term appointed. . .' (III:145).*

(2) *'Allah created you from dust, then from a little fluid, then He made you pairs (the male and female). No female beareth or bringeth forth save with His Knowledge. And no one groweth old who groweth old,*

nor is aught lessened of his life, but it is recorded in a Book. Lo! That is easy for Allah' (35:11).

(3) *'Every Soul will taste of death . . .'* (III:185).

(4) *'He it is Who gathereth you at night and knoweth that which ye commit by the day. Then He raiseth you again to life therein, that the term appointed (for you) may be accomplished. And after-ward unto Him is your return. Then He will proclaim unto you what ye used to do'* (VI:60).

(5) *'Allah receiveth (men's) souls at the time of their death, and that (soul) which dieth not (yet) in its sleep. He keepeth that (soul) for which He hath ordained death and dismisseth the rest till an appointed term. Lo! herein verily are portents for people who take thought'* (39:42).

The amazing similarity between science of genetics and the Holy Quran makes it clear that the science of genetics regarding life-span of man, that senescence is written and is pre-programmed into the genetic script at birth as normal development programmed is very much in consonance with the above noted verses from the Holy Quran. All this similarity and concord clearly prove that the Holy Quran is the Word of the Creator (Who is Allah) and is His message for mankind to believe in the existence of one Allah and to obey and worship Him according to the guidance revealed by the Holy Quran.

Besides the genetic destiny and the biological cause for the death of a man as pre-programmed in the genetic script, the term for the death of man is appointed which shall occur either biologically or due to any other physical cause as per the law of casualty and chance.

The Similarity of the Science of Astrophysics and Biology on the Chemical Composition of Man with the Quranic Verses on Man's Creation and the Contribution by Stars, the Sun and the Moon and the Earth

The following Holy verses are quoted for contemplation :-

(1) *'And He has constrained the night and the day and the sun and the moon to be of service unto you and the stars are made subservient by His Command. Lo! herein indeed are portents for people who have sense'* (16:12).

(2) *'Have not those who disbelieve known that the heavens and the earth were one piece, then We parted them, and We made every living thing of water. Will they not then believe?' (31:30).*

(3) *'And He it is Who hath sown you broadcast in the earth and unto Him ye will be gathered' (23:79).*

(4) *'And Allah has caused you to grow as a growth from the earth. And afterwards, He maketh you return thereto. And He will bring you forth once again' (71:17).*

From the above Holy verses it is revealed that there is a great similarity between the findings of the Astrophysicists studying the chemical composition of stars and Biologists investigating the chemical composition of human bodies. It is found that the chemical composition of man consists of much the same allotment of elements as are found in our galaxy. Moreover, the metal found in trace elements in human bodies on earth appear to have been found in the explosions of stars that died before the sun was born, seeding space with the metal rich dust and gas from which our solar system and eventually, ourselves were formed.

The above facts of science are in similarity with the Quranic verse (31:30) quoted above which states that the heaven and the earth were one piece i.e. the universe, our galaxy and our solar system and earth were all one piece and then Allah parted them and Allah made every living thing of water. Again the Holy verse (16:12) quoted above reveals that the sun and the moon are for the service of mankind and that Allah has constrained the sun and the moon, the night and the day for the service of man. Moreover, the stars are made to contribute and serve and to promote some end and they are made useful for man in a subordinate capacity and they come in usefulness after the sun and the moon.The stars are therefore made subservient to man by the Command of Allah and in the existence of this reality indeed there are portents for people who have knowledge and sense to grasp and understand the meanings encompassed in the Holy verse mentioned above.

The Holy verses quoted above reveal that the sun and the moon and stars and the earth (which is the abode of man), are all contributing in the growth and the sustenance of man on earth. The stars are making contribution in the chemical composition of man on earth, when the stars during their evolution exploded, thereby, seeding space with the metal rich dust and gas from which our solar system and eventually, ourselves were formed. Similarly, the sun, the moon and the earth contribute in the growth and development of man as a growth from the earth, where Allah has caused and has sown man broadcast in the earth.

From the similarity of the science of Astrophysics (revealing the composition of stars and galaxies) and the science of Biology (revealing the chemical composition of man) with the Holy Quranic verses quoted above, it has become evident that the Holy Quran is full of Wisdom, Knowledge, Information and Guidance and that the source of Quran is Allah Himself. The Quran is the inspired word of Allah revealed on Prophet Muhammad (PBUH) for the guidance of all mankind. The similarity of science on physical matters of the physical universe and man, with the Holy Quran, clearly and directly indicate the portents of Allah, which in turn, indicate the existence of Allah as the Creator of all things, the Holy Quran as His Message for mankind and Prophet Muhammad (PBUH) as His Last Messenger.

The above Holy verses reveal the ultimate fate of mankind and that they will be gathered or assembled and resurrected by Allah to stay immortal in the 'Hereafter'.

An abstract of an article from New York Times Magazine by Timothy Ferris, entitled 'Probing the Mysteries of the Galaxies', published in Reader's Digest, August, 1979, is found to be in consonance with the substance and the sense in the above quoted Holy verses.

The abstract from the article is as follows :-

> 'Deeper connections between ourselves and the galaxies are being discerned. Astrophysics studying the chemical composition of stars and Biologists investigating the Chemical composition of our bodies, have found that we are made up of much the same allotment of elements as is our galaxy. The metals found in trace elements in our bodies appear to have been found in the explosions of stars that died before the sun was born, seeding space with the metal-rich dust and gas from which our solar system and eventually, ourselves were formed'.

The composition of galaxies is beginning to reveal itself through the eyes and ears of new astronomical tools — X-ray satellites, ultra-violet senors, computer simulation techniques etc.

Science in agreement with the Holy Quran on reproduction of human life. Creation of Adam as the first human being and his spores sown broadcast in the earth

The Holy Quran clearly and repeatedly reveals that after death, mankind shall be revived. They will be brought back to life and their remains will be gathered at molecular and atomic level precisely and perfectly to the original form of each man. The life of mankind and the life of the universe is appointed for a period, when the universe shall catastrophically collapse. After the great physical event, mankind shall be gathered by Allah, recollected and revived back to life. All this shall occur on the Doomsday or the Day when the physical universe shall catastrophically collapse, and mankind on revival shall pass over or shall find themselves in the next world which is eternal and where mankind shall be immortal. That world is called, the 'Hereafter' i.e. the World of 'Life after death' which is certain as is revealed by the Holy Quran. The Holy Quran reveals absolute truth and now it is for man whether to believe it or believe not, but it is the true word of Allah, whereof there is absolutely no doubt.

Man — A Living Matter and a Portent or a Token of Allah's Creation on Earth

Allah addresses mankind in the Holy Quran that there are portents in the heavens and the earth for those people whose faith is sure and that mankind themselves and their creation is a portent if they see and ponder over it and have the wisdom and knowledge to grasp it. Man is created by Allah out of clay and water and then He breathed His spirit into him and gave him life. Then Allah created man from a draught of despised fluid and then fashioned and proportioned him and gave him the best stature, shape and anatomy and perfected him with a soul and inspired him with conscience and gave him the faculty of hearing, seeing, feeling and thinking etc., and so raised mankind as the best community. Allah's design of man is perfect.

The Holy Quran in this respect reveals the following verses :-

(1) *'Lo! in the heavens and the earth are portents for believers'. (45:3).*

(2) *'And in your creation and all the beasts that He scattereth in the earth, are portents for a folk whose faith is sure' (45:4).*

(3) *'And in the earth are portents for those whose faith is sure'. (51:20).*

(4) *'And (also) in yourselves, can ye then not see? (51:21).*

(5) *'These are the portents of Allah which we recite unto thee (Muhammad) with truth. Then in what fact, after Allah and His*

portents, will they believe?' (45:6).

(6) *'He began the creation of man from clay' (32:7).*

(7) *'And He it is Who hath created man from water' (25:54).*

(8) *'Then He made his seed from a draught of despised fluid' (32:8).*

(9) *'Then He fashioned him and breathed into him of His spirit and appointed for you hearing and sight and hearts. Small thanks give ye!' (32:9).*

(10) *'Who created thee, then fashioned, then proportioned thee?' (82:7).*

(11) *'Surely We created man of the best stature'. (XCIV:4).*

(12) *'And a soul and Him Who perfected it. (XCI:7).*

(13) *'And inspired it (with conscience of) what is wrong for it and (what is) right for it' (XCI:8).*

(14) *'Ye are the best community that hath been raised upon for mankind'. Ye enjoin right conduct and forbid indecency; and ye believe in Allah' (68:110).*

(15) *'Verily We have honoured the Children of Adam. We carry them on the land and the sea, and have made provisions of good things for them and have preferred above many of those whom We created with a marked preferment' (17:70).*

Structurally man himself is merely frail clay and water but Allah perfected man with a soul and created him of the best stature when Allah fashioned and proportioned him and breathed in him His spirit to make him a living man and gave him the power of sight, hearing, thinking, feeling and inspired him with conscience of what is wrong for him and what is right for him. Allah has honoured man by preferring him above many of those whom Allah created with a marked preferment.

Allah created man as living matter and gave him the power of speech, intelligence, wisdom, thinking capability and conscience and created him as responsible creature and as a portent and a token of living matter on earth with complete and automatic and self-generating and self-adjustable human body with the vital organs and all with marvel designs and functions.

Human body or structure without life is a piece of clay but the moment the Holy Spirit was blown into the body, it acquired life with numerous functions and powers. Life and spirit or soul is unknown to medical science and to the science of Biology, Physics and Chemistry. So, man himself does not know what he is and how he functions as a living intelligent creature. All living creatures of the animal world on earth and man are the portents and the marvels of

Allah and a living man is the most superior token of all the creations as above Holy verses reveal.

Professor Dr. Glenn Clark writes :-

'In the Physics and Chemistry Laboratories we find that the body is fluid and is not a solid thing. It is not permanent, it is changing every hour, every minute and every second. Human body contains between 85 to 90 per cent fluid i.e. water. Human structure and all its organs are so perfect and appropriate in design and in its creation and operation that no worldly machine could ever match it'.

The Holy Quran reveals :-

(1) *It is He Who created all things and ordered them in due proportions'. (25:2).*

(2) *'Allah knoweth that which every female beareth and that which the wombs absorb and that which they grow. And everything with Him is measured' (13:8).*

(3) *'Who created thee, then fashioned, then proportioned thee' (82:7).*

Loius Pasteur was amazed and shocked when he looked through the microscope at a small piece of human flesh and cried:

'I am seeing a whole in a part'.

A part of (human body) had acquired qualities and characteristics of the whole or the whole had manifested itself in a part (human body).

Human Structure
Inner Man

Of the billions of people on earth, not one duplicates another. Not even identical twins. This uniqueness is only one astonishing fact of that assembly of some 600 muscles, 206 bones, 60,000 miles of blood vessels, 60 to 75 trillion cells, your body.

Human structure is composed of about 75 trillion cells, each having a membrane a bare .0000001 millimeter thick. Each cell carries an identification tag recognized by other cell membranes.

Millions of cells die everyday and are replenished instantly. It is amazing that 75 trillion cells of human body can live in such harmony, each minding its own business, efficiently performing its own task, is something to ponder and is a marvel of Allah.

Dr. Andren Conway, a Famous Physiologist writes :-

> 'In the science of Physiology, when one studies growth, development, maintenance and repair of the body, it is found that each cell almost without exception 'knows' its role in carrying out design or purpose for the welfare of the body as a whole'.

Various parts and organs of the human body and their functions and designs are wonders of nature.

The Human Brain

Take the human brain which itself is a tremendous complicated and complex structure. The number of neutron in one brain is more than 25 billion. No computer can duplicate all its myriad functions. Even when one is asleep, it continues handling traffic that would swamp all the world's telephone exchange. The wonders performed by human organs are due to the creative powers wielded by the Holy Spirit lodged by Allah in the body.

The Nervous System

Look at the nervous system which functions day and night when millions of messages pour through its billions of cells, telling the heart when to beat, limbs when to move, lungs when to draw in air. Consider the sensory nerves which tell us whether curry is tasty, a piece of music is pleasing, a view is inspiring.

See the marvels of human circulatory system. It is longer than any railway, it has an estimated 60,000 to 100,000 miles of route. Silently, automatically working day and night it normally provides the exact blood flow required by any tissue or organ, carrying food to and wastes away from several hundred million million customs the body cells. The circulatory system even produces its own rolling stock, the red and white cells. In a single second, it manufactures millions new red cells to replace an equal number of cells that have perished.

The Human Liver and the Spleen

This wonder human organ the liver, is a three pound gland tucked under the ribs of the right side of one's body. It is a chemical wizard whose manifold magic performance have dazzled modern scientists and medical experts. More than 500 Liver functions have been catalogued todate and new ones are constantly been discovered. Each second ten million of one's red blood cell die and must be disposed of. The spleen breaks them down; then the liver helps salvage the component parts. Such as iron for re-use in building new blood cells.

A cut on hand could mean death, but the liver produces fibrinogen and protherombin that help clot blood. The liver also manufactures antibodies that fight invading viruses and bacteria. Without these antibodies, even the smallest infection could cause death.

The Human Heart

The human heart weighs nearly 12 ounces and hangs by ligaments in the centre of one's chest. It is hardworking four-chambered pump-actually two pumps, one to move blood in the lungs, the other to push it out into the body. Everyday, the heart pumps blood (through 60,000 miles of blood vessels). In one's life time it pumps 300,000 tons of blood. The heart generates its own electricity and sends out pulses to trigger contraction. (What makes heart to beat is still unknown to scientists)

The Human Lungs

The lungs are inflated 500 million times by a human being in an average life time. No man-made machine can stand wear and tear for such a long period without overhauling. The lung has grape-like branches of minute air sacs 750 million microscopic air sacs called alveoli.

The Human Kidney

The kidney contains more than a million little filtering units called nephrons. Blood passes through it continuously it cleans and filters it, ridding it of wastes that are potentially deadly. It helps production of red blood cells. Controls water balances — ensures that blood is neither too acidic nor too alkaline. Every hour kidneys filter twice the total blood in one's body. It does hundreds of other jobs, still unknown to scientists.

The Human Eyes

The human eye contains nearly 130 thousand million light receptors which are equal to the number of stars in the Milky Way.

The body organs shuttle and work day and night under the mysterious divine force We call soul or spirit. Some famous scientists are of the opinion that the soul abides in the heart and some that it lives in the brain. But no one knows what it is and where it is lodged by the Creator Allah. In fact it is the presence of this Holy Being in the clay cassette which makes it a universe in miniature and a marvel of Allah.

The Holy Quran reveals :-

> *'They will ask thee concerning the spirit, Say: The spirit is by the Command of my Lord and of knowledge Ye have been vouchsafed but little'* (17:85).

Science has no knowledge about the spirit. Practically man does not know anything about the spirit. The spirit is only by the order of Allah and is something divine. It is not physical. As regards the reproduction of mankind, Allah knows the sex of a child, the moment what the womb absorbs and which it grows and that Allah has measured all the human organs and create them in due proportions and in true proportions and has perfectly designed and measured the organs for specific functions in the human body as briefly discussed above.

The Holy verses reveal :-

(1) *'And everything with Him is measured'* (13:8).

(2) *'Who created thee, then fashioned, then proportioned thee?'* (82:7).

In the light of the above verses, it is for man to contemplate how miraculously the various human organs function to maintain human body. In addition to the organs mentioned above, there are numerous other organs which play equally marvellous part in functioning and in contributing to the overall human system. Their achievements and basic functions are yet to be discovered. Their functions are still hidden from human observations. It may take hundreds or thousands of years to discover the hidden mysteries underlying the human body. The skin, the eyes, the ears and the heart, the brain the kidney, the lungs etc., have vital functions to perform in the human body.

The human body and its vital organs on the whole function as recording and broadcasting station. Vital human organs have also the characteristics to function as cassettes by recording all intelligent messages and deeds and actions of events in which vital parts, such as, skin and the sense of touch, the nervous system, the brain, eyes and ears etc., are involved. The signals and impulses by the skin, nervous system, brain etc. are of great significance. The functions of human skin and the sense of touch is discussed in the Chapter on Accountability of man. Human being is physical but the spirit part of him is metaphysical. Therefore, there could be many invisible functions performed by the human body under the invisible divine power as is the man's spirit.

The Holy Quran reveals and warns man in the following verses that :-

(1) *'Ye did not seek to hide yourselves, lest your hearing your sight and your skins should bear witness against you. But ye did not think that God know not many of the things that ye used to do'* (41:20:22).

(2) *'Behold, two (guardian angels) appointed to take note (of his doings) one sitting on the right and one on the left. Not a word does he utter but there is a sentinel by him ready (to note it)'* (50:17).

The Holy Quran reveals that even the skin of man has the power of speech and would testify against him for what he did. May be that man's skin and his brain while receiving impulses and messages be tapping them and may also serve as the bugging devices and as the built-in storage of recorded cassettes, or serve as amplifier for signalling hidden impulses somewhere, which would be used for the purpose of man's accountability on the Day of Judgement in the Hereafter.

The Holy Quran reveals :-

(1) *'Till, when they reach it, their ears, and their eyes and their skins testify against them as to what they used to do' (41:20).*

(2) *'And they say unto their skins: Why testify Ye againstus? They Say: Allah has given us speech who giveth speech to all things and who created you at the first, and unto whom ye are returned' (41:21).*

(3) *'Ye did not hide yourselves lest your ears and your eyes and your skins should testify against you, but ye deemed that Allah knew not much of what ye did' (41:22).*

The human mind is still in a stage of infancy and evolution and man does not know the location of the soul or the Holy Spirit. Man will never know his most vital invisible part, the soul or the spirit. But man may or may not know the invisible functions of human organs, such as, the power of speech by the skin and many other hidden functions by the various organs. The tremendous coded genetic information in the DNA is also a great miracle of Allah.

Allah has designed human beings in such a way that he has placed great capabilities in human body. Some of these capabilities are known and are visible whereas some are invisible and unknown and some are hidden from mankind and are not yet discovered.

Allah has therefore, created man as a token and as His marvel and has gifted him with all essential qualities of a superior creation. Man is a combination of physical stature operated by divine spirit. The physical qualities and the constituting organs or parts of man are visible and known and are still being discovered but the numerous invisible functions of the organs and human body are unknown and may remain unknown in respect of many of the organs. May be these organs be in communication through hidden processes with the metaphysical world for accountability. However, God inheres everywhere and is more nearer to man than his jugular vein.

So, man is extraordinary improbable object but he is a great reality and is very much in existence with all his wondrous organs and their functions wondrous both visible and invisible in the marvellous creation of man. In fact, man is a living universe in miniature.

Science in agreement with the Holy Quran on reproduction of human life. Creation of Adam as the first human being and his spores sown broadcast in the earth

Life Creating God Exists

Scientists Establish Existence of the Creator by Mathematics

Adam (The First Man) and his Spores Beamed to Earth from beyond space (the garden)

Science and the Holy Quran in Similarity

Science is man's attempt to know the reality, but the Holy Quran reveals the absolute truth.

British Astronomer Sir Fred Hoyle and Sri Lanka born Astronomer Chandra Wickrama Singhe have written an amazing book just published in England under the title (Evolution from Space,) which reveals that life-creating God exists. One of the big surprises of the creation-science trial in Arkansas last December, 1981, was the appearance, as a Key witness against Darwinnian Evolution, of Chandra Wickrama Singhe, a distinguished astro-physicist from University College, Cardiff, in Wales. Even more surprising was his revelation that he and his eminent collaborator, Sir Fred Hoyle both former disbelievers in a life-creating God, are now persuaded that such God exists. Not only, that but they believe that the existence of a Creator can be established by mathematics, with a probability greater than 10 ^{40,000} (10 followed by 40,000 zeros) to 1. The Holy Quran reveals that Allah Who is the One God, the Unimaginable Supreme Being', exists beyond all doubts and that He is the Creator of all things and of mankind and that He is of Infinite Power, Infinite Wisdom and of Infinite Knowledge.

Hoyle gave a startling account of their revolutionary theory in a lecture in January 1982 at the Royal Institution, London. Hoyle and his friend do not deny that most of life on earth, including human beings, evolved from simple forms that first appeared on the planet several billion years ago. What they do claim is that natural laws cannot account for life's origin, and that Darwinian natural selection cannot explain its development.

Their argument is a mathematically sophisticated form of ancient proof of God by design. Put all the parts of a watch in a barrel, goes a familiar version, and you can shake the barrel until Doomsday without producing a watch. Hoyle's favourite analogy concerns Rubik's Cube. Give a scrambled cube to a blindfolded person, let him make a random move each second and it will take a hundred times as long as the age of the earth to solve the cube. Life depends on long amino-acid chains, each link selected from 20 possible amino-acids. Calculations show, Hoyle reported that the chances of forming a typical chain by randomly combining amino-acids are about the same as the chances of solving Rubik's cube by haphazard twists.

Conventional revolutionary theory says: Given the size of earth's premeval seas, and millions of years for molecules to swirl around in this 'Organic soup', amino-acid could take shape by blind chance alone. No way, says Hoyle. Even if you assume that all of space is an organic soup, the universe is still too young to make it likely that the necessary amino-acid chains could have resulted from blind shuffling. Moreover, there is noway random mutations can account for the rapidity with which new species arose after life began on earth.

Then how can life be explained? One must assume, Hoyle declared that an Intelligence within the universe is directing the constant creation of micro-organisms in intersteller gas. These organisms ride the galaxy on light wave. A few billion years ago some of them were carried to the earth by comets according to a theory proposed by Hoyle and Wickrama Singhe in their earlier book, 'Life Cloud' and more recently, in a somewhat different form, defended by Francis Crick in 'Life Itself'.

But that is only half the story. To direct the course of evolution, the Intelligence has for billions of years been showering micro-organism (perhaps even insects!) on the earth, where they interact with life forms to promote the large mutations necessary to explain what seems to be sudden jumps in the fossil record. Small DNA copy-error mutations do no more than fine-tune a species. The last big leap, from beast to human, is so enormous that Hoyle cannot conceive of it as being the result of DNA replication errors. He says there is noway a Darwinian struggle for survival can explain 'the emergence of a Mozart, a Shakespeare or a Karl Friedrich Gauss'.

But if an Intelligence inside our universe directed all this, by what process did this Intelligence come into being? Did it arise from the actions of some now extinct Intelligence in a cycle of the universe that preceded the Big Bang or from the action of a higher Intelligence outside the Universe? Is there an infinite hierarchy of intelligences? Hoyle has no answers to these transcendent questions, writes Martin Gardner in Discover March, 1982 issue.

What can a skeptic say about this latest bombshell from the greatest maverick among living astronomers? On the apparent gaps in the fossil record. Stephen Jay Gould and other 'Punctuationists' (none of whom is mentioned by Sir Fred) are providing plausible hypothesis. As for the old argument that blind chance cannot explain the origin of life, whoever imagined, as Issac Asimov asked many years ago, that molecules combine by blind chance? Spill a thousand jelly beans on a rug and the probability that they will form beautiful hexagonal patterns is indeed near zero. But myriads of such patterns form when snow is falling. All this is under the directions of Allah.

When agitated by outside energy, said Asimov organic molecules in earth's primeval soup could form the required building blocks of life by the workings of 'unblind chance'. It would be chance guided by natural laws about which so little is yet known that no one can even begin to figure the odds. Not even Hoyle.

The Holy Quran, which is the word of God reveals many things about such questions. The Holy Quran gives description of Allah (Chapter 2 of this book), Who is the Creator of heavens and the earth out of naught and is the Shaper and the Fashioner of all things and the Knower of all things. Allah created man in perfect human form and as a superior creature and then beamed him to the earth by His Divine Power along with human spores. Allah has appointed man as the viceroy of earth. Allah's Simple Command: Be! and it is', is uncomprehensible. Man is created by Allah and is then genetically programmed, but His Will prevails. He is broadcast in earth and is designed to grow as a growth from the earth. Similarly, man is subject to programmed events and circumstances where laws of casualty and chance and other unknown laws are at work, but at the same time, man is inspired with conscience so that he may think and choose and then join to follow one out of the infinite designed programmes' of the Creator Allah, but under all circumstances His Will is Supreme.

The creation of universe and all that it contains including the creation of man and their perfect systems and perfect working serve as the tokens or signs of Allah, and lead mankind to feel the existence of Allah and know Him as the Creator of all things. Science is the means to understand the Holy Quran which reveals absolute truth, and reveals many things which man must know and follow so that he knows his Creator and feels his responsibilities towards his Creator and towards man.

Life Span or Life Term of each Man is Appointed and is Preprogrammed by Allah in the Genetic Script (DNA) at Birth as Genetic Destiny

Science of Genetics Regarding Senescence and Death in Similarity with the Holy Quran

Whether the aging is programmed in the brain when at a set time the pituitary gland releases a "death" harmone or the existence of an "aging" gene, maintaining that senescence is written into the genetic script at birth as part of the normal developmental programme. The aging gene, or genes, "swithch on" at a preprogrammed time. Once activated, the genes act to slow down or halt manufacturing processes crucial to the life of the cell. The genetic machinery—the DNA and its associated protein-making apparatus centres at the cellular level. Whatever be the cause of aging, the maximum age of each person is preprogrammed by Allah and the time, the Day, the Hour and the moment of death is fixed and appointed by Allah, as is revealed by the Holy Quran.

The Holy Quranic verses are:-

(1) *"No soul can ever die except by Allah's leave and at a term appointed . . ." (III:145).*

(2) *"Allah created you from dust, then from a little fluid, then He made you pairs (the male and female). No female beareth or bringeth forth save with His Knowledge. And no one groweth old who groweth old, nor is aught lessened of his life, but it is recorded in a Book. Lo! That is easy for Allah" (35:11).*

(3) *Every Soul will taste of death . . ." (III:185).*

(4) *"He it is Who gathereth you at night and knoweth that which ye commit by the day. Then He raiseth you again to life therein, that the term appointed (for you) may be accomplished. And after-ward unto Him is your return. Then He will proclaim unto you what ye used to do" (VI:60).*

(5) *"Allah receiveth (men's) souls at the time of theiz death, and that (soul) which dieth not (yet) in its sleep. He keepeth that (soul) for which He hath ordained death and dismisseth the rest till an appointed term. Lo! herein verily are portents for people who take thought" (39:42).*

The amazing similarity between science of genetics and the Holy Quran makes it clear that the science of genetics regarding life-span of man, that senescence is written and is preprogrammed into the genetic script at birth as normal development programme is very much in consonance with the above noted verses from the Holy Quran. All this similarity and concord clearly prove that the Holy Quran is the Word of the Creator (Who is Allah) and is His message for mankind to believe in the existence of one Allah and to obey and worship Him according to the guidance revealed by the Holy Quran.

Besides the genetic destiny and the biological cause for the death of a man as preprogrammed in the genetic script, the term for the death of man is appointed which shall occur either biologically or due to any other physical cause as per the law of causalty and chance.

Chapter 9

MAN PERFECTED WITH SPIRIT, GIFTED WITH CONSCIENCE TO CHOOSE THE PATH OF HIS CONDUCT

Allah, Who is the Creator of the universe and the earth, created living man and perfected him with spirit and inspired him with conscience and thinking power to distinguish between right and wrong and to choose the path of conduct. These gifts bestowed by Allah make man superior to other creations and responsible to Allah for keeping good conduct among mankind as per teachings of the Holy Quran:-

The Holy Quran reveals:-

(1) *'And the heaven and Him Who built it'. (XCI:5).*
(2) *'And the earth and Him Who spread it'. (XCI:6).*
(3) *'And a soul and Him Who perfected it'. (XCI:7).*
(4) *'And inspired it (with conscience of) what is wrong for it and (what is) right for it'. (XCI:8).*

The understanding from the above Quranic verses is clear that Allah created man from the materials of the heaven or the universe and has spread him on the earth and perfected him with a soul or with a spirit and bestowed him with 'conscience' so that he

chooses the path of his conduct. The 'conscience' of living man is the inspired gift or power from Allah to mankind to think and decide what is wrong for him and what is right for him and to choose independently whatever man likes. The conscience makes man responsible and responsibility makes him answerable and accountable to Allah for his deeds and actions on planet earth. The Holy Quran reveals that the deeds of mankind are minutely observed and precisely recorded through the most sensitive visible and the invisible systems by Allah, the Creator of the heavens and the earth and all in between them, for accountability of man on the Appointed 'Doomsday' and on the 'Day of Judgement' on his 'Resurrection' in the 'Hereafter'.

Religion of Islam — A Link between Metaphysical and Physical or Physics

Man of profound learning and erudition will find tremendous wisdom encompassed in the Holy Quran if he thoroughly contemplates and studies the verses word by word so as to understand the arcane meanings contained in the Holy verses. The study of the Holy Quran is most revealing in the context of the knowledge of modern sciences which help in its proper understanding. Knowledge, wisdom and faith are very vital to understand the substance of the Holy Quran describing the physical universe and man and also to understand the revelations giving description of the events beyond the physical universe, or all that is going to happen after the Doom of the Universe i.e. all about the metaphysical world, or the world of the 'Hereafter'. Man while in the physical universe has a very strong link with the metaphysical world, as per revelation of the Holy Quran. The Holy Quran teaches man to believe in the unseen and to believe what is revealed on Prophet Muhammad (PBUH) and be certain of the 'Hereafter'. The Holy Quran spans the two worlds in knowledge and reveals the reality of the physical universe and of the 'Hereafter' and is a strong link between the two.

Profound knowledge of the physical sciences to know the physical universe, and deep faith in Allah, the Creator of the heavens and the earth and in His Messenger Prophet Muhammad (PBUH) and in His Message the Quran and faith in the Unseen and in the Hereafter is vital to fully understand the substance of the Holy Quran. These are some of the major and basic doctrines of Islam to fully grasp and understand all physical and metaphysical matters including all the unseen and the invisible realities, described by the Holy Quran. These doctrines also include mainly the realities of the 'Doomsday', the 'Resurrection of man, the existence of a perfect system for the observation of man's deeds and actions for 'Accountability', the 'Day of Judgement', the 'Hereafter' and the Oneness of God as the Creator of all things (physical and metaphysical) and the Lord of the worlds and the Owner of the Day of Judgement. It would be found that there is a definite relationship between the physical sciences to understand the universe and man, and the science of religion of Islam and the revelations of the Holy Quran to understand the doctrines of Eschatology of the metaphysical universe. The Holy Quran is a link of revealing realities of the metaphysical world and the Physics or physical world. The Holy Quran invites attention of mankind to ponder over the meanings of the Holy verses, which already contain in the form of guidance, the most modern concepts of science about the physical universe and gives information and inspiration which reveals the absolute reality of the Oneness of God, Who is the Absolute, the Eternal and is the Creator of the universe and man, and of the 'Hereafter'.

Anti-Matter

In Islam, science is complementary to other ways of knowing and apprehending the truth, so that true science in Islam becomes one of the languages in which the attributes of God are described. Science is admitting us to glimpses of the grandeur and the mysteries of the physical universe. Man has some knowledge of the constituents and properties of matter, but is confounded to discover the existence of anti-matter. Allah has created everything with a purpose to perform and nothing is created in vain or in sports. Anti-matter and anti-space too have a purpose to perform. Knowledge of Science teaches that when anti-space composed of anti-matter, approach space then, matter and anti-matter annihilation will take place on fantastic scale. May be that anti-matter finally becomes one of the causes for the appointed 'Doomsday'.

The Unknowable Reality of Living Man

The masterword of heredity, the key to genetics is the discovery of DNA molecule which forms a chemical code and is the most wonderful of all universal mysteries as the DNA molecule

(Deoxyribonucleic Acid) of each man contains coded biological information equivalent to about 100,000 pages of the size of the Encyclopaedia Britannica. (Refer Encyclopaedia Britannica Volume — 10, page 894) 1979. Allah has therefore, coded and packed in a perfect manner all the genetic instructions and informations, with complete biological description of each man from birth to death. All these instructions are recorded in the DNA. There are numerous Quranic verses which give the allegorial and symbolic indications of the coded biological informations about the genes of man. These Holy Quranic verses give symbolic indication about DNA and reveal the truth that 'Allah is the Knower of Every Creation' and that He has created man and Hereafter, Allah will revive mankind once again the same way as He produced them at the first and that everything is recorded with Him in a Book.

The symbolic verses of the Holy Quran hinting towards the DNA as a Book where genetic instructions from birth to death of each man are recorded by Allah in a Book and that is easy for Allah, are quoted below:-

(1) *'Allah created you from dust, then from a little fluid, then He made you pairs (the male and female). No female beareth or bringeth forth save with His knowledge. And no one groweth old who groweth old, nor is aught lessened of his life, but it is recorded in a Book. Lo! that is easy for Allah'. (35:11).*

(2) *'Say: He will revive them who produced them at the first for, He is the Knower of every creation'. (36:79).*

(3) *'Everything have We recorded in a Book'. (78:29).*

(4) *'We know that which the earth taketh of them, and with us is a recording Book'. (50:4).*

The understanding and the sense that these Holy Quranic verses convey is as follows:-

The above Holy verses symbolically indicate that the DNA (Deoxyribonucleic Acid) or as the Holy Quran reveals and call it the recording Book or recorded in a Book' is the source of coded instructions recorded by Allah in the DNA of each man. It is surprising to know that the the DNA molecule serves as a code or a book containing record in which genetic instructions and informations are stored and recorded and fed by the Creator Allah Who is the Knower of every creation. The spirit or the electron or the atom of Divine force or element or the vital force joins to lead the DNA of each man to acquire the state of life to follow the coded instructions recorded by Allah in the DNA or a Book of each man. The Holy Quran hints in the above Holy verse (35:11) that the aging process with the growth of man is in accordance with the instructions coded in the DNA or a 'Book' till he becomes old. The process of life go on following the coded instructions in the DNA (a Book) till 'the appointed time' for his death reaches which is recorded in (a Book) and is followed by the DNA. The life span of man fixed in the Book by the Creator Allah can neither be lessened nor increased and the DNA shall have to behave and act accordingly.

On the death of man, Allah will revive him once again exactly the same way as it was done at the first creation. Allah is the Knower and Creator of all creations. Allah has recorded everything in the Book. He knows the constituents and the elements which constitute and frame the physical body of man that ultimately goes to the earth on his death. Allah will therefore, revive the dead as He is the Knower of every creation and all things are recorded in the Book with Allah. This means Allah knows all things and He is Able to do all things. To explain these further, a diploid human cell contains DNA, which stores the genetic information that give rise to the chemical and physical properties of living organism. The biological role of DNA is that it is the ultimate carrier of heredity. Genes are composed of DNA in which genetic information is contained in the form of codes. Each single strand of DNA builds up an exact complementary copy of itself. The information contents of a single cell has been estimated as around 10^{12} bits. (comparable to about a hundred million pages of Encyclopaedia Britannica.) Allah has preserved coded instructions or information in the DNA, and Allah has the DNA record of every man with Him in a Book, which is revealed in the Holy Quran and is symbolically indicated as 'Everything We have recorded in a Book'. (76:29) and that Allah is the Knower of it. So DNA is symbolically indicated with a Book. The science of Molecular Biology and Genetics is therefore in similarity with the verses of the Holy Quran. The DNA, therefore; contains a perfect and complete genetic record of each man which is preserved with Allah Who is the Knower of every creation. As such, having the specific DNA of each person recorded with Allah in a Book, Allah will create by reviving the dead man and recollect and gather him atom-wise or electron-wise or at any level to his perfect original shape with exactly the same biological characteristics and with all the necessary constituents as are in the wet earth from which man was originally created by Allah. To explain it briefly, the same man shall be resurrected in the same perfect order at the age as Allah desires and when He says: Be! and all mankind shall be resurrected and that is easy for Allah.

The Holy Quran reveals:-

(1) *'Allah is Able to do all things'. (24:45).*
(2) *'Verily, We shall give life to the dead'. (36:12)..*
(3) *'That is easy for Allah'. (36:79).*
(4) *'And He is Able to gather them when He will'. (42:29).*
(5) *'Lo! Thy Lord is Doer of What He will'. (11:107).*

The above Holy verses are clear and self-explanatory. The sense contained in the Holy verses is that Allah is Able to do all things and that He is able to gather mankind with all his constituents from the earth as explained above, as and when He wishes. Allah is the Doer of what He Will. He shall verily give life to all the dead mankind on the Day of Resurrection and that is easy for Allah. The Creator Who is Able to do all things can create or revive the same man again and that is easy for Allah.

The knowledge of science is very vital to study such realities so that man understands the absolute reality of the Holy Quran and the Creator Allah. Let man ponder to understand himself in the context of the knowledge of modern sciences as the Holy Quran reveals in its verses (45:3-4) and (51:21) quoted in this chapter. The Holy Quran is the Divine Book, the Word of Allah, and man must have resolute faith in it and understand and follow its teachings which are for the guidance of mankind.

Science must continue to strive for a better grasp of the inner laws of being, of the vast and complex combination of cells (in which DNA is a tiny part of a cell), of the chemicals, tissues and consciousness but without claiming to know, the unknowable reality. Science in Islam is only one of the 'peep hole into the infinite'. The Eternal and Infinite Power of Allah as the source of all creations that delivers man from the fear of the unknown and unknowable.

Man copying Nature on DNA Pattern

Scientists are working on the pattern of DNA and are taking help from nature by copying nature's biological technology of the DNA molecule, in preparing a crystal computer to be called 'biological crystal computer', for storing and encoding the contents of millions of books from libraries when 10^{10} information units shall feed the crystal computer, which is equivalent to the contents of 20,000 books, occupying volume equal to an ordinary match box. The speed of crystal computer will be measurable in Nano-second and Pico-second which is one-tenth and one-hundredth million part of a second. Revolutionary achievements would be possible within the next few decades or in a period of less than a century.

Allah is the Creator of mankind. Allah knows the elements which constitutes each man including his DNA which is the masterword of heredity and is the key to genetics. Information of every creation is on record with Allah in a Book and the spirit is at His Command. Allah has All Knowledge, All Wisdom and All Power and on the Day of Resurrection Allah will revive all dead mankind back to life and Allah is Able to do all things and that is easy for Him.

The Holy Quran is God's Message for the guidance of All Mankind

The unthinking atheists, who do not believe in Allah and in the heavenly religions, and those who follow other religions than Islam, are invited to pay serious heed to the verses of the Holy Quran in the context of modern knowledge of sciences without prejudice and with open mind. They will be wonder struck to find that the Holy Quran is full of knowledge, wisdom, information and guidance. They will find truth in the teachings of the Holy Quran which is the word of Allah for the guidance of mankind and they will know that the Holy Quran is not a man-made Book. Those who are astray will find light of wisdom in the Holy Quran and will know their Creator. The striking and amazing similarity of the knowledge of natural sciences of Physics, Chemistry, Astronomy, Astrophysics, Cosmology, Cosmogony, Relativity, Quantum Mechanics, Bio-Chemistry, Genetics and Biology, Anatomy, Embryology, Chemical Kinetics, etc, with the verses of the Holy Quran and the sense that it contains on the creation, evolution and ultimate fate of the physical universe and man, are excitingly astonishing and prove beyond all doubts that the Holy Quran is indeed a Heavenly Book and is not man-made and cannot be man-made for containing all those miracles and wonders of divine wisdom and knowledge for all times. The Holy Quran revealed on Prophet Muhammad (PBUH) 1400 years ago when there was knowledge hardly worth the name, contains miraculous revelations full of most modern scientific concepts which must be studied with an open mind to find the reality. It will be found that the sense and the substance and the absolute reality of the Holy Quran will become more and more clear and understandable with the achievement of more and more knowledge and with the passage of time. It will be found that Divine reality revealed by the Holy Quran 1400 years ago stands true for ever and that science which is in search of the truth shall always be found to be in complete consonance with the Holy Quran, the absolute truth and the word of Allah. The revelations of the Holy Quran are true from the beginning to the end of the physical universe and stand true in the 'Hereafter' as it is the word of the Creator Who is the Knower of every creation.

Sound Knowledge and Faith in the Holy Quran, the Means to know Creations and the Creator of all Creations including Man in Human Form

Creationists *vs* Evolutionists

In the United States of America there is a great awakening in search of the absolute truth and the belief in one God as the Creator of all things who created man as the best of creatures in human form and not as an animal like ape as the evolutionists believe.

In the struggle between those who believe in Darwin's Theory of Evolution called evolutionists and those who believe in 'Creation Science' called creationists has been taken to the courts in more than 20 states. The creationists emphasize that 'Creation Science' must be taught in schools as science subject. They believe that life is created by 'The Unimaginable Supreme Being', Allah, and the Holy Quran confirms their faith. Darwin's Theory is only a theory and is a misleading one. 'Creation Science' similar to exobiology is a vital and new discipline of science to know the Creator. Presently, the people of U.S.A. and of other countries as well are taking more interest to know the Religion in the context of science, as science is 'trained and organized common sense'.

'Creation Science' is basically a discipline of science with two components, where man tries to understand its physical aspects through the knowledge of physical sciences and its spiritual aspect through the knowledge of the science of Religion which leads man to know the Creator of all creations including human life. In reality the science of Religion of Islam taught by the Holy Quran is the 'absolute science' revealing realities beyond physical limits. Creation Science' is therefore a discipline of science to know absolute science or reality (physical and metaphysical). It is only the Holy Quran, the Last unaltered heavenly Book which reveals perfect truth and the established sciences in all disciplines are in perfect agreement with the Holy Quran. Islam is the only Religion with which modern science is in total agreement. In reality, besides many other things, the Holy Quran is the only Divine Book or the Word of God which teaches 'Creation Science' with knowledge and wisdom and gives informations and guidance to all mankind.

One of the groups sympathising 'Creation Science', is known as FLAG (Family Life and America under God). Mrs. Mary Ann Miller who believes in 'Creation Science', says: 'I believe we are all made in God's image and if our children are taught that they came from animals they are hopelessly defrauded. We want them taught moral law, but evolutionists recognize only animal law and that leads to crime, prostitution and abortion'.

Mrs. Mary Ann Miller is very correct in her belief. She will find the best support for her belief in the Holy Quran which teaches the religion of Islam. The Holy Quran is clear for people with open mind and is clear for people who have sound knowledge of physical sciences and of many other things including man's common sense and conscience which leads him to the right faith.

The Holy Quran is a divine guide of perfect reality, in the light of which, the tussle between the evolutionists and the creationists can be settled once for all. The Holy Bible and other heavenly Books and God's messages which were revealed on Prophets Moses and Jesus and other Prophets are finally consummated in the Holy Quran the Last Message from God revealed to the Last Prophet Muhammad (PBUH) for all mankind. In the light of the Last Revelation or the Final Revelation (which is also the latest but absolute and final), the people who believe in other religions than

Islam are invited and are welcome to read the Holy Quran with open mind and try to understand and grasp its sense and substance. Once they do so, they will find that the Holy Quran is full of wisdom, knowledge, information and guidance. They will get all that which they search for. The Holy Quran is absolutely in its original form and is unaltered by man.

Notwithstanding all that, the revelations in the Holy Quran are not incompatible with science at any level. The Holy Quran reveals perfect truth whereas science is knowledge of physical things, which is limited and is subject to human intelligence level and capacity. Science is therefore in pursuitof the truth regarding physical things. It does not go beyond that. So far man has found that science at the level of Molecular Biology and Particle Physics is in perfect agreement with the Holy Quran. The Quranic verses reveal that knowledge or science is the means to know the religion of Islam and the teachings of the Holy Quran. Thus, science and the religion of Islam are not in competition but are in consonance.

Regarding the creation of man, the Holy Quran reveals that man is created in perfect human form when God said: Be! and Adam was created.

The following Quranic verses are quoted:-

(1) *Verily We have honoured the children of Adam. We carry them on the land and the sea and have provisions of good things for them, and have preferred them above many of those whom we created with a marked preferment'.(17:70).*

(2) *'Lo! the likeness of Jesus with Allah is as the likeness of Adam, He created him of dust then He said unto him Be! and he is'. (61:59).*

(3) *'And When, I have fashioned him and breathed into him of My Spirit then fall down before him prostrate'. (15:29).*

(4) *He said: O Iblis! What hindereth thee from falling prostrate before that which I have created with My hands art thou too proud or art thou of the high exalted?'. (38:75).*

(5) *'This day have I perfected your religion for you, completed My favour upon you and have chosen for you Islam as your religion' (5:4).*

(6) *Allah created not (all) that save in truth, He detaileth the revelations for people who have knowledge'. (10:5).*

(7) *'Allah it is Who hath created Seven heavens, and of the earth the like thereof. The Commandment cometh down among them slowly, that*

Ye may know that Allah is Able to do all things and that Allah surroundeth all things in knowledge'.(66:12).

(8) *'See yet not how Allah hath made serviceable unto you whatsoever is in heavens and whatsoever is in the earth and hath loaded you with His favours both without and within? Yet of mankind is he Who disputeth concerning Allah without knowledge or guidance or a Scripture giving light'. (31:20).*

(9) *'Nay, but they denied that, knowledge whereof they could not compass and whereof the interpretation (in events) hath not yet come unto them. Even so did those before them deny. Then see that what was the consequences for the wrong doers'. (10:39).*

(10) *'Surely We created man of the best stature'. (XCIV:4).*

(11) *'And a Soul and Him Who perfected it'. (XCI:7).*

(12) *'And inspired it (with Conscience of) what is wrong for it and (what is) right for it'. (XCI:8).*

(13) *'He created the heavens and the earth with truth and He shaped you and made good your shapes and unto Him is the journeying'. (64:3).*

(14) *'Allah it is Who appointed for you the earth for a dwelling-place and the Sky for a canopy, and fashioned you and perfected your shapes and hath provided you with good things. Such is Allah, your Lord. Then blessed be Allah, the Lord of the Worlds!' (40:64).*

In the above verses, the Holy Quran reveals that man is not the decendent of animal like ape. God created man as the best of creations or creatures in perfect human form, with best stature and shape and has inspired him with conscience and asked the angels to fall prostrate before him. Thus, God created man and has preferred him above many of those whom Allah created with a marked preferment. Man has therefore a very high station and an honoured position among all creatures. Man is inspired with conscience so he is responsible to obey His Creator and submit to His Will as revealed in the Holy Quran. Because of such a high station and because of the inspired conscience man is responsible to God and is accountable for his deeds and actions in this physical world. The Holy Quran reveals that God created man with His own hands which means the greatest honour to mankind. Man's obedience and his submission to God's Will includes that he is of the righteous and should bear decent moral and social behaviour and comply with religious laws as the Holy Quran teaches.

Creation Science is not a religion, but it has its deep roots in all the physical sciences and beyond. Absolute realities which lie beyond physical sciences and are beyond human perception and power of understanding are revealed on mankind by Allah through divine revelations. The Holy Quran reveals all that which is necessary for man to know and which lie beyond the limits of physical sciences. Faith in the divine revelations is religion. So, religion is the knowledge of absolute realities and the knowledge about the Creator Allah and the Knowledge about all that physical and metaphysical creations which the Holy Quran reveals. To know the physical creations, we make attempt and try to know it through the acquired knowledge of the physical sciences. But the metaphysical creations are beyond man's power and beyond the approach of physical sciences. Islam as religion is perfected by God and is chosen by Allah for mankind and the Holy Quran teaches man about all creations and creatures and reveals that there is One God, the Creator Allah Who created all things. Science or knowledge is the means to know the religion of Islam and the religion of Islam reveals about the Creator Allah, the One God and His physical and metaphysical creations.

'Creation Science', is therefore science plus 'something more than science'. This 'something more than science' is man's inspired conscience plus his wisdom and knowledge of physical sciences and faith in the Holy Quran which is the message of God. Science calls physical reality, a reality and in this attempt tries to know the perfect reality. Scientists have never tried to know who created the physical reality. 'Creation Science' is therefore a discipline which has the two components which includes the physical knowledge of creations and the knowledge about the Creator Who is behind the creations. When physical reality is established as perfect reality then man wants to know 'something beyond'; i.e. the Absolute Reality of the Source Who created all these physical creations. But the Creator of physical realities and of the metaphysical realities is the 'Unimaginable Supreme Being' who is beyond the understanding and comprehension of man as man is merely a creature. At this stage, the science of the religion of Islam and the Quran guides man to understand all that which is metaphysical and is beyond the physical understanding of man. The Holy Quran, the word of God teaches man about both i.e., the physical realities of the universe and the metaphysical realities of the 'Hereafter', i.e. Life after death.

'Creation Science in the Light of the Present Form of Bible and the Holy Quran

The creationists who advocate 'Creation Science' are very right to demand that creation science should be taught in schools, as it is science plus conscience plus wisdom and knowledge and faith in the Creator Who created the creations and created the creatures.

Life is certainly created by 'the Unimaginable Supreme Being' Who is Allah as the Holy Quran reveals. 'Creation Science' is therefore, a very vital discipline of science and wisdom for man to know and to learn about creations and the Creator. Darwin's Theory of Evolution is misleading and is not based on reality. It is merely a theory and there are many un-explainable missing links. It is based on conjunctures and not on facts. The teaching of incorrect science about the creation of human life is disservice to young generations and to the humanity on the whole.

The Holy Quran consummates all the previous heavenly messages of Allah to mankind. The Holy Quran is a guide for mankind. It contains wisdom, knowledge and informations. The original message of God in the Bible has been changed by man and the signs of the various human manipulations are found in the Gospels and the original text of the Old Testament. The Gospels were drastically altered. The authenticity of all the above Holy Books is extremely dubious. The Holy Scriptures of Judeo-Christian if examined in the light of modern knowledge would show that their authenticity is questionable because numerous manipulations, changes, additions and alterations were made. In these Scriptures, there exist a lot of contradictions, improbabilities and incompatibilities with modern scientific data, which is very surprising and prove clear manipulation by man. Most of the statements are contradictory and scientifically unacceptable.

For detailed analysis of these Holy Scriptures and for their comparative study with the Holy Quran (which is absolutely free from human manipulations, contradictions, incompatibilities etc., and is absolutely in original form), reference may be made to the valuable scientific study conducted by Dr. Maurice Bucaille, a French Surgeon, in his book entitled 'The Bible, the Quran and Science'. It is found that modern science is in perfect agreement with the Holy Quran. A complete agreement of modern scientific data with the Holy Quran must serve as a great eye opener and it leads one to a positive conclusion that the Holy Quran is the conclusive word of God. The Holy Quran is not the work of man and can never be the work of man. The presence of scientific realities revealed by Prophet Muhammad:(PBUH) 1400 years ago is a miracle and proves that the Holy Quran is heavenly Revelation which the believers learned it by heart. The Holy Quran is the only heavenly Book, the word of God which is perfectly in its original form. The Holy Quran provides perfect guarantee of authenticity. The presence of modern scientific knowledge, wisdom and information in allegorial form and in direct form, when studied today, is a challenge to explanation in human terms. The Quran vividly shows that it is the word of God for man and that it can never be changed, manipulated or altered by man. The believers have memorized the whole Quran by heart from the day of revelation till today and it will be so for all times.

The creationists would be surprised to find a tremendous support from the knowledge, wisdom, information and guidance encompassed in the verses of the Holy Quran. They must therefore rely on the Holy Quran to defeat the evolutionists and their utterly wrong concepts of the creation of man by the process of evolution and not accepting the reality of the creation of man as the most superior creature in human form. The Holy Quran describes man's first creation in perfectly human form and describes the stages of his reproduction, his high position among the creatures, his conscience and his nature. All these points are of tremendous significance. Science of Biology in all disciplines is in perfect agreement with the Holy Quran on the creation and reproduction of man and on man's all other aspects as is described in the various Chapters of this book. Besides man and the physical sciences related to human life, like, Molecular Biology, Astrophysics, Cell Biology Genetic Engineering, the sciences of Cosmogony, Cosmology, Astrophysics, Physics, Chemistry, Relativity, etc., are all in perfect agreement with the Holy Quran. In the light of such Revelations Darwin's Theory which is based on conjunctures has no place in science. It violates Second Law of Thermodynamics. Creation of life is not through pure chance. Even a single living cell is so complex that it is only the act of divine creative power and is not a matter of chance. The idea that simple form of life develops into complex life is not correct.

The Creationists who believe in 'Creation Science' must study the Holy Quran, so as to achieve their mission and establish the truth of their concept that 'Creation Science' is science of the creation of life, science of the creation of human being and science of the creation of universe about which the Holy Quran gives clear hints and indications so that men of sound knowledge may grasp and understand the substance and the sense of the Holy verses contained in the Holy Quran.

If the Creationists take support from the Bible, which no longer is in its original heavenly form, they will face many problems and their arguments based on the teachings of the manipulated Bible would scientifically be unacceptable and would be unrealistic. The Creationists may study and examine the Scriptures themselves in the light of modern scientific knowledge and they will find the Holy Quran as a divine document of miracles. The Holy Quran reveals that science and reasons should always be referred to for establishing the truth and authenticity.

Dr. Maurice Bucaille states in his book, 'The Bible, the Quran and Science' that:

> 'I had to acknowledge the evidence in front of me: the Quran did not contain a single statement that was assailable from a modern scientific point of view'.
>
> There is the illustration of an unusual application of science to a Holy Scripture, the contribution of modern secular knowledge to a better understanding of certain verses in the Quran which until now have remained enigmatic, if not incomprehensible. Why should we be surprised at this when we know that, for Islam, religion and science have always been considered twin sisters?
>
> These scientific considerations, which are very specific to the Quran, greatly surprised me at first. Up until then, I had not thought it possible for one to find so many statements in a text compiled more than thirteen centuries ago (fourteen centuries) referring to extremely diverse subjects and all of them totally in keeping with modern scientific knowledge'.

> There is in any case absolutely no opposition between the data, in the Quran on the creation and modern knowledge on the formation of the universe. This fact is worth stressing for the Quranic Revelations , whereas it is very obvious indeed that the present day text of the Old Testament provides data on the same events that are unacceptable from a scientific point of view. The description of the creation given in the Quran is quite different from one in the Bible'.

The Holy Quran is the message of God which is obligatory on all mankind and is meant for the guidance of all mankind. As already mentioned there are contradictions, improbabilities and incompatibilities between Gospels and science whereas, there is absolutely no disagreement between the most modern physical sciences and the Holy Quran. The Holy Quran must be studied with an open mind so as to know its reality. The Holy Quran is a miracle and clearly shows that it is the word of God as most modern knowledge of science in all branches and the physical facts concerning the universe and man, are contained in the Holy verses and are already present in the Holy Quran revealed by Prophet Muhammad (PBUH) 1400 years ago when nothing about physical science was known to man.

The presence of highly scientific facts in the Holy Quran concerning universe and man which when studied today, are matter of bewilderment and clearly show that the Holy Quran is a heavenly Book/Message for mankind.

The Holy Quran is a divine document of miracles for all times. Its study must seriously be undertaken by all the nations of the world in their own interest as the Quran is for all mankind. There is no compulsion of religion in Islam. Read the Holy Quran, ponder over it seriously, try to understand its substance and sense and then it is for you to believe it or not and once you believe in it, then follow it properly and correctly and with a firm mind as the Holy Quran guides.

The creationists would face many confrontation between the statements of the Bible and Scientific data because all the Gospels and the Old Testament were changed and manipulated and many additions and alterations were made in the original text of these Holy Scriptures. The Holy Quran is the only Scripture whose original divine text is absolutely intact and all natural phenomena and scientific data is in total agreement with the Holy Quran and the Holy Quran could only be properly understood through modern scientific knowledge.

Statements in the Bible like the world was created about 10,000 years ago, contradict science and are unacceptable. Revelations if in their original form shall never contradict or be in confrontation with real facts. Science is always found to be in perfect agreement with unaltered text of the Revelations as are found in the Holy Quran. The creation of the world in six days means the creation of the world in six periods. The concept of a day on earth for man is different to the one mentioned in the Holy Quran and the Holy Bible.

It is strongly advisable that Creation Science' may be studied by the Creationists in the light of the Holy Quran and not in the light of the Bible for their tussle with the evolutionists who have already gone to the courts in many of the states of USA.

Part III

THE INVISIBLE AND THE HIDDEN LIVING CREATION PARALLEL TO MAN

THE EXTRA—TERRESTRIAL LIFE IN THE UNIVERSE

SCIENCE IN SIMILARITY WITH THE HOLY QURAN ON LIFE IN SPACE

(vi) Science on the search for extra-terrestrial life.

(vii) Intelligent Life beyond the Solar system.

(viii) God is All Engineer, All Mathematician, Creator, Shaper, Fashioner of All things, and the Creator of life on earth in the Solar system of the Galaxy.

Chapter 10

THE INVISIBLE AND THE HIDDEN LIVING CREATION

QURAN ON THE JINN — THE INVISIBLE LIVING AND INTELLIGENT CREATION BEYOND THE PERCEPTION OF PHYSICAL SCIENCES

Science or the knowledge of physical matters by man is confined to the frontiers of the visible objects upto the observable limits of the boundless universe and to the invisible objects of the detectable type. Beyond that, man's science or knowledge and efforts are helpless. The Holy Quran reveals truth beyond all frontiers and spans in knowledge all things in the physical and metaphysical worlds. The Holy Quran teaches and guides to believe in the unseen which is permanently beyond man's knowledge. It reveals to believe in the invisible of the heavens and the earth. Faith and belief in the revelations is therefore the most basic doctrine of Islam which the Holy Quran teaches so as to know and understand the hidden, the invisible and the unseen realities of the physical and metaphysical worlds. Man's knowledge of the physical sciences is confined only to physical matters of the visible and the detectable invisible type. Quran reveals truth about all matters of the physical universe, and man's knowledge of sciences finds it to be in complete similarity with the revelations of the Holy Quran. The Holy Quran, at the same time, reveals absolute truth about the matters of the metaphysical worlds, but it is beyond the scope of physical sciences to know anything of the metaphysical worlds. Faith and belief in the Holy Quran that it is the word of Allah is the fundamental doctrine which the Holy Quran teaches. Man should also draw inferences for knowing the realities of the metaphysical worlds from the realities of the physical world which the Quran truthfully describes, use his senses, wisdom and conscience and believe in the 'Unseen' as the Holy Quran teaches in the verse (3:3) which is as follows:-

> *'Who believe in the unseen and establish worship and spend of that We have bestowed upon them' (3:3).*

The jinn falls under the category of the invisible of the undetectable type of this world, therefore, it is beyond the scope of physical sciences to know what jinn is! How they exist and what is their form and composition etc. The Holy Quran reveals knowledge, wisdom, information and guidance to mankind about the hidden things in the universe and jinn is the invisible and the hidden creation.

The Holy Quran reveals:-

(1) *'Verily We have brought them a Scripture which We expound with knowledge, a guidance and a mercy for the people who believe'(7:52).*

(2) *'This is the Scripture whereof there is no doubt, a guidance unto those who ward off evil' (3:2).*

(3) *'Who believe in the unseen and establish worship and spend of that We have bestowed upon them' (3:3).*

The Holy Quran is set forth point by point with knowledge for people who believe and whose faith is sure and there is no doubt in the Holy Scripture, which is a guidance from Allah for mankind who ward off evil. The Holy Quran truthfully reveals knowledge and reality about the invisible and the unseen which it describes. The jinn is one of the creation of Allah.

Jinn is the invisible and the hidden living creation parallel to mankind and is a totally different form of creation than mankind. Jinn is created out of essential fire or smokeless fire. It appears they live in some life supporting zone suited to their form near to the earth with in the solar system. There are a few verses in the Holy Quran which reveal about this invisible living and intelligent creation which is basically created out of entirely different substance than man and exists in absolutely different environment, shape and form.

The following Quranic verses reveal some information about the jinn which indicate that jinns are living creation of intelligent and powerful type but are not perceptable to man's senses and to his visual observations and to the knowledge of science to physically detect him. It is beyond man's comprehension to know about the jinns except what is revealed by the Holy Quran.

The Holy Quranic verses reveal:-

(1) *'And the jinn did We create afore time of essential fire'. (15:7).*

(2) *'And the jinn did He create of smokeless fire' (2V:15).*

(3) *'I created the jinn and mankind only that they might worship Me' (21:37).*

(4) *'We shall dispose of you, O ye two dependents (man and jinn)' (53:31).*

(5) *'Yet they ascribe as partners unto Him the jinn, although He did create them, and impute falsely, without knowledge, sons and daughters, unto Him. Glorified be He and high exalted above (all) that they ascribe unto Him' (VI:101).*

(6) *'The Originator of the heavens and the earth! How can He have a child, when there is for Him no consert, When He created all things and is Aware of all things' (VI:102).*

(7) *'O Ye assembly of the jinn and human kind! Came there not unto you messengers of your own, Who recounted unto you My tokens and warned you of the meeting of this Your Day? They will say: We testify against ourselves. And the life of the world beguiled them. And they testify against themselves that they were disbelievers' (VI:131).*

(8) *'And We inclined towards thee (Muhammad) certain of the jinn, who wished to hear the Quran and when they were in its presence, said: Give ear! and when it was finished, turned back to their people, warning' (46:29).*

(9) *'Say (O Muhammad): It is revealed unto me that a Company of Jinn gave ear and they said: Lo! it is a marvellous Quran' (72:1).*

(10) *'Which guideth into righteousness, so we believe in it and we ascribe no partners unto our Lord' (72:2).*

(11) *'And (the jinn who had listened to the Quran said): we had sought the heaven but had found it filled with strong warders and meteors' (72:8).*

(12) *'And we used to sit on places (high) therein to listen but he who listened now findeth a flame in wait for him' (72:9).*

(13) *'And we know not whether harm is boded into all who are in the earth or whether their Lord intendeth guidance for them'* (72:10).

(14) *'And among us there are righteous folk and among us there are far from that. We are sects having different rules'* (72:11)

(15) *'And we know that we cannot escape from Allah in the earth, nor can we escape by flight'* (72:12).

(16) *'If they (the idolaters) tread the right path, we shall give them to drink of water in abundance'* (72:16).

(17) *'And there were gathered together unto Solomon his armies of the jinn and human kinds and of the birds they were set in a battle order'* (27:17).

(18) *'Till they reached the valley of the ants, an ant exclaimed: O ants enter your dwellings lest Solomon and his armies crush you unperceiving'* (27:18).

(19) *'And Solomon smiled, laughing at her speech, and said My Lord, arouse me to be thankful for Thy favour wherewith Thou hath favoured me and my parents, and to do good that shall be pleasing unto Thee and include me in (the number of) Thy righteous slaves'* (27:19).

(20) *'And unto Solomon (We gave) the wind, whereof the morning course was a month's journey and the evening course was a month's journey, and we caused the found of copper to gush forth for him, and (We gave him) certain of the jinn who worked before him by permission of his Lord. And such of them as deviated from Our Command, them we caused to taste the punishment of flaming fire'* (72:26).

(21) *'(He is) the Knower of the Unseen and He revealth unto none His Secret'* (72:26).

(22) *'Whom neither man nor jinn will have touched before them'.* (56:74).

(23) *'Of the jinn and of mankind'* (CXII:6).

(24) *'And (remember) when We said unto the angels: Fall prostrate before Adam and they fell prostrate, all save Iblis. He was of the jinn, so he rebelled against his Lord's Command. Will ye choose him and his seed for your protecting friends instead of Me, when they are an enemy unto you? Calamitous is the exchange for evil-doers?* (18:50).

(25) *'Oh, company of jinn and men, Ye have power to penetrate (all) regions of heavens and the earth, then penetrate (them)! Ye will never penetrate them save with (Our) sanction'* (55:33).

According to the Holy Quran, Allah created two apparently parallel species of creatures, the jinn and the mankind. The former

from smokeless fire or essential fire and the latter from wet earth. The Holy Quran is centrally concerned with man and has revealed little about the jinn, although it is implied that the jinn are endowed with reasons and responsibility but are more prone to evil than man. Jinn, like man, can choose its path of conduct. Jinns are invisible living intelligent creatures or beings parallel to mankind.

Jinns are capable of changing various forms and shapes as they are created from smokeless fire or essential fire and existed before man was created on earth. Jinn is a creation and is an altered form of 'living energy' or something like living radiation, created out of smokeless fire as man is an altered form of 'living matter' created out of wet earth or clay. One should carefully ponder and see the difference between human body in the form of flesh, bones and blood but in reality is clay and water. The true substance out of which jinn is created is some basic form of fire. Jinns are mortal as human beings but are some sort of Astro-biological creatures. May be that the jinns be living in a hot spot with a tenuous environment like the ring around the planet Saturn, which may provide proper type of the life supporting zone of a plasma cloud of ionized gases for them. The environment in the doughtnut around Saturn is so tenuous that it contains only 30 charged particles per cubic foot, emptier than the best vacuum on earth. Jinns are not visible to human eyes and are not detectable by the physical laws of science known to mankind. The jinns are a kind of living creature which are transmutable, transonic, transpierceable and transmissible astro-biological creatures. They are capable of swift movements changing shapes at will, at terrific speed. One can just pass along the jinn without feeling and noticing him. However, man physically knows nothing about the jinn who is an unseen and an invisible reality. Man and jinn are different types of creatures and exist fundamentally in absolutely different forms and environments under different life supporting zones, and are not detectable by man and his knowledge of physical sciences. Man is in altered matter form. The jinn is in altered smokeless fire form, which may be some form of a living radiation of the undetectable type. Both are subject to different laws and forces and as such, there are fundamental barriers and limitations between them. Thus, they do not feel the existence of one another (man and jinn), unless man is favoured by Allah with divine power to see the jinn, as Prophet Solomon was favoured and certain of the jinns worked before him by permission of his Lord. So, jinns were brought under his command and this is a great miracle.

Prophet Solomon also knew the languages of birds and ants, which is another miracle and an act of favour bestowed by Allah on Prophet Solomon, as is revealed by the Holy Quran in verses quoted above. The audibility of sound, the visibility of vision, the knowledge of languages, the power of perception, are all subject to certain barriers and limitations which can be removed and relaxed and supernatural capability given to overcome these physical limitations and barriers to whom Allah wishes. And Allah gave all these powers to Prophet Solomon to do miracles.

The Holy Quran reveals:-

> *'Lo! Ye are those who argue about that whereof ye have some knowledge; why then argue ye concerning that whereof ye have no knowledge? Allah knoweth. Ye know not'* (III:66).

If man cannot physically perceive and imagine the reality of the unseen and the invisible (including the jinn), which is revealed by the Holy Quran, then conscience, wisdom, common sense, logic and faith guide man not to argue such matters. Because one can only argue to some extent matters of which man has some knowledge. It is only Allah the Creator who knows the Unseen and the Invisible of His creation and men do not know anything about such matters. It is of no use to argue about such unseen matters whether physical or metaphysical of which man has absolutely no knowledge. Arguments without knowledge shall merely be irrelevant and irrational conjectures. Man cannot describe the absolute truth of the existence of jinn which is apparently invisible and unseen and is hidden from man and is beyond the scope of his perception and knowledge, but its existence is absolute reality as the Holy Quran reveals. In such events faith and belief in the guidance of the Holy Quran is the only right path to know the absolute reality.

In reality there are invincible barriers on both the creatures to perceive and feel each other i.e. the jinns and the human beings. Besides the barriers of the invisibility, lack of audibility and the lack of the sense of feeling and perception of the form and the substance, there may be many more barriers of nature unknown to man. This is why the two creatures made of different substances and in different forms are not at logger-head and do not interfere with each other as they have nothing in common to acquire and have no relevance to one another and cannot enter the domain and environment and the life support zone of one another in which each creature live. The jinn were inclined by Allah and they gave ear and heard the Holy Quran (the word of Allah), and turned back to their people and warned them about the Quran. Allah is the Creator of both the creatures, the jinn and the mankind and of all other things. The jinn after hearing the Holy Quran said: Lo! It is a marvellous Quran. And the jinn used to sit on (high) places to listen but now they cannot as they are harmed and cannot escape from Allah in the earth by flight. The jinns like the mankind really wonder about human beings and they cannot meet each other due to natural barriers. Jinn is a miracle for man and vice versa.

Jinns have various sects with different rules and among them some are good folk and some far from that. Allah gave power to Prophet Solomon and certain of the jinn worked before him by the Command of Allah. It is therefore, wrong to argue and doubt about the existence of jinn — the living intelligent creature parallel to man, simply because the jinns though absolute reality, are not detectable and are not visible to mankind. The mention of jinn in the Holy Quran is a clear proof of the existence of jinn as the living, intelligent creatures, created out of the smokeless fire. May be that the jinns are some sort of the undetectable living energy in altered form, but are beyond man's power to perceive them. Man only knows to the extent which the Holy Quran reveals.

The Angels

The Angels are very superior type of living creatures, created out of some divine type of light. They are in the high heavens and can travel or transmit themselves from heaven to heaven or from any heaven to earth and back to heaven, and from the metaphysical world to the physical world by the Command of God. Angels remain all the time in the service of God and are inborn obedient. The universe is freely violable for them when God Commands them. They are free from the applicability of the physical laws. They can adopt any human shape. They are of multiple wings or rank and dimensions and powers. Wings allegorially denote powers and dimensions and rank. Therefore, time and distance for them is no hurdle. Allah has created Angels rank on rank and Allah has assigned them various wings or dimensions ranging from two, three, four and a multiple of these to perform various acts in the heavens and on earth and in between them and in the metaphysical worlds as God Commands them to do.

The Holy Quran reveals:-

> *'Praise be to Allah, the Creator of heavens and the earth, which appointeth the angels as messengers having wings two, three and four. He multiplieth in certain what He will. Lo! Allah is Able to do all things'* (35:1).

The Angels are the messengers of Allah. Unlike the man and the jinn who can choose the path of their conduct, the angels always remain obedient to Allah. Angels are given powers of various degrees, to perform various acts in the heavens and earth.

The sense contained in the word wings in the above Holy verse indicates the rank and power of an angel to perform any act ordered by God and shows the power of transcendency of the angels.

Chapter 11

QURAN AND SCIENCE ON LIFE IN THE OUTER SPACE

A number of the Holy Quranic verses reveal that intelligent life exists in outer space and that many languages are spoken over there. The fundamental and the major restraint on man to probe life in space is the natural restraint of the 'constancy' of the velocity of light at 186,000 miles per second which is the ultimate speed of the infinitesimal material particles. This has resulted in the inviolability of the physical universe due to its boundlessness. Moreover, restraints due to limited life span of man (about 70 to 80 years)' the need for a special environment to support life and other unknown, unseen restraints are in addition.

Man is helpless to probe life in space by space travel either in our near galaxy (Milky Way) or in the billions of galaxies scattered all over in the boundless space. The living creation in space may be thousandsor millions or billions of light years away. It is therefore physically as well as technically impossible to contact in person or communicate with them even at the speed of light which is the ultimate physical speed. Meaningful signals from earth could hardly be transmitted up to a thousand light years away in space. Suppose there is life a thousand light years away, the return signals would take another 1,000 light years. The total time taken for such a message would take 2,000 years. It means about 40 generations of man must have passed away on earth before the return signals could reach the earth. It is, therefore, impossible for man to physically probe life in space by space travel and to know about it in view of many restraints and in view of the inviolability of the universe and the constancy in the velocity of light, i.e. 186,000 miles per second.

When man and his knowledge of the physical sciences become helpless to explore and know life in space, the Holy Quran is always there to guide man. The Holy Quran reveals that life exists in the universe. The universe which is in perfect celestial mechanic, is not created in vain or in play by Allah. It has a purpose to perform. It serves as the token of Allah's creation and is for the benefit of mankind. Moreover, man is not the lone creation in the boundless universe though he is the best community raised up for mankind. The Holy Quran reveals about the existence of the extra-terrestrial life in the universe. The more one knows about the mysteries of the universe, the greater one finds the universe to be mysterious.

It is not only the jinn and the mankind which exist as the intelligent living creatures alone in the universe. There are certainly other living creatures which exist in the boundless and inviolable universe besides the earth.

A number of verses of the Holy Quran clearly reveal that life do exist in the boundless space. The Holy Quran although is centrally concerned with man on earth but has made some mention of the existence of jinn, which is basically and totally a different form of life unconceivable by man. Man and the jinn are the two living and intelligent forms of creations who are basically very much different in substance and characteristics. Man is a miracle to jinn and jinn is a miracle to man. Similarly, many other types of life in numerous different forms and different life support zones and environments do exist in the universe at many places which may or may not be detectable and may or may not be visible to man. These beings and living creatures elsewhere in the universe are besides the Angels. However, man cannot conceive the form of life in the universe and the way he exists. Whether, the life in the universe elsewhere is like the man form or the jinn form or is totally different to both, is not known. Moreover, the Angels too are a living and superior form of very obedient creation created out of divine form of light (the substance of their creation) quite different to man and jinn but these are inconceivable and undetectable by the physical laws. Only Allah knows about the unseen and the invisible in the universe and beyond the universe (whether living or non-living, physical or metaphysical). As far as man is concerned, there are many physical limitations and restraints on his conceiving power and understanding capability, besides the innumerable physical barriers on his sense of perception,vision, hearing, sense of feeling and touch and on his movements and requirements, besides his basic life support requirements of a special environment as on earth. Mankind, therefore, can never probe and penetrate deep into the space because of man's physical shortcomings, sustenance requirements and life-span.

The following Quranic verses besides many more, reveal the existence of intelligent life beyond any doubt in the universe:-

(1) *'And unto Allah maketh prostration, whatsoever is in the heavens and whatsoever is in the earth, of living creatures and the Angels (also) and they are not proud'. (16:49).*

(2) *'He Said: My Lord knoweth, what is spoken in the heaven and the earth. He is the Hearer, the Knower'. (21:4).*

(3) *'Not one of the beings in the heavens and the earth but must come to God Most Gracious as a servant' (19:88-93).*

(4) *'While all creatures in the heavens and on earth have willing or unwilling, bowed to His Will and to Him shall they all be brought back'. (3:83).*

(5) *'And thy Lord is best aware of all who are in the heavens and the earth'. (17:35).*

(6) *'And (remind them of) the Day when the Trumpet will be blown, and all who are in the heavens and the earth will start in fear, save him whom Allah Willeth. And all come unto Him, humbled'. (27:87).*

(7) *'The seven heavens and the earth and all that is therein praise Him'. (17:44).*

(8) *'Unto Him belongeth whosoever is in the heavens and the earth. And those who dwell in His presence are not too proud to worship Him, nor do they weary'. (21:19).*

(9) *'And unto Allah falleth prostrate whosoever is in the heavens and the earth, willingly or unwillingly, as do their shadows in the morning and the evening hours'. (13:15).*

(10) *'All that are in the heavens and the earth entreat Him. Everyday He exerciseth (Universal) Power'. (55:29).*

(11) *'There is none in the heavens and the earth but cometh unto the Beneficent as a slave'. (19:93).*

(12) *'Allah it is Who hath created seven heavens, and of the earth the like thereof. The commandment cometh down among them slowly, that ye may know that Allah is Able to do all things, and that Allah surroundeth all things in knowledge'. (66:12).*

Earth like Planets in Space

The above verses make it very clear that besides the earth we live in, there are earths or planets the like of our earth elsewhere in the universe. The indication is more than enough for scientists to ponder. These earths or planets must be inhabited by living intelligent creatures. We do not know, what type of creature they are? But they certainly exist.

The above Quranic verses and many more like that clearly reveal that various forms of life certainly exist in the universe, where many languages are spoken and that man and jinn are not the only creations in this inviolable universe. The angels also are living creations of the most obedient inborn nature. But they are in high heavens. The Holy Quran reveals reality that living creatures exist in the universe and that the inviolable universe and its vast expanse and systems are not created in play or in vain, but everything that is created in all the seven heavens have definite purpose to perform and that all things created have specific role to play. All things are on record with Allah, everything is given a function of its own to perform. The creation of planets, the stars, the galactic systems and the substance of the universe with mere non-living matter and energy become purposeless without intelligent life. The vital purpose of the universe is to support life and to serve as God's portent for mankind. The universe has therefore definite purpose and function of its own to perform, both, as one whole, and as well as system wise, to support living and intelligent creations and to serve as portent of Allah for man, to know God's inviolable creation. The universe serves as the abode of living creatures of various forms created out of various substances and serve as the source of sustenance for them. The earth can be quoted as an example which is the abode of man who is created out of plastic clay or wet earth. The jinn also live somewhere within the solar system and are created from essential fire or 'smokeless fire'. May be the jinn be living in the type of environment like the ring around the planet Saturn or somewhere else. Similarly, other unseen or invisible and hidden creatures created out of some unknown substance or creatures created out of some known substance, such as, man like or jinn like creatures may be living on and around the celestial bodies in the universe under life support zones suited to them and to the substance of which they are created. May be, some of these creatures are not affected by the force of gravity due to their inborn property and they may be governed by laws unknown to man and beyond the power of perception of man. Whatever the form or shape, it is certain that living creatures of various types do exist in space in the boundless universe as the Holy Quran reveals.

The following Quranic verses on the creation of universe are very clear, revealing that all things created have a function to perform:-

(1) *'And We created not the heavens and the earth and all that is between them, in play'. (XLIV:38).*

(2) *'Not without purpose did we create heaven and earth and all that is between them in vain. That is the opinion of those who disbelieve. And woe into those who disbelieve in the Fire'. (38:27).*

(3) *'Everything have We recorded in a Book'. (LXXVII:29).*

Nothing is created by Allah without a purpose or just in vain. Everything has a definite part to play and functions to perform. Hence, the jinn and the mankind, both the living and intelligent creatures can choose the path of their conduct and are created only that they may worship Allah. So, they are all on trial. The Holy Quran is a complete guidance for mankind and reveals the existence of other living creatures in the inviolable universe.

Life of Various Types in the Universe

Allah created the living creations who are intelligent, responsible and gifted with conscience, and the living creations who are un-intelligent and who live by instinct. Allah created the living creations in the universe who are visible, invisible and unseen. Allah created all these living creations in the universe out of different substances, in different forms and to live in different life support zones and environments. Different creatures have different characteristics, functions, powers and limitations. Creatures live in various regions of the earth and the heavens and in the environments created for them. The Holy Quran reveals that man is created out of 'clay' and water in an 'atmosphere' to live on earth and the jinn is created out of essential 'fire'. The jinn must be living somewhere in suitable life support zone within the solar system, which man cannot possibly locate. The acquatic life exists in the 'Hydrosphere' on earth. This indicates that life in different form on earth is designed to exist in water where man dies. The acquatic creatures have different mechanism and the hydrosphere is the life support zone for them. It is, therefore, possible that various types of life, i.e. visible and invisible is existing in the universe in different forms and different environments. Even on earth life exists in extraordinary environments.

Life can exist and grow in extraordinary wide range of ecological nitches. The alga cyanidium caldarium can grow in concentrated solution of hot sulphuric acid. Other bacteria, alga and fungi can live in extremely acidic (Ph of 0) or extremely alkaline (Ph near 13) environments. Procaryotic bacteria live at temperature above 90° C (194° F) almost at the boiling point of water. Sulphate reducing bacteria are reported to grow and reproduce at 104° C or (219° F) under very heavy pressure. Moreover, life exists in a temperature of 200° C, or 392° F. This is really something fantastic.

Similarly, very mysterious types of life may be existing under mysterious environments and life supporting zones from the point of view of man. But, intelligent and technical civilization of some kind and form must be existing in numerous planets similar to earth in the inviolable universe containing uncountable billions of planets in the boundless universe.

Life in Space

The Quranic verse (24:45) clearly reveals that:

'Allah creates what He will. Lo! Allah is Able to do All things.'. (24:45).

It is easy for Allah to create life in the visible or in invisible form out of any 'substance' under any 'environment', anywhere in space. The Holy Quran has revealed that Allah has created intelligent life out of 'wet clay' in the form of living matter and out of smokeless fire in the form of 'living energy' or radiation. Allah has created the 'Angels' out of some divine form of light. The Holy Quran has clearly revealed that life does exist at many places in the universe. What kind of life and what form of life and out of which 'substance' is it created, whether visible, or invisible and hidden and in what type of environment it exists i.e. whether technical civilization on planets, in luminous bodies, or around planets or around the luminous bodies, or it is anywhere in suspension in space or it is in specific ranges of temperature and pressure-that only Allah knows. Allah is Able to do all things. May be that the form of life is created out of unknown and unseen substance and is unaffected by any of the physical constraints known to man. All that is easy for Allah. The universe is very vast and is inviolable. There are many possibilities of unimaginable form and type of life existing in space.

In the inviolable universe, there are billions and billions of galactic systems and each galactic system has billions and billions of stars and planets which are millions of light years apart within each system. Allah has not created all this vast expanse and the innumerable systems just in vain or without any purpose or in play. These are all the portents of Allah and indicate to man the Infinite Power of creation of Allah and the existence of One Allah of Infinite attributes with each attribute to Infinity and serve as a matter for heed and invites men's attention to ponder over all the creations in the light of the Message of Allah — The Holy Quran. The whole creation in the universe has a definite function to perform and a purpose to achieve. Basically man is created to submit to the Will of Allah and worship Him and obey Him in the light of the guidance of the Holy Scripture. Man is created objectively. Man may or may not realize the purpose of his creation as it depends on his knowledge, wisdom and faith but on the revelation of the Holy Quran, man certainly knows that he has a definite purpose to achieve during his life time and that is, complete obedience and submission to the Will of God-the Creator of man and of all things. The message in the Holy Quran is the Will of God revealed to Prophet Muhammad (PBUH) for the guidance of mankind. Similarly, the universe and its governing forces are appointed for performing precise functions till the appointed day which also amounts as worship to Allah the Creator of All things.

The Holy Quran reveals:-

(1) *'Not without purpose did We create heaven and earth and all that is between them in vain. That is the opinion of those who disbelieve. And woe unto those who disbelieve in Fire'. (38:27).*

(2) *'And We created not the heavens and the earth and all that is in between them, in play' (44:39).*

Science on Extra-terrestrial Life beyond Our Own

Radio Astronomers are searching life elsewhere in the universe. This is because, most astronomers now believe that the creation of planets is a natural by-product of the birth of stars from clouds of gas and dust in space. Among the countless stars in the universe there must be millions with planetary systems - and so millions of worlds where life can or does exist.

Chemicals of Life in Space

Analysis of meteorites has shown that they contain chemicals like those obtained in experiments simulating primitive earth conditions. It seems that the chemical 'building blocks' of life can be made under the most hostile conditions in space. This has encouraged biologists to believe that life may be quite common throughout the universe. All life on earth is carbon - based, and carbon is prevalent around emerging stars, so that extra-terrestrial life would presumably be carbon-based like that on earth. Radio-Astronomers have discovered about 40 different types of molecules in space, including several that are thought to have been involved in the original creation of life on earth. These range from simple compounds, such as water and ammonia, to more complex compounds, such as formic acid and methylamine, which can react together to give the amino acid known as glycine.

The numerous chemicals 'building blocks' that result could have assembled themselves to form the first living cells on earth. It is believed that these chemical 'building blocks' of life may be widespread in space. Investigations of space by radio astronomy have shown that these basic chemicals are being formed from the widely distributed atoms in the clouds of gas around newly forming stars.

These clouds are mostly composed of hydrogen and helium, the two most abundant chemicals in space. Helium is comparatively inert, but hydrogen is one of the major atoms in the bodies of living things. With oxygen it forms water, the basic liquid of life. Furthermore it forms many types of compounds with carbon, an atom whose affinity for linking into complex chains makes it the chemical backbone of life.

Life Support Zones

Not only are the right chemicals needed to produce life - a favourable environment is also essential. Starts warm the space around them, like fires. The strength of the stellar fire governs how large an area around the star is at the right temperature to support life. In our own solar system the Sun's life support zone, as it is called, stretches for some 80 million miles, with earth near its centre. Outside this zone, conditions are too hot or too cold to sustain life as we know it. There are about a quarter of the stars in the Milky Way like the sun and it is believed the life building chemicals may be widespread around it and elsewhere in space.

Listening for Messages

If only one star in every 100,000 of the 100,000 million stars that exist in the Milky Way alone has one planet which bears Earth - like life, that still means there may be a million such planets that could communicate with Earth. However, the distance between the stars are so great that any message travelling at the speed of light would take many thousands of years to reach its destination. This is a formidable task, and is one which does not fit in well with normal radio - astronomical observations.

The Holy Quran reveals information and is a guide in giving wisdom and knowledge to man for all matters and for things beyond the scope of man and his knowledge of physical sciences. Regarding the extra-terrestrial life, the Holy Quran clearly indicates that life exists in the universe at many places and that Allah knows the various languages spoken there. This means intelligent civilizations exist who speak many languages, but still man appears to be the most intelligent technical civilization in the universe as far as one can understand from the Holy Quran. The living creations elsewhere in space obey and worship Allah and as the Holy Quran reveals nothing is created in the universe without a purpose or in vain. So, each celestial system in the universe has a definite part to play and that the hundred thousands million of stars in each galaxy and the hundred thousands million of the galaxies in the observable space are not created in play.

Biologist Billingham wonders whether extra-terrestrial life, like life on earth would be carbon-based and directed by DNA. We don't know that DNA is the only way to make life," he says, "but it's possible that it's the best way." We, are not clever enough chemists to dream up anything better than DNA and carbon proteins, but maybe that's a question we'd answer. Some scientists have suggested that silicon, which is almost as versatile chemically as carbon, could serve as the basis for life.

Divine Invitation to Man for Space Probe

Amazingly, there exists a standing invitation for mankind in the verse (55:33) of the Holy Quran for penetration in space as far deep as possible. Man and the jinn are addressed by Allah in the Holy Quran to penetrate the regions and barriers in space and in the earth to the limits of their power and knowledge that they can possibly penetrate. The substance of this reality in the verse could not be realized till the recent past when space travel has been made possible only 24 years back. Till then the interpretation in events had not taken place and the sense and knowledge encompassed in the verse was not understandable. The sense contained in the verse (55:33) is now understandable when space travel has practically been made possible. This shows that the Holy Quran revealed wisdom and knowledge 14 centuries ago, and for understanding the wisdom of the Holy Quran, sound knowledge is very important thing to grasp the sense and substance of the Holy Quran. The Holy Quran invites mankind and the jinn to explore space and the earth to any limit that they can do, and this invitation is beautifully encompassed in the Quranic verse (55:33) quoted below. This means that open invitation for space travel by man already exists in the Holy Quran. The existence of this reality in the Holy Quran is a miracle and is very surprising and astonishing. It evidently shows the existence of Allah the Creator Who knows all things and the Holy Quran as His message for mankind. It is a standing divine invitation to mankind in the Holy Quran for space probe which indicates that the Holy Scripture is the word of Allah revealed to the unlettered Prophet Muhammad (PBUH) 1400 years ago when knowledge about space travel was at zero level. The predating of the recent events in space travel by the Holy Quran, the knowledge of which man could not compass and whereof the interpretation (in events) had not come to man, is a miracle and shows that it is a divine revelation and that the Holy Quran is not man-made, and cannot be man-made.

The Holy Quran reveals:-

(1) *'Oh, Company of jinn and men, ye have power to penetrate (all) regions of heavens and the earth, then penetrate (them)! Ye will never penetrate them save with (Our) sanction'. (55:33).*

(2) *'Nay, but they denied that, knowledge whereof they could not compass and whereof the interpretation (in events) hath not come unto them. Even so did those before them deny. Then see what was the consequences for the wrong-doers'. (10:39).*

(3) *'And verily in the heaven We have set mansions of the stars and We have beautified it for beholders'. (15:16).*

(4) *'Lo! We have adorned the lowest heaven with an ornament, the planets'. (37:6).*

The context of the Holy verse (55:33) has been explained above. The sense conveyed by the Holy verse is that if man can overcome the earth's gravitational force and other similar forces or barriers in other regions of space, then let man penetrate space as far deep as he has the power to do so. However, he can never penetrate through all regions and beyond certain limit, without the Sanction of Allah. Allah has created man with a frigile constitution who depends on many basic requirements. The human mechanism, his life span and living design system and requirements has limited inborn capacity and capability within a specific life supporting zone. As such, man can probe space up to that limit and not beyond that unless with the sanction of Allah.

Allah invites both the groups of intelligent creatures, the jinn and mankind to penetrate the earth and the universe and all its regions and barriers in space according to their inherent power, given capacity and knowledge and their respective physical form and according to the means at their disposal for space travel to any limit in the universe. This is an open invitation by Allah to man and the jinn to do so which requires power and knowledge to develop and harness, so as to overcome the barrier of gravity of the earth by mankind and to overcome similar barriers by the jinn, and to achieve a break-through the first region of the gravity of earth by man, then to go to the moon, the first and the nearest planet to earth, and then to go to the next planet and cross other barriers, and so on till man could go as far deep in space as possible.

Mankind and the jinn will never be able to penetrate all the regions or barriers in space in the inviolable universe or in the earth but to the limit and extent of the power and knowledge and the physical capability that Allah has given to man and as Allah allows or grants sanction to the penetration of the limits and the regions as He wishes and allows to penetrate in space.

The above verse (55:33) openly invites man for space travel to the possible limit. This would of course be subject to his knowledge, power and physical capacity. But man will never penetrate all regions in space except by the Permission or Sanction of Allah as there are limitations, constraints and barriers which man cannot penetrate or overcome.

The physical capacity of man permits penetration in space only to a certain limit as there are many inconquerable obstacles, like the principle for the physical 'constancy' in the speed of light and the inviolability of the universe, the black holes, and other similar unconquerable regions and gravitational barriers and hostile environments making life impossible to exist for space probe in addition to man's own physical limitations. However, the theoretical knowledge of man about the universe has penetrated reasonably deep and this knowledge will go on developing to reveal the mysteries and the realities of the boundless universe and to know its Creator Allah, as the mysterious universe is a portent of Allah and its creation is one of the attributes of the Creative Power of Allah.

Regarding the physical possibilities of space travel by man, one has to keep in mind certain invincible and hostile regions and barriers or physical limitations as revealed by the Quranic verse (55:33), which cannot be overcome without the Sanction of Allah.

The principle governing the constancy in the speed of light (which is the ultimate speed of an infinitesimal material particle) is one of such basic physical limitation or constraint in space travel as nothing can travel faster than the speed of light. Besides this, there are many other forces and unsurmountable limitations and hurdles to face for crossing other regions which man can never physically overcome. (To travel faster than light a body would have to lie — as a four dimensional object — in a space-like direction instead of a time-like one.) Time itself was created along with the creation of the universe. Something divine guided can travel in Time' beyond infinite time.

Einstein argued that as bodies near the speed of light their mass (This is nearly the same as their weight) becomes greater and so greater force is needed to move them. It would be impossible to have a force great enough to move a body at more than the speed of light. What is true about speed is also true about distance. Of course, we cannot go tearing round the universe. We shall never be able to do so. We may have to limit our journeys to our own solar system or at the most in the vicinity of the nearest star. Nothing can travel faster than the speed of light. This is so great that it would circle seven times round the earth every second. But it would take eight minutes to reach the sun and over four years to get to the nearest star. It would take a hundred thousand years to travel from one side of the Milky Way (near galaxy) to the other and two million years to reach the Andromeda Nebula. It would take well over five thousand million years to get towards the fringes of the inviolable and expanding universe at present visible in the largest telescopes. It is going to be difficult for men, who have a life-span of perhaps seventy or eighty years, to go on journeys which would last for billions of years without mentioning all the difficulties of the space travel itself. So, it is impossible for man to physically go beyond a specified limit in space travel and cross all regions. Something very divine is required to travel deep into space and that is only with the Sanction of Allah.

Man, can probe with telescopes from earth far deep into space and see the mysterious universe full of mansions of stars, the wonderful creations of Allah. In this respect the Holy Quran reveals the verses (15:16) and (37:6): as already mentioned above.

Till recent times man probed into space up to 2 billion light years away but very recently, man has probed in the observable universe up to 10 billion light years away from earth with the most modern equipments, which is a fantastic achievement for man but is insignificant in terms of the boundless universe. The invitation to man to travel and explore as far as possible in the universe is to see the marvels and mysteries of Allah and the creation of His inviolable universe, and to achieve unlimited benefits of the bounties of nature, from space travel and from space laboratories by conducting various types of experiments and gain innumerable benefits and observe space as far deep as possible. What a miraculous, wonderful and a perfect Book is the Holy Quran revealed on Prophet Muhammad (PBUH) 1400 years ago and which is full of Divine guidance and teachings for all men and for all times! It reveals surprising and astounding realities to man, which man cannot compass in knowledge till interpretation (in events) takes place.

The more knowledge you acquire and the more you study and ponder over the Holy Quranic verses, the greater understanding one has of the Holy Quran. The understanding of the Holy Quran, therefore, goes with the level of knowledge and wisdom of man and his faith. In reality, the Holy Quran is wisdom and knowledge and a guidance and teaches absolute reality. It depends on man how much knowledge and faith he has and to what level he understands and can grasp the wisdom and sense contained in the Holy Quran. The knowledge and wisdom encompassed in the verses of the Holy Quran holds perfectly good for all times. Perfect faith and sound knowledge would give a thorough understanding of the Holy Quran and of the absolute reality that it teaches. The Holy Quran is a heavenly Book truthfully revealed by Allah on Prophet Muhammad (PBUH) and all mankind must have unflinching and resolute faith in it. Read the Holy Quranic verses distinctly and word by word and read each word separately, ponder over it and if you have sound knowledge and faith, you will find treasures of wisdom and knowledge and perfect truth in it. The Holy Quran is the conclusive word of Allah for mankind.

Allah invites man and the jinn to penetrate space and the earth to the possible limits to achieve the benefits and to see the mysteries and marvels of the wonderful creations of Allah which are His portents for mankind so that man knows the Creator Allah through His wonderful creations and believe in His message and in His messenger Prophet Muhammad (PBUH).

Science on the Search for Extra-terrestrial Life

Exobiology, a term coined by a U.S. Biologist, J. Lederberg, for the study of extra-terrestrial life, has been called a science without a subject matter. Exobiology, has deep significance even if extra-terrestrial life is never found. A given planet may possess life of a simple sort or life of a quite complex bio-chemistry, physiology and behaviour. It may possess intelligent life and a technical civilization.

It is not known what aspects of living systems are necessary in the sense that living systems everywhere must have them, it is not known what aspects of living systems are contingent in the sense that they are the result of evolutionary accident, so that somewhere else a different sequence of events might have led to different characteristics. In this respect the possession of even a single example of extra-terrestrial life, no matter how seemingly elementary in form or substance, would represent a fundamental revolution in Biology. It is not known whether there is a vast array of biological themes and counterpoints in the universe, whether there are places that have fugues, compared with which our one tune is a bit thin and reedy. Or it may be that our tune is the only tune around. Accordingly the prospects for life on other planets must be considered in any general discussion of life.

Life on earth is structurally based on carbon and utilizes water as an interaction medium. Hydrogen and Nitrogen have significant accessory structural roles; phosphorus is important for energy storage and transport, sulphur for three dimensional configuration of protein molecules and so on. But must these particular atoms be the atoms of life everywhere, or might there be a wide range of atomic possibilities in extra-terrestrial organisms? What are the general physical constraints on extra-terrestrial life? The creation of jinn out of 'smokeless fire' must have a totally different combination of the substance which may never be known to mankind.

Intelligent Life beyond the Solar System

For thousands of years man has wondered whether he is alone in the universe or whether there might be other worlds populated by creatures more or less like himself. Many mythologies populated the sky with divine beings, certainly a kind of extra-terrestrial life. Many early philosophers held that life was not unique to the earth.

Metrodorus, an Epicurean Philosopher argued that:

> 'To consider the earth the only populated world in infinite space is as absurd as to assert that in an entire field sown with millet, only one grain will grow'.

The probability of advanced technical civilizations in our galaxy depends on many controversial issues. The number N of extant technical civilizations in the galaxy can be expressed by the socalled 'Green Bank Formula'.

How distant could the transmitting and receiving planets be for intelligible signals to be transmitted and received? The answer is rather astonishing 1,000 light years. Within a volume centred on the earth, with a radius of 1,000 light years, there are over 10,000,000 stars.

The search for extra-terrestrial intelligence is an extraordinary pursuit, in part because of the enormous significance of possible success, but in part because of the unity it brings to a wide range of disciplines; studies of the origin of stars, planets and life of the evolution of intelligence and of technical civilization; and of the political problem of avoiding man's self-annihilation.

The Holy Quran reveals:-

'Man is self destroyed: How ungrateful'. (80:17).
'Self destroyed is he; how he planned'. (74:19).

Suppose, there is a technical civilization (possibly the nearest) within a range of 1,000 light years away, even then mankind, may hardly communicate to know that such a civilization exists as questions, answers, from and to, without language problem and without other unforeseen circumstances, shall take more than 2,000 years between earth and the nearest civilization in space. However, it may never be possible for man to contact technical civilizations existing in far off space. The Holy Quran hints in verses (16:49) and (21:4) that there are many civilizations existing in space and Allah knows what is spoken there. The relevant verses from the Holy Quran on life in outer space have already been quoted on page172 in this Chapter. These verses clearly indicate that life definitely exists at numerous places in space.

God is All Engineer, All Mathematician, Creator, Shaper, Fashioner of All Things and of Creating Life Support Zone on Earth in the Solar System of the Galaxy

The following Holy Quranic verses are quoted for deep contemplation and for word by word analysis to understand the sense and the substance of the Holy verses:-

(1) *'Assuredly the creations of the heavens and the earth is greater than the creation of mankind; but most of mankind know not'. (40:57).*

(2) *'He is Allah, the Creator, the Shaper out of naught, the Fashioner'. (60:24).*

(3) *'It is He Who created the heavens and the earth in true proportions'. (VI:73) and (39:5-6).*

(4) *'It is He Who created all things and ordered them in due*

proportions'. (25:2).

(5) *'And the Sky He hath uplifted and He has set the measure'. (55:7).*

(6) *'Have not those who disbelieve known that the heaven and the earth were one piece and then We parted them and We made every living thing of water. Will they not then believe?' (21:30).*

(7) *'And the earth have We laid out, how gracious was the Spreader (thereof)!'. (51:48).*

(8) *'Lo! in the heavens and the earth are portents for believers'. (45:3).*

(9) *'And in your creation and all the beasts that He scattereth in the earth, are portents for a folk whose faith is sure'. (45:4).*

(10) *'There are the portents of Allah which we recite unto thee (Muhammad) with truth. Then in what fact, After Allah and His portents, will they believe?' (45:6).*

(11) *'And of His portents is the creation of the heaven and the earth and of whatever beasts He hath dispersed therein. And He is Able to gather them when He Will'. (42:29).*

(12) *'Is it not for the sun to overtake the moon, nor doth the night outstrip the day. They float each in an orbit'. (36:40).*

(13) *'And hath made the moon a light terrain and made the sun a lamp'. (71:16).*

(14) *'And Allah hath made the earth a wide expanse for you'. (71:19).*

(15) *'And He it is Who created the night and the day, and the sun and the moon. They float, each in an orbit'. (31:33).*

(16) *'Allah it is Who raised up the heavens without visible supports, then mounted the throne, and compelled the sun and the moon to be of service, each runneth into an appointed term; He ordereth the course; He detaileth the revelations, that happily ye may be certain of the meeting with your Lord'. (13:2).*

The above Holy verses reveal great wisdom on the creation of the universe, the solar system, the earth and on the creation of life support zone on earth.

Allah has created the earth and the universe as one piece of spinning gaseous mass as clouds of dust. Allah then parted the earth from the whole and created the fundamental known four forces and the physical laws governing them. Allah ordered the creation of life support zone on earth after its suitable location in the solar system and thus suitable environment on earth was created for which Allah located the earth at a suitable distance from the Sun and the Moon and installed it in an appointed orbit, with a specific speed and made it revolve around its own axis at a specific angle so as to create suitable environments for the creation of life, its growth and sustenance and to ensure a proper life support zone within the solar system at the specific location from the sun.

All this was calculated and engineered to create proper environments and life support zone for man the viceroy of Allah on earth along with other living creatures and the wild life all over the earth by a simple wish of Allah and by His Divine Creative Power.

The attention of scientists is invited to ponder over the Holy Quranic verses in the context of the perfect laws of all sciences such as, Cosmology, Cosmogony, Astrophysics, Physics, Chemistry and Biology and on the interaction of the basic known four forces (now converted into three by Dr. Salam of Pakistan and the other two scientists) and then observe the marvels and the portents of Allah in the creation of earth and life support zone on earth including the creation of intelligent man who is inspired with conscience.

The act of the entire creation and all these phenomena and the reality of life and of earth and of the universe and of all that which the universe contains is by the simple wish of Allah: Be! and it is. The All-Wise Creator, Engineer, Mathematician, Shaper and Fashioner is behind all this creation which is for the benefit of mankind and which serve as the tokens of Allah so that man knows Allah from His attributes.

The motion of earth and the moon are the tokens of Allah for men of knowledge (Scientists) who ponder on the rotation of earth around its axis at a speed of about one thousand miles an hour to create day and night of proper duration. If the earth rotated with a speed of one hundred miles an hour, the duration of days and nights would have been ten times longer. The longer hot days would burn all things on earth and make animal life and vegetation growth impossible Similarly, longer cold nights would freeze everything and create unfavourable environments to support life on earth.

It is a matter of wisdom to ponder in the light of the Quranic verses who made the earth to rotate at the most favourable speed to support life?

Again life would be impossible if the sun would have been a few thousand miles nearer to earth and if it had been a few thousand miles farther, then life on earth would have freezed solid. This is something very precise and pre-calculated and shows the act of All-Wise Creator and His Existence as the Creator of universe.

The earth is tilted precisely at an angle of 23 degree, which results in change of season and helps in the growth of various kinds of vegetation, crops, fruits, flowers and animal life. It creates beauty on earth and beauty in life.

If the moon would have been 25,000 miles farther, there would have been no tides in the sea and no facilities of transportation of big oceanic vessels to ports.

In the context of the above scientific explanation of the creation of earth to support life on earth, the Holy Quran reveals the following verse:-

> *'Lo! in the creation of the heavens and the earth, and the difference of night and day and the ships which run upon the sea with that which is of use to man, and the water which Allah sendeth down from the sky, thereby reviving the earth after its death, and dispersing all kinds of beasts therein, and (in) the ordinance of the winds and the clouds obedient between heaven and earth: are signs (of Allah's Sovereignty) for people who have sense'. (II:164)*

Each word of the above Holy verse convey great sense of creating favourable life supporting environments and for it the creation of day and night and the creation of tides in the sea and the transportation of ships carrying merchandise and the creation of seasons and the formation of weather, the winds, the clouds and the rains and the growth of vegetation like forests, crops, fruits and the creation of animal life on earth. All these provisions are for the sustenance of man on earth and shows the Sovereignty of Allah, the Creator of all things in the heavens and the earth.

Again, if the crust of the earth would have been deeper by another ten feet, all carbon dioxide and oxygen would have been absorbed and nothing would have been left for the growth and sustenance of animal and plant life on earth.

Another phenomenon of the solidifying or freezing of water on earth is miraculous in the sense that when water freezes, its density gets lighter and it expands and the ice thus formed floats at the surface of water. It does not become denser and heavy to sink. Allah keeps balance and everything with Him is measured and He is the Sustainer and the Protector of all things and provides safety in all weathers to acquatic life on earth. The floating of ice at the surface of water enables it to receive warmth from the sun rays and this makes water below the ice to be warm enough to support acquatic life there and also avoid freezing of the entire water depth as in that case acquatic life would have been impossible.

Allah has created and ordered all that what is required, right from the origination of the universe and earth to all the infinite processes of evolution required for the earth to adjust in solar system at the distance of life supporting zone and to create life supporting environments on earth with all its pre-requisites.

The Holy Quran reveals that all things are done the moment Allah intends to do. In this respect the Holy Quran reveals:-

> *'And Our Word unto a thing when We intend it is only that We say unto it: Be! and it is'. (16:40).*

Allah has created man as a superior living intelligent creature and has inspired him with conscience and has given him the power of thinking, hearing, knowing and the ability to conceive the Creator Allah and has revealed the Holy Quran to guide him and to know his Creator Allah. It is, therefore, for man to study and observe the creation of Allah and His marvels which are His tokens and to have unflinching faith in Allah and in His Message and in His Messenger and in His Sovereignty overall things.

Part IV

(a) SCIENCE ON THE GRAVITATIONAL COLLAPSE OF THE UNIVERSE IS IN COMPLETE SIMILARITY WITH THE HOLY QURAN ON THE DOOMSDAY'.

(b) SCIENCE IN COMPLETE SIMILARITY WITH THE HOLY QURAN ON THE CREATION OF THE UNIVERSE OUT OF 'NOTHING' AND THE OBLITERATION OF THE UNIVERSE TO 'NOTHING'.

(c) SCIENCE IN COMPLETE SIMILARITY WITH THE HOLY QURAN ON THE RE-EMERGENCE OF THE UNIVERSE AND EARTH AFTER OBLITERATION OF UNIVERSE TO NOTHING OR THE RE-CREATION OF A SIMILAR UNIVERSE AND A SIMILAR EARTH OUT OF 'NAUGHT'.

(d) THE SCIENCE OF 'BLACK HOLES', THE INVISIBLE OBJECTS IN THE UNIVERSE IN SIMILARITY WITH THE INVISIBLES OF THE HEAVEN MENTIONED BY THE HOLY QURAN AND ALLEGORIALLY QUOTED AS 'HEAVEN FULL OF PATH'. 'PATH' IS A SIMILI FOR BALCK HOLE'.

thing', a similar universe shall repeat its creation from 'nothing' as before.

(iii) Science in miraculous similarity with the Holy Quran on the 'Doomsday'.

(iv) Science in miraculous similarity with the Holy Quran on the 'Doomsday'.

(iv) Science in similarity with the Holy Quran on 'black holes'—the Pathways to other Universes.

(v) The Sciences of Cosmogony, Cosmology, Astronomy and Astrophysics in similarity with the Holy Quran on the Creation of the Universe from nothing, the Evolution of the Universe and on the obliteration of the universe to 'nothing'. The entire universe becoming as the Invisible Black Hole.

(vi) Mankind will be Resurrected, brought back to life and may be transfigured to stay immortal in the wonderful world of the 'Hereafter'.

(vii) The Apocalypse of Gravitational Collapse: Wheeler, Einstein and Niels Bohr's Scientific concepts in similarity with the Holy Quran.

CHAPTER XIII

(i) Allah the Originator, the Creator at Will, the Shaper out of naught, the Sustainer of the Universe and man, and the Bringer of the Doomsday and the Creator of the 'Hereafter'.

(ii) Sustenance in Earth for Man and for all who search or ask.

(iii) Allah's Will governs the universe whether it is the Law of Casualty or the Quantum Theory.

(iv) Quran reveals that everything in the Universe works perfectly according to the set Physical laws governing the Fundamental forces in the Universe and explains the working of the Universe as a whole.

(v) Quranic Miracles when Physical Laws yield before the Will of God.

(vi) The Quran as the Documentary miracle of the Last Prophet Muhammad (Peace be Upon Him).

Chapter 12

SCIENCES OF COSMOGONY, COSMOLOGY, ASTROPHYSICS AND ASTRONOMY IN SIMILARITY WITH THE HOLY QURAN ON THE CREATION OF THE INVIOLABLE UNIVERSE OUT OF NOTHING AND ON THE DOOMSDAY (GRAVITATIONAL COLLAPSE) OF THE UNIVERSE INTO NOTHING, AND THE RE-EMERGENCE OF SIMILAR UNIVERSE AND SIMILAR EARTH OUT OF NAUGHT

QURAN ON THE DOOMSDAY OR THE GRAVITATIONAL COLLAPSE OF THE UNIVERSE AND ON THE WAY TO SINGULARITY AND ZERO VOLUME

The science of creation of the universe and of the obliteration of the universe is miraculously in similarity with the Holy Quran.

The sciences of Astrophysics, Cosmogony and Cosmology are in miraculous similarity with the Holy Quran on the 'Doomsday' which is the greatest and the heaviest physical event in the universe for its complete gravitational or catastrophic collapse.

Similarly, science is in similarity with the doctrines of Eschatology of the Quran which is discussed in Chapter 14.

There exists a definite relationship between the physical sciences and the science of religion taught by Islam. It means there is a link of the metaphysics of the Holy Quran with the physics or physical.

The Holy Quran reveals:-

(1) *'And, O my people! Lo! I fear for a Day of Summoning'*. (40:32).

(2) *'Lo! the Hour is surely coming, there is no doubt thereof: ye most of mankind believe not'. (40:59).*

(3) *'This is the Day of Decision. We have brought you and the men of old together'. (76:38).*

The approach to the 'Doomsday' and the 'Doomsday' itself is a great heavy physical event of the future of the universe and of mankind and is closely linked and followed by metaphysical events of Hereafter as revealed by the Holy Quran, such as Death, Resurrection, Accountability, Judgement and Immortality in the Hereafter.

The Holy Quran reveals and describes the events of the 'Doomsday' whereas the Sciences of Astrophysics and Cosmology describe it as 'the catastrophic collapse or the gravitational collapse' of the universe.

The Holy Quran in its numerous verses reveals the events approaching the 'Doomsday' and decribes the physical condition of the earth, the moon, the sun, the stars, the sky and of the entire space and time and of the physical universe including all the cosmological bodies in the cosmos on the Doomsday. The Holy Quran gives the physical proof of the 'Doomsday' or of the 'Catastrophic collapse' of the universe in the following Holy verses:

Quran on the Doomsday or the Last Day — the Great event to the 'Hereafter'.

(a) *The State of Earth on the Doomsday*

Attention of mankind is invited to the absolute reality of the gravest event to befall on mankind and on earth as is revealed by the Holy Quran. Science is in complete similarity with the Holy Quran on the gravitational collapse and on the events to occur on earth, in the solar system and in the whole universe and indicates very clearly the re-emergence of similar universe and similar earth.

The Holy Quran reveals:-.

(1) *'The calamity'. (C:1).*
(2) *'What is the calamity'. (C:2).*
(3) *'A day wherein mankind will be as thickly scattered moth'. (C:4).*

(4) *'When the event befalleth'. (56:1).*
(5) *'Abasing (some) exalting (others)'. (56:3).*
(6) *'There is no denying that it will befall'. (56:2).*
(7) *'When the earth is shaken with a shock'. (56:4).*
(8) *'When the earth is shaken with her (final) earthquake'. (XCVIII:I).*
(9) *'And the hills are ground to powder'. (56:5).*
(10) *'So that they become a scattered dust'. (56:6).*
(11) *'And the mountains will become as carded wool'. (C:5).*
(12) *'And earth yieldeth up her burdens'. (XCVIII:2).*
(13) *'On the day when the earth and the hills rock and the hills become a heap of running sand'. (73:14).*
(14) *'That day she will relate her chronicles'. (XCVIII:4).*
(15) *'And when the Hills are moved'. (81:3).*
(16) *'And when the mountains are blown away'. (77:10).*
(17) *'And the Hills are set in motion and become as a mirage'. (78:20).*
(18) *'When the seas are poured forth'. (82:3).*
(19) *'And the sepulchres are overturned'. (82:4).*
(20) *'And when the sea rise'. (81:6).*
(21) *'And the earth with the mountains shall be lifted up and crushed with one crush'. (69:14).*
(22) *'And the mountains move away with (awful) movement'. (52:10).*
(23) *''And thou seest the hills thou deemest solid flying with the flight of clouds; the doing of Allah Who perfecteth all things. Lo! He is informed of what ye do'. (27:88).*
(24) *'And the hills become as flakes of wool'. (70:9).*
(25) *'Nay, but when the earth is ground to atoms, grinding, grinding'. (89:21).*
(26) *'And thy Lord shall come with angels. rank on rank'. (89:22).*
(27) *'And Hell is brought near that day, on that day man will remember, but how will the remembrance (then avail him)?' (89:23).*
(28) *'The day when the sky will become as molten as copper'. (70:8).*
(29) *'On the day when the heaven will heave with (awful) heaving'. (52:9)*

The above Holy verses reveal the state of earth on the Doomsday when fundamental forces shall run wild and yield to the Command of Allah, the Creator the Shaper, the Compeller of the universe and man and of all things.

(b) Quran on the Catastrophic Collapse of the Cosmos on the Dooms Day

The Holy Quran further reveals the conditions of the solar system and of other cosmological bodies and of the cosmos on the whole in the following Holy verses:-

Science and the Holy Quran in agreement on the gravitational collapse of universe to singularity and zero volume and its re-emergence

(1) *'But when the sight is confounded'. (75:7).*

(2) *'And the moon eclipsed'. (75:8).*

(3) *'And when the sun and the moon are united'. (75:9).*

(4) *'So When the stars are put out'. (76:8)*

(5) *'And heaven is opened and becometh as gates'. (78:19).*

(6) *'And heaven will split asunder, for that day it will be frail'. (69:16).*

(7) *'When the sun is overthrown'. (81:1).*

(8) *'And when the sky is torn away'. (71:11).*

(9) *'When the heaven is cleft asunder'. (82:1).*

(10) *'And when the heaven splitteth asunder and becometh rosy like red hide'. (55:37).*

(11) *'When the planets are dispersed'. (82:2).*

(12) *'And when the stars fall' (81:2).*

(13) *'And when souls are united' (81:7).*

(14) *'And when the pages are laid open' (81:10).*

(15) *'The day when We shall roll up the heavens as a recorder rolleth up a written scroll. As We began the first creation, We shall repeat it. (It is) a promise (binding) upon us. Lo! We are to perform it' (21:104).*

(16) *'Allah effaceth what He will and establisheth (what He will), and with Him is source of ordinance'. (13:39).*

(17) *'On the Day when the earth will be changed to other than this earth, and heavens (also will be changed) and they will come-forth unto Allah, the One, the Almighty'. (14:48).*

(18) *'Have they not seen that Allah Who created the heavens and the earth is Able to create the like of them and hath appointed for them an end whereof there is no doubt? But the wrong-doers refuse aught save disbelief (17:99).*

(19) *'Is not He who created the heavens and the earth Able to Create the Like of them? Aye, that He is! for He is All-Wise Creator' (36:81).*

(20) *'They ask thee of the (destined) Hour, when will it come to port. Say: Knowledge thereof is with my Lord only. He alone will manifest it at its proper time. It is heavy in the heavens and the earth. It cometh not to you save unawares. They question thee as if thou couldst be well informed thereof. Say: Knowledge thereof is with Allah only, but most of mankind know not' (VII:187).*

(21) *'And unto Allah belongeth the unseen of the heavens and the earth, and the matter of the Hour (of Doom) is but as a twinkling of the eye, or it is nearer still. Lo! Allah is Able to do all things'. (16:77).*

(22) *'But watch thou (O Muhammad) for the day when the sky will produce visible smoke' (44:10).*

(23) *'That will envelop the people. This would be a painful torment' (44:11).*

From the Big Bang to Big Crunch

Universe to be Vast Cataclysmic Inferno on the Dooms Day, then turn into Black Hole and Efface into Nothing

The above Quranic revelations clearly depict the events and the state of condition of the main features of the earth and of the solar system and of the entire universe. The earth and its people will be filled with visible smoke on the 'Doomsday'. The Holy Quran gives a very vivid picture of what shall happen and the way it shall look like to an on-looker or an observer, though there would be no observer except Allah, the Master of the Day of Judgement. The Holy Quran describes the various stages of the events and the destruction of the main features of the earth, the hills, the mountains and the seas and of the sun, the moon, the stars, the galaxies and of the entire universe as a whole and describe these in such a way that as if one looks at the slow motion picture of the various stages of the process of obliteration due to gravitational collapse of the earth, and of the solar system and of the whole cosmos on the very day of happening i.e. the 'Doomsday'. All the fundamental forces of nature shall run wild and completely yield. The entire cosmos shall become like molten copper and a vast cataclysmic inferno. The entire universe and the earth shall roll up to the point of singularity and zero volume and shall be effaced to nothing or 'naught'.

While describing the Doomsday, the revelations of the Holy Quran are mostly in the form of direct verses. The Doomsday is very clearly described. The Holy Verses are easy to understand the calamity to befall on the 'Appointed Day'. The Quranic verses give vivid picture of the various stages of the gravitational collapse and happenings of the approaching physical events on the 'Doomsday' when the mountains will be lifted and crushed with one awful crush and when the earth will be shaken with earthquake and the hills being ground to powder as scattered dust or carded wool and fly like clouds. The hill rock would become a heap of running sand and thus the hills shall move and set in motion and become as a mirage. The earth is ground to atoms, (grinding, grinding). All the seas on earth shall rise by evaporation. This may be due to the intense heat of the sun on its expansion into 'red joint' before turning into 'black hole'. All these physical events show that there would be severe catastrophic cosmological upheavel due to intense gravitational changes in all luminous and non-luminous bodies and the sun, besides the severe disorder in all the fundamental forces with an ultimate catastrophic collapse and roll up into naught of all things. In the process, the earth may start wobbling, the sun may have burnt out its internal thermonuclear fire and may expand and collapse in the process of turning into black hole and engulf all its planets. The sight in the cosmos will be totally confounded as soon as the events to the 'Doomsday' approaches, as the moon will be eclipsed and then the sun and the moon are united and the stars are put out i.e. turn into black holes and the heaven will split as under as that day it will be frail and the heaven will be opened to become as gates. The entire universe will turn into black hole, singularity and zero volume and then to nothing. In the process, the sun will be over-thrown and the stars shall fall and the sky torn away, and the heaven shall become as rosy like red hide. Everything will be crushed into each other to become a cataclysmic inferno in the collapsing cosmos. The entire universe and the heavens shall roll up as a recorder rolls up a written scroll and everything shall be effaced into nothing. That will be the 'Doomsday' On the 'Doomsday' souls shall be united with their bodies and mankind shall be resurrected, assembled and brought back to life, may be all this is at the atomic level but Allah knows the best and then accountability will start, and the pages of the recorded deeds and actions of mankind shall be laid open for Judgement as that will be the Day of Judgement or Decision.

The above is the Quranic description of the Dooms Day', revealing the events to happen and the catastrophy to befall on the cosmological bodies in the cosmos as a whole and the calamity to be faced by the fundamental forces which shall become asymmetrical and incomprehensible heading towards the ultimate catastrophic gravitational collapse of the universe as a whole, and shrinking the entire universe into infinite density and to a point of singularity and zero-volume and then disappear into 'nothing' or 'naught' as it was before. This would be the 'Big Crunch' before the 'Big Bang!'

The Holy Quran reveals that after obliteration of the universe to 'Nothing', a similar universe shall begin and repeat its creation as before and science is in similarity with it

After the Big Crunch, again to the Big Bang, to Re-create the like of this Universe and this Earth

The Holy Quran further reveals and assures mankind that Allah shall repeat the creation of the heavens and the earth as promised by Allah in the Holy Quran and Who made the re-emergence of the universe a binding on Himself and He is to perform it. Allah is Able to do all things and He is the Lord of the unseen and the invisible in the heavens and in the earth. He knows everything and may be that the Hour of the Doom be near, as it is a matter as a twinkling of the eyes or still nearer than that as the Quran reveals. Allah has the power to efface and establish whatever He wishes and whenever He wishes. Mankind shall return to Allah, Who is the One and the Almighty. The Holy Quran reveals in the above quoted verses (21:104) and (14:48) that on the Day when the present earth and universe shall be changed to other than this earth and universe, then new universe and new earth shall be created. Allah promises the return of new worlds after the catastrophic collapse of the physical universe and the earth.

The Holy Quran reveals:-

(1) *'We created not the heavens and the earth and all that is between them save with truth and for a term appointed. But those who disbelieve turn away from that whereof they are warned'. (46:3).*

(2) *'Allah it is Who hath revealed the Scripture with truth and the Balance. How canst thou know? It may be that the Hour is nigh' (42:17).*

(3) *'And unto Allah belongeth the Unseen of the heavens and the earth and the matter of the Hour (of Doom) is but as a twinkling of the eye or it is near still. Lo! Allah is Able to do all things'. (16:77).*

(4) *'The Day when We shall roll up the heavens as a recorder rolleth up a written scroll. We began the first creation, We shall repeat it. (It is) a promise (binding) upon Us. Lo! We are to perform it'. (21:104).*

(5) *'Allah effaceth what He will and establisheth (What He Will), and with Him is source of ordinance'. (13:39).*

(6) *'On the Day when the earth will be changed to other than this earth, and heavens (also will be changed) and they will come forth unto Allah, the One, the Almighty'. (14:48).*

(7) *'And they esteem not Allah as He hath the right to be esteemed, when the whole earth is His handful on the day of Resurrection and the heavens are rolled in His right hand. Glorified is He and High Exalted from all that they ascribed as partner (unto Him'. (39:67).*

The above Holy verses reveal that Allah has created the universe for an appointed period and that all the unseen matters of the heavens and earth belong to Allah and that the bringing (of Doom) for Him is so easy and quick like a twinkling of the eyes or nearer than that and He is Able to do All things. Allah shall roll up the heavens and efface all things to 'naught' and He will establish and recreate all things with changed universe and changed earth in the same way as He began the first creation and with Him is source of Ordinance. Man must esteem Allah as All-Wise Creator and the Doer of All things as He has the right to be esteemed for His Infinite attributes and that Allah is Able to do all things. So, the earth and the heavens on the Day of Resurrection are rolled up at His Command. Allah is glorified and He is High Exalted and is above all things.

Science on the Fate of the Universe — The Gravitational Collapse in miraculous similarity with the Holy Quran

How stunningly close and amazingly correct, science revealing the fate of the universe by gravitational collapse is in similarity with the verses of the Holy Quran on the Doomsday or the Catastrophic collapse of the universe and its re-emergence with changed earth and changed universe. The clear similarity between the two is the greatest miracle of all times and is eyes opener for all mankind. Modern concepts and findings which science has discovered now, are found to be already present in the Holy Quran revealed more than 1400 years ago. The similarity of science with the Quranic verses on the 'Doomsday' is excitingly astonishing and flabergasting. It is absolutely miraculous. Men of sound knowledge, wisdom, understanding and faith may seriously pay heed to the truthful miracles of the Quranic revelations on the 'Doomsday' and to all other revelations and listen to the word of God attentively, obey His teachings as revealed in the Holy Quran and worship Him and ask for His mercy and guidance to follow the right path. Profound similarity of science with the Holy Quran on the Doomsday should serve as an eye opener for all mankind. The Quran is the bearer of good tidings for all mankind.

Scientists describe what they call it as the 'fate of the universe' by the eventual catastrophic collapse and then its replacement or change by similar creation of new worlds. This explanation is given on page 1011, Volume 18 of the Encyclopaedia Britannica, 1979, an extract from which is quoted below:-

> 'As the end approaches, first the galaxies and then the stars are crushed into each other in an over-whelming cataclysmic inferno, in which ultimately the collapsing cosmos reverts to the primeval chaos of the big bang. Whether the universe rises again phoenix-like is not known, and it depends perhaps on whether it can preserve identifying qualities as it passes through an inchoate quantum cosmological state of a nearly infinite density'.

The Abbe Lemaitre, in the Primeval Atom (1931) has written:-

> 'Standing on a cooled cinder, we see the slow fading of the suns and we try to recall the vanished brilliance of the origin of the worlds. The brilliance has gone; the suns are doomed; but the vanished brilliance and with it new worlds may once again return'.

The miraculous similarity of science describing the fate of the catastrophically collapsing universe, and the direct and clear verses of the Holy Quran describing the physical collapse of the cosmological bodies and the whole cosmos on the Doomsday are remarkably astonishing and absolutely stunning. The description of science on the catastrophically collapsing universe is very much the same or similar to the Quranic revelations on the 'Doomsday '. What does all this Quranic miracle show? It shows beyond all doubts that the Holy Quran is the Word of God and is not man-made. It cannot be man-made for revealing such miraculous informations 1400 years ago. And that Allah is the Creator and the Oblitrator of the universe. And that Allah is of Infinite attributes and is Able to do all things.

The scientific and Quranic descriptions of earth and of the cosmos on the Doomsday give exactly similar and definite sense on the ultimate cataclysmic collapse of the universe. The fact is that the Holy Quran revealed it 1400 years ago whereas physical science discovers it now. The Quranic revelations are the absolute truth beyond all doubts and are the Divine words of Allah and that modern knowledge of science about the creation, evolution and ultimate fate of universe and of mankind is found to be in complete congruity with the Quranic verses revealed more than 1400 years ago on the unlettered Prophet Muhammad (PBUH) when there was no such knowledge available at that time and the beginning of such knowledge was not made even more than a thousand years after the revelations. The amazing similarity of physical facts and events with the Quranic revelations instantaneously inspires the wisdom and conscience and the common sense of man to the unflinching and resolute belief in the existence of One Allah and faith in the Holy Quran as the true word of Allah and in Prophet Muhammad (PBUH) as His Messenger. The progressively increasing knowledge of science which is in constant pursuit of finding the reality, helps man in clearly understanding and grasping the substance of the Holy Quranic verses on the Doomsday ' and finds it as the absolute truth and this conviction shall become more and more strong with the achievements of more and more knowledge which surrounds all things. Hence, science or sound knowledge for knowing the reality of physical objects in the universe is the most important factor. Knowledge is the means to understand and grasp the substance and the sense contained in the verses of the Holy Quran which leads to the unflinching faith in the existence of One Allah and in the existence of the metaphysical world or the 'Hereafter' and in other unimaginable, invisible, hidden and unseen matters revealed by the Holy Quran.

The Holy Quran reveals:-

(1) *'Allah it is Who hath created seven heavens and of the earth the like thereof. The commandment cometh down among them slowly, that ye may know that Allah is Able to do all things and that Allah surroundeth all things in knowledge'. (66:12).*

(2) *'And of His signs is the creation of the heavens and the earth and the difference of your languages and colours Lo! herein indeed are portents for men of knowledge'.* (30:22).

(3) *'A Scripture whereof the verses are expounded, a lecture for people who have knowledge'.* (41:3).

(4) *'Say: Believe therein or believe not, Lo! those who were given knowledge before it, fall down prostrate on the faces, adoring'.* (17:107).

(5) *'(This is) a Scripture that We have revealed unto thee full of blessing that they may ponder its revelations and that men of understanding may reflect'.* (38:29).

The above Holy verses and many more like these lay great emphasis on knowledge and on men of knowledge, and on men of understanding Who pay heed and reflect, as Allah has surrounded all things in knowledge. Attention is invited to carefully read the Holy Verses (III:7-66) and (31:27), in this context which are mentioned in this book in Chapter 2 and 5.

The Holy verses reveal that if men believe in the revelations or believe not, it is for them to choose, but those who were given knowledge before it, believed in Allah's revelations and they fall down in humility and submission before Allah in Divine worship. The Scripture of Allah in Arabic is full of blessings for mankind and people who have knowledge and ponder over the revelations will know that Allah is Able to do all things and that Allah surroundeth all things in knowledge. In order to grasp the sense and to know the real meanings of the Holy Quranic verses, knowledge with 'faith' is required for its full understanding.

More examples and further details of the research work done by various scientists and their views expressed are given to show how science of Cosmogony, Cosmology and Astrophysics is in congruity with the Holy Quran on the Creation of the Universe out of 'nothing' and the Obliteration of the universe to nothing. In this respect, the evolutionary process of the conversion of luminous bodies (Stars) into the formation of 'Black Holes', is discussed, which is again in similarity with the allegorial verse (51:7) of the Holy Quran for miraculously conveying the sense of Black holes.

Black holes — The Pathways to Other Universes

As already mentioned, the Holy Quran clearly describes the Doomsday and the events approaching the Doomsday. The verses indicate that all things in the universe will be effaced and all the heavens and the earth will be rolled up by Allah, as the matter of the Hour of Doom for Allah is so quick and so easy as the twinkling of the eyes or it is still nearer than that when all things will be effaced into naught. All the unseen and the invisible matters of the heaven belong to Allah. Black hole falls under one of such matters of the heaven and it indicates and gives proof how luminous celestial bodies undergo changes when ultimately they reduce by achieving near infinite density and become invisible and ultimately by further gravitational collapse they reduce to zero volume and to a point of singularity.

The Holy Quran clearly hints on the truth of the black holes but in allegory. Men of knowledge, wisdom and understanding if ponder on the Holy verse (51:7) and (51:8) quoted below will be able to grasp the sense and the substance contained in these verses, which refer to numerous black holes in the universe. Moreover, other verses of the Holy Quran on the Doomsday and on other matters of the heaven indicate processes in the formation of the black holes and the mysterious Qausars something like anti-matter, ultimately causing the catastrophic collapse of the universe into singularity and zero volume and into 'naught'.

The Holy Quran reveals:-

(1) *'By the heaven full of path:' (51:7).*

(2) *'Lo! Ye, foresooth, are of various opinions (concerning the truth)'. (51:8).*

(3) *'And We have created above you seven paths, and We are never unmindful of creation'. (23:17).*

(4) *'And heaven is opened and becometh as gates'. (78:19).*

(5) *'And there is nothing hidden in the heaven or the earth but it is in a clear record'. (27:75).*

(6) *'He is the Knower of the invisible and the visible, the Great, the High Exalted'. (13:9).*

(7) *'(He is) the Knower of the unseen. Not an atom's weight, or less than that or greater, escapeth Him in the heavens or in the earth, but*

it is in a clear record'. (34:3).

(8) *'This is the Scripture whereof there is no doubt, a guidance unto those who ward off evil'. (3:2).*

(9) *'Who believe in the unseen and establish worship and spend of that We have bestowed upon them'. (3:3).*

(10) *'His are the Keys of the heavens and the earth and they who disbelieve the revelations of Allah such are they who are the losers'. (39:63).*

(11) *'Lo! Allah is the Knower of the Unseen of the heavens and the earth. Lo! He is Aware of the secrets of (men's) breasts'. (35:58).*

(12) *'He is Allah, the Creator, the Shaper out of naught, the Fashioner. His are the most beautiful names. All that is in the heavens and the earth glorifieth Him and He is the Mighty, the Wise'. (60:24).*

Out of the above Holy verses, the Holy verses (51:7-8) are very short and are all in allegorical form. The sense contained in the verses is explained below in the context of knowledge of modern sciences and after thoroughly grasping and understanding the substance encompassed in the verses. The Holy Quranic verse (51:7) referred above is as follows:-

'By the heaven full of path'. (51:7)

The above Quranic verse indicates that the heaven or the universe is 'full of path'. Now, one must contemplate and try to understand first of all, the allegorial Quranic sense of the 'path', and then of the 'heaven full of path'. One must ponder, what is path? And what sense does it convey? How could the heaven be full of path? All this is to be contemplated in the context of Cosmology and Astrophysics.

In order to grasp and understand the allegorial meanings of the above Holy verse, sound knowledge of Physics, Astronomy, Astrophysics, Cosmogony and Cosmology, with wisdom and faith is required. In this context a few paras from the 'Reader's Digest' Library of Modern Knowledge Volume-1, Page 41' describing 'Black hole' is quoted. From the scientific description of 'Black hole' one can grasp and understand the Quranic allegorial sense of 'heaven full of path', from the similarity between the two. This is because Cosmology, Astronomy and Physics explain that the universe is 'full of black holes'. Thus, science explains all this and is in similarity with the Holy Quran that a 'black hole' in the universe is like a 'path' in the universe. This becomes more clear from another verse which reveals that 'And heaven is opened and becometh as gates'. (78:19), and from the following scientific explanation of the characteristics of the black holes:-

> 'According to some theories, black holes act as pathways to other universes, so that matter flowing into black holes may be pouring into other regions of space and time of which we have no knowledge'.

This makes it clear that a 'black hole' is a 'path' leading to the 'Gate way' of the universes. In order to further support this, guidance from the next Quranic verse can be taken, which reveals:-

> *'And We have created above you seven paths, and We are never unmindful of creation'. (23:17).*

This Holy verse conveys great sense that above the mankind (and earth), Allah has created seven paths. Here paths convey sense and means universes and that Allah is not unmindful of His creation. The above quoted Quranic verses further reveal, that even an atom's weight or less than that (which means sub-atomic particles) are in Allah's notice and are in a clear record. (34:3). The Holy Quran reveals absolute truth and there is no doubt about it. The Holy Quran teaches to believe in the unseen and establish worship to Allah Who is the Knower of all things. What lies in other universes, or what is hidden there elsewhere and whatever is unseen or is invisible, is in a clear Record with Allah as He is the Creator and the Knower of all things. And 'He is Allah the Creator, the Shaper out of naught, the Fashioner of All things'. (60:24). Allah is the Originator and the Creator of all things. Things, invisible, hidden and unseen are not known to man and are beyond his power of perception. Man must have faith in all such unseen and invisible and hidden realities revealed by Holy Quran.

What is a Black Hole?

Sound knowledge in Astrophysics would reveal the nature of Black holes to some extent.

When a star with a mass more than 20 times that of the sun explodes as supernova, 'bombshell' (Temperature 3500,000,000 degree centigrade), it may leave behind a core so massive that even a neutron star is not its final state. The object's gravity may be so great that it goes on collapsing for ever, crushing the matter within it to an unimaginable state. As the object's density gets greater and greater, the force of gravity rises even more until nothing can escape — not even light. The object has become a 'black hole'. At the centre of the 'black hole', the remains of the former star would be crushed to infinite density, in zero volume. This point is termed as 'singularity'.

According to modern theories of Astrophysics there is nothing that can stop the endless collapse of massive star core under its own gravity. There could be as many as 10 millions black holes in the Galaxy, formed after the supernova explosions of massive stars.

The Making of a 'Black hole'

Among the most enigmatic objects in the universe are the so-called 'black holes', believed to be formed after massive stars erupt as brilliant supernovae at the end of their lives. The dense core of such a star, left behind after the explosion, continues collapsing under the inward pull of its own gravity until it vanishes in a black hole from which not even light can escape. Some astronomers think black holes act like giant 'plug holes', through which material pours out of our universe In a way, black holes are as mysterious as quasars. They don't seem to obey the rules of Physics; they are, for instance, inherently invisible.

As a star more than ten times heavier than the Sun exhausts its energy, its outer layers collapse towards the centre. The star then erupts in a supernova explosion, throwing off its outer layers.

After the explosion, the dense core of the star is left behind, possibly as a highly compressed object known as neutron star. Spinning neutron stars are detected as flashing radiation sources, or pulsars. If the mass of the star's remaining core is too great, it continues contracting under the force of its own gravity to become a black hole. Into such a hole matter can fall, but out of it nothing can escape.

As their names implies, black holes are invisible because they emit no light. Black holes although invisible, can nonetheless be detected as it gives off x-rays when it tears off the neighbouring star and engulf its material by sucking.

Black holes act as pathways to other universes, so that matter flowing into black holes may be pouring into other regions of space and time of which we have no knowledge'.

From the above explanation of a black hole, it is clear that a black hole is one of the detectable, 'invisible' of the heaven. The Holy Quran very often mentions the invisible and the unseen and hidden matters of the universe. Again, Science of Astrophysics, Astronomy and Cosmology explain that black holes act as path ways to other universes. The Holy Quran allegorially reveals that heaven is full of path. Science explains that there are 10 million black holes in the Galaxy alone. The science of black hole is very recent but the presence of its allegorial mention in the Holy Quran revealed 1400 years ago is a great miracle and leads to the fact that the Holy Quran is the word of God. It is for all mankind to believe the revelations of the Holy Quran.

The similarity of modern science of Astrophysics, Astronomy and Cosmology, with the verses of the Holy Quran indicates that the Holy Quran is the Message of God and is a heavenly Book revealed by inspiration. The similarities in all fields of sciences serve as tokens or portents or the signs of Allah to indicate to mankind that Allah exists and is the Creator and the Knower of all things. The Holy Quran shows that it is full of Wisdom, Knowledge and Information and is for the guidance of all mankind. It always gives a documentary proof in respect of many things either in allegory or directly and full of sense, wisdom and knowledge and clearly proves that the Holy Quran is not man-made and cannot be man-made. The Holy Quran is revealed for the guidance of mankind, so it is for man to read it and ponder over it and obey what it teaches as it is from the Creator of mankind and brings a message of good tidings from Allah to mankind.

As explained before, Allah created the heavens, and the earth out of 'nothing' or 'naught'. Then He turned to the heaven when it was 'smoke' and formed the universe and the earth out of the smoke or the materials of heavens and earth. Then Allah ordered them seven heavens in two Days or two periods and decked our heaven or the near universe with stars.

The same way, the Holy Quran reveals:-

(1) *'But Watch thou (O Muhammad) for the Day when the sky will produce visible smoke'. (44:10).*

(2) *'That will envelop the people. This would be a painful torment'. (44:11).*

On the Doomsday , the sky will again produce visible smoke and Allah will roll up the universe like a written scroll and efface everything and revert back to 'nothing' or 'naught' as it was before. Allah has promised to repeat the creation of the universe and the earth, the like of this universe and the like of this earth and this is a promise which Allah made a binding on Himself.

Science of Astrophysics in congruity with the Holy Quran on the Creation of the Universe out of 'Nothing' or 'Naught' and the Obliteration of the Universe to Naught

The Holy Quran reveals :-

'He is Allah, the Creator, the Shaper out of naught, the Fashioner. His are the most beautiful names. All that is in the heavens and the earth glorifieth Him and He is the Mighty, the Wise'. (60:24).

The incredible similarity and congruity of the modern knowledge of science with the Holy Quran is simply exciting and amazing in respect of the catastrophic collapse of the universe as Science of Astrophysics explains, and the events of the Doomsday as the Holy Quran describes, then the black holes or the invisible 'Collapsed' stars, as science explains, and the 'invisible' of the heavens and the 'path' in the heaven as the Holy Quran refers. Also, there is miraculous similarity and concord of the physical sciences of the 20th Century dealing with creation and reproduction of man, the creation and evolution of the universe, the expansion of the universe as per Hubble's Law, the inviolability of the universe, the structure of atom built with might and as indicated by Einstein's equation $E = mc^2$ the interaction of matter and energy, the creation of the universe from 'naught' or 'nothing' and the obliteration of the universe to 'naught' or 'nothing' molecular biology, cell biology, water in protoplasm, the DNA, of mankind, the chromosomes and genetic engineering, the Law of Casualty by Einstein and the uncertainty principle, the Quantum Theory of incomprehensibility by Niels Bohr, and of Max Planck, Newton's Law of motion, particle physics or higher mathematics, theory of Relativity, the Einstein Relation, the Law of Conservation of Matter and Energy, the Quantum Theory of Light, the process of annihilation and the process of electron-positron creation, the mutual conversion of matter and energy, the Laws of Thermodynamics, the Law of Definite Proportion, the process of radio-activity, the process of nuclear fusion of hydrogen in the sun, the process of conversion of solar energy into plant material through photosynthesis, etc. with the Holy Quranic verses either in the form of allegory or by the direct revelations. Science is helpless and cannot probe about the invisible, the hidden and the unseen of the universe and of the Hereafter, whereas, the Holy Quran reveals hints about them either directly or in allegory. The Holy Quran, therefore, bridges the two worlds in knowledge for the guidance of mankind, i.e. the physical universe and the 'Hereafter'.

Allah, the Creator of all things, the One, is the Greatest Unseen and the Invisible and the Unimaginable for mankind. Among His attributes some are that He is Omnipresent, Omnipotent, Omniscient and Omnificent and is Self-Evident.

Allah is the Lord of this World and of the 'Hereafter' and of all things in the heavens and the earth. The 'Hereafter' is unseen and lie beyond the jurisdiction of physical science, but the Holy Quran truthfully reveals it as the next and the eternal abode for mankind.

The 'Hereafter', i.e. life after death is one of the act of creation of Allah and is unseen as the Holy Quran reveals. The 'Hereafter' is an eternal World, where man shall be resurrected to live as immortal being and where the accountability for his worldly deeds and actions shall take place and a Judgement pronounced to reward or punish him with Paradise or Hell, according to the performance of his deeds in the universe. The Holy Quran reveals that deeds of all mankind are minutely observed and recorded, which shall be laid open before each individual on the 'Day of Judgement'. The reality of Eschatology is discussed in Chapter 14 of this book.

The knowledge of science cannot tell man, phenomena and events in the Hereafter like the resurrection, the observation of man's deeds, his accountability, the Day of Judgement, the Paradise, the Hell, the Hereafter and all that is to happen before Allah on the Day of Judgement. These Phenomena are all invisible, and unseen matters. The revelations of the Holy Quran, therefore, describe the Unseen, the Hidden and the Invisible realities. Quran reveals physical realities, and the same way it reveals metaphysical realities. The jinn is one of the hidden creation of Allah. The jinns are unseen and invisible and are intelligent living creatures very much in existence.

They are an absolute reality and are clearly described in the Holy Quran. There are many things in the physical universe, which are invisible, hidden and unseen but exist as absolute reality. Refusal to recognize such realities simply because man does not happen to know it through his limited knowledge of Sciences and to deny them is simply senseless and an illogical conclusion. Similarly, the 'Hereafter' is unseen but is an absolute reality. When science becomes helpless and human knowledge and capacity to understand and perceive cannot penetrate due to human limitations, then the teachings of the Holy Quran are always there as Divine guide for mankind about matters of the physical universe, the invisible and the unseen and about the metaphysical matters and events of the 'Hereafter'. Man must have faith in them. The Holy Quran is the only unaltered and perfect heavenly Book and the source of guidance which spans the two worlds in knowledge and is the source of divine light and wisdom for mankind and for those who believe and pay heed and ponder over the Holy Quranic verses, and its meaningful and allegorial verses which are encompassed with knowledge about all the creations of Allah, including the universe, man, the spirit, the jinn, the Angels, the Doomsday, the Resurrection, the Eschatology, the 'Hereafter', the Paradise and the Hell.

Entire Universe becoming as the Invisible Black hole

Out of the many unseen and the invisible, one of the invisible of the physical universe which the sciences of cosmology and astronomy and astrophysics describe, is a black hole' in space which has already been discussed. The black hole is a mysterious 'invisible' celestial body that devours matter, curves space and warps time. The evolution of the universe may ultimately turn the entire universe as 'black hole' or invisible, and may roll up the entire, matter, energy, space and time and reduce it to a point of singularity and zero volume and then disappear into 'nothing' or 'naught'.

The Holy Quran reveals the following verses and the science of black holes and of the gravitational collapse is found to be in complete similarity with the substance of the Quranic verses :-

The Holy verses on gravitational Collapse are:-

(1) *'When the sun is overthrown'. (81:1).*

(2) *'And when the stars fall' (81:2).*

(3) *'So When the stars are put out'. (76:8).*

(4) *'When the planets are dispersed'. (82:2).*

(5) *'And when the sun and moon are united' (75:9).*

(6) *'Nay, but when the earth is ground to atoms grinding, grinding'. (89:21).*

(7) *'And when the sky is torn away'. (81:11).*

(8) *'When the heaven is cleft asunder'. (82:1).*

(9) *'And when the heaven splitteth asunder and becometh rosy like red hide'. (65:37).*

(10) *'The day when the sky will become as molten Copper'. (70:8).*

(11) *'And unto Allah belongeth the unseen of the heavens and the earth and the matter of the hour (of Doom) is but as a twinkling of the eye, or it is nearer still. Lo! Allah is Able to do all things' (16:77).*

(12) *'The Day when We shall roll up the heavens as a recorder rolleth up a written scroll. As We began the first creation, We shall repeat it. (It is) a promise (binding) upon Us. Lo! We are to perform it'. (21:104).*

(13) *'Allah effaceth what He will and establisheth (what He will) and with Him is source of Ordinance'. (13:39).*

(14) *'And they esteem not Allah as He hath the right to be esteemed, when the whole earth is His handful on the Day of Resurrection and the heavens are rolled in his right hand. Glorified is He and High Exalted from all that they ascribe as partner (unto Him)' (39:67).*

(15) *'He is the Knower of the invisible and the visible, the Great, the High Exalted'. (13:9).*

(16) *'He is the Knower of the Unseen and He revealeth unto none his Secret'. (72:26).*

(17) *'Lo! Allah is the Knower of the Unseen of the heavens and the earth'. (35:38).*

(18) *'And there is nothing hidden in the heaven or the earth but it is in a clear record'. (27:75).*

Science reveals that the black holes are gobbling up celestial matter by exerting incredible gravitational force and that these invisible 'collapsed' stars may hold the key to mankind's ultimate fate. Black hole is among the invisibles of the heaven. The Holy

Quran gives clear indications in the verse :-

'So when the stars are put out'. (76:8).

And again, the Holy verse reveals :-

'And when the Stars fall' (81:2).

Extract from the article written by John L. Wilhelm appeared in the Reader's Digest in November 1977 is much relevant in the above context and is quoted below. This may be read in the light of the revelations of the Holy Quran, revealed on the creation, evolution and the final fate of the universe. The extract of the article is as under :-

> The violent bursts of X-rays spewing forth from massive streams of stellar gas from constellation cygnus (the Swan) in the sky are examined through telescopes. The gas streams appear to be hurtling from a bright, visible star toward this mysterious unseen companion'. All the evidence so far strongly supports one of the eeriest hypotheses ever conceived by the mind of man: The idea of an invisible 'black hole' in space that devours matter, curves space and warps time'.
>
> 'Black holes exert incredible gravitational force where matter is crushed beyond recognition, scrunching atoms together into a mass of infinite density. This is the remnant of a collapsed star whose fires have burnt out, a star once so huge that its top-heavy gravity crushed it down to the size of golf ball, then further, to 'nothing', so it disappears'.
>
> 'Because of its incredible density, the collpased star's gravitational attraction has swelled to overwhelming proportions. All that passes within its reach falls into this stellar maelstorm, there to be trapped for ever. Even light rays cannot escape, so no one can see it, or into it. The former star has become like a fathomless pit in space. These are celestial ghosts and are called 'Black holes'.

> Today, some scientists think that gigantic black holes may be gnawing at the centres of most galaxies, including our Milky Way, devouring entire stars at a gulp. Perhaps as much as 90 per cent of the entire mass of the universe has already disappeared into black holes. Perhaps the mysterious quasars, those noisy cauldrons of violent energy heard out on the edges of space, are stupendous black holes gobbling up the hearts of whole galaxies. Herbert Gursky at the Harvard-Smithsonion Centre for astrophysics makes an even more mind-boggling suggestion. The ultimate black hole may be the universe itself'.
>
> British Scientists J.B.S. Haldone once observed :-
>
> 'The Universe is 'not only queerer than we suppose, but queerer than we can suppose'.

The two necessary conditions for the formation of black holes are: a truly huge mass,. concentrated within a truly small distance. Giant stars provide the mass. When they grow old and begin to burn out their internal thermonuclear fires no longer can withstand. the inward gravitation crush of the outer layers. Consequently, these outer layers begin to fall toward the centre, packing atoms together, shrinking the star. Then Newton's inverse square law begins to run wild. As the atoms jam closer and closer, the force of gravity grows much more rapidly, accelerating the collapse inward. The process feeds on itself. More shrinkage means closer atoms, hence more gravity. More shrinkage ...... more gravity ...... more shrinkage. At a critical point, the imploding star may be held in check. A small star lacking the gravitational wallops to jam its electron and closer together ends up as a tremendously dense, hot cinder called a 'White Dwarf', a somewhat large star in which all the electrons have been squeezed into the protons of atomic nuclei, forming neutrons. Or the star undergoes final collapse to a single point of infinite density. The speed of this final cave-in approaches the velocity of light and can happen in less than a second. The star disappears; it literally 'winks out', and a black hole is born. The Holy Quranic verses(16:77), (76:8), (81:11) and (81:2) quoted above may be read again in the light of the above scientific explanation.

Every large, bright star boils off a solar wind of particles and radiates in all directions. A neighbouring black hole feeds on this solar wind. Matter sucked down a black hole beats up to a billion degrees as it smashes in. As a consequence, the infalling matter radiates a chaotic flow of intense X-rays which scatter throughout space and can be detected. Because X-radiation is absorbed by the earth's thick mantle of air, scientists on track of black holes must launch their X-ray detectors aboard rockets or satellites which soar above their interfering mantle.

We have known for five decades that the universe is expanding, and that the expansion is the result of a primordial explosion that blew apart the gigantic 'cosmic egg' of matter from which all was formed. Will the universe continue to expand, flying outward for ever with matter getting spread out more thinly? Or will the gravitational attraction of the stars and galaxies eventually arrest this expansion and cause the universe to start contracting? The equations and ideas of Einstein predict that the universe will one day do exactly this, collapse upon itself.

At present, astronomers have not found upon enough matter in the universe to produce strong enough gravity to reverse the current expansion. However, some scientists suggest that a significant part of the 'missing matter' needed to close the universe may be locked up in black holes. If so, then there is sufficient gravity to force the universe to collapse upon itself in a blinding rush of self annihilation, destroying not only all existing matter but time and space as well. Galaxies collide and even cannibalize each other, and may hold enough matter to make the universe collapse in a big crunch. The above Holy Quranic verses (21:104), (16:77) and (30:67) clearly indicate the same.

Thus, if we can unravel the riddle of black holes—this riddle of utmost gravity—then almost certainly we will explode our vision of reality and substitute a conception that well may provide an answer to the over-riding riddle of mankinds ultimate fate.

Einstein's Theory of Relativity predicts that black hole theory, is a theory of 'Space-time', and in it time, as well as space, performs strange tricks. To an outside observer, time slows down near a black hole.

Just how does one go about searching the heavens for something so strange and so invisible as a hole in space? Once a star collapses to a black hole, gravity is all that stays behind. And gravity can be detected, because it will cause a nearby star to wobble in orbit around it.

The Holy Quran reveals :

> *'He is Allah, the Creator, the Shaper out of naught, the Fashioner. His are the most beautiful names. All that is in the heavens and the earth glorifieth Him, and He is the Mighty, the Wise'. (60:24).*

Hereafter, the Enduring Home for the Believers with Better, Comfortable and Lasting Life and a Wonderful Fate for Mankind on Resurrection

The fate of mankind after the collapse of universe—a gift of welcome awaits the righteous of mankind in the Hereafter

So, the science of black hole or the invisible of the heaven as the Holy Quran describes lead to the conclusion that the universe will ultimately turn into 'black hole' and then to 'nothing' or 'naught' from which it was originally created as the Holy Quran reveals. Similarly, after the collapse of the universe and in the metaphysical world, the fate of mankind is absolutely certain and is resurrection in the 'Hereafter' which is an eternal world and is the real, more comfortable, better and more lasting and permanent home of mankind. A gift of welcome for the righteous of mankind awaits in the Hereafter from the Lord of the Worlds. These are the revelations from the Holy Quran to mankind, whereas, man's knowledge of science does not go beyond the physical universe and cannot tell him about the more comfortable and enduring life of the 'Hereafter' as the ultimate fate of mankind. Undoubtedly, the Holy Quran confirms the exposition of that which is decreed for mankind. The Holy Quran has made clear revelations on the fate of mankind. It is for man to follow the revelations and act accordingly so that he builds up his real and comfortable fate in the 'Hereafter'.

More Scientific views and informations from scientists on the annihilation of the physical universe are given.

Universe will Fade away into a Tiny Matter

'London, July 10, 1981: When the universe dies, it will just fade away, particle physicists have argued. But there will still be a tiny amount of matter left to tell the tale, claim two U.S. Physicists, Dr. Don Page and Dr. Randall Mckee.'

They have taken to its logical conclusion the theory current among high energy physicists that ultimately (after some 1000 billion billion billion years) the nuclear constituents of atoms will decay, leaving only leptons: light electron, positrons, and massless neutrons.

Uptil now, physicists have argued that the process should be further, because the universe is electronically neutral. There must be balance or as many electrons as positrons (which have opposite charges) in the final state, given indefinite time they should annihilate one another.

The result would be just a cloud of photons (a glow of light and heat), mass-less neutrines and gravitons, the phsothetical particles of the gravitational field. Such a universe is called radiation dominated because most of the energy in it is in the form of massless particles which move at the speed of light. By contrast, the universe is presently matter dominated: Most of the energy is in the form of massive particles, whose state of lowest energy is to be at rest.

But Dr. Page and Dr. Mckee say if the universe is expanding and the density is low the electrons and positrons will never get the chance to get together. The rate of recombination will be so slow that separation will overcome annihilation. But according to the Quranic verse (11:107), it is the Will of Allah which ultimately prevails and which decides the method for the catastrophic collapse of the universe.

The result, the physicists show, is that the universe will remain dominated by matter after all, although it will still be a wraith like universe, nothing like the world of stone and water that we know. In the end, it seems we shall all be a cloud of leptons .

Science is in pursuit to unravel the visible realities of man and the universe but it is far behind to catch it. It is Allah who knows the best, for He is the Creator, the Obliterator and the Compeller Knowledge of all natural sciences acquired so far by man is found to be in congruity with the Holy Quran on the catastrophic collapse of the Universe but it cannot tell about the absolute truth of the ultimate fate of the universe and of man as when and how they are to meet their destined fate. The Holy verse (11:107) quoted below may be contemplated. The Holy Quran reveals all things. It reveals the absolute truth of the physical world and of the world of the 'Hereafter'. The Holy Quran truly reveals the ultimate fate of mankind and of the universe. The cloud of leptons mentioned by the scientists in the wraith like universe is also in similarity with the Quranic verse (44:10).

The Holy Quran reveals :-

> *'But Watch thou (O Muhammad) for the day when the sky will produce visible smoke'. (44:10).*

The apocalypse of gravitational collapse of the universe as John Archibald Wheeler explains and as Einstein and Neil Bohr held views, besides the research work of Professor Stephen Hawking are quoted as these are found to be completely in similarity with the verses of the Holy Quran on the Doomsday already mentioned and as mentioned below.

The Holy Quran reveals :-

(1) *'Abiding there so long as the heavens and the earth endure save for that which thy Lord willeth. Lo! thy Lord is Doer of what He will'. (11:107).*

(2) *'They ask thee of the (destined) Hour, when will it come to port. Say: Knowledge thereof is with my Lord only. He alone will manifest it at its proper time. It is heavy in the heavens and the earth. It cometh not to you save unawares. They question thee as if thou couldst be well informed thereof. Say: Knowledge thereof is with Allah only, but most of mankind know not'. (7:187).*

(3) *'The Day when We shall roll up the heavens as a recorder rolleth up a written scroll. As We began the first creation, We shall repeat it. (It is) a promise (binding) upon us. Lo! We are to perform it'. (21:104).*

(4) *'And unto Allah belongeth the Unseen of the heavens and the earth, and the matter of the Hour (of Doom) is but as a twinkling of the eye, or it is nearer still. Lo! Allah is Able to do all things'. (16:77).*

(5) *'Man is made of haste. I shall show you My portents, but ask Me not to hasten'. (21:37).*

(6) *'And Allah Who hath revealed the Scripture with truth and the Balance. How canst thou know? It may be that the Hour is nigh' (42:17).*

The Holy verse (11:107) and others quoted above indicate that the catastrophic collapse of the universe may be due to anyone of the physical reasons in the normal evolutionary process as long as the universe could endure or abide. Notwithstanding all this and as and when Allah willeth, He may trigger off the catastrophic collapse of the universe any moment as He is the Doer of what He will. And the matter of the Hour of Doom for Allah is but as a twinkling of the eye, or it is nearer still. Allah will manifest the Doom at its proper time which is only in the knowledge of Allah, when Allah shall roll up the universe as a recorder rolleth up a written scroll. But the Holy Quran reveals that man is made of haste and Allah says that I shall show you My portents, but ask Me not to hasten.

As long as the universe endure or abide under the normal evolutionary process, the Catastrophic collapse of the universe could be due to any one of the following reasons as sciences of black holes and of the particle physics indicate :

(1) Due to the Black hole formation.
(2) Due to matter and anti-matter annihilation by collision.
(3) Due to the end of Proton.
(4) Due to the decay of the nuclear constituents of atoms when they can no longer endure or abide.

Andrei Sakharov a well-known Russian Physicist was worried about the fact that the universe did not seem to contain enough anti-matter. Indeed, it seemed to contain very little, less than on part in 10 billion. But most notions of symmetry required that there may be equal quantities. If protons could decay, Sakharov deduced, then even if the universe started with equal quantities of matter and anti-matter, there ultimately be more protons than anti-protons.

However, the protons could not live for ever but only for about 10^{32} years when everything will fade away into nothing or naught.

It must be noticed that Allah has not bound himself to wait till the decay of protons to live or endure for 10^{32} years. The knowledge of the collapse of the universe or the Doom is only with Allah. The Hour of the Doom is Appointed by Allah and it can happen any moment and any hour with the Will of Allah and Allah will manifest it at its proper time. Stephen Hawking says :

> 'One of the most amazing things is that the Universe should be so close to the dividing line between collapsing and expanding'.

And this is what the Holy Quran has revealed it 1400 years ago. Again, 'if the universe is closed, it could perhaps, keep bouncing back and forth in a cycle of different universes. If that is the case, the universe that we inhabit would be just one of many'. Attention of the reader is invited to the Holy verses (14:48), (36:81) and (17:99), besides the Holy Quranic verses quoted above.

Science and the Holy Quran in Agreement on the Roll up of Universe to Singularity and Zero Volume

In addition to what is already explained, imagine the universe running in reverse, an 18 billion-year reeling in of the galaxies and all other matter back toward the moment of birth—the condition prevailing at or near 'Zero Second'-T-equals zero—the moment of cosmic ignition. The Holy Quran reveals that the gravitational collapse of the universe shall happen at (the Hour of Doom) but as a twinkling of the eye or nearer still when Allah shall roll up the universes as a recorder rolleth up a written scroll.

After it Allah shall repeat the creation of the universe as He began the first creation. This is a promise given by Allah and He will perform it as Allah is the Creator, the Shaper out of naught, the Fashioner. All this is clearly revealed in the Holy Scripture with truth. Attention is invited to the Holy Quranic verses (16:77), (21:104), (7:187), (11:107), (42:17), (21:37), (13:39), (39:67), (60:24), (14:48)as quoted in this Chapter. The Holy Quran draws attention of mankind to the roll up of the universes and then to the re-emergence of the universe when the earth will be changed or fashioned to other than this earth and the universe will also be changed. The Holy verse (14:48) refers.

Science of Astrophysics is found to be in perfect similarity with the Holy Quranic verses. Attention of Scientists all over the World is invited to Study the Holy Quran and to thoroughly ponder over these holy verses which shall utterly surprise them.

As we approach zero, even the very best theory of space, time and gravitation - Einstein's theory of general relativity - seems to break down. It has the universe crunching down to a 'Singularity' - a single point of infinite density. It's beyond knowing. At zero seconds, the universe does what it pleases and there is no way it is going to tell us what it had in mind (Science 1981, June Issue, 'Why is the Cosmos 'Lumpy''? by Ben Patrusky).

From the above scientific description and in view of the Quranic verses it is very clear that science fact or knowledge achieved by man so far is in complete similarity and concord with the Holy Quran which lays great emphasis on learning and on knowledge. The similarity on the gravitational collapse of the universe is simply amazing and it leads to a clear proof that the Holy Quran is the Word of God revealed 1400 years ago on the last Prophet Muhammad (PBUH) for the knowledge, information and guidance of all mankind on earth. The ignorance of modern man of the lack of knowledge of the Holy Quran is a great misfortune and deprivation from Divine Mercy.

The above verses of the Holy Quran are to the point and the sense encompassed in them is very specific and direct and is in complete consonance with the most modern findings and facts of the science of Astrophysics and on the fate of universe. This is a clear token or portent of God for man to know and to ponder over the absolute realities. All these similarities and facts of science lead to the absolute conclusion that the Holy Quran is not man-made and cannot be man-made. It is the message of Allah for mankind Who is the Unimaginable God of mankind. It is for all mankind to take heed, ponder and take guidance from His message and follow the absolute truth revealed in the Holy Quran as it is the Word of God - the Creator of mankind, the heavens and the earth and of all that is in between them. The Holy Quran reveals physical and metaphysical events on and after the gravitational collapse of the universe i.e. of the Doomsday and of the Hereafter. Many facts are beyond man's comprehension. Chapter 14 on man's accountability before God in the Hereafter is an attempt to show that the metaphysics of Quran has a link with the physical universe and man and that physical events are linked with the metaphysical realities of the Holy Quran.

The Apocalypse of Gravitational Collapse

Wheeler, Einstein and Niels Bohr'sMax Planck and Professor Hawking's Scientific Concepts in similarity with the Holy Quran

The Scientific contribution by Einstein, Niels Bohr, Max Planck, Wheeler and Stephen Hawking on the universe and its physical laws for the interaction of matter, energy, time and space and for the Apocalypse of gravitational collapse are found to be in similarity with the Holy Quran describing the `Doomsday' 14 centuries ago.

John Archibald Wheeler says :-

> `We will first understand how simple the universe is when we recognize how strange it is".

John Archibald Wheeler is one of the most brilliant physicists who has helped to invent the theory of nuclear fission, contributed heavily to the design of the atomic and hydrogen bombs and made many other achievements. At present, he is working on `black hole' and other grant contingencies of nature, with an eye towards the `apocalypse of gravitational collapse' which the Holy Quran calls it the `Doomsday'. The revelations made by the Holy Quran clearly and directly describe the cataclysm and all the events of the Doomsday and give a complete picture of all the happenings to take place on earth and in the cosmos. The Quran describes the terrible state of the crushing of mountains and the powdering of the hills, all ground to atoms and the evaporation of the seas on earth as the events on the Doomsday . It further describes the gravitational collapse of the celestial bodies, the putting out and falling of stars, the engulfing of the moon by the sun, the gravitational collapse of the sun, the tearing away of the celestial bodies, the turning of the cosmos as molten copper and its becoming rosy like red hide and the opening of the heaven to become as gates for the next greatest event to be faced by man in the other world, i.e. the world of `life after death', i.e. the Hereafter.

The Holy Quran further describes that it will be the day when the heaven shall roll up, effacing all things and the sky will produce visible smoke. After it, Allah will repeat the creation of similar universe and similar earth and establish it according to His will, when on the Day, the earth and the universe will be changed to other than this earth and this universe. It is beyond all doubts that Allah has appointed an end to this earth and to this universe and He is able to create the like of them for He is All-wise Creator. The concerned verses of the Holy Quran on the Doomsday are quoted in the beginning of this Chapter .

Wheeler is one of the greatest Scientists who sifts and

weighs the provisory concepts of physical law, searching for what he calls 'the glittering central mechanism of the universe', and according to him, 'the Goal is to understand the plan of Creation'.

In short Wheeler actually wants to know the 'Creator' and then wants to know 'the Plan of His Creation'. For achieving the objective, first of all it is necessary to know the creation as far as possible. After studying the creation, one would know that the creation is one of the attributes of the Creator. Once one knows the attributes, then it is easy to know 'the glittering central mechanism of the universe' and 'the plan of creation'. Wheeler will be able to find tremendous knowledge, informations and guidance if he reads the Holy Quran and tries to grasp and understand the sense of the Holy verses in the context of his knowledge of the universe.

Niels Bohr is responsible for the development of Quantum Theory, which had revolutionized science. The uncertainty principle, a cornerstone of that revolution, placed fundamental limits on what could be known about nature. For example, it is impossible—even in theory—to determine simultaneously both the position and momentum of an electron. Measuring one quantity destroys the capability to measure the other, leading to severe paradoxes of nature.

Wheeler says: Conversations with Niels Bohr really convinced me that people like Buddha, Jesus, Moses and Confucius existed. This means Wheeler believed in them for what they did. Heavenly Books reveal, specially the Last Holy Book, the Quran, that Moses and Jesus were prophets of the Creator (Allah) and they performed miracles with the permission of Allah. The acts of miracles are not explainable by the physical laws. These are paradoxes of nature and make the ordinary physical laws of nature as incomprehensible. But all such miracles performed by the prophets of Allah, were with the Will of Creator Allah and were all perfect reality and these miracles actually happened. May be Quantum theory be able to explain the miracles!

Niels Bohr operated according to the dialectical notion that without paradox there is no hope of progress, a belief he deeply instilled in Wheeler 'A great truth', according to Bohr, 'is a truth whose opposite is also a great truth'.

According to Einstein's Theory, gravity is just geometry; space is warped by the presence of matter or energy just as a mattress sags under a heavy body. The greater the local concentration of mass, the tighter the curvature of space around it.

What happens to stars when their thermonuclear fires ran out of fuel and gravity crushed them inward.

A star the size of our sun would shrink to a white dwarf about as big as the earth, while gravity could hammer heavier stars into a solid ball of neutrons weighing billions of tons per teaspoonful—a joint atomic nucleus 20 miles in diameter. The neutron—star stage, further contracts to such a density that space would be warped around it like a black fist; neither light nor anything else would ever be able to leave the star. The remains of the star would be squeezed to an infinitely dense point crushing itself out of existence, space would be infinitely curved. The result is a cosmic dead and called a singularity, where general relativity, space, time and even the Laws of Physics break down.

On an Appointed Day, the prevailing of such conditions in the whole Universe is described by the Quran in the verse (21:104) as follows:-

> *'The Day when We shall roll up the heavens as a recorder rolleth up a written scroll. As we began the first creation. We shall repeat it. (It is) a promise (binding) upon us. Lo! We are to perform it' (21:104).*

Wheeler realized that if one takes general relativity seriously, this gravitational catastrophe is a real possibility and he gave this strange creation of nature, the name of 'black hole'. The Holy Quran refers to such things as the 'invisible' of the heaven. To Wheeler a 'black hole' is only a rehearsal for the ultimate cataclysm that he believes will ring down the curtain of creation at the end of the universe. In this so called Big Crunch, the bell tolls for us all.

According to the Holy Quran this 'ultimate cataclysm' is the Doomsday . And the Day fixed for the Doomsday is only in the knowledge of Allah. The Holy Quran makes the following revelations :-

(1) *'Abiding there so long as the heavens and the earth endure save for that which thy Lord Willeth, Lo! thy Lord is Doer of what He will'. (11:107).*

(2) *'They ask thee of the (destined) Hour, when will it come to port. Say: Knowledge thereof is with my Lord only. He alone will manifest it at its proper time. It is heavy in the heavens and the earth. It cometh not to you save unawares. They Question thee as if thou*

couldst be well informed thereof. Say: Knowledge thereof is with Allah only, but most of mankind know not'. (7:187).

(3) '*Allah effaceth what He will and establisheth (What He will) and with Him is source of Ordinance*'. (13:39).

(4) '*But watch thou (O Muhammad) for the day when the sky will produce visible smoke*' (44:10).

(5) '*The Day when the sky will become as molten copper*'. (70:8).

(6) '*On the Day when the heaven will heave with (awful) heaving*'. (52:7).

(7) '*Those who disbelieve say: The Hour will never come unto us. Say: Nay, by my Lord, but it is coming unto you surely. (He is) the Knower of the Unseen. Not an atom's weight or less than that, or greater, escapeth Him in the heavens or in the earth, but it is in a clear record*'. (34:3).

(8) '*And unto Allah belongeth, the unseen of the heavens and the earth and the matter of the Hour (of Doom) is but as a twinkling of the eye, or it is nearer still. Lo! Allah is Able to do all things*'. (16:77).

(9) '*And they esteem not Allah as He hath the right to be esteemed, when the whole earth is His handful on the Day of Resurrection, and the heavens are rolled in His right hand. Glorified is He and High Exalted from all that they ascribe as partners (unto Him)* (39:67).

(10) '*Man is made of haste. I shall show you My portents, but ask Me not to hasten*'. (21:37).

The Holy Quran in the above verses, confirms the apocalypse of the gravitational collapse of the universe. Allah is the Knower of the unseen of the heavens and the earth which all belongs to Him. The Quran reveals that not an atom's weight or less than that i.e. a sub-atomic or sub-nuclear particles or greater, escapes the notice of Allah and that everything is in a clear Record.

Today Wheeler refers to black holes as 'gates of time'. It is not the blackness of their surface that interests him, it is the utter oblivion at their centre. 'There is no 'after' after the big crunch, just as there is no 'before' before the big bang', he stresses, therefore, 'Space and time are not fundamental categories of nature'. In fact time dies.

As a star or the universe contracts to microscopic dimensions, even geometry has to pay its dues to the uncertainty principle, destinies become probabilities.

If the universe contracts according to the laws of black hole physics, there is a chance says Wheeler—that a new universe could emerge with a different geometry. The big crunch would turn into another big bang. The result would be an oscillating universe, an endless cycle of cosmic expansion and contraction. The changing of the universe from shape to shape takes place on a stage that Wheeler calls super space, an abstract infinite dimensional space in which each point corresponds to an entire configuration or geometry of the universe. 'Super space is not some poetic fancy', insists Wheeler. 'It is the dynamic arena of general relativity'. As it evolves, the universe—according to this theory—traces a slightly fuzzy line from one point, the big bang, to another, the big crunch. At that point does another line, another universe take off?

Answer to this question already exists in the Holy Quran, which certainly says Yes! Another universe shall take off and that is a Promise from God which He made Binding on Himself: The Holy verse (21:104) given below refers.

The above scientific concepts and findings of Wheeler are in congruity with the revelations of the Holy verses of Quran on the Physical universe as given below :-

(1) *'The day when We shall roll up the heavens as a recorder rolleth up a written scroll. As We began the first creation, We shall repeat, it. (It is) a promise (binding) upon us. Lo! We are to perform it'. (21:104).*

(2) *'On the Day When the earth will be changed to other than this earth, and heavens (also will be changed) and they will come-forth unto Allah, the One, the Almighty'. (14:48).*

(3) *'Is not He Who created the heavens and the earth Able to create the like of them? Aye, that He is: for He is All-Wise Creator' (36:81).*

(4) *'Have they not seen that Allah Who created the heavens and the earth is Able to Create the like of them and hath appointed for them an end whereof there is no doubt? But the wrong doers refuse aught save disbelief' (17:99).*

The above Quranic verses are in great similarity with the ultimate cataclysm and gravitational collapse of the universe and with the contraction of the universe to microscopic dimension and with the primordial nothing, and then with the laws of black hole physics, which indicate that a new universe could emerge with a different geometry.

Wheeler says: Such a re-emergent universe—reprocessed by gravity's eraser—might not resemble our own. Super-space is an infinite ensemble of possible worlds; there is room for universes, in which all stars are red or blue or in which there are no stars at all. Most of these universes, Wheeler notes, are 'still born', they contain no life. The question is—Is life possible in any of these alternatives? Wheeler and other cosmologists have suggested that our own universe is uniquely tuned to produce life, the way a plant exists to grow a flower. We might be in effect, the crown of creation. By this admittedly self centered logic, known as the anthropic principle, the universe is the way it is because we are here having some how selected it from the super universe of possibilities.

The following Quranic verses grouped as A, B and C which are in similarity with science, are quoted for the guidance of cosmologists and physicists :-

(A) (1) *'Then He ordained them seven heavens in two days and inspired in each heaven its mandate: and We decked the nether heaven with lamps, and rendered it inviolable. This is the measuring of the Mighty, the Knower' (41:12).*

(2) *'Lo! We have adorned the lowest heaven with an ornament, the planets' (37:6).*

(3) *'And verily in the heaven We have set mansions of the stars and We have beautified it for beholders' (15:16).*

(B) (1) *'Ye are the best community that hath been raised up for mankind. Ye enjoin right conduct and forbid indecency; and Ye believe in Allah' (68:110).*

(2) *'Surely We created man of the best stature' (XCIV:4).*

(3) *'And inspired it (with Conscience of) what is wrong for it and (what is) right for it' (XCI:8).*

(4) *'Verily We have honoured the Children of Adam. We carry them on the land and the sea, and have made provision of good things for them, and have preferred them above many of those whom We created with a marked preferment' (17:70).*

(C) (1) *'And We created not the heavens and the earth and all that is in between them, in play' (44:38).*

(2) *'Not without purpose did We create heaven and earth and all that is between them in vain, that is the opinion of those who disbelieve. And woe unto those who disbelieve in the Fire' (38:27).*

The above three sets of the verses (A, B and C), reveal that there are seven heavens or universes, each created with a different mandate. Out of these the lowest universe or the nearest universe or our universe is decked with stars and is beautified for beholders. It is also adorned with planets which are like ornaments of the universe, as are the earth and the moon and other planets. Man is created in this universe as the most superior creation and he is given conscience of what is wrong for it and what is right for it. Man is therefore, created as a responsible being and according to Wheeler he is rightly 'the crown of creation', as the Holy Quran reveals that man is preferred above the creations Allah created with a marked preferment. The universe is not created without purpose or in play but is created for mankind who are the crown of creation and because we are here.

The above Holy verses make it clear that nothing is created without a purpose and that every creation is created with a purpose to perform.

Einstein wondered whether God had any choice in the creation of the world; so does Wheeler. They and other cosmologists will find answer to their question in the following Holy Quranic verses :-

(1) *'Abiding there so long as the heavens and the earth endure save for that which thy Lord willeth: Lo! thy Lord is Doer of What He will' (11:107).*

(2) *'Allah effaceth what He will and establisheth (What He will) and with Him is source of Ordinance'. (13:39).*

(3) *'Allah it is Who hath created seven heavens and of the earth the like thereof. The Commandment cometh down among them slowly, that ye may know that Allah is Able to do all things, and that Allah surroundeth all things in knowledge'. (66:12).*

(4) *'Allah createth what He will. Lo! Allah is Able to do all things'. (24:45).*

(5) *'And Our word unto a thing, when We intend it is only that We say unto it: Be! and it is'. (16:40).*

(6) *'The Originator of the heavens and the earth! When He decreeth a thing. He saith unto it only: Be: and it is' (II:117).*

(7) *'But His Command, When He intendeth a thing, is only that He saith unto it: Be! and it is' (36:82).*

(8) *'Glory be to Him: When He decreeth a thing, He saith unto it only. Be! and it is' (19:35).*

(9) *'He it is Who created the heavens and the earth in truth. In that day when He saith: Be! and it is' (6:73).*

(10) *'Hast thou not known that Allah knoweth all that is in the heaven*

and the earth? Lo! it is in a record. Lo! that is easy for Allah' (22:70).

The above Holy verses reveal that God is the Originator of the heavens and the earth. Allah is Doer of what He will and with Him is source of Ordinance. When Allah orders a thing, He says unto it only, Be! and it is. Allah is All Powerful, All Knowledgeable and All-Wise Creator. Allah has Infinite choices and the power in the creation of any thing He wills. The creation, extinction and re-creation of the universe is not a process of a mechanical repeater, without an All Powerful Mechanic behind it. There is a 'Creative Will' of the Creator behind the creation. Force or a machine has no Will. It is the 'unimaginable Supreme Living and Eternal Being' Who has the Will to do any thing He likes and He is Allah, the Lord of the worlds.

Man should not forget that there is limitation on human observational power. Science is a human enterprise, carried out by human beings, employing sense organs, muscular structure and a nervous system, as well as auxiliary tools of manipulation and observation. There could be many things which are hidden, invisible, unseen, unimaginable and inconceivable which lie beyond the observation and the power of human understanding and capabilities. The existence of such realities cannot be denied simply because these are beyond the power of observation or understanding of human beings and that human beings are not designed to perceive all such matters.

The Holy Quran frequently mentions the invisibles of the heavens and the earth and the unseen. These include the jinn, which is a parallel creation to man but is not perceivable to man and are not detectable by known physical laws. Similarly, the Holy Quran reveals that life exists in space, which may be created out of different substance to live in various unimaginable environments. The subject is already discussed in the relevant Chapter of this book.

Wheeler's present position has evolved to embrace a new concept he terms 'Observership'. He now believes that 'Unless the blind dice of mutation and natural selection lead to life and consciousness and observership at some point down the road, the universe could not have come into being in the first place'.

Wheeler's thinking has expanded from super-space and black holes to the concept of what he terms an observer-dependent, participatory universe. Wheeler has the concept that the plan of creation is intimately related to the quantum uncertainty principle. 'In some strange sense the quantum principle tells us that we are dealing with a participatory universe', he concludes. Without an observer, there is no physics', the strange sense of the quantum principle indicates and leads one to the belief that We are dealing with a participatory universe and that without the Creator Allah, there is no matter, energy, time, space and the physical laws for interaction and changes. This is what the Holy Quran reveals in the verse given below :-

> *'He is Allah, the Creator, the Shaper out of naught, the Fashioner. His are the most beautiful names. All that is in the heavens and the earth glorifieth Him and He is the Mighty, the Wise'. (60:24).*

Wheeler wonders if this principle could be a prescription for building the Laws of Physics out of the primordial nothing—a command to create, to counterpose against the black hole's urge to destroy: The gates of time tell us that physics must be built from a foundation of no physics'. In this respect the Holy Quran guides as follows :-

(1) *'But His Command, when He intendeth a thing, is only that He saith unto it only, Be! and it is' (19:35).*
(2) *'But Ye prefer the Life of the World'. (88:16).*
(3) *'Although the Hereafter is better and more lasting'. (88:17).*
(4) *'That We may transfigure you and make you what Ye know not'. (56:61).*
(5) *'A gift of welcome from the Forgiving, the Merciful'. (41:32).*

The above Quranic verses indicate that Allah establishes what He will and with Him is source of Ordinance. (13:39). He commands: Be! and it is done. On the gravitational collapse of the universe and its extinction to primordial nothing, man will find himself into the gates of the 'Hereafter' on his resurrection. There, he will be free of time. He will enter a better and eternal world, which is a gift from Allah. May be that man find himself in somewhat different form in the 'Hereafter'.

Wheeler's philosophy of science is much more radically relativistic than Einstein. Wheeler would make all physical law relative to observers. He has us creating physical laws by our existence. In principle, if the role of observer in the universe is as essential as he imagines, life may even create physical laws by conscious decision. This is a radical departure from the objective reality in which Einstein believed so firmly. Explains physicist Freeman Dyson of the Institute for Advance Study.

Boiled down, Wheeler's new intellectual adventure is summarized by these succinct words of his :-

> Of all strange features of the universe, none are stranger than these: 'Time is transcended, Laws are mutable and observer - participancy matters'.

From the above intellectual conclusion and from the theories of 'genesis and observership' of Wheeler, one finds that Wheeler is a great genius, a man of great mental capacity and one of the greatest scientists whose cosmological findings are of far-reaching consequences and revolutionary in nature in the sense that his concepts are very close to know the reality of nature and to know the reality of the existence of Allah and Allah as the Creator of the heavens and the earth as is revealed by the Holy Quran. Wheeler's concepts are in similarity with the Holy Quran in respect of the physical universe, its cataclysmic collapse and its re-emergence and in respect of the 'Hereafter', when he concludes that time is transcended.

Wheeler says: 'Time is transcended'. This means time is separate from or beyond the material universe, and is beyond human knowledge or is existing apart from the material universe. This is as of the 'Hereafter' and is a hint to the Hereafter. The Holy Quran reveals that the 'Hereafter' is certain.

Again, Wheeler says: 'Laws are mutable'.

This means the physical laws are changeable. The change is because of 'the Will of the Creator of the Law' according to His Will and plan of creation. The Holy Quran reveals that the Creator is the Doer of What He Will and is Able to do all things and that is easy for Him.

Finally, Wheeler says:-

> 'And observer-participancy matters'.

This conveys sense that the will or the command of the Creator over His creations or the universe matters. The Creator has the absolute power over His creations which will participate and obey and submit to the will of the Creator and act perfectly according to the appointed physical laws of the Creator.

Wheeler Says:-

> The best way to find oneself outside the ranks of science is to find oneself inside the rank of mysticism'.

The doctrines or beliefs of mystics are that it is possible to achieve communication with God through contemplation and love without the medium of human reason. Mysticism is the possibility of attaining knowledge of spiritual truths through intuition acquired by fixed meditation.

— Wheeler wonders if nature can be thought of as a giant, self-organizing computer. The reply to such an unreligious observation is that a computer must have a creator and a Creator of Infinite dimensions, with Infinite power, Infinite knowledge and Infinite wisdom to feed the computer with Infinite functions so that everything fits together. To create life and all physical things, and build the structure of atom with might, and then to expand the innumerable galactic systems in the cosmos and then its evolution, sustenance and a perfect celestial order and again its catastrophic collapse and its re-emergence could never be the act of any mechanical, electrical, nuclear or a similar force, or a machine. These forces are the created one. Mere force of any amount is nothing as mere force is not living and thinking and has no sense, knowledge and wisdom and the will to act. The Will of Allah the Alive, the Eternal, is the 'creative energy' of the Divine Command, Be! and its becoming, when matter and energy was created and the structure of the atom with sub-atomic particles was built with might 'in a set measure, in true proportions' and in due proportions' as the Holy Quran reveals:-

Wheeler says:-

> 'If there is one thing in physics I feel more responsible for than any other it's this perception of how everything fits together. I like to think of myself as having a sense of judgement. I am willing to go anywhere, talk to anybody, ask any question that will make headway. I

confess to being an optimist about things, especially this question about our hopes of being able to understand how things are put together'.

More important than 'how everything fits together' in physics, is 'how everything is created' beyond physics, and who created? Physics only deals with physical matter already in existence either in the form of matter or energy. The Creator is beyond physics. One knows the Creator from His physical creations and from the sense of judgement and from the revelations of the Holy Quran (the Word of God) If Wheeler wants to make headway, he is advised to get knowledge, wisdom, information and guidance from the verses of the Holy Quran and grasp the sense out of it in the context of his knowledge of physics and cosmology. He (Wheeler) will know the Creator from the attributes of the Creator as is already mentioned in the relevant Chapter. The Creator of Inifinite dimensions and attributes is behind the glittering central mechanism of the universe and the Holy Quran is the key to understand the plan of His Creation. Wheeler will find the right answers to his questions and shall know the absolute reality of the existence of Allah as the Creator of all things i.e. the physical universe with time and space, man, all the invisible the hidden and the unseen, the jinn, and all the physical undetectable matters and things, and the 'Hereafter'. It is Allah Who manages how everything fits together.

The Holy Quran beautifully reveals :-

> *'(He is) the Knower of the Unseen. Not an atom's weight, or less than that or greater, escapeth Him in the heavens or in the earth, but it is in a clear record'. (34:3).*

Man must study nature and know its Creator Who created all things at sub-atomic and sub-nuclear level out of 'naught' so that he knows how everything fits together. It is the sound knowledge, faith and the wisdom which reveals the wonders of nature and which enables man to grasp and understand the Holy Quran as the word of Allah and know Allah the Creator of all things in the physical universe and in the Hereafter.

Dr. Robert Jestrow, Director of NASA's Goddard Institute for Space Studies and Professor of Astronomy and Geology at the Columbia University said in an article in 'The New York Times' that:

'for the Scientist who has lived by his faith in power of reason the story ends like a bad dream. He has scaled the mountains of ignorance, he is about to conquer the highest peak, as he pulls himself over the final rock he is greeted by a band of theologians who have been sitting there for centuries'.

Similarly, **Napoleon Bonaparte** said :-

'I hope the time is not far off when I shall be able to unite all the wise and educated men of all the countries and establish a uniform regime based on the principles of the Quran, which alone are true and which alone can lead men to happiness'. (Napoleon Bonaparte et l' Islam' by Cherfils, Paris, pp. 105—125).

Science and the Quran on the Creation of the Universe from the State of Singularity and Zero Volume and from 'Naught'

The Convergence of all Forces into Singularity and Zero Volume and the Emergence of all forces from Infinite Density and Zero Volume at the time of Big Bang

Stephen Hawking Professor of Applied Mathematics and Theoretical Physics at Cambridge University, England, is a distinguished scientist. Some scientists believe that Hawking may be able to postulate the single theory that will unite the two branches of physics that have been at odds with one another for half a century. Quantum Mechanics, which describes the behaviour of matter at the atomic level, and General Relativity, which explains the workings of the universe as a whole.

Hawking's arena is the physics of black holes, those theoretical regions of space so dense and so distorted by Einsteinian Gravitational effects that nothing, not even light, can escape from them. However, Hawking showed that tiny black holes could emit radiation and eventually explode. It was a startling proposition. It convinced Hawking and others that long-sought, single unifying theory—the so-called Holy Grail of Physics—that would explain all the interactions of matter and all the forces that control them lay within the black hole.

Black hole lives most of its life as an ordinary star, withstanding a tug-of-war between the powerful outward force of its heat and radiation and the strong inward thrust of gravity. But when the star's nuclear fuel is spent, it dies, collapsing under its own weight to a point where gravity is so strong that not even light can escape. It is there in the black hole, which defies all the laws of physics, that Hawking hopes to unite the twin pillars of 20th century physics. Einstein's theory of General relativity and Max Planck's quantum theory. So far the two theories have been as incompatible as fire and water. No one, not even Einstein, has been able to unify them.

Einstein's great achievement, the General Theory of Relativity, says that gravity, which affects the behaviour of the universe, its planets, stars, and galaxies is a basic property of 'curved' space—a kind of tension in the interstellar void.

Quantum theory, on the other hand describes the behaviour of atoms and their sub-nuclear particles. At the heart of quantum mechanics is the uncertainty principles, which states that certain pairs of quantities, such as the position and momentum of particle, cannot be measured simultaneously. This means that the electron, for example, is not only a particle, as classical physicists had envisioned it, but a wave that would have to be smeared out around the nucleus of the atom.

Thus the paradox: General relativity says that large objects—rocks, foot-balls, planets, stars, behave in a predictable manner, while quantum theory maintains that at the atomic level, matter behaves randomly. Clearly there cannot be separate rules for different parts of the universe. Einstein spent the last 30 years of his life trying to resolve the problem. 'God does not play dice with the Universe', he said, rebelling against the randomness of quantum mechanics.

Unifying quantum theory and general relativity would remove the last barrier to understanding why the universe is the way it is and that is the goal toward which Stephen Hawking is working.

At Cambridge Hawking Collaborated with Penrose and they used a new mathematical system they had devised. They developed a number of theories about singularities, those cosmic specs of infinite density and zero volume in the middle of black holes. They were able to show with intricate mathematics that the universe as a whole was a singularity when the Big Bang occurred 16 to 17 billion years ago. 'In other words, time has a beginning', says Hawking.

The Holy Quran reveals that the universe is created by Allah with His creative Power out of 'naught' which in the process indicates that the universe was created from a singularity and zero volume and before that from absolutely naught. Almighty God shaped and set the measure for all physical laws to emerge from the state of singularity and zero volume when Quantum Mechanic and General Relativity, uncertainty principles, all the four (now three) kinds of interactions or fundamental forces were united into one and emerged from one source i.e. out of naught' with the 'Creative Force' of Allah.

The Holy Quran reveals :-

(1) *'He is Allah, the Creator, the Shaper out of naught, the Fashioner. His are the most beautiful names. All that is in the heavens and the earth glorifieth Him and He is the Mighty, the Wise' (60:24).*

(2) *'Lo! We have created everything by measure' (54:49).*

(3) *'.....And everything with Him is measured' (13:8).*

Hawking reasoned, again mathematically, that millions of minuscule black holes, the size of protons in the nucleus of an atom could be squeezed into existence by the cataclysmic force of the Big Bang. He calculated that these mini-holes were created within the first 10^{-20} seconds after the Big Bang. That is a decimal point followed by 19 zeros and a one which expresses a vanishingly small fragment of time. Hawking's mini-black holes explained so many previously unexplained phenomena supplying the so-called missing mass, for instance, needed to close the universe that the idea quickly won wide acceptance.

What Hawking proposed was that black holes, in defiance of every known principle, emit a steady stream of particles. What had convinced him that black holes a creation of general relativity, could emit particles under the right conditions was the application of quantum theory to the problem. He reasoned that the uncertainty principle, the back bone of quantum mechanics, declares that space is active and cluttered. Pairs of elementary particles like electrons and their anti-matter opposites, positrons, spontaneously come into being and exist for a fraction of a second before uniting and cancelling each other out. Hawking argued that the energy for this instantaneous creation and annihilation could come from a gravitational field nearby.

If such an event were carried out at the edge of the black hole at the event horizon, as it is called one of the particles might wander down into the black hole never to be seen again. But the other particle theoretically could escape. To an observer, it would appear as if the particle had been ejected by the black hole.

Still aghast at his own findings, Hawking demonstrated that black holes evaporate over a long period of time because these 'virtual' particles that Hawking envisions need energy to escape.

This was Hawking's first step toward merging general relativity with Quantum Theory. But evaporating and exploding black holes were so out of sync with conventional wisdom that Hawking, usually sure of his intellectual creations, doubted his own results.

In February 1974 Hawking presented a paper called 'black hole Explosions', which stunned and confused his colleagues.

Hawking radiation, as black hole emission is called, demonstrates that the holes are not cut off from the rest of the universe as scientists used to think but are part of the continuum of space and time. In a quiet rejoinder to Einstein, Hawking says: 'God not only plays dice (with the universe) but also sometimes throws them where they cannot be seen'. Here Hawking refers to the unseen of the universe.

In this context Einstein once said to Niels Bohr in the context of General Relativity, Quantum theory and uncertainty principle:-

> 'Do you believe that God plays dice with the Universe'.

In the same context Niels Bohr replied:-

> 'Do not tell God what to play'.

Recently Hawking has gone further and he says :-

> 'God not only plays dice (with the universe), but also sometimes throws them where they cannot be seen'

All these remarks on the behaviour of matter and energy in the universe progressively indicate that God exists with Infinite Power, Knowledge, Wisdom and His 'Creative Power' has created matter, energy and life out of 'naught', a stage or a period before singularity and zero volume. Later on or in the next stage or period things were brought to the stage or period of singularity and zero volume and then in the third stage the Big Bang occurred and in the subsequent stage or period (probably the fourth stage or period), the expansion of the universe and its evolutionary process is taking place by the interaction of fundamental forces under the physical laws i.e. Quantum Mechanics, General Relativity,Special Relativity, Uncertainty principle, and all the four (now three) fundamental interacting forces took effect. The planet formation (earth) and the creation of life on it are probably the remaining fifth and sixth stages or periods. The Holy Quran indicates all these stages or periods with a similitude of 'Day' in the creation and formation of the Seven heavens including our universe and the earth. To understand the Holy Quran, one has to go to the level of sub-atomic or sub-nuclear particles, and to the level of particle physics in respect of the universe and to the level of atom and Molecular Biology in respect of life where creation of life and the Resurrection of life are indicated by Allah in the Holy Quran.

Allah's 'Creative Power' at the level of sub-atomic particle or sub-nuclear particle and at the level of atomic and molecular level with the spirit at His Command does all things as He likes. So, the creation of universe and its form, and its obliteration and the creation of life and death and its Resurrection and the creation of eternal world as the 'hereafter' and the resurrection of mankind to stay immortal in the Hereafter is an easy matter for Allah, as Allah is Able to do all things. Man would know all these things if he achieves sound knowledge and have faith in the Revelations of the Holy Quran. A few Holy verses are quoted for thorough pondering in the context of sciences.

The Holy Quran reveals :-

(1) *'Then He ordained them seven heavens in two days and inspired in each heaven its mandate; We decked the nether heaven with lamps and rendered it inviolable. That is the measuring of the Mighty, the Knower'. (41:12).*

(2) *'And He it is Who created the heavens and the earth in six days and His Throne was upon water that He might try you, which of you is best in conduct. Ye it thou (O Muhammad) sayest: Lo! Ye will be*

raised again after death! Those who disbelieve will surely say: This is naught but open magic.

(3) *'Allah Createth what He will. Lo! Allah is Able to do all things'. (24:45).*

(4) *'Allah is the Originator of the heavens and the earth and He ordered in that Day when He said: Be! and it is'. (29:35)(6:73) (2:117).*

(5) *'He is Knower of every creation'. (36:79).*

(6) *'Everything have We recorded in a Book'. (77:29).*

(7) *'Verily, We shall give life to the dead'. (36:12).*

(8) *'That is easy for Allah'. (64:7).*

(9) *'He is the Knower of the invisible and the visible, the Great, the High Exalted'. (13:9).*

(10) *'He is the Knower of the Unseen, Not an atom's weight, or less than that or greater, escapeth Him in the heavens or in the earth, but it is in a clear record'. (34:3).*

(11) *Abiding there so long as the heavens and the earth endure save for that which thy Lord willeth. Lo! thy Lord is Doer of What He will'. (11:107).*

(12) *'And Our Commandment is but one (Commandment) as the twinkling of an eye'. (54:50).*

(13) *'And with Him are the keys of the invisible. None but He knoweth them. And He knoweth what is in the land and the sea. Not a leaf falleth but He knoweth it, not a grain amid the darkness of the earth, naught of wet or dry but (it is noted) in a clear record' (6:59).*

The above Holy verses clearly indicate the Creative Power of Allah, His Infinite Knowledge, Infinite Power and Infinite Wisdom and the interaction of the fundamental forces at His Command and clearly indicate His created laws governing them and their single source of singularity and zero volume out of which they emerge and to which they converge. The verses indicate about the General Relativity, Special Relativity, Quantum Mechanics Uncertainty principles and all the fundamental forces governing matter and energy. Above all, the Holy Quran indicates much beyond all this and reveals that Allah is the Creator and the Knower of all things. The Holy verses indicate the creation of the universe, the stages of creation, the emergence of forces from a single source, the creation of earth, the creation of life on earth, the creation of man, a strange assembly of atoms infused with life, and above all reveals about the Creator, Who is the Knower of all things and who have recorded everything in a Book and Who shall give life to the dead by

Resurrection in the Hereafter and which is easy for Him as Allah is Able to do all things. Lo! Allah is Doer of What He will. He knows the visible, the invisible, the hidden and the unseen. Everything is in His knowledge. Not a leaf fall but He knows it. All things are in clear Record. And Allah is the Originator of the universe and the earth and He ordered in that Day when He said: Be! and it is. Allah created seven heavens or universes in two Days or in two period or stages and the universes and the earth in six days or stages or periods. The sciences of Cosmogony, Cosmology, Astrophysics, and Quantum Mechanics, the uncertainty principle and the science of Biology and Genetics reveal the same.

The Creator Allah has revealed the Holy Quran a Holy Document of miracles on Prophet Muhammad (PBUH) for the guidance of all mankind. The Holy Quran, therefore, reveals hints about the creation of universe and man. These hints are portents for mankind to know the Creator through the knowledge and wisdom of the Holy Quran and through the study and observations of God's Creation of the universe and of man, by man with his inspired conscience which enables him to know what is wrong and what is right. The more science advances, the more you know about God's Creation and the more you have faith in the Holy Quran as the word of God or the message of Allah revealed on Prophet Muhammad (PBUH) for the guidance of all mankind. Allah is beyond all these physical things and beyond matter and energy. Allah is the Alive, the Aware, the Subtile, the Seer, the Eternal, the Creator of the All things, the Shaper out of naught, the Fashioner, the Omniscient, the Omnipresent, the Omnipotent and the Omnific. He is the Creator of All things. He is the unimaginable Supreme Being, with Infinite Power, Infinite Knowledge, Infinite Wisdom and Infinite of All things.

The Inviolable Universe is being Hit by Black holes and Singularities Ultimately Turning it into the Inevitable Nothingness. Beyond that Lies the World of the Hereafter where Space and Time have no Meanings. The Hereafter is the World of Immortality where Mankind shall be Resurrected by Allah as Revealed in the Holy Quran

Man on death is destined for the Hereafter in the meta-physical world which lies beyond the seven heavens or the physical worlds of space and time. The gravitational collapse of the physical universe, literally to nothing or naught is an inescapable feature of a gravity powered cosmos as the Holy Quran reveals and as the science of Astrophysics shows. The gravitational collapse or the roll up of the universe into the state of singularity, zero volume and nothingness is a process which is decreed by Allah as the Holy Quran reveals. As is evident, black hole and singularity establishes a bridge into the enigmatic parallel worlds which lie one above the other. This universe is connected with a different cosmos above it. The Holy Quran reveals seven universes one above the other. Our universe is the lowest and is decked with stars which is connected through pathways or through the interiors of the black holes with the one above it. When singularity hits the universe, then nothing remains physical. The singularity is certainly nature's greatest crisis. The singularity marks the end of the physical world and the end of physics as well as the end of the space and time. Physicist Paul Davies says that there can be nothing 'beyond' that is in any sense relevant to the affairs of our world, for no influence whatever can cross the barrier of the singularity. Of course, one can imagine all manner of things to be located on the far side of a singularity, but that is idle speculation, because no observation or experiment can ever be performed to test the idea or to support one picture rather than another. The singularity seems to mark the edge of anything that we can know. These views are expressed by Paul Davies, theoretical physicist at the University of Newcastle-upon-Tyne, under the article 'Exploring The Naked Singularity', published by Science Digest May, 1982. Paul Davies has also written 'Other Worlds' and 'Runaway Universe' and 'The Edge of Infinity', published by Simon and Schuster.

Paul Davies further says that if these ideas are right, it is clear that the details of gravitational collapse and space time singularities will be profoundly modified when the star shrinks to these unimaginable minute dimensions. In that case, a singularity need not necessarily be regarded as an edge of the physical universe but, less drastically, as an edge of space and or time only, what lies beyond space and time we do not know.

Einstein on religion once said:-

> "Science without religion is lame, religion without science is blind".

Science and the Holy Quran in agreement on the gravitational collapse of universe to singularity and zero volume and its re-emergence

As per revelation of the Holy Quran, Islam is perfected by God as a religion and then chosen it for man to follow it.

The Holy Quran is a Divine message for all mankind and clearly reveals knowledge and wisdom, information and guidance about the singularity and the roll up of the universe into nothing and the re-emergence of a similar universe out of nothing. It reveals about the Hereafter, which is life after death and is existence beyond the Physical worlds, where mankind shall be resurrected and shall stay immortal. The Holy Quran further reveals that the world of the Hereafter which awaits mankind has the Paradise which is as wide as the seven heavens besides the Hell. It clearly means that the metaphysical world of the Hereafter is boundless.

The glorious Quran reveals about all these things either in allegory or in direct form and men of sound knowledge and wisdom can find answers to such questions as raised by Paul Davies. These are:

(1) Have Scientists discovered the boundary of physical universe?

(2) Or have they come upon a world where space and time have no meanings?

(3) What lies beyond space and time?

Answers to the above questions in the light of Holy Quran are as follows:-

(1) In reality there are seven universes. The nearest physical universe which is ours is decked with stars and galaxies and is expanding and has been rendered inviolable even for the velocity of light. So, the universe in which we live is boundless. It is therefore beyond man's power and ability to find the boundary of even the nearest physical universe, what to speak of others which lie above this one.

(2) Beyond the seven heavens or universes is a world of the Hereafter where space and time have no meaning. Mankind is destined there via the singularities where he will be immortal on resurrection.

(3) Beyond space and time lies the world of immortality a metaphysical world or the world of the Hereafter. On the Doomsday and on resurrection, when there is

Accountability and Judgement, mankind shall be in the world of the Hereafter and after accountability man would either go to the Paradise or to the Hell with reference to the performance of his deeds in the Physical world, which are even recorded by the skin and its bio-chip molecular computers serving as bugging devices on man and function as God's envoys. The details on Accountability are given in Chapter 14 and Chapter 17 deal with the Hereafter.

Understanding the Miracles, the Doctrines and the Teachings of the Holy Quran — The Message of God in the Context of and at the Level of Quantum Theory which Ultimately Merge at a Microscopic Level with the Law of Casualty (Cause and Effect)

The Holy Quran reveals that sound knowledge gives a clear understanding of the wisdom encompassed in its Holy verses. This wisdom is understandable and can be interpretted in the context of quantum theory, particle physics, singularity and zero volume, molecular and cell biology, RNA, DNA and genetic engineering in respect of universe and man.

Quantum, a Latin word meaning "how much", is used by scientists to denote some very difficult ideas, says Heinz R. Pagels, Associate Professor of Physics at Rockefeller University New York City, in his book, The Cosmic Code, the comments on which are made by Malcolm W. Browne as appeared in Discover, May 1982 issue. The quantum pioneers are personalities like, Planck, Bohr, Heisenberg, Pauli, Dirac and the rest.

Quantum theory is the foundation of all branches of Science. It reveals something very disquieting about the tenuous foundation of human existence. Human beings live in a world dominated by cause and effect, a world seemingly remote from the quantum realm of the atom, where a wholly different set of rules applies. But, as Bagels points out, the world perceived by human beings is constructed from that other world, and the two actually merge at a microscopic level. We cannot help being affected in subtle ways by quantum principles, many of which fly in the face of experience, intuition, and logic. The revelation of the Holy Quran on Prophet Muhammad (PBUH), which is a Divine act and an absolute reality as its sense and substance its wisdom and knowledge reveals, must clearly be understandable in the context of quantum theory and other physical laws and with faith as the means to understand all that which lie beyond the comprehension of man.

Experience tells us that a single object cannot be in different places at the same time, and yet quantum particles disobey this rule without violating their own peculiar logic; the expression 'either or' loses meaning at the microscopic level; one can never say that a particle must be either in one place or another. For that matter, the quantum particles that make up everything in the universe are not even objects, in the usual sense, but can be viewed as expressions of abstract waves of probability implies possibility (even when possibility is very remote), magical, impossible things seem to happen in the quantum world.

For example, it is impossible by definition for anything to penetrate an impenetrable barrier, and yet electrons, riding on the magic carpets of probability waves, do adjust that, materializing in places that ordinary logic would deny them.

This is no mere theory. It is the basis of tunnel diodes, transistors, and many of other practical marvels of present-day society. The philosophical implications are staggering. Quantum probability statistics make it conceivable for an entire universe to spring unbidden from the void of non-existence in a titanic "Quantum fluctuation", in fact, quantum physicists hold that the big bang of creation may have been just such a causeless, random fluctuation in the all encompassing vacuum.

Ideas like these, which may seem to border on mysticism, did not emerge full blown from the minds of the founders of quantum physics, but took shape over decades of hard thinking, debating and experimentation.

While quantum physics is solidly buttressed by experimental evidence and coherent theory, it still rests upon the foundation that defies human comprehension, in this it seems to share at least one dimension with other kinds of faith, mysticism included.

The revelation made in the Holy Quran and the sense and substance encompassed in its verses which are the words of the Unimaginable Supreme Being, the Creator Allah, are understandable in the context of quantum theory. Faith in the Holy Quran and faith in Allah and in His Messenger Prophet Muhammad (PBUH) on whom the Holy Quran is revealed, is the vital dimension to understand the Creator and to understand His Infinite Power, Infinite Wisdom and Infinite Knowledge in the creation of universe and in the creation of man and to understand all that which exists and all that which happens and which shall happen and all beyond that. Sound faith in the Holy Quran, therefore, leads man to know the absolute realities, physical and metaphysical both, which are otherwise beyond the comprehension of man and are not explainable under the law of casualty (cause and effect). Faith leads man to believe in such facts which are beyond the converging point where quantum theory and law of casualty meet. The revelations of the Holy Quran and the miracles performed by the leave of Allah by Prophets, like, Moses, Zachariah, Marry, Jesus, David, Solomon and others as mentioned in the Holy Quran and the revelation of the greatest miracle of the Holy Quran itself revealed on the Last Prophet Muhammad (PBUH) the greatest of the Prophets, are all the absolute realities, which are understandable in the context of quantum theory. It is for mankind to have firm faith in it and to believe it and to understand it at all level of sound knowledge. It reveals the Absolute Truth about all things, some of which are beyond the comprehension of man and beyond quantum theory and beyond all other physical laws. So, faith is the fundamental means to grasp all that which the Holy Quran reveals whether physical or metaphysical.

Chapter 13

ALLAH THE ORIGINATOR, THE CREATOR AT WILL, THE SHAPER OUT OF NAUGHT, THE SUSTAINER OF THE UNIVERSE AND MAN AND THE BRINGER OF DOOM AND THE CREATOR OF THE HEREAFTER

Allah is the Creator of What He Will, the Shaper out of naught and the Sustainer of the universe and of man and the Creator of all other known and unknown and invisible form of life and of the unseen worlds. All things that are created in the universe and on earth and the numerous events that took place, serve as Allah's portents for mankind so that man knows Allah through His marvels of creations of all kinds and from the revelations of the Holy Quran which describe numerous creations and the events in allegory or directly. Faith in Allah the Creator of man and of all things and in His revelations, and to obey and worship Him is the purpose of man's creation as man is under-trial on earth. Man's fate is resurrection in the 'Hereafter', an immortal world and a reality of great significance and there the requital for his deeds depends on his performance in the present world. Modern Sciences dealing with the physical universe and man with all their modern concepts and discoveries are in congruity with the Holy Quran and the science of religion of Islam revealed on Prophet Muhammad (PBUH) 1400 years ago. This similarity is miracle upon miracle and leads to the absolute reality of the existence of God and the Holy Quran as His message for mankind.

The Holy Quran reveals:-

> *'Allah is the Originator of the heavens and the earth and He ordered in that Day when He said: Be! and it is'.* (29:35) (6:73) (2:117).

The 'Will' of Allah is the Creative Energy of the Divine Command 'Be' and its becoming, i.e. the Cosmogony taking place in the original form of the chaotic matter, something like smoke or vapour or gaseous mass or suspended particles or radiation or might or power or energy and matter or the substance for the formation of the universe governed by the created and the measured universal physical laws and the fundamental forces maintaining a perfect celestial Mechanic.

The Holy Quran reveals:-

(1) *'Then turned He to the heaven when it was smoke and said unto it and unto the earth: come both of you, willing or loth. They Said: We come obedient'. (41:11).*

(2) *'Then He ordained them seven heavens in two Days and inspired in each heaven its mandate; We decked the nether heaven with lamps and rendered it inviolable. That is the measuring of the Mighty, the Knower'. (41:12).*

(3) *'And He it is Who created the heavens and the earth in six days and His Throne was upon water — that He might try you, which of you is best in conduct. Ye if thou (O Muhammad) sayest: Lo! Ye will be raised again after death! Those who disbelieve will surely say: This is naught but open magic'. (11:7).*

(4) *'Say (O Muhammad, unto the idolaters): Disbelieve ye verily, in Him Who created the earth in two days and ascribe ye unto Him rivals? He (and none else) is the Lord of the Worlds' (41:9).*

(5) *'He placed therein firm hills rising above it, and blessed it and measured therein its sustenance in four days, alike for (all) who ask' (41:10).*

(6) *'Allah has created every animal of water. Of them is (a kind) that goeth upon its belly and (a kind) that goeth upon two legs and (a kind) that goeth upon four. Allah createth what He will. Lo! Allah is Able to do all things'. (24:45).*

The above Quranic verses indicate the Science of Sub-nuclear Particles, Astrophysics and Particle Physics and reveal that before the formation of seven heavens, there was 'smoke' or radiation or energy or might or something else. Then out of the created substance or 'smoke' or 'radiation', or 'energy' or 'might' or something, the near heaven and the earth were created. Then the heaven was ordered to be seven heavens or universes and each heaven or universe assigned its own mandate. Our heaven, i.e, the near heaven or our universe was decked with stars and made inviolable i.e. secure from the trespass by any thing and rendered it as a boundless universe. Man can judge or measure the Infinite Might of Allah and His Infinite knowledge from the inviolability of our universe or of the near heaven. Then above the seven heavens, lay the tremendous Throne of Allah, the Lord of the Worlds, which was upon water. The Tremendous Throne was floating above the seven heavens upon water or may be something of hydrogen and oxygen, the constituting elements of water and the basic elements of the universe or the heaven.

The above-mentioned Quranic verse (41:10) reveals that in the earth, Allah has placed all the amenities for the sustenance of man and of all kinds of life which He created. Allah created all living creatures, i.e. of all kinds of animals, birds, insects, plant life and human beings etc., of water on the earth and has provided sustenance for all in the earth. Allah is Able to do all things.

Sustenance in Earth for Men and for All Who Search or Ask

Allah has blessed the hills and the earth with sustenance in measured quantities for all who search and ask for it and on which all kinds of life depend and derive benefits to sustain themselves: (41:10). Allah has provided all kinds of natural resources in measured quantities in the hills and in other parts of the earth for man and for all other living creatures i.e. sustenance from forests, and deserts, plains, hills, mountains, rivers and seas etc which yield all kinds of produce for sustenance i.e. fodder, food, shelter and mineral wealth, from which man and other living creatures derive benefits. All kinds of animals and birds live in forests and feed in forests and hills and in the seas. All living creatures make efforts to seek their sustenance in earth. The Holy Quranic verse (41:10) clearly reveals that Allah has blessed the earth and its hills with sustenance for all those who make efforts to take benefit out of them and get them. Man explores the hills and the land resources and the resources from the seas and rivers on earth and conducts investigations and carry out excavations to get mineral wealth and food which are provided in 'measured quantity'. During the process of evolution, each of the earth's constituting elements of the specific quantity took specific time in getting solidified in the shape of various mineral compounds in the hills and mountains on earth and scattered all over its surface including the seas. The hills and lands and the seas of the earth are blessed with measured quantity of minerals and forests wealth and food and provide sustenance for human beings, birds, insects and animals and for all other known and unknown wild life and the acquatic life.

The Holy verses are:-

(1) *'He placed therein firm hills rising above it, and blessed it and measured therein its sustenance in four days, alike for (all) who ask'. (41:10).*

(2) *'Give us sustenance, for Thou art the Best Sustainers'. (5:114).*

Allah—The Sustainer of the Universe and of Man and of All other Creatures

The Holy Quran reveals:-

'We have built the heaven with might and We it is Who make the vast extent (thereof)'. (51:47).

The 20th Century Scientists have established that the Universe is expanding. Edwin Hubble's Law is in congruity with the above Quranic verse and states that the universe is expanding isotropically. Einstein's Theory of Relativity is also in consonance with the above Quranic verse.

The Holy Quran reveals:-

(1) *'Have not those who disbelieve known that the heavens and the earth were of one piece, then We parted them, and We made every living thing of water? Will they not then believe?' (21:30).*

(2) *'Verily We have brought them a Scripture which We expound with knowledge and guidance and a mercy for people who believe'. (7:52).*

(3) *'And maketh the sun and the moon constant in their courses, to be of service unto you and hath made of service unto you the night and the day'. (14:33).*

The Holy verse (21:30) questions the disbelievers that do they know that the heaven and the earth were one piece and then

Allah parted the earth from the heaven and then Allah created all living creatures on earth of water. In spite of all these facts, the disbelievers do not believe the realities revealed in the context of all these creations. Allah has revealed the scripture for the knowledge and guidance of mankind and Allah will have His mercy on him who believe in the Scripture. Allah has created the sun and the moon, the day and the night for the service of mankind which provide sustenance for mankind on earth. The sun and the moon in various forms are the sources of sustenance for life on earth. Human life, animal life, acquatic life and plant life depend on the energy of the sun. The formation of seasons, the weathers, clouds, rains, floods and the growth of green vegetation on earth also depend on the sun and the moon. The change of weathers, the change of seasons, the pleasant reflected light of the moon, the phases of moon for reckoning time and its other numerous benefits, the formations of tides due to the pull or gravity of moon, sleep and rest during the formation of night and work during the formation of day and so many other vital factors for sustaining life on earth depend on the service of the sun and the moon and in creating life supporting zone and life supporting environments on earth. The sun and the moon are made constant in their respective courses at specific distances from earth for the service of mankind, as they provide life supporting energy and life supporting environments on earth. The sun and the moon are for the service of mankind on earth. The sun's rays or energy is absorbed by the green vegetation in the earth which helps in the growth of all sorts of green forests, harvests and orchards and green trees which convert and store the solar energy through the process of photo-synthesis. The green trees or forests or green vegetation, ultimately convert into coke, coal, charcoal, gas, petrol etc., a product which ultimately converts into the Hydro-carbon family, which is stored energy and is for the service of mankind and Allah has appointed energy or fire in the green tree and its ultimate product of the hydro-carbon compound. All this is for the service of mankind. The tree or its ultimate product when burnt gives fire or energy which mankind kindles from it for numerous uses. This is one of the most vital provision on the earth from the sun for the sustenance of mankind both directly and indirectly. The sun's energy is ultimately available in the form of storage of fuel, fire, food and fodder for animal and human consumption and uses. The Holy Quran is full of Knowledge, Wisdom, Guidance, Information and a Mercy for those who believe in it.

In this context the Holy Quran reveals the following verses which are of great significance:-

(1) *'Who hath appointed for you fire from the green tree and behold! Ye kindle from it' (36:80).*

(2) *'Have Ye observed the fire which Ye strike out?' (56:71).*

The above verses of the Holy Quran convey tremendous sense if one ponders in the context of sciences and make it clear that the sun and the moon are for the sustenance and service of mankind on earth. Sun is the ultimate source of energy, which sustains vegetation life on earth. On vegetation life depends the animal life as animals feed on vegetation. Human life consumes both i.e. the vegetation and the animals. Actually, it is the same energy or might with which the universe is built but is in different form due to different interactions. Energy is found either in one form or the other and as such the entire universe is built of might. Energy and matter are the same and are mutual convertible by interaction.

Allah is the Creator and the Sustainer of man. The earth, the hills, the trees and all green vegetation, the sun, the moon, the stars and all things in the universe are created for the sustenance of man. Allah is the Shaper out of naught and He is the bringer of the 'Doomsday' and the Creator of the 'Hereafter'. The ultimate fate of man lies in the 'Hereafter' when life after death starts as that is the permanent abode for mankind.

Allah's Will Governs the Universe whether it is the Law of Casualty or the Quantum Theory

Out of Infinite attributes of Allah as revealed by the Holy Quran, a few are as follows:-

(1) *'He begetteth not nor was begotten'. (CXII:3).*

(2) *'And there is none comparable unto Him'. (CXII:4).*

(3) *'Say: He is Allah, the One!'. (CXII:I).*

(4) *'Allah the eternally Besought of all!'. (CXII:2).*

(5) *'Lo! Thy Lord is Doer of what He Will'. (11:107).*

(6) *'Allah createth what He Will. Lo! Allah is Able to do all things'. (24:45).*

(7) *'That is easy for Allah'. (36:79).*

The sense in the above Holy verses can be explained as follows:

The above Holy verses show that Allah is the Creator. He is the Law Maker and Source of Ordinance lies with Him. He is the One, the Eternal and there is none comparable to Him. Allah is neither father to nor son of anyone. He is above the Law of Casualty and the Law of Incomprehensibility and the Quantum Theory, which are all His creations for governing the physical objects in the universe including man. Allah has created these physical laws for governing His physical creations, but His Will always prevails the way He wants and everything yields.

Einstein believed the universe was governed by one logical set of laws in which all events are determined by the Law of Casualty i.e. the belief that a definite cause produces a definite effect. Niels Bohr, however, denounced this and thought that physical phenomena were determined not by casualty but by chance. He held the view that probability and chance rather than determination guided the occurrence of all events in the physical universe. This is known as the Quantum Theory.

Einstein asked Niels Bohr:-

'Do you believe that God plays dice with the Universe'.

Niels Bohr replied:

'Do not tell God what to play'.

The literal meaning of the Holy verse (CXII:3) is that God is neither father to nor son of any one. Metaphorically speaking, father can be regarded as the cause and the son as effect. God is neither father nor son and He is beyond cause and effect, and beyond the law of casualty and chance. The physical universe and the physical laws and forces governing the universe and propounded and discussed by Einstein and Niels Bohr are the creation of God. These laws and forces give-in before the Will of God as these are for the 'created' things and the created laws of God govern them as God Will, and God is the Doer of What He Will.

The Holy Quran reveals:-

(1) 'Allah createth what He Will. Lo! Allah is Able to do all things'. (24:45).

(2) *'Abiding there so long as the heavens and the earth endure save for that which thy Lord willeth. Lo! thy Lord is Doer of what He Will'. (11:107).*

(3) *'And Our word unto a thing, when We intend it is only that We say unto it: Be! and it is'. (16:40).*

As far as the Law of Casualty and Chance to govern the universe is concerned, the above Holy Quranic verses (24:45) and (11:107) are the true guide and tell which of the concepts of either Einstein or Niels Bohr are more nearer and more applicable to the created universe or both are applicable in their respective sense and originate from the same (single) source.

Ordinarily Allah has appointed set laws which are assigned to perfectly govern the universe but at the same time His Will' or His Creative Power always prevails and is above everything and the governing laws of nature for the universe become incomprehensible.

Allah's Will or a word into a thing or merely Allah's intend into a thing when Allah say Be! and it is done accordingly. The Creator Allah is the Eternal, the Living and that He is the One and the Uncomparable and that whenever He enforces His Will, the laws become incomprehensible. All universal laws and forces yield before His Will. The Will' of Allah is one of the attributes of Allah. The attribute of will or His Creative Power clearly shows that Allah is All Wise, All Powerful, the Eternal and the Living and the Will is essential quality of the Wise Living, the Omniscient Being. Allah is All Wise, All Knowledgeable and All Powerful. He exercises the powers the way He likes. From the type, nature and the extent of the 'Creations' one knows the attributes of the 'Creator' and from the attributes one knows the Supremeness of the Creator.

Allah governs the universe according to His own assigned and set laws as long as the universe and earth endure and last unless He brings changes in the laws at will. And Allah is Doer of What He will and in a manner that the change from the previous laws to the new one, by itself become the law of nature. The Will' of Allah is the Law of nature. The Will of Allah prevails and He creates the 'creation' the way He wants. Allah is Able to do all things. Therefore the laws becoming incomprehensible and asymmetrical is no matter.Such a situation indicates the implementation of the Will of Allah in a way as He orders. The performance which appears to man as miracle or as unusual act is no matter for Allah, as Allah is source of Ordinance. Everything is easy for Allah. Allah performs miracles when He will. Allah gifted powers to prophets to perform miracles with His permission so that a miracle be a portent of Allah for man to know Allah and His Powers.

Numerous examples of the law of casualty and chance about the universe and man are already present in the Holy Quranic verses which are mentioned either allegorically or direct and to the point.

A few out of the numerous Holy verses on the creation of the universe which are in consonance with each concept and physical law are quoted below. These contain the general Relativity, the special Relativity , Quantum Mechanics or Max Planck's Quantum theory, uncertainty principle and physical laws relating to all the fundamental forces. In addition, the Holy Quran gives indication about the creation of life at molecular level.

The Quranic Verses which Reveal that Everything Works according to Perfectly Set Physical Laws Governing the Fundamental Forces in the Universe and explains the Working of the Universe as a Whole

The Holy Quran reveals:

(1) *'And maketh the sun and the moon constant in their courses, to be of service unto you and hath made of service unto you the night and the day'. (14:33).*

(2) *'Allah causeth the revolution of the day and the night, Lo! herein is indeed a lesson for those who see'. (24:44).*

(3) *'The sun and the moon are made punctual'. (55:5).*

(4) *'It is not for the sun to overtake the moon, nor doth the night outstrip the day. They float each in an orbit'. (36:40).*

(5) *'And He hath constrained the night and the day and the sun and the moon to be of service unto you, and the stars are made subservient by His Command. Lo! herein indeed are portents for people who have sense' (16:12).*

(6) *"And the Sky He hath uplifted; and He hath set the measure". (55:7).*

(7) *"Lo! We have created everything by measure". (54:49).*

(8) *"And Our Commandment is but one (Commandment) as the twinkling of an eye". (54:50).*

(9) *"It is He Who created the heavens and the earth in true*

proportions". (6:73) and (39:5-6).

(10) *"It is He Who created all things and ordered them in due proportions". (25:2)*

(11) *"And with Him are the keys of the invisible. None but He knoweth them. And He knoweth what is in the land and the sea. Not a leaf falleth but He knoweth it, not a grain amid the darkness of the earth, naught of wet or dry but (it is noted) in a clear record". (6:59).*

(12) *"And made of him a pair, the male and female". (76:39).*

(13) *"And that He created the two spouses, the male and the female". (53:45).*

(14) *"He it is Who produceth, then reproduceth". (85:13).*

The above Holy verses reveal that the entire universe and all things in the universe whether visible or invisible, living or non-living, are created by Allah in due proportions and in true proportions and with a set measure. Allah has set the measure for the sky and for all things in it and has established celestial mechanic in the whole cosmos. All celestial bodies including the sun and the moon are made punctual and constant in their orbits so that they are of service to mankind. Everything is governed by the physical laws and by the four known fundamental forces.

Man is created as male and female and it is Allah who produces and reproduces man according to His set physical laws and also the way He wants.

All systems, therefore, run in perfect order and in accordance with set physical laws which govern everything according to the assigned orders of Allah. But Allah's Will always prevails and He is the Doer of what He Will.

The laws of universe becoming incomprehensible and asymmetrical and the performance of miracles are by the same source Who runs everything according to perfectly set laws as is clear from the Holy verses of the Quran. The act of miracles show the Will of Allah as the Creator and the Doer of all things according to His Will and the Phenomena become unusual and not subject to the normal laws of nature. In such events the laws become incomprehensible and this is not something bewildering as Allah is Able to do all things and He is the Doer of what He Will.

A few examples of miracles are quoted from the Holy Quran which show that Allah is the Doer of What He Will..In such cases the normal laws of nature yield and change over to laws which are incomprehensible and unusual. Allah creates what He Will and Allah is the Doer of What He Will. The Will of Allah is the Divine energy for creation and for doing all things. Normal Physical laws automatically change, adjust and perform acts or phenomena to the Will of Allah Who is Source of Ordinance. The deviation from the ordinary laws of nature, which we call as miracles, serve as portents of Allah, so that man knows the Infinite Powers, Wisdom and Knowledge of Allah, Who is Able to do all things as He wishes.

A few miracles from the Holy Quran are quoted. These were performed by the various prophets with Allah's leave. so that mankind should know the Creator Allah and His Infinite Powers to do All things.

Quran on the Miracles Performed by various Prophets

The following miracles are quoted from the Holy Quran performed by various Prophets of God with permission of Allah. The act of miracle is the Will of God when normal physical laws give-in. The miracles are tokens of Allah for man to believe in the existence of Allah and show that Allah is the Doer of What He will.

The Miracle of the Creation of Son to a Barren Woman from Infirm Old Man (Zachariah)

The Holy Quran reveals in the verses given below a miracle of the creation of son to a barren woman from infirm old man, though biologically and genetically it is impossible for a barren woman to conceive and bear child from infirm old man. But the miracle happened as Allah Does what He Will :-

(1) *'He said: My Lord! How can I have a son when age hath overtaken me already and my wife is barren? (The Angel) answered: so (it will be), Allah doth what He Will (III:40).*

(2) *'He said: My Lord! How can I have a son when my wife is barren and I have reached infirm old age? (19:8).*

(3) *"He said: So (it will be) Thy Lord saith: It is easy for Me, even as I created thee before, when thou wast naught". (19:9).*

(4) *"Peace on him the day he was born and the day he died and the day he shall be raised alive! (19:15).*

The above verses reveal deviation from the set laws of nature, as a barren woman conceives a son from an infirm old man as Allah said it will be. Thus the laws of genetics and biology yielded and became incomprehensible, but were true in obeying the Will of Allah.

The Miracle of the Creation of Son to Marry without Spouse

The creation of son to Marry without spouse is the greatest miracle of genetics in the Science of Biology as conception without male to a female is genetically impossible and contrary to physical laws of the science of Biology and Genetics. Allah creates what He Will. Allah is Able to do all things. His word unto a thing: Be! and it is. And that is easy for Allah.

The Holy Quran reveals in the verses quoted below a miracle of the creation of son to Marry without husband. Under the ordinary laws of nature, it is again impossible and is very much incomprehensible, but it is the Will of God and He said it will be and Marry got conceived by miracle and gave birth to Jesus. The process of birth after miraculous conception took place under the normal and ordinary laws of nature :-

The Holy Quranic verses reveal:-

(1) *'She said: How can I have a son when no mortal hath touched me, neither have I been unchaste? (19:20).*

(2) *'He said: So (It will be) Thy Lord saith: It is easy for Me. And (it will be) that We may make of him a revelation for mankind and a mercy from Us and it is a thing ordained'. (19:21).*

(3) *'And She conceived him and She withdrew with him to a far place'. (19:22).*

(4) *'And her Lord accepted her with full acceptance and vouchsafed to her a goodly growth; and made Zachariah her guardian. Whenever Zachariah went into the sanctuary where she was, he found that she had food. He said: O Marry! Whence cometh unto thee this (food)? She answered: It is from Allah. Allah giveth without stint to whom He Will (III:37).*

(5) *'Then She brought him to her own folk, carrying him. They said: O Marry! Thou hast come with an amazing thing'. (19:27).*

(6) *'O Sister of Haroon! Thy father was not a wicked man nor was thy mother a harlot'. (19:28).*

(7) *'Then she pointed to him: They said: How can we talk to one who is in the cradle, a young boy?' (19:29).*

(8) *'He spake! Lo! I am the slave of Allah. He hath given me the Scripture and hath appointed me a Prophet'. (19:30).*

(9) *'Peace on me the day I was born, and the day I die and the day I shall be raised alive! (19:73).*

(10) *'Such was Jesus, son of Marry: (this is) a statement of the truth concerning which they doubt'. (19:34).*

(11) *'It befitteth not (the Majesty of) Allah that He should take unto Himself a son. Glory be to Him! When He decreeth a thing, He saith unto it only: Be! and it is'. (19:35).*

A miracle is an event or action by the Will of God which apparently contradicts known scientific laws but is due to the act of God. A miracle is a portent and a token of Allah so that man knows that Allah exists and is the Doer of what He will. An act of a miracle is deviation from the scientific physical laws. Miracles can only be performed by the Will of Allah and with the permission of Allah when physical laws give way and wonders are performed. Miracles show that there is 'Unimaginable Supreme Being', Who has the Power to do what He likes and Who is the Creator of all things. Allah gave powers to His Prophets to perform miracles with His leave so that the miracles serve as portents and tokens of Allah, for mankind to believe in Allah and in His Prophets and in His Book or Message. The Holy Quran reveals a number of miracles performed by various prophets to their people to serve as the tokens of Allah.

The Miracles of Prophet Messiah Jesus Son of Marry the Prophet of Allah

Messiah Jesus son of Marry is the Prophet of Allah. Almighty God, bestowed on Jesus divine power and as such he was able to perform a number of miracles. The first miracle is that Jesus was born to his Mother Marry without a biological father. Then he was made able to speak while he was in cradle. He made a bird out of clay and then he breathed into it, and by Allah's leave, the bird became alive. Jesus was given the healing power and he could cure a born blind and a leper. He raised the dead by Allah's leave and could tell the people which they have eaten and which they have stored in their houses. These are all portents for mankind to know Allah and to know His Power and believe in Him. Jesus has neither been slewed nor crucified but it looked so. This is again a miracle.

And this is absolutely certain and is an absolute reality. These are all acts of miracles where the will of Allah prevails and the ordinary laws of nature yield and become incomprehensible. Allah gave powers to (His Messenger) the Prophet Jesus to perform these miracles with His leave so that the people know about their Creator Allah and worship Him alone. In order to teach the people of that period and to convince them at their level of understanding, Allah gave some divine powers to Prophet Jesus to perform certain miracles so that the people know that Jesus is Allah's messenger Prophet, and that he has brought the message of goodwill. It was therefore necessary to convince the uneducated and ignorant people in a manner which shall appeal them most. The medium of communication chosen by Allah for informing people was through His Prophets to whom Allah gave the divine powers of performing miracles so that these miracles serve as tokens of Allah and the people believe in what the prophet said. Prophet Jesus, the son of Marry performed the greatest miracles of raising the dead by Allah's leave. Ordinarily, it is an act most unimaginable and utterly impossible. Similarly, he breathed life into clay in the form of bird and it was a living bird by Allah's leave. Allah gave powers to His Prophet Jesus to perform miracles with the permission of Allah Who is Able to do all things.

The Holy Quran reveals :-

(1) *'She said! My Lord! How can I have a child when no mortal hath touched me? He said: so (It will be). Allah createth what He will. If He decreeth a thing, He saith unto it only Be! and it is' (III:47).*

(2) *'And she who was chaste, therefore We breathed into her (something) of Our Spirit and made her and her son a token for (all) people' (21:91).*

(3) *'Lo! this, your religion, is one religion, and I am your Lord, so worship Me' (21:92).*

(4) *'He will speak unto mankind in his cradle and in his manhood and he is of the righteous'. (III:46).*

(5) *And will make him a messenger unto the children to Israel, (saying): Lo! I come unto you with a sign from your Lord. Lo! I fashion for you out of clay the likeness of a bird, and I breathe into it and it is a bird by Allah's leave. I heal him who was born blind and the leper and I raise the dead by Allah's leave. And I announce unto you what ye eat and what ye store up in your houses. Lo! Herein*

verily is a portent for you, if ye are to be believers'. (III:49).

(6) *'And because of their saying: We slew the Messiah Jesus son of Marry, Allah's Messenger—They slew him not nor crucified, but it appeared so unto them and Lo! those who disagree concerning it are in doubt thereof; they have no knowledge thereof save pursuit of a conjecture; they slew him not for certain' (IV:157).*

The Miracle of the People of the Cave who fled for Refuge, Slept there for 309 years but felt that they lived in the Cave for a day or less than that

This is a miracle and a Portent of Allah where men took refuge in a cave for 309 years. They went into sleep and were under conditions that if observed closely would have created terror, but when they woke after 309 years, they were fresh and thought that they were asleep for a day or part of a day. Allah is the Doer of what He will. Allah sustained and preserved the people for 309 years in the cave and then they were woken alive. Such divine miracles make the universal physical laws of nature to become ineffective. The law under the circumstances become incomprehensible and the Will of Allah prevails.

The Holy Quran reveals:-

(1) *'Or deemest thou that the people of the cave and the Inscription are a wonder among Our portents?'(18:9).*

(2) *"When the young men fled for refuge to the cave and said: Our Lord! Give us mercy from Thy presence and shape for us right conduct in our plight". (18:10).*

(3) *"When We sealed up their hearing in the Cave for a number of years:" (18:11).*

(4) *"And afterward We raised them up that We might know which of the two parties would best calculate the time that they had tarried". (18:12).*

(5) *"We narrate unto thee their story with truth. Lo! they were young men who believed in their Lord and We increased them in guidance". (18:13).*

(6) *"And thou wouldst have deemed them waking though they were asleep and We caused them to turn over to the right and the left and their dog stretching out his paws on the threshold. If thou hadst*

observed them closely thou hadst assuredly turned away from them in flight and hadst been filled with awe of them". (18:18).

(7) *"And in like manner We awakened them that they might question one another. A speaker from among them said: How long have ye tarried: They said: We have tarried a day or some part of a day, (others) said: Your Lord best knoweth What Ye have tarried. Now send one of you with this your silver coin unto the city and let him see what food is purest there and bring you a supply thereof. Let him be courteous and let no man know of you". (18:19).*

(8) *"And (it is said) they tarried in their cave three hundred years and add nine". (18:25).*

(9) *"Say: Allah is best aware how long they tarried. His is the invisible of the heavens and the earth. How clear of sight is He and keen of hearing! They have no protecting friend beside Him and He maketh none to share in His Government". (18:26).*

The Miracles of Prophet Moses to Pharoah and His People

Allah gave powers to Prophet Moses to perform miracles so that Pharoah and his people who were evil living people should know the tokens from Allah through His Prophet Moses and that they should believe in Allah, the One God, the Creator of mankind and the universe and worship Him. The first miracle was that Allah spoke to Moses direct. The second miracle was that the staff of Moses turned into a serpent and then returned to its former state. The third miracle was that when Moses put his hand into his arm pit, it came forth white without being hurt. The fourth miracle was that Moses parted the sea with his staff when he hit it and then crossed over to safety. The fifth miracle was that Moses asked Allah for water for his people and Allah said to Moses to smite the rock with his staff when twelve springs gushed out therefrom. And so on.

These miracles were to serve as portents of Allah performed by His Prophet Moses to let Pharoah and his people know that whatever the prophet says is from Allah and is absolutely true. The miracles were used to assure the people that what Moses said was from Allah. That was the way to convince the people at their level of understanding. Pharoah and his people were unbelievers in God.

The Quranic verses describing the miracles of Moses and his meeting with Allah are:-

(1) *"Lo! I, even I, am Allah. There is no God save Me. So serve Me*

and establish worship for My remembrance". (20:14).

(2) *'And what is that in thy right hand, O Moses?' (20:17).*

(3) *"He said this is my staff whereon I learn and wherewith I beat down branches for my sheep and wherein I find other uses". (20:18).*

(4) *'He said: Cast it down, O Moses! (20:19).*

(5) *'So he cast it down, and Lo! it was a serpent glinding'.(20:20).*

(6) *'He said: Grasp it and fear not. We shall return it to its former state'.(20:21).*

(7) *'And thrust thy hand within thine arm pit, it will come forth white without hurt (That will be) another token'.(20:22).*

(8) *'And when he reached it, he was called from the right side of the valley in the blessed field, from the tree: O Moses! Lo! I, even I, am Allah, the Lord of the worlds:' (28:30).*

(9) *'Throw down thy staff. And when He saw it writhing as it had been a demon, he turned to flee headlong (and it was said unto him): O Moses! Draw nigh and fear not. Lo! thou art of those who are secure'.(28:31).*

(10) *'Thrust thy hand into the bosom of thy robe, it will come forth white without hurt. And guard thy heart from fear. Then these shall be two proofs from your Lord unto Pharoah and his Chief: Lo! They are evil living folk'.(28:32).*

(11) *'But when he reached it, he was called, saying: Blessed is whosoever is in the fire and whosoever is round about it. And glorified be Allah, the Lord of the Worlds'.(27:8).*

(12) *'O Moses! Lo! it is I, Allah, the Mighty, the Wise'.(27:9).*

(13) *'And throw down thy staff! But when he saw it writhing as it were a demon, he turned to flee headlong; (but it was said unto him): O Moses! Fear not! Lo! the emissaries fear not in My presence'.(27:10).*

(14) *'And put thy hand into the bosom of the robe, it will come forth white but unhurt. (This will be one) among nine tokens unto Pharoah and his people. Lo! they were ever evil living folk'.(27:11)*

(15) *'Then We inspired Moses, saying: Smite the sea with thy staff. And it parted and each part was as a mountain vast'.(26:63).*

(16) *'And when Moses asked for water for his people, We said: smite with thy staff the rock. And there gushed out therefrom twelve springs (so that) each tribe knew their drinking-place. Eat and drink of that which Allah hath provided and do not act corruptly, making mischief in the earth'.(II:60).*

The greatest miracle of Moses is the greatest event when Allah Himself called Moses from a blessed tree in a blessed field on the right side of the valley and it was said to him. O Moses! Lo! I, even I, am Allah, the Lord ot the Worlds.

The Holy verses further reveal that Allah gave powers to Moses to perform miracles as tokens of Allah to Pharoah and his people who were evil and sinful so that they believe in Moses as the Prophet Messenger of Allah and believe in Allah as the One God, Obey Him and Worship Him.

The Holy Quran reveals a miracle about the dead body of pharoah pertaining to the time of Prophet Moses when Pharoah died by drowning thousands of years before the revelations of the Holy Quran but his dead body was found in 1898 preserved as mummy and lying in the tombs of Thebes on the bank of river Nile, after more than 1300 years of the revelation of the Holy Quran. The mention of recently revealed fact by the Holy Quran is a miracle as at the time of revelation of the Quran, it was an event of the past thousands of years and of the future and the body of Pharoah was found intact so as to serve as token from Allah for the coming generations after him as revealed by the Holy Quran. This is again a Quranic miracle and people should not be heedless of this miracle (portent).

The Miracle of Quranic Revelations on Pharoah's Drowned Body to serve as Portent for People after him

The Holy Quran reveals:-

(1) *'But Pharoah rebelled against the messenger whereupon We seized him with no gentle grip' (74:16).*

(2) *'And We brought the children of Israel across the sea and Pharoah with his hosts pursued them in rebellion and transgression, till, when the (fate of) drowning overtook him, he exclaimed: I believe that there is no God save Him in Whom the Children of Israel believe and I am of those who surrender (unto Him)'.(10:90).*

(3) *'But this day We save thee in thy body that thou mayest be a portent for those after thee. Lo! most of mankind are heedless of Our portents'.(10:92).*

(4) *'So, when they angered Us, We punished them and drowned them every one'. (43:55).*

(3) *'And We made them a thing past and an example for those after (them)'. (43:56).*

It is not known whether it was Rameses II, the greatest of the Pharoahs or his successor Merneptah who was drowned in the Nile and whose body is preserved as a mummy till to day. According to the Holy Quranic verses (74:16), (10:90-92) and (43:55-56) quoted above, Pharoah cried:-

> *'I believe that there is no God save Him in Whom the Children of Israel believe, and I am of those who surrender unto Him'. God replied: What now! when hitherto thou hast rebelled and be of the wrong doers?But this day We save thee in thy body that thou mayest be a portent for those after thee' (10:90-91-92).*

Could any scientist believe 1400 years ago how the Pharoah's body was preserved for thousands of years? When the Prophet Muhammad (PBUH) revealed this fact to mankind how could he know that the body was lying preserved as a mummy in the tombs of Thebes opposite Luxor on the other bank of the Nile? It was only discovered in 1898. Dr. Maurice Bucaille, a surgeon from Paris who has written an illuminating book, 'The Bible, the Quran and Science', is doing research on these mummies to establish, if possible, which Pharoah was drowned during the Israelis exodus.

The Miracles of Prophet David who knew the Languages of Birds and Iron was made soft for him

Allah bestowed on David the unusual power to understand the languages of birds. This is the first miracle of Prophet David. The second miracle of the Prophet David was that iron was made soft for him. These are the favours of Allah on Prophet David and indicate that the powers of Allah are Infinite and that He is the Doer of what He will. The performance of the unusual phenomenon or miracle through His Prophet is very easy matter for Allah as Allah has Infinite powers to do what He will.

The Quranic verses reveal as follows:-

(1) *'And assuredly We gave David grace from Us (Saying): O Ye hills and birds, echo his psalms of praise! And We made the iron supple unto him' (34:10).*

(2) *'And Solomon was David's heir. And he said: O Mankind! Lo! We have been taught the language of birds and have been given (abundance) of all things. This surely is evident favour'.(27:16).*

The Miracles of Prophet Solomon, when Jinns were made under His Command and the Wind was under his Control and He knew the language of Birds

Allah bestowed on Prophet Solomon, knowledge and the power of judgement. Allah subdued the hills and the birds to obey Solomon and David. Allah gave power to Solomon and the wind was made under his control and the copper was discovered to him in abundance, from which Prophet Solomon prepared garments of War for protection. Allah made the jinns under the control of Prophet Solomon and they worked before him by the permission of Allah. Prophet Solomon was taught the language of birds and the ants. These were the miracles which were performed by Prophet Solomon with the permission of Allah so that people may know Allah and obey Him and worship Him.

During those days there was almost no knowledge, therefore such kinds of miracles were necessary to let people know about the existence of One God (The Creator of man and the Universe and of all that which is in between them). Also miracles were performed so that people may know that Allah has the power to do anything He likes as Allah is Able to do all things.

The Holy Quran reveals:-

(1) *'And We made Solomon to understand (the case); and unto each of them We gave judgement and knowledge. And We subdued the hills and the birds to hymn (his) praise along with David. We were the doers (thereof)' (21:79).*

(2) *'And unto Solomon (We subdued) the wind in its raging. It set by His Command toward the land which We had blessed. And of everything We are aware' (21:81).*

(3) *'And We taught him the art of making garments (of male) to protect you in your daring. Are ye then thankful' (21:81).*

(4) *'And unto Solomon (We gave) the wind, whereof the morning course was a month's journey and the evening course a month's journey, and We caused the fount of copper to gush forth for him and (We gave*

him) certain of the jinn who worked before him by permission of his Lord. And such of them as deviated from Our Command, them We caused to taste the punishment of flaming fire' (34:12).

(5) *'And We verily gave knowledge unto David and Solomon and they said: Praise be to Allah, Who hath preferred us above many of His believing slaves' (27:15).*

(6) *'And Solomon was David's heir. And he said: O Mankind! Lo! We have been taught the language of birds and have been given (abundance) of all things. This surely is evident favour' (27:16).*

(7) *'And there were gathered together unto Solomon his armies of the jinn and human-kind, and the birds and they were set in a battle order' (27:17).*

(8) *'Till, when they reached the Valley of the Ants, an ant exclaimed: O ants! Enter your dwelling lest Solomon and his armies crush you, unperceiving' (27:18).*

(9) *"And (Soloman) smiled, laughing at her speech and said: My Lord, arouse me to be thankful for Thy favour where with Thou has favoured me and my parents and to do good that shall be pleasing unto thee and include me in (the number of) Thy righteous slaves". (27:19).*

(10) *"And he sought among the birds and said: How is it that I see not the hoopoe or is he among the absent?' (27:20).*

(11) *"But he was not long in coming and he said: I have found out (a thing) that thou apprehendest not and I come unto thee from Sheba with sure tidings". (27:22).*

The above Holy verses reveal the miracles performed by Prophet Solomon with the permission and with the Will of Allah. And Allah is the Doer of What He Will. His Will is the Divine Creative Power which becomes the law of nature. Ordinarily, Allah has set all the laws of nature to function in perfect order. Allah has created and set all things in perfect balance with 'a set measure'. All things are created by Him 'in true proportions' and their interaction is in 'due proportions' with no deviation at all. The fundamental forces interact on matter and energy in time and space in perfect order and there is no dislocation. These are the laws of nature perfectly designed and set by Allah. Anything which is done beyond the applicability of the ordinary laws of nature, becomes incomprehensible and appears to be a miracle. In reality, the miracles obey the Laws of nature and work according to the Creative Power of Allah, Who is Able to do all things.

The two actions or events of nature i.e. the one as per normal and existing laws of nature and the other behaving differently and becoming incomprehensible for sometimes and for some purpose show that the All Wise, All Powerful Creator (Allah) exists and that He is Able to do all things whenever He wishes. The change is a token or a portent of Allah and invites attention of mankind so that man knows that Allah is Able to do all things at His will. The change and the incomprehensibility of laws are for some purpose. It shows the existence of God and His will to do what He likes. The Holy Quran gives clear exposition of all this reality. The miracles show the existence of Allah and show that Allah is the Creator of all things and the Doer of all things at will. The miracles show that Allah is Able to do all things. Allah is the sustainer of the universe in perfect order with His perfect physical laws on the interaction of matter and energy in time and space. The Will of Allah overrules everything for He is All Wise Creator. Thus, Einstein and Niels Bohr, both are correct in their respective concepts and the way they perceived and looked at nature and its physical laws.

Quran as the Documentary Miracle of the Last Prophet Muhammad (PBUH)

The revelations of the Holy Quran as the infallible word of Allah on Prophet Muhammad (PBUH) is the greatest miracle containing wisdom, knowledge, information and guidance for all times. The Holy Quran is revealed with a 'Balanced' script by inspiration on Prophet Muhammad (PBUH) for the guidance of all mankind.

The Holy Quran teaches the doctrines of Islam and submission to the Will of One Allah. It reveals about the 'Doomsday' the Resurrection of mankind, his accountability on the Day of Judgement, and about the immortal life after death in the Hereafter. The Holy Quran is a treasure of documentary miracles for men of wisdom, knowledge and understanding and is the divine word of the Creator Allah for mankind to act upon. The Holy Quran reveals all about the past, the present and of this temporary physical world and of the future of mankind, and all about the unseen world in the 'Hereafter', which is eternal and is the permanent abode of mankind. The revelation of the 'Hereafter' is the Unique revelation to mankind by the Quran.

The Holy Quran is therefore, the unique heavenly document full of miracles revealed on Prophet Muhammad (PBUH) by Allah - the Creator of the heavens and the earth and all that is between them. Science in all the branches is found to be in complete similarity with the Holy Quran. There can be no miracle greater than the Quran. What more miracle or documentary proof greater than this is required by knowledgeable man to know Allah, the Creator of all things, who has bestowed man with conscience so that he chooses between the right and the wrong and created him as an intelligent and responsible living being from an assembly and miraculous combination of atoms infused with life. Whatever the Quran reveals is from God and is the absolute truth.

Muhammad (PBUH) is the Last of the Prophets. The Holy Quran is the last of the heavenly Books. There would be no more prophets and no more heavenly Books. The Holy Quran the word of Allah is the Unique heavenly documentary message which contains knowledge, wisdom, information and guidance for the whole mankind on earth. Quran is a miracle of the modern times and of all times. It is a miracle of knowledge, wisdom, information and a guidance for people of knowledge having faith and very high understanding of modern knowledge of sciences.

It is, therefore, easy for the people of the present time and more convincing to find the miracles of the absolute truth in the verses of the Holy Quran, in a documentary form of a Book which reveals all kinds of things. To a modern man with faith, knowledge and wisdom, the Holy Quran is the greatest miracle word by word and verse by verse. It is for mankind to read the Holy Quran revealed on the Messenger of Allah Prophet Muhammad (PBUH) and know Allah the Creator of man, the Almighty, the Hearer, the Seer and act on the teachings of Allah revealed in the Holy Quran.

The Holy Quran reveals:-

(1) *'Nay, but their hearts are in ignorance of this (Quran) and they have other works, besides, which they are doing'.(23:63).*

(2) *'They measure not Allah His rightful measure Lo! Allah is strong, Almighty'.(23:74).*

(3) *"Allah chooseth from the angels messengers and (also) from mankind. Lo! Allah is Hearer, Seer". (23:75).*

(4) *"And strive for Allah with the endeavour which is His right. He*

hath chosen you and hath not laid upon you in religion any hardship; the faith of your father Abraham (is yours). He hath named you Muslims of old time and in this (Scripture), that the messenger may be a witness against you and that Ye may be witnesses against mankind. So establish worship, pay the poor due and hold fast to Allah. He is your Protecting Friend. A blessed Patron and a blessed Helper". (23:92).

(5) *"Lo! This, your religion, is one religion, and I am your Lord, so worship Me". (21:92).*

(6) *"And they have broken their religion (into fragments) among them, yet all are returning unto Us.' (21:93).*

Quran the Document of Miracles from God with Truth and Justice, revealed with a Multimiracle Balanced Script of Substance and of Words and Divisible by the Code Number 19 to show the Miracle of Script as Token of Allah

The Holy Quran is revealed by Allah as a multimiracle script and a document of miracles with absolute truth. One of its miracles is that the Quranic script is written with 'the Balance of absolute truth and justice' and with 'the Balance of alphabets, letters and words', with reference to the first Holy verse (Bismillahir-Rahmanir-Rahim), (In the name of Allah, the Beneficent, the Merciful) which consists of 19 key letters. These are the key letters of the Quran besides other abbreviates and alphabets indicated before the beginning of Surah (Chapter). Moreover, the verses of the Holy Quran which reveal wisdom, knowledge and hidden information about man and the universe and about all that is created, is miraculously and surprisingly in similarity with the most modern knowledge of physical facts discovered by man, and science or knowledge is found to be in complete similarity with the Holy Quran. Thus, the Quranic 'Balanced Script', with the use of balanced alphabets its substance and its words, its style and the sense contained in the Holy verses is full of wisdom, knowledge, information and guidance and is a Divine act of Allah and is a documentary miracle upon miracle for all times. All this is revealed by the Quran in the following Holy verses:-

(1) *"And if Ye are in doubt concerning that which We reveal unto Our slave (Muhammad), then produce a 'Surah' of the like thereof and call your witness besides Allah if ye are truthful". (11:23).*

(2) *'And this Quran is not such as could ever be invented despite of Allah; but it is a confirmation of that which was before it and exposition of that which is decreed for mankind-therein is no doubt from the Lord of the Worlds' (10:37).*

(3) *'And Allah Who hath revealed the Scripture with truth and the Balance. How canst thou know? It may be that the Hour is nigh' (42:17)*

(4) *'Say: Verily, though mankind and the jinn should assemble to produce the like of this Quran, they would not produce the like thereof though they were helpers of one another' (17:88).*

(5) *'And verily We have displayed for mankind in this Quran all kinds of similitudes, but most of mankind refuse aught save disbelief' (17:89).*

(6) *"Above it are nineteen". (74:30).*

(7) *"And the Even and the Odd". (89:3).*

The above Quranic verses clearly reveal that this Quran is not man-made and is such that man can never invent it and that it cannot be man-made and that it is the divine word of Allah which confirms what it was said before it in the previous heavenly Books revealed on the previous Prophets of Allah and that it explains and sets-forth the facts which are ordered for mankind by Allah. Allah has revealed the Holy Quran with absolute truth and with the Balance in all respects i.e. balance of truth, balance of words and alphabets and balance of sound and of symphony. Allah says, that if man and jinn, both together make their utmost efforts, they would never be able to produce the like of this Quran. It obviously implies that the Holy Quran is the divine word of Allah and that it is not man-made.

The script of the Holy Quran has thoroughly been studied and analysed for a number of years with the help of computers and some miraculous results have been achieved as a result of the analysis of the Holy Script and its alphabets during such studies. The miracle of the Script is that the whole of Quranic Script is exactly divisible by 19 Key Letters of (Bismillahir-Rahmanir-Rahim) and by some more key alphabets and words before the beginning of Surah or Chapter. It has been found that the numerical (code number) of the Holy Quran is 19. The Script analysis of the Holy Quran reveals that it is always divisible by the numerical number 19. These informations are published and released by the

Islamic Productions 5937 E, Pima Street, Tucson, Arizona 85712, (USA) in 1976; (19x104).

The miraculous writing of Quranic scripture, in a miraculous alphabetical order is perfectly balanced by the use of selected alphabets and words and is made divisible by a miraculous Code Number 19. This is a scriptural miracle of the Holy Quran which gives a mathematical and a physical proof by the wonderful arrangements of words of the Quranic Script proving that it is truly a heavenly divine message from God and is revealed 'with truth' and 'with the Balance' of justice in its substance and with the Balance of alphabets in its script so that the Scriptural miracle of the Quran be a token of Allah and be safe from human manipulation. All this clearly proves that the Holy Quran can never be man-made. The miracle writing of the scripture and its divisibility by the number 19 is a documentary portent and a token of Allah for mankind to know Allah, as the Creator of man, the heavens and the earth and all that is in between them. The Quranic script is written in a manner so as to be a portent for mankind, besides the unlimited miracles of wisdom, knowledge, guidance and information encompassed allegorially or direct in each verse of the Holy Quran. The divisibility of the Script of the Holy Quran by 19 and by the Key letters and alphabets is a great sign of Allah. It is humanly impossible to produce such a script whose alphabets, abbreviates and words of the same type which are repeatedly used, when totalled, be always divisible by the miracle number 19, and at the same time be written in a Script full of wisdom, knowledge and information. The Divine words of the Scripture are so arranged that these always maintain a balance when divided by all the 19 letters of the first Quranic verse of Bismillahir-Rahmanir-Rahim.

Allah says that all kinds of similitudes are displayed for mankind in the Holy Quran, but most of mankind disbelieve in the revelations. The Holy verse (74:30) which reveals 'Above it are nineteen', definitely displays a similitude for mankind to understand. Another verse (89:3) reveals 'and the Even and the Odd' is also of significance and relevance, but is in symbolic form. It allegorically mentions about the even number and the Odd number, which convey sense that odd number 19, evenly divides the key letters and alphabets of the Holy Scripture.

The number 19 is a common denominator and is a sort of Quranic 'numerical code'. It is surprising that every word and part of the verse Bismillahir-Rahmanir-Rahim wherever used in the whole of Quran is exactly divisible by the miraculous number 19. How could it be possible that an unlettered Prophet reveal a meaningful Book full of perfect wisdom, sense and substance describing the visible and the invisible realities of the universe and man and then at the same time its script is written in a manner so that when all the key letters, alphabets and words used in the Holy Scripture are totalled, will always be found to be divisible by the number 19? For example, the word 'Allah' has been used 2698 times and it is exactly divisible by the number 19 i.e. 2698 19=142. Again the word 'Ism' has been used 19 times. The word (Ur-Rehman) has been used 57 times i.e. (19x3). The word (Ur-Rahim) has been used 114 times which is (19x6).

Again, all the abbreviates mentioned in the beginning of the (Surah) Chapters are the key letters and are always found to be divisible by the number 19. For details reference may be made to the research done and detailed chart released by the Islamic Productions, Tucsen, Arizona, USA. All these miracles with such a script prove that the Holy Quran is not man-made and can never be man-made. The Script further proves that the Holy Quran comes to us perfectly preserved, intact and without distortion, alteration or loss. It is perfectly original and heavenly document or Book of guidance for mankind. The Holy Quran itself states in the verse (74:30) that any one who claims that Quran is man-made will have the number 19 over him. This Odd number 19, is always evenly divisible by the numerous key letters, alphabets and words repeatedly used in the Holy Quran. The Holy Quran is the perpetual document of miracles revealed on Prophet Muhammad (PBUH), for the guidance of all mankind.

Part V

THE REVELATIONS OF THE HOLY QURAN AND THE DOCTRINES OF ESCHATOLOGY:

(DEATH, RESURRECTION, ACCOUNTABILITY, JUDGEMENT AND IMMORTALITY IN THE HEREAFTER)

THE ABSOLUTE REALITY OF METAPHYSICAL WORLD OF THE HEREAFTER AS MAN'S ETERNAL ABODE.

CHAPTER XIV

(i) The Resurrection of Mankind in the Hereafter:

(a) The Metaphysics of Quran has Link with Physical Man.

(b) The Spirit or Soul of Mankind.

(c) Water in Protoplasm.

(d) Role of DNA in the Resurrection.

(ii) Accountability of Man on the Day of Judgement in the Hereafter:

(a) Physical events linked with the Metaphysical Realities of the Quran.

(b) Record for Accountability.

(c) Science in similarity with the Quran on God's Invisible Watch on Man and by His Envoys for his Accountability. Man's own

Organs serve as witnesses and Watchmen of Allah.

(d) The Skin of Man as the witness of Allah for Man's Accountability. Science in similarity with the Quran on the role and behaviour of Skin.

(iii) The Day of Judgement in the Hereafter for the Requital of Man's Physical Performance, Deeds and Actions:

(a) Link of the Metaphysics of Quran with the Physical Universe and Man.

(b) Similarity of scientific concepts, observed facts and laws with Quranic verses lead to the proof of Absolute Reality.

(c) The 'Hereafter' or the Life after Death.

Chapter 14

THE DOCTRINES OF ESCHATOLOGY OF THE QURAN (DEATH, RESURRECTION, ACCOUNTABILITY, JUDGEMENT AND IMMORTALITY IN THE HEREAFTER)

The Holy Quran reveals on mankind the doctrines of Enchatology, i.e. the doctrines dealing with Death, Resurrection, Accountability, Judgement and the Immortality in the 'Hereafter'. All these vital doctrines of Islam as the Holy Quran reveals are explained in separate sections of this Chapter on Eschatology under the various sub-heads of Resurrection, Accountability, Judgement and Immortality in the Hereafter. As already discussed science cannot probe into these metaphysical realities revealed by the Holy Quran. Therefore, the Holy Quran beautifully guides man and reveals :-

(1) *'Who believe in the unseen and establish worship and spend of that we have bestowed upon them'. (3:3).*

(2) *'Lo! Ye are those who argue about that whereof ye have some knowledge: Why then argue ye concerning that whereof ye have no knowledge? Allah knoweth. Ye know not'. (III:66).*

The above Holy verses make it very clear that man may argue about all that of which he has some knowledge. But what is the use of arguing those matters or metaphysical realities which are unseen and are invisible and hidden and of which man has absolutely no knowledge and is totally unaware. In the context of the above verses, these realities are beyond man's probe and comprehension. But, Allah Who is the Creator, surely knows all things about His creations, whether physical or metaphysical, whereas man does not know and cannot know. The Holy Quran teaches that the faithful are those who believe in the Unseen and establish worship to God and help the poor. The above verses have great sense and wisdom. It is beyond man's physical capacity and understanding to know the realities which are unseen. Man has no alternative but to believe in the Word of Allah and in the unseen and in the invisible and help the poor which is a part of worship to Allah.

The Holy Quran reveals that on the Last Day, when the world would come to an end, the dead shall be resurrected and a Judgement shall be pronounced on every person in accordance with his deeds, which are recorded in a Book. The actual evaluation, however, will be for every individual whatever the terms of reference of his performance. In order to prove that the resurrection will occur, the Holy Quran gives moral and physical arguments. Because not all requital is meted out in this life, a final Judgement is necessary to bring it to completion. Furthermore, Allah is All Powerful and has the Ability to destroy and bring back to life all creatures, and revive similar universe, as Allah has Infinite Power, Knowledge and Wisdom.

The Holy Quran reveals :-

> *'Then have patience (O Muhammad) even as the stout of heart among the messengers (of Old) had patience and seek not to hasten on the doom for them. On the Day when they see that which they are promised (it will seem to them) as though they had tarried but an hour of the day light. A clear message. Shall any be destroyed save evil living folk?'. (46:35).*

The above verse reveals that on the Doomsday when man will be resurrected in the Hereafter, the whole of his life-span in the physical world would appear to him as if he has spent an hour and this is a clear message of God to man. So, it is for man to do good in this temporary and short-lived world and get its reward in the eternal world of the Hereafter.

The Resurrection of Mankind in the 'Hereafter'

The Metaphysics of Quran has Link with Man

Immediately on the 'Doomsday' is the 'Day of Resurrection' which is the first and the greatest metaphysical event for mankind in the 'Hereafter'. The Holy Quran reveals in numerous of its verses that mankind shall be resurrected on the 'Doomsday' for 'Accountability' on the 'Day of Judgement' in the 'Hereafter'. The Holy Quran is an exposition of that which is decreed for mankind. There is a definite relationship between physical sciences and the science of religion taught by the Holy Quran specially in respect of man in the context of physical universe and the Hereafter. The metaphysics of Quran has a link with the physical universe, man and his conduct, which is constantly under Divine observation for the purpose of Accountability and Judgement on the Day of Resurrection so that he is rewarded or punished in the Hereafter. Man, created as an intelligent being and inspired with conscience to distinguish between right and wrong, is responsible and answerable to his Creator in the light of Quranic teachings. Man is therefore on trial. Man'sobedienceto the Will of Allah as per the message contained in the Holy Quran is worship to Allah.

Some of the Holy Quranic verses on Resurrection are given below :-

(1) *'He asketh when will be the Day of Resurrection?' (75:6).*

(2) *'But When sight is confounded'. (75:7).*

(3) *'A day when the trumpet is blown and ye come in multitudes'. (77:18).*

(4) *'And the moon is eclipsed'. (75:8).*

(5) *'And the sun and the moon are reunited'. (75:9).*

(6) *'And when souls are united'. (81:7).*

(7) *'And when the pages are laid open'. (71:10).*

(8) *'And they used to say: When we are dead and have become dust and bones, shall we then, foresooth, be raised again'. (23:16).*

(9) *'Then Lo! on the Day of Resurrection ye are raised again'. (23:16).*

(10) *'Will all be brought together to the tryst of an appointed day'. (56:50).*

(11) *'Verily We shall give life to the dead'. (36:12).*

(12) *'Say, He will revive them Who produced them at the first, for He is knower of every creation'. (31:79).*

(13) *'Those who disbelieve assert that they will not be raised again. Say (unto them, O Muhammad): Ye verily, by my Lord! Ye will be raised again and then ye will be informed of what ye did and that is easy for Allah. (64:7).*

(14) *'Have they not seen that Allah, Who created the heavens and the*

earth and was not wearied by their creation, is Able to give life to the dead? Aye, He verily is Able to do all things'. (46:33).

(15) *'And because the Hour will come, there is no doubt thereof and because Allah will raise those who are in the graves'. (22:7).*

(16) *'Your creation and your raising (from the dead) are only as (the creation and the raising of) a single soul. Lo! Allah is Hearer, Knower'. (31:28).*

(17) *'And of His portents is the creation of the heaven and the earth and of whatever beasts He hath dispersed therein. And He is Able to gather them when He will'. (42:29).*

(18) *'Every soul will taste of death. And Ye will be paid on the Day of Resurrection only that which ye have fairly earned. Whoso is removed from the Fire and is made to enter Paradise, he indeed is triumphant. The life of this world is but comfort of illusion'. (III:185).*

(19) *'And (remind them of) the Day when the Trumpet will be blown, and all who are in the heavens and the earth will start in fear, save him whom Allah willeth. And all come unto Him, humbled'. (27:87).*

(20) *'And then Trumpet is blown and Lo! from the graves they hie unto their Lord'. (36:51).*

(21) *'Crying: Woe upon us! Who hath raised us from our place of sleep? This is that which the Beneficent did promise and the messenger spoke truth'. (36:51).*

(22) *'And He it is Who gave you life, then He will cause you to die, and then give you life again. Lo! man is verily an ingrate. (22:26).*

(23) *'When we are dead and have become dust (shall we be brought back again)? That would be far return! (50:3).*

(24) *"That We may transfigure you and make you what ye know not'. (56:61).*

(25) *"We know that which the earth taketh of them, and with us is a recording Book".(50:4).*

(26) *"Everything have we recorded in a Book". (77:29)*

(27) *"And He is Able to gather them when He will "(42:29).*

(28) *'And they say: When we are lost in the earth, how can we then be recreated? Nay but they are disbel [illegible] in the meeting with their Lord". (32:10).*

(29) *"Say: the angel of death, who hath charge concerning you will gather you and afterward unto your Lord Ye will be returned".(32:11).*

(30) *"Then when He will, He bringeth him to life". (80:22).*

(31) *"Is not He (who doth so) able to bring the dead to life". (76:40).*

(32) *'Thinketh man that We shall not assemble his bones?' (75:3).*

(33) *'Yea, verily. Yea, We are able to restore his very fingers! (75:4).*

(34) *'The Day when they come forth from the graves in haste, as racing to a goal'. (71:43).*

(35) *'The day when they will hear the (Awful) cry in truth. That is the day of coming forth (from the graves)'. (50:42).*

(36) *'With eyes aghast, abasement stupefying them: Such is the Day which they are promised'. (71:44).*

(37) *'On the day when the earth splitteth asunder from them hastening forth (they come). That is a gathering easy for Us (to make). (50:44).*

(38) *'And He hath coined for Us a similitude and hath forgotten the fact of his creation, Saying: Who will revive these bones when they have rotted away' (36:78).*

(39) *'Say: He will revive them who produced them at the first, for He is Knower of every creation'. (36:79).*

(40) *'There is not an animal in the earth, nor a flying creature flying on two wings, but they are peoples like unto you. We have neglected nothing in the Book (of our decrees). Then unto their Lord they will be gathered'. (6:38).*

(41) *'How disbelieve ye in Allah when ye were dead and He gave life to you! Then He will give you death, then life again, and then unto Him ye will return'. (II:28).*

The sense which the above Holy Quranic verses on Resurrection convey are clearly understandable. Some of the verses are allegorial but others are direct. On the whole, the verses give a very vivid picture of the Resurrection when souls are united and Accountability starts on the Day of Judgement and every Individual shall be informed of what he did. All this is easy for Allah, and Allah is Able to gather all of them and He has the Book of record with Him.

The Holy Quran reveals verses on 'Resurrection' and also informs man about the certainty of the 'Hereafter':-

(1) *'And who believe in that which is revealed unto thee (Muhammad) and that which was revealed before thee and are certain of the Hereafter' (2:4).*

(2) *'Then Lo! On the Day of Resurrection ye are raised (again)' (23:16).*

(3) *'Praise be to Allah, unto whom belongeth whatsoever is in the heavens and whatsoever is in the earth. His is the praise in the Hereafter and He is the Wise, the Aware'. (34:1).*

It is a divine declaration of absolute reality that all dead mankind shall be brought back to life on the 'Day of Resurrection' in the 'Hereafter'. The 'Hereafter', i.e. 'Life after Death' is certain and is an absolute metaphysical reality. It is beyond the scope of physical science to provide any direct explanation for metaphysical and Divine matters. This is why, there is no scientific explanation as to what life is? And how it is created? Though life is a reality in the physical universe and shows the divine act of creation. Similarly, there is no scientific explanation as how, the dead could be revived and brought back to life. But this is also a divine reality and man shall be resurrected in the Hereafter. Science is helpless and cannot probe into the metaphysical matters. Resurrection is beyond the scope of science and is subject to the Divine Command. The only link from the physical to metaphysical is through the Holy Quran which is the divine scripture giving light of wisdom, information and guidance to all mankind. Allah is the Creator of the Physical Universe and of the 'Hereafter'. Men of sound knowledge who pay heed to the revelations and reflect shall find truth in the Holy Quran.

Quran — The Revelation from Allah

The Holy Quran reveals about itself:-

(1) *'With truth We have sent it down, and with truth hath it descended. And We have sent thee as naught else save a bearer of good tidings and a warner'. (17:105).*

(2) *'Say: Believe therein or believe not, lo! those who were given knowledge before it, when it is read unto them, fall down prostrate on their faces adoring'. (17:107).*

(3) *'A revelation from Him Who created the earth and the high heavens'. (20:4).*

(4) *'This is the Scripture whereof there is no doubt, a guidance unto those who ward off evil'. (2:2).*

(5) *'Who believe in the unseen and establish worship and spend of that We have bestowed upon them'. (2:3).*

(6) *'That (this) is indeed a noble Quran'. (56:77).*

(7) *'In a Book kept hidden'. (56:78).*

(8) *'This is a glorious Quran (inscribed) in a guarded tablet'. (85:21-22).*

(9) *'See Ye not how Allah hath made serviceable unto you whatsoever is*

in skies and whatsoever is in the earth and hath loaded you with His favours both without and within? Yet of mankind is he who disputeth concerning Allah without knowledge or guidance or a scripture giving light'. (31:20).

(10) *'And when thou bringeth not a verse for them they say: Why hast thou not chosen it? Say: I follow only that which is inspired in me from my Lord. This (Quran) is in sight from your Lord and a guidance and a mercy for a people that believe'. (VII :203).*

(11) *'And this Quran is not such as could ever be invented despite of Allah: but it is a confirmation of that which was before it and exposition of that which is decreed for mankind — There is no doubt-from the Lord of the worlds'. (X:37).*

(12) *'Nay, but they denied that, knowledge whereof they could not compass and whereof the interpretation (in events) hath not yet come unto them. Even so did those before them deny. Then see what was the consequences for the wrong-doers'. (10:39).*

(13) *'Lo! this (Quran) is a conclusive word'. (86:13).*

The Holy Quran enlightens mankind and is the only source to reveal all the divine events, as Quran itself is the inspired word of Allah and is an all-time guidance for mankind. In order to understand the substance of the Holy Quran and the reality of all divine matters, one has to possess knowledge, wisdom and firm belief.

The sense in the Holy Verse (31:20) quoted above is that mankind should take guidance or be enlightened from the Quranic revelations for which they must possess knowledge to understand its meanings, as to dispute concerning Allah without knowledge is wrong and is an act of ignoratioelenchi in the light of His revelations.

Man is such that he denies the reality of the Quranic revelations when he is unable to grasp and understand the sense which is contained therein, till the interpretation events takes place with the passage of time and more knowledge find the revelations as absolute truth. This is what the Quran indicates.

The Spirit or Soul of Mankind

In the verses on Resurrection, the Holy Quran clearly

mentions that Allah is the Knower of every creation and that everything is 'recorded in a Book' with Him. This is a hint and a guidance in symbolic form, meaning that everything including the DNA and other physical constituents of man created out of wet earth are known to Allah besides the spirit or soul which Allah breathed into him. Moreover, Allah knows the environments required for life as on earth. The Quran reveals that Allah shall revive the dead exactly the same way as He gave life at the first. And that Allah is Able to gather them when He Will. Allah perfectly knows the arrangement of those basic elements at the electronic, atomic and molecular level for resurrection which constitutes living man from wet earth to which Allah breathed His Spirit, or soul, of which man has but little knowledge.

Regarding the Spirit, the Holy Quran reveals:-

> *'They will ask thee concerning the Spirit: Say: The Spirit is by command of my Lord and of knowledge ye have been vouchsafed but little'. (17:85).*

The Holy Quran guides that Allah will resurrect mankind in the 'Hereafter' and that He may transfigure man and make man which he cannot perceive and know as Allah is Able to do all things. May be that on resurrection, man is given some other type of form to live eternally in the 'Hereafter' which at present cannot be conceived by man. Basically he will be the same person in all respects. May be that on transfiguring man (56:61), Allah may bring some changes in his living cells, the surrounding fluids and its nutrients or something else which man cannot perceive. All this is a divine matter and is beyond the perception of man.

Taking guidance from these verses and then examining man's material or physical composition from the elementary matter, it is obvious that 'living man' is a combination of the atoms of matter plus 'Divine Spirit', out of this, 'Divine Spirit' or 'soul' or 'vital force' or an 'atom of Divine Force' is immortal and has no source in the physical world, for being Divine in nature. Therefore, 'Spirit' is not subject to man's physical observations and verification. 'Spirit' is above and beyond the sphere of material universe and cannot scientifically be detected or observed, it is totally beyond man's comprehension. The 'Spirit' is indestructible and is under the knowledge of God and man is not given knowledge of it except that the 'Spirit' is by Allah's Command. On the death of man, the 'Spirit' returns to its original element or source in the heaven. Regarding the 'Matter' part of man's body, it also returns to its original place in the bio-sphere of the earth from which substance it was originally created.

The Holy Quran reveals:-

(1) *'Verily, We created man from a product of wet earth'. (23:12).*

(2) *'We know that which the earth taketh of them, and with Us is a recording Book' (50:4).*

On death, man's body simply decays, changes form, disintegrates and in due course of time reverts into the original matter or elements of the earth's constituents forming the biosphere. The immortal 'Spirit' leaves its body when death of man occurs. The vital elements or the constituents forming man's body from the earth's biosphere are:

(1) Carbon,
(2) Hydrogen,
(3) Nitrogen,
(4) Oxygen,
(5) Phosphorus, and
(6) Sulphur,

which all return to earth, to its basic state. The major constituent or human body of which it is made is 'Water'. Human body is mortal and all its constituting elements simply disintegrate, but are not destroyed as far as the physical laws of science go.

All these elements undergo chemical and physical changes and simply change form on disintegration after the immortal spirit leaves behind the mortal body. It otherwise amounts to the fact that nothing is materially destroyed when living mankind die, except the change of form and the separation of living substance i.e. life and spirit in the human body from the non-living assembly of atoms and mechanism. On death, the 'divine spirit' returns to its original immortal element in the metaphysical world by the Command of God and the body is left to be disintegrated and is subjected to the process of physical and chemical laws in the physical world. Allah has the 'Record' and 'Measure' of every man for his gathering by recombination and may be that the gathering is at the electron or the atom or the molecule level. Allah may order for the assembly or 'gathering' of these physical elements of man's body with Divine element of spirit for resurrection at a simple divine Command of Be! when all mankind shall be gathered and revived or brought back to life or resurrected. Allah has All Knowledge, All Power and the Ability to resurrect mankind, the same way as He first created him, when He said: Be! and Adam was created. Allah is Able to do all things. He is the Doer of what He will. And that is easy for Him.

The Holy Quran reveals:-

(1) *'We know that which the earth taketh of them and with Us is a recording Book'. (50:4).*

(2) *'Everything We have recorded in a Book'. (76:79).*

The above Quranic verses reveal absolutely clear divine message, indicating in allegory that Allah knows the remains of human body which the earth takes after the death of mankind and that Allah has a system which completely records and has already recorded everything and that Allah has the knowledge of all things. The knowledge of natural sciences is found to be in congruity with the above Quranic verse (50:4) to an astonishing degree. The Holy verses reveal miracles but in allegory and in symbolic form and men of knowledge and understanding on contemplation will always find wisdom, knowledge, guidance and information about the absolute reality in the Holy Quran and know the Absolute Powers of Allah.

The 'Recording Book' mentioned in the Holy Quran is a symbolic indication for the complete coded biological information of the DNA molecule and of other Constituents which Allah has recorded in the Book and He has direct knowledge of all things about each of the mankind. Allah has coded the information in the DNA of every man. The DNA molecule has complete and perfect coded biological information from birth to death of each man. Allah has a permanent record of the various components of living man, about the cell and about the different substances of the cell, which collectively is called protoplasm. The structure of the protoplasm and the DNA etc. contains complete coded information about the genes of each mankind besides all other body-building-blocks or constituents.

The Holy Quran reveals :-

(1) *'Verily, We created man from a product of wet earth'. (23.12).*
(2) *'We made every living thing of water'. (21:30).*
(3) *'Allah hath created every animal of water'. (24:45).*
(4) *'He is Knower of every creation'. (36:78).*
(5) *'Everything have We recorded in a Book'. (78:29).*
(6) *'Verily, We shall give life to the dead'. (36:12).*
(7) *'That is easy for Allah'. (64:7).*
(8) *'Allah is Able to do all things'. (24:45).*

The above Quranic verses are direct, clear and self-explanatory. These Holy verses do not require any interpretation. Men of understanding shall find great wisdom and light in the above verses which mention such events and metaphysical matters, which are closely related with the physical matters. The metaphysics of Quran has a link with the physical universe, man and his conduct. It is surprising to find the great consonance of science with the verses of the Holy Quran, specially the water content of the protoplasm with the Holy Quranic verses which reveals :-

(1) *'Have not those who disbelieve known that the heaven and the earth were of one piece, then We parted them, and We made every living thing of water', Will they not then believe'? (21:30).*

(2) *'And He it is Who hath created man from water, and hath appointed for him kindred by blood and kindred by marriage; for thy Lord is Ever-Powerful' (25:54).*

The above Holy verses reveal that all 'Living things' contain water. Science is in complete similarity with the Quran which reveals that it is the 'protoplasm' of living man and of living things which contain 85 per cent to 90 per cent water, and is discussed under the heading, 'Water in protoplasm'.

Water in Protoplasm

It is a miracle and an astounding fact to find that modern concepts about the structure of human cell containing water already exists in the Holy Quran revealed more than 1400 years ago on the Holy Prophet Muhammad (PBUH). Biologically, water is the dominant constituent of living matter.

Scientific analysis shows that the predominant and the major constituent forming the structure of man is of water. Human structure is composed of 60 to 75 trillion living cells that can survive indefinitely and can even reproduce itself, provided its surrounding fluids contain appropriate nutrients. The cell is made up of different substances which collectively is called protoplasm. The protoplasm is composed mainly of five basic substances; water, electrolytes, proteins, lipids and carbohydrates.

The fluid medium of all protoplasm is water, which is present in a concentration between 85 and 90 per cent. This is surprisingly in consonance with another Holy Quranic verse which reveals :-

'And Allah hath created every animal of water'. (24:45).

Next to water is proteins which normally constitute 10 to 20 per cent of the cell mass. Lipids are 2 to 3 per cent and carbohydrates 1 per cent. The electrolytes play important role. According to the knowledge of science, the protoplasm is a living substance and the basis of all living matter in which water plays the most vital role. According to the Holy Quran, man is created from water. The following verses are quoted :-

(1) *'And He it is Who hath created man from water'*. (25:54).
(2) *'Allah made every living thing of water'*. (21:30).
(3) *'Allah hath created every animal of water'* (24:45).

The similarity between the revelation of the Holy Quran and the physical reality of the protoplasm (which is mostly water) in man and in every living thing is most astonishing and is consequential of the great reality, both the physical and Divine. The similarity of modern science and the Quran revealed 1400 years ago, is a direct and positive proof that there exists beyond all doubts and most certainly, the All-Wise Creator of man and of universe, Who is Able to do all things and Who will resurrect mankind.

Role of DNA in the Resurrection

As discussed, DNA is the source of coded information and it has to play a very vital role on the Day of Resurrection as all the biological information about each man is encoded in the DNA which is on 'record' with Allah in the 'Recording Book'. The substance of all mankind shall be raised and gathered by Allah by His simple command: Be! and it is; when the whole mankind will be raised. For Allah, the raising of all mankind is like the raising of one man.

The Holy Quran reveals :-

(1) *'He is Knower of every creation'*. (36:79).
(2) *'And with Us is a recording Book'*. (50:4).
(3) *'Everything have We recorded in a Book'*. (76:29).
(4) *'Verily, We shall give life to the dead'*. (36:12).
(5) *'That is easy for Allah'*. (64:7).
(6) *'Allah is Able to do all things'*. (24:25).

Thorough contemplation on the above Quranic verses, amazingly reveal that science is in full congruity with the Holy verses and that the DNA of mankind, is recorded in a Book with Allah and that man's creation from the 'Wet Earth', with water as the major constituent of the protoplasm, is noted with Allah in a recording Book or the Book of Knowledge. Allah is the Knower of every creation and everything is recorded with Him. On the Day of Resurrection, Allah, verily will give life to the dead and that is easy for Allah, and He is Able to do all things. The mystery of DNA, its tremendous coded biological information and the complete genetic instructions in a DNA molecule of man are facts which are in similarity with the Holy Verses and are the portents and marvels of Allah and show His Infinite Knowledge, Infinite Power, and Ability to do all things. The coding of tremendous genetic informations in a DNA molecule is a miracle and a divine act of God. The biological role of DNA has already been discussed. DNA tape for a single human cell is able to contain coded information equal to a hundred million pages of Encyclopaedia Britannica. Allah has coded a perfect and complete genetic record or recording Book of biological information in the DNA molecule of each man. A DNA molecule looks like a long twisted braid of computer tape and a gene is just a minute section of instructions on that tape. The DNA tape in one human cell would stretch several feet if straightened out; but, awkwardly wadded up inside a cell's nucleus, they form specks so tiny they can barely be seen with a light microscope. The Holy Quran reveals that Allah is Knower of every creation. (36:79). And that Allah has recorded everything in a Book. (77:29) and that Allah is Able to do all things'. (24:45). And that 'Allah verily, shall give life to the dead'. (36:12). And that is easy for Allah'. (64:7).

The Holy Quran in its numerous verses has revealed in clear and direct form as well as in allegory and in symbolic form that man shall be resurrected in the 'Hereafter' and that Allah has a complete record of each man and has All Knowledge, All Power and Ability to revive him again and it is easy for Allah to give life to the dead. On thorough reading of the Holy verses on Resurrection and on thorough contemplation in the context of known knowledge about human beings, it becomes evident that the science of human biology and genetics is in similarity with the Holy Quranic verses. All this similarity clearly indicates that the Holy Quran is the Word of Allah and is a Book of Divine guidance revealed on Prophet Muhammad (PBUH) for the guidance of mankind. Science of human biology is in congruity with the numerous Quranic verses, in respect of the creation of man and with the process of reproduction of man, and the various stages of the growth and development of man in the womb of mother and with the anatomical description of the womb in Three-fold gloom or the three layered embryonic membrane, and specially in respect of the DNA molecule with the coded genetic informations and with the protoplasm and with the living cell of man. The all-round similarity clearly leads one to the reality that the Holy Quran is undoubtedly a divine revelation which completely describes man and contains absolute truth and that mankind must believe it and have faith in the revelations from Allah. The same is true in respect of the description of the creation, evolution and the ultimate fate of the universe. The scientific observations and scientific concepts and facts about the physical universe and man are in complete agreement with all that the Holy Quranic verses reveal. The same is true about all the Quranic revelations on metaphysical events. Man's conscience, and his inner feelings and senses and his sound knowledge and faith in the revelations and thorough contemplation on the same shall guide man to believe in the Divine revelations as the Word of God and the absolute truth.

From a thorough study, analysis and after deep contemplation on all kinds of allegorial and direct Quranic verses on universe and man, one finds and comes to the ultimate conclusion that science in all branches describing man and universe is in complete congruity with the Holy Quran. The similarity of science with the

Holy Quran, directly indicates that the Holy Quran is undoubtedly the inspired revelations from Allah on Prophet Muhammad (PBUH) and is not man-made and cannot be man-made. The Holy Quran teaches man to obey and worship Allah and reveals wisdom, knowledge, information and guidance for the good of all mankind. The Resurrection of man as revealed by the Holy Quran is the absolute reality and shall take place on Doomsday in the 'Hereafter'. Allah is Able to do all things and that is easy for Him. On the Day of Resurrection all generations of mankind i.e. from the first man on earth till the last of mankind upto the Doomsday , shall be uniformly resurrected for their accountability and shall be answerable to all that which they did in the physical world on the Day of Judgement in the Hereafter.

Accountability of Man on the Day of Judgement in the Hereafter

Physical Events linked with the Metaphysical Realities of the Quran

On Resurrection, man stands accountable to Allah in the 'Hereafter' for his deeds which are perfectly recorded to serve as evidence on the 'Day of Judgement'. Thus, the process of accountability starts immediately on the 'Doomsday'. This is the time when temporary physical life and the physical universe come to an end, and the permanent immortal life in the metaphysical world of the Hereafter begins to live for ever.

Earth being the abode of man, the viceroy on earth, has been frequently mentioned in the Holy Quran.

The Holy Quran reveals :-

> *'Have not those who disbelieve known that the heavens and the earth were one piece, then We parted them and We made every living thing of water? Will they not then believe?' (21:30).*

Mankind is created to live on earth and nowhere else in the universe under specific life supporting environments with suitable atmosphere, temperature, pressure, gravity, seasons and weathers The solar energy from the sun provides sustenance to support life on earth which is placed in a life supporting zone from the sun.

Therefore, earth has a great importance in the universe for being the birth planet of mankind. Allah has assigned mankind a specific tenure of life on earth which shall terminate on the 'Doomsday' Therefore, Allah addresses mankind through the revelation of the Holy Quran to adopt good conduct and to believe in Allah and has inspired man with conscience to choose the path of his conduct either the right path or the wrong path as he wishes. And as such, man is created as the best community and has been blessed with the revelation of the Holy Quran for his guidance so that he knows and follows the right path.

The Holy Quran reveals :-

(1) *'Ye are the best community that hath been raised up for mankind. Ye enjoin right conduct and forbid indecency; and ye believe in Allah'. (68:110).*

(2) *'And inspired it (with conscience of) what is wrong for it and (what is) right for it'. (XCI:8).*

(3) *'Surely We created man of the best stature'. (XCIV:4).*

(4) *'I created the Jinn and Mankind only that they might worship Me'. (LI:56).*

Man is not created as an irresponsible savage on earth. He is rather created with marked preferment above many of the preferred creations of Allah. Man is inspired with conscience to do what is right for him. He is created as an intelligent and responsible being. He is accountable to God for his actions and deeds which are minutely observed, photographed and recorded right from man's birth to his death, at the speed of light or much faster than what could be imagined through the hidden divine forces. All his utterances and all the impulses signalled by his brain, and by his skin through the sense of touch and the nervous system are automatically recorded in a divine manner whether these are uttered, whispered or simply imagined in mind. The recorded cassette of man's actions and intentions shall be produced in evidence on the Day of Judgement in the 'Hereafter'. There would be many other hidden and invisible sources for the record of man's deeds and actions and for the impulses and signals being transmitted from the various parts of the body.

The following Quranic verses clearly reveal a thorough watch and observation by Allah on man's actions for accountability on the 'Day of Judgement' after resurrection in the 'Hereafter'. It is for mankind to objectively contemplate on these verses and take full advantage of his 'inspired conscience' to do right things during his tenure of life in the material world where we presently live.

The Holy Quranic verses on the observation of deeds and conduct of mankind are as follows :-

(1) *'Behold, two (guardian angels) appointed to take note (of his doings) one sitting on the right and one on the left. Not a word does he utter but there is a sentinel by him ready (to note it)'. (50:17-18).*

(2) *'Ye did not seek to hide yourselves, lest your hearing, your sight and your skins should bear witness against you. But ye did not think that God knew not many of things that ye used to do'. (41:22).*

(3) *'He uttereth no word but there is with him an observer ready'. (L:18).*

(4) *'Or deem they that We cannot hear their secrets thoughts and private confidences? Nay, but Our envoys, present with them, do record'. (43:80).*

(5) *'Nay! but ye deny the Judgement, while verily over you (are appointed angels) to watch you, honest and honourable, writing down your deeds. They know all that ye do'. (82:9-10-11-12).*

(6) *'Allah is informed of what ye do'. (27:88)*

(7) *'This our record speaks about you with truth: for we were won't to put on record all that ye did' (45:28-29).*

(8) *'When the two Receivers receive (him) seated on the right hand and on the left'. (L-17).*

(9) *'Lo! Allah is the Knower of the Unseen of the heavens and the earth. Lo! He is aware of the secrets of (Men's breasts)'. (35:38).*

(10) *'Lo! We it is Who bring the dead to life. We record that which they send before (them) and their footprints. And all things We have kept in a clear register'. (36:12)*

(11) *'And say unto them: Act! Allah will behold your actions and (so will) His messenger and the believers and ye will be brought back to the Knower of the invisible and the visible and He will tell you what ye used to do'. (IX:105).*

(12) *'And Allah is the Invisible of the heavens and the earth and unto Him the whole matter will be returned. So worship Him and put thy trust in Him. Lo! thy Lord is not unaware of what ye (mortals) do'. (11:123).*

(13) *'We verily created a man and We know what his soul whispereth to him and We are nearer to him than his Jugular Vein (50:16).*

(14) *'He knoweth all that is in the heavens and all that is in the earth and He knoweth what ye conceal and what ye publish. And Allah is aware of what is in the breast (of men)'. (64:4).*

(15) *'On the day when there tongues and their hands and their feet testify against them as to what they used to do'. (24:24).*

(16) *'Till, when they reach it, their ears and their eyes, and their skins testify against them as to what they used to do'. (41:20).*

(17) *'And they say unto their skins: Why testify Ye against us? They say: Allah hath given us speech who giveth speech to all things and who created you at the first, and unto whom ye are returned'. (41:21).*

(18) *'Ye did not hide yourselves lest your ears and your eyes and your skins should testify against you, but ye deemed that Allah knew not much of what ye did'. (41:22).*

(19) *'And We task not any soul beyond its scope and with Us is a Record which speaketh the truth and they will not be wronged'. (23:62).*

(20) *'And the earth shineth with the light of her Lord and the Book is set up and the prophets and the witnesses are brought, and it is judged between them with truth and they are not wronged'. (39:69).*

(21) *'And each soul is paid in full for what it did. And He is best aware of what they do'. (39:70)*

(22) *'This Our Book pronounceth against you with truth, Lo! We have caused (all) that Ye did to be recorded'. (45:29).*

(23) *'Vision Comprehendeth Him not, but He comprehendeth (all) vision. He is the Subtile, the Aware'. (6:104).*

The above verses of the Holy Quran clearly reveal that Allah has appointed two guardian angels on each man who serve as His watch forces and that the angels incharge take notes of every man's doings. The angels are appointed as sentinel or as observers and the moment he utters a word and pass a concept in mind or makes intention when impulses are formed and released by the brain which are instantaneously recorded by them through their divine system which is invisible, hidden and unseen to mankind. Thus, no action or deed, either open or secret, can be hidden from the notice of Allah and His angel messengers, as on the Day of Judgement even the hearing, the sight and the skins of each man shall bear witness against him for his deeds and doings which are automatically observed and recorded by man's own body and somewhere else outside the body also. Thus, one cannot deny the judgement as whatever one did that has been photographed and recorded in writing by angels appointed over each man who are honest and honourable and constantly watch you. And Allah is informed of everything what man has been doing in his life time. The record of deeds of every man is being compiled which shall speak the truth on the 'Day of Judgement' and on the Day of Resurrection in the 'Hereafter'. Thus, every man is accountable before Allah. For this purpose each man shall be properly received in the 'Hereafter' by the two 'Receivers' who will in the 'Hereafter' by the two 'Receivers' who will be seated on Man's right as well as on his left on the 'Day of Judgement'. A complete record of every man shall be available for a thorough accountability on the Day of Judgement before Allah in the 'Hereafter'.

The Two (Guardian) Angels who are appointed over each man as incharge to watch and record his activities are constantly observing and compiling the actions and deeds, the intentions and thoughts, the photographs of all deeds and actions, the sound, the impulses from the nervous system and the brain and the impulses due to the sense of touch from the skins and the whispers and intentions and feelings of each mankind. All good and bad acts are recorded and computerized by the invisible forces through a system which is perfect in all respects.

The angels incharge of the forces of light, sound and electrical impulses from the skin, the brain and from other parts of human body and other hidden and invisible forces that are constantly focussed on each man are recording and preserving man's actions for the purpose of accountability right from the day he is born till his death. This means the deeds of each man are recorded in a sort of cassettes by the appointed envoys and angels of Allah through the help of visible and invisible, known and hidden forces and through the electromagnetic force, light and sound and some other divine forces. The above Holy Quranic verses clearly convey knowledge, sense and the meanings that the record for evidence is compiled with great precision and in great details which shall be produced and laid open and played back and shown to each man on the Day of Judgement in the 'Hereafter' for the purpose of each man's accountability. For this purpose Allah has made arrangements for all that which man does to be recorded by His invisible messengers.

The Quranic verses on man's conduct and his accountability

reveal clear hints about the existence of a perfect, flawless, perpetually automatic recording phenomena either physical or divine or both operating in the universe where all relevant forces, known and hidden, unseen and invisible under the charge of angels having various wings or rank or dimensions are at work to note and record (the deeds) and doings of mankind. In this respect, Allah has assigned the Angels specific functions to perform with all necessary forces at their disposal which record everything in the Book of conduct of each man.

In this regard the Holy Quran reveals:-

> *'And the Book is placed and those seest the guilty fearful of that which is therein, and they say: What kind of a book is this that leaveth not a small thing nor a great thing but hath counted it?' 'And they find all that they did confronting them, and thy Lord wrongeth no one'. (18:49).*

The above-mentioned Quranic verses clearly hint that there is a perfect invisible recording system appointed by the Creator Almighty God to watch mankind and to precisely record all his deeds and doings. The complete record of watch on man's actions is kept by Allah for the purpose of 'Accountability' on the Day of Judgement' in the 'Hereafter'. In this regard the Holy Quran reveals the following verses on the record or the written document of performance or evidence of all persons:-

Record for Accountability

The Holy Quranic verses reveal:-

(1) *'And when the pages are laid open'. (81:10).*
(2) *'Nay, But the record of the righteous is in Iliyin'! (84:18).*
(3) *'Ah, What will convey unto thee what Iliyin is!' (84:19).*
(4) *'A Written Record'. (84:20).*
(5) *'Everything have We recorded in a Book'. (77:29)*
(6) *'Nay but the record of the vile is in sijjin'. (83:7).*
(7) *'Ah! What will convey unto thee what Sijjin is'! (83:8).*
(8) *'A written Record'. (83:9).*
(9) *'Lo! there are above you guardians'. (82:10).*
(10) *'Generous and recording'. (82:11).*

(11) 'Who know (all) that Ye do'. (82:12).

The above Holy verses clearly and directly reveal that Allah is observing and is maintaining a written record of the good and bad deeds and actions of mankind for the purpose of accountability to be laid open before mankind on the 'Day of Judgement'. It is, therefore, in the interest of man to be of good conduct and decent, just and peaceful and obedient to Allah, his Creator and act according to the revelations from Allah revealed on Prophet Muhammad (PBUH) in the Holy Quran for the guidance of mankind. The record of the righteous and the record of the vile are maintained and kept separately for the purpose of accountability.

Man himself is the most improbable object but he is a living reality with conscience, power of thinking and intelligence. His apparent and hidden parts and systems of his body and their functions are mysterious and miraculous. His brain is the most mysterious of all and his skin also which convey all sorts of messages to the brain. The brain has a highly complex structure with more than 25 billion neutrons. The surface area of the skin has an enormous number of sensory receptors. The Creative Power of Allah lodged spirit in man's body which runs the brain and his nervous system, where millions of messages pour through its billions of cells. Man is therefore a universe in miniature. It maintains its own record of what man does and thinks. It has unlimited capacity for record and storage of informations and all that which pass in his mind. All this information which is recorded in something like cassette or something parallel or similar to DNA will be replayed when Allah desires. The soul or the spirit of man which is divine substance or element or energy has a great fundamental role.

God's Invisible Watch on Man and by His Envoys for his Accountability

Man's Own Organs serve as Witnesses and Watchmen of Allah

The Holy Quran reveals that man's doings and deeds are perfectly observed, watched and recorded and that Allah knows and is informed by His messengers or angels or envoys what man does. This means, man is watched by the invisible forces under the

Divine directions. Moreover, Man's own vital organs and their senses assist and perform the functions of observers and watchmen in noting and recording the doings of each man. These vital organs and their senses will bear witness against the man for his deeds. The moment man utters a word that is recorded as Allah has appointed invisible observers and envoys who watch and write down and prepare record of the deeds of every man. Light and sound and the impulses from the vital organs of man play a very vital role of a 'watch' on man. The various forces are at work in photographing, sound recording and in detecting, observing, noting and recording the signals and impulses of each man for his doings and deeds. Invisible Divine Processes like the television transmission by means of cameras, which are focussed on each man, are transmitting scenes of man which are received by the television receivers to reproduce the original images. The life deeds cassettes parallel to DNA are recorded and preserved, which would not merely show the film with sound and pictures of the doings of each man but the impulses signalled by the skin through the brain are recorded to note the doings of each man alongwith his intentions and feelings which he plans and which are in his mind. The role played by the skin is therefore of great importance. In this respect the following Quranic verses are quoted below :-

The Holy Quran reveals :-

(1) *'Nay! But ye deny the judgement while verily over you (are appointed angels) to watch you, — honest and honourable, writing down your deeds. They know all that ye do'. (82:9—12).*

(2) *'Behold, two (guardian angels) appointed to take note (of his doings) one sitting on the right and one on the left. Not a word does he utter but there is a sentinel by him ready (to note it). (50:17-18).*

(3) *'This Our record speaks about you with truth: for We were wont to put on record all that ye did'. (45:28-29).*

(4) *'Lo! We it is Who bring the dead to life. We record that which they send before (them) and their footprints: And all things We have kept in a clear register'. (36:12).*

Allah is the Knower of the unseen and of the invisible of the heavens and the earth (9:105) and (12:123) and is Aware of the secrets of men's breasts. The Holy Quran further reveals that there is no need to hide yourself as your hearing, your sight and your skins shall bear witness against you and that your ears, eyes and skins shall testify what you used to do. Man will then ask his skin, 'why are you testifying against me?' The skin will sav.'Allah has given us the power of speech and He created you and ultimately you shall have to return to Him.'

Observation and watch on man's doings has been discussed above in the context of the Quranic verses, but a few verses of the Holy Quran which reveal the functions of the skin and the part played by the skins of man are quoted again. The 'Power of speech' to the skin convey sense in allegory. This has to be grasped in the context of modern knowledge of science about the skin and its sense of touch which has the extraordinary ability to pick up and transmit, a wide variety of signals and responses. Thus for versatility of communication the skin ranks next to brain.

The Holy verses are :-

(1) *'Ye did not seek to hide yourself, lest your hearing your sight and your skins shall bear witness against you. But ye did not think that God knew not many of the things that ye used to do'. (41:20-22).*

(2) *'And they say unto their skins: Why testify ye against us? They say: Allah has given us speech Who giveth speech to all things and who created you at the first and unto whom ye are returned' (41:21).*

(3) *'Till, when they reach it, their ears and their eyes and their skins testify against them as to what they used to do'. (41:20)*

(4) *'Ye did not hide yourselves lest your ears and your eyes and your skins should testify against you, but ye deemed that Allah knew not much of what ye did'. (41:22).*

From the above holy verses of the Quran, it is evident, that besides the sense of hearing from the ears and the power of speech by the tongue and the sense of vision from the eyes which are observed and recorded through physical forces and through the invisible and hidden processes, there is another vital sense, which is the (sense of touch) from the skins. The skin represents the external nervous system of the organism and its sensitivity and ability to pick up and transmit a variety of signals is simply tremendous. The sensitivity of the skin has extraordinarily a wide range of responses which exceeds that of all other sense organs and that for versatility it comes next to the brain. Skin is therefore the most vital organ to detect and record all the doings of man right from his birth to his death. Some of the major characteristics of the skin allegorially revealed by the Holy Quran are described below. It will become evident how important is the role of the skin of man and the sense of touch and other senses and what a great similarity is found between the science of the sense of touch from the skin and the verses of the Holy Quran on the role of skin and of other organs on man's accountability.

The Skin of Man as the Witness of Allah for Man's Accountability

The skin as a tactile organ covering man's body plays vital role not alone physically but also behaviourally. It is the largest organ of the body. J. Lionel Taylor describes the sense of touch from the skin in his book titled The Stages of Human Life' as the chief sense. A quotation from his book is given below :-

> The greatest sense in our body is our touch sense. It is probably the chief sense in the process of sleeping and waking; it gives us our knowledge of depth or thickness and form; we feel, we love and hate, are touchy and are touched through the touch Corpuscles of our skin'. (J. Lionel Taylor, The Stages of Human Life, 1921 page 157).

Ashley Montagu in his book Touching --the Human Significance of the Skin' explains that the skin is the oldest and the most sensitive of man's organs. It is the first medium of communication and our most efficient protectors. In the evolution of senses the sense of touch is the first to come into being. Touch is the parent of our eyes, ears, nose and mouth. It is the sense which became differentiated into others and is the mother of the senses. Perhaps next to brain, the skin of man is the most important of all organ systems. The sense most closely associated with the skin, the sense of touch, is the earliest to develop in the human embryo.

The skin in common with the nervous system arises from the outermost of the three embryonic cell layers, the ectoderm. The nervous system is, then, a buried part of the skin or alternately the skin may be regarded as an exposed portion of the nervous system. The skin is as the external nervous system of man. Skin as the largest sense organ of the body enables the organism to learn about its environment. It is the medium, in all its differentiated parts, by which the external world is perceived. The face and the hand as 'sense organs' not only convey to the brain a knowledge of the environment but convey to the environment certain information about the 'Internal Nervous System'. The skin, as we know from human faces, carries its own memory of conditions experienced in the remote and immediate past.

The surface area of the skin has an enormous number of sensory receptors receiving stimuli of heat, cold, touch, pressure, and pain.

Transmitted through the atmospheric environment, in addition to air movements, are gases, particles, changes in pressure, temperature, humidity, light, radiation and much else. To all these stimuli the skin is equipped to respond with extraordinary efficiency.

A voice makes one's skin 'tingle'. A dread fear makes one's skin 'creep'. The skin, in fact, does creep — it contracts, and this is the reason why one's hair sometimes stands on end (the pilomotor reflex). Not only our geometry and our physics, but our whole conception of what exists outside us, is based upon the sense of touch.

The finding of physiologists, anatomists, neurologists, psychiatrists, psychologists and other investigators is that the various elements comprising the skin have a very large representation in the brain. As a sensory system the skin is much the most important organ system of the body. A human being can spend his life blind and deaf and completely lacking the senses of smell and taste, but he cannot survive at all without the functions performed by the skin. When other senses fail, the skin can perform to an extraordinary degree for their deficiencies. The brain must receive sensory feedback from the skin in order to make such adjustments as may be called for in response to the information it receives. The feedback from skin to brain, even in sleep, is continuous. The skin is a good conductor of electricity. Electrical changes can be measured at the skin surface such as by psychogalvanometer or as is called 'lie detector'. Emotional changes acting through the autonomic nervous system usually produce an increase in the electrical conductance of the skin (a decrease in resistance) across the palms of the hands or feet. There can be little doubt that in tactile stimulation electrical changes are transmitted from one individual to the other.

Since the skin is derived from the same embryological

ectodermal layer as the eyes, several investigators have maintained that in such individuals the skin has retained some primitive optical properties and it is this that enables them to see with the skin. We all have stereognostic ability i.e. the ability to perceive objects or forms by touch. Most human being can almost 'see' the form of the object they have touched. Tips of the fingers have the greatest sensitivity in 'reading' that is in stereognising, the form of objects by touch. If anv evidence were required to demonstrate the mind of the skin it could rest on the sensory capacities of the finger tips alone. Those capacities, in the form of sensory receptors that pick up the stimuli, in turn transmit them to the brain in the form of complex nervous impulses.

The skin and the retina of the eye are unique in that their sensory receptors are laid out in a pattern. This enables both the retina and the skin to pick-up regularities and patterns of stimuli and to convert them readily into images in the brain.

The spatio-temporal perceptive capacities of the skin are quite remarkable. Time is handled almost as well by the skin as by the ear. The skin can pick-up a break of about 10 thousands of a second in a steady mechanical pressure or tactile buzz. Eye discriminations are about 25—35 thousands of a second. The skin picks up the location of distances on its surface very much more efficiently than the ear is able to locate sounds at a distance.

Gildard has shown that the possibility of communicating through the skin was, indeed a remarkable piece of prescience. The skin, Gildard has demonstrated, is capable of receiving and reading rapid and sophisticated messages. There is every likelihood', he says, 'that skin languages of great subtlety and speed can be devised and used. Perception through skin by means of its properties is a reality. The skin possesses the ability to respond to a large variety of modalities. The vibrotactile or electrotactile signal cannot be shut out. Nor can the skin close its eyes; it cannot even hold its ears—in this respect it more closely resembles the ear than the eye. The skin may be unique in combining the spatio-temporal dimensions of hearing and vision, the ear being best in the temporal and the eye in the spatial dimension.

The skin itself does not think, but its sensitivity is so great, combined with its ability to pick up and transmit so extra ordinarily wide variety of signals and make so wide a range of responses, exceeding that of all other sense organs, that for versatility it must be ranked second only to the brain itself. The skin, in fact, represents the external nervous system of the organism.

Gescheider has shown that the skin is able to localize sound waves of different intensities with remarkable accuracy which suggests all sorts of possibilities.

The skin as the sensory receptor organ which responds to contact with the sensation of touch, a sensation to which basic human meanings become attached almost from the moment of birth, is fundamental in the development of human behaviour.

From the above scientific explanation of the characteristics and quality of the skin and its sense of touch, it is found that there is a great similarity with what the science of skin explains and the verses of the Holy Quran on the observation of man's deeds and actions reveal for the purpose of man's accountability and judgement in the Hereafter, where man's own organs serve as Allah's witnesses and his own vital organs watch on him and on his conscience and mind. Man's deeds and actions are watched invisibly and recorded through invisible processes by Divine order and man's own hearing, sight and his skins bear witness and shall testify on the Day of Judgement against him for what he used to do. Man, therefore, should not think that God does not know what he has been doing during his life time (from birth to death) as his own ears, eyes and skins testify against him for what he used to do.

The Day of Judgement in the 'Hereafter' and the Requital for Man's Physical Deeds in the Metaphysical World

There is definite relationship between the 'Creator' and the 'created' or the Creature. The created has to submit and obey his Creator and worship Him as per His revelations and guidance. The love, obedience and respect by man (the created intelligent being), must be supreme for his Creator Allah, as Allah has the right to be esteemed, loved, obeyed and worshipped by the creature (man) in the light of guidance and teachings of the Holy Quran.

The Holy Quran reveals:-

(1) *'I created the jinn and the mankind only that they might worship Me'. (21:57).*

(2) *'And they esteem not Allah as He hath the right to be esteemed, when the whole earth is His handful on the Day of Resurrection and the Heavens are rolled in His right hand. Glorifie· He and High*

Exalted from all that they ascribed as partner (unto Him)'. (39:67).

The Holy Quran is the Word of Allah, the Creator of the heavens and the earth and of all things and of the 'Hereafter'. The Holy Quran further reveals as follows:-

(1) *'This is the scripture whereof there is no doubt, a guidance unto those who ward off evil'. (2:2).*

(2) *'Who believe in the unseen and establish worship and spend of that We have bestowed upon them'. (2:3).*

(3) *'With truth We have sent it down, and with truth has it descended and We have sent these as naught else save a bearer of good tidings and a Warner'. (18:105).*

(4) *'They believe in Allah and the Last Day and enjoin right conduct and forbid indecency, and vie one with another in good works. They are of the righteous'. (69:114).*

Allah has perfected and then chosen the religion of Islam for mankind. Islam means submission and obedience to the Will of One Allah and acceptance of His Commands as revealed in the Quran. For the guidance of mankind, Allah has revealed the Holy Quran as the perfect Code of Instructions for Human Conduct.

The Holy Quran describes Allah with absolute truth and describes His creations of the Physical universe, mankind, the jinn and all the visible, the invisible, the hidden and the unseen things, and the creation of the 'Hereafter' or the metaphysical worlds with absolute truth. As man is the created or the creature so he is bound to obey his 'Creator'. The created or the creature has to perform a role before his Creator for which he stands accountable during his life tenure. For accountability, the record of deeds and actions of mankind is observed for which he stands answerable in the 'Hereafter' on the Day of Resurrection which is the 'Day of Judgement'. The Judgement is on the basis of good or bad deeds of mankind performed by him during his life time in the physical universe, and man has to get its requital after his proper accountability in the 'Hereafter'. Accordingly, man with reference to his conduct either goes to the Paradise or the Hell. There is definite relationship and similarities between physical sciences and the Science of Religion taught by the Holy Quran as knowledge is the source to grasp and understand the substance of the Quran. The metaphysics of Quran has a link with the physical universe and man, and with his conduct which is under constant divine observation for accountability and judgement so that on the Day of Resurrection in the Hereafter he is rewarded or punished.

The Holy Quran reveals:-

(1) *'The Reality'. (69:1).*
(2) *'What is the Reality'. (69:2).*
(3) *'Ah, What will convey unto thee what the Reality is!'. (69:3).*
(4) *'Woe unto the repudiators on that day'. (83:10).*
(5) *'Those who deny the Day of Judgement'. (83:11).*
(6) *'There is but one shout and lo! they behold'. (37:19).*
(7) *'And say! Ah Woe for us! This is the Day of Judgement'. (37:20)*
(8) *'Couldst those but see when the guilty hang their heads before the Lord, (and say): Our Lord! We have now seen and heard, so send us back; We will do right, now we are sure'. (32:12).*
(9) *'And if We had so willed, We could have given every soul its guidance, but the word from the concerning evil doers took effect: that I will fill hell with the jinn and mankind together'. (32:13).*
(10) *'So taste (the evil of your deeds). For as much as ye forget the meeting of this your Day, Lo! We forget you. Taste the doom of immortality because of what ye used to do'. (32:14).*
(11) *'Ah, what will convey unto thee what the Day of Judgement is'. (83:17).*
(12) *'Again, what will convey unto thee what the Day of Judgement is'. (83:18).*
(13) *'A day on which no soul hath power at all for any (other) soul. The (absolute) Command on that day is Allah'. (83:19).*
(14) *'And we used to deny the Day of Judgement'. (74:48).*
(15) *'Till the inevitable came unto us'. (74:47).*
(16) *'Assuredly the Day of Decision is the term of all of them'. (44:40).*
(17) *'This is the Day of Decision. We have brought you and the men of old together'. (76:38).*
(18) *'Lo! the Day of Decision is a fixed time'. (78:17).*
(19) *'A day when the trumpet is blown and ye come in multitudes'. (78:18).*

The sense contained in the above Holy Quranic verses is very clear and understandable that the inevitable Day of Judgement shall come and man will know the Day of Resurrection in the

'Hereafter'. Mankind shall then realize and be sure of the 'Day of Judgement' and the guilty among the mankind will hang their heads and say to Allah: Our Lord, We have now seen and heard, please send us back and we will do the right but Allah will give hell to the evil-doers among the mankind and the jinn. As they forgot when they were in the physical universe of meeting their Lord on the 'Day of Judgement' in the 'Hereafter'. So, the evil-doers will taste the doom of immortality for what they used to do in the physical world.

Link of the Metaphysics of Quran with the Physical Universe and Man

There is a strong link of the metaphysics of Quran with the physical universe and man. In order to know and understand the reality of the metaphysics of Quran, one has to know the physical universe and man and also know about their creation, evolution and their purpose to perform and finally their ultimate fate or physical death for which they are destined or fated to meet the end. All physical acts of man have link or relation with the life to follow after death and beyond the physical universe i.e. in the 'Hereafter'. The 'Doomsday' or the Catastrophic collapse of the physical universe and man is certain and shall be the heaviest event to be faced by the physical universe and mankind as is revealed by the Holy Quran and as the Science of Astrophysics and Cosmology indicate and are found to be in complete concord and congruity with the Holy Quran. The Doomsday or the Catastrophic collapse of the universe is inevitable and is a must. Its taking effect or occurrence shall be the basic step for the transformation of mankind from the 'Physical state' to the 'metaphysical', or the step for the entry of mankind into the 'Hereafter'. Then in the Hereafter all events mentioned by the Holy Quran shall take place, namely, the 'Resurrection of man' his 'accountability' and trial (on the basis of his conduct and deeds and his performance in the physical universe) and the assessment of man for the purpose for which Allah created him and guided him with the wisdom of the Holy Quran. A 'Judgement' on his conduct shall be pronounced which shall decide either entry for him into the 'Paradise' or into the 'Hell'. All this is to happen in the 'Hereafter' which is eternal and where man shall live eternally and shall be immortal.

Similarity of Scientific Concepts, Observed Facts and Laws with Quranic Verses Lead to the Proof of Absolute Reality of the Existence of God

Now, analysing and linking all these metaphysical events with the physical events and realities of the universe and man, one feels absolutely certain of the existence of the Creator Allah. While pondering over the absolute realities contained in the allegorial and direct verses of the Holy Quran encompassed with knowledge and wisdom, one is baffled to discover the existence of highly modern concepts of science to be already present in the Holy Quranic verses reveald 1400 years ago. The facts and similarities show the portents and the tokens of Allah and prove His Act of creation and of His existence. The similarity of the sense and substance of the Holy Quran, with recently discovered and established facts of science clearly indicates that there is a definite and absolute link between the Holy Quran as the Word of God and of the realities of the physical creations discovered by man through the knowledge of sciences. This link leads mankind to know the ultimate reality behind the creation of universe and man and serves as a clear proof of the absolute reality of the Creator and makes man believe in the absolute truth of the Oneness of Allah and believe in the Quranic revelations as the Divine Words of Allah, intermittently revealed over a span of 23 years on the Last Prophet Muhammad (PBUH), the unlettered Messenger of Allah, for the guidance of all mankind. The Holy Quran is, therefore, the true message of Allah to mankind and is the absolute reality, revealing events to mankind for his guidance in the physical universe and the events to follow in the 'Hereafter'.

The tremendous wisdom and knowledge that has been coded allegorially and also expressed directly in each verse of the Holy Quran, prove beyond all doubts that the revelations are Divine which describe the origination and the creation of the universe and man, and tells about the events in the past, the present, and the future and tells about the hidden matters and about the visible, the invisible and the unseen matters and of the 'Life after death', i.e. the 'Hereafter'. The Holy Quran perfectly and truthfully describes the gravitational or the catastrophic collapse of the physical universe i.e. the 'Doomsday' or the Last Day of the physical universe and reveals about the re-emergence or the new creations of similar worlds to come again in existence after the Doom of the universe.

Science, is fully in consonance with the Holy Quran either directly or indirectly on physical matters, and by inferences and indirectly, one can easily draw the same conclusion for the absolute truth of the metaphysical matters. It is a matter of knowledge, understanding and faith that counts in grasping the sense contained in the Holy Quran. Man's knowledge of science is the means to understand physical creations. His faith and wisdom is the means to understand the metaphysical realities. Man's knowledge, wisdom and unflinching faith in the Holy Quran as the Word of God, gives total understanding of the Quranic doctrines of Eschatology and in the Oneness of Allah and in Prophet Muhammad (PBUH) as His Messenger, and the belief in the 'Hereafter'.

Physical sciences have barriers and limitations to probe even into the physical matters in the physical universe, but the divine matters and the metaphysical events in the Hereafter are permanently beyond the scope of science. It is only the science of religion of Islam, revealed to mankind by divine revelations which truly and perfectly tells about the absolute realities of the Physical universe and about the 'Hereafter' and about all the metaphysical events in the Hereafter. True science helps to understand the meanings of the Holy Quranic verses within the limits of observed or known knowledge in the observable universe, beyond that it is impossible to know even the existing physical realities of the mysterious and wonderful world. Science is confined to the knowledge of the physical matters which one can only observe through the physical laws. Therefore, it is beyond the scope of physical sciences to directly know about any thing which is metaphysical and pertains to the 'Hereafter'. It is only the Holy Quran which truthfully reveals to man the events of the metaphysical world. However, thorough knowledge of science and man's wisdom and his conscience and faith helps in clear understanding of the verses of the Holy Quran which reveals both the physical and metaphysical realities. Man can also know the realities of the events of the metaphysical world in the Hereafter by inferences from the similarity of science with the sense and substance contained in the Holy Quran. These realities in turn, lead the conscience, the faith and the common sense of man to believe in the unseen which the Holy Quran reveals and which is the absolute truth. Men of knowledge and understanding shall find to their surprize that modern scientific concepts, laws and facts of great fundamental importance and of far reaching consequences are encoded arcanely in the Holy verses of the Quran revealed on mankind by Prophet Muhammad (PBUH) 1400 years ago. These are found to be in amazing similarity on all fundamental aspects of man and the universe. The contents of the Quranic verses reveal miracles upon miracles and lead to the firm belief that the Creator Who created all things in 'true and due proportions' and 'with a set measure', fully knows His creations which He has described and encompassed with inexhaustable sense in short Arabic verses in a unique language style of the Holy Quran.

It is incumbent on all mankind and specially on scientists, intellectuals and scholars the world over, to study the Holy Quran as it is the Message of God to mankind full of Wisdom which describes great physical and metaphysical events of absolute truth and that man as superior creation is responsible to ponder over the revelations to find what does it say! And what does it reveal for the guidance of mankind! And then respond to the Message from the Creator to His Creature. The substance of the Holy Quran contains all kinds of subjects to guide man. On the moral side, it reveals to man, who has a faltering nature to live in a single brotherhood and to behave with proper conduct worthy of the lofty station given to mankind by Allah, the Creator.

Man is responsible and is answerable to God for his deeds on the 'Day of Judgement'. The Holy Quran guides him to obey and worship God in the light of the teachings of the Holy Quran. The love for God and the fear of God amounts to the remembrance of God which is also worship and obedience to Allah.

The 'Hereafter' or the Life after Death

The 'Hereafter' is life after death and is existence beyond life on resurrection. There lies the ultimate future of mankind after their death along with the death of the earth and the death of the entire universe on the appointed 'Doomsday' or on the gravitational and Catastrophic collapse of the universe to 'nothing'. Man will be resurrected on the 'Doomsday'. He will be revived and brought back to life once again for his accountability on the 'Day of Judgement' in the 'Hereafter'. He will be treated with reference to his deeds and actions in the physical world. He will either go to Paradise as wide as seven Heavens or to the Hell. The world of the Hereafter is the eternal world where man shall be immortal. That is a wonderful world, more pleasing and man will get all that for which his soul desires.

The 'Hereafter' to which is the journeying, is the ultimate abode of mankind on his Resurrection. Quran is the true word of Allah and it lays great emphasis on mankind that there is certainly 'Life after death', the 'Hereafter' which is one of the fundamental doctrines of Islam revealed by the Holy Quran. Among the fundamentals of Islam, the most important is the belief in the Oneness of Allah, the belief that Muhammad (PBUH) is the Last of the Prophets of Allah on whom the Holy Quran (the Word of Allah) was revealed by inspiration for the guidance of all mankind and the belief in the 'Hereafter', i.e. the 'Life after death' and the belief in the doctrines of Eschatology i.e. the 'Doomsday' and the 'Resurrection' of man, his 'accountability' on the 'Doomsday' or the 'Last Day' and the 'Day of Judgement' and the belief in the immortality of the 'Hereafter' when man shall either be rewarded to go to Paradise or punished with Hell, with reference to his deeds and actions in the present world.

Islam is perfected and is the chosen religion for mankind by God, which strongly invites attention of mankind to the 'Hereafter', i.e. 'Life after death' This is a great contribution by Islam to civilize mankind in the present world so that man is ready for accountability of his deeds on the Day of Judgement for the requital of his deeds when he is resurrected to answer. The eternal life begins in the 'Hereafter', which is absolutely another world and is excellent abode than the one in which we are now living and where life is short and a temporary one.

The Holy Quran describes the 'Hereafter' in a number of the Holy verses A few are quoted as below :-

(1) *'Those who have been given knowledge see that what is revealed unto thee from thy Lord is the truth and deadeth unto the path of the Mighty; the Owner of Praise'. (34:6).*

(2) *'Hath he invented a lie concerning Allah, or is there in him a madness? Nay, but those who disbelieve in the Hereafter are in torment and far error'. (34:8).*

(3) *'And We have not sent thee (O Muhammad) save as a bringer of good tidings and a warner unto all mankind, but most of mankind know not'. (34:28).*

(4) *'Say Lo! my Lord hurleth the truth. (He is) the Knower of Things Hidden' (34:48).*

(5) *'And who believe in that which is revealed unto thee (Muhammad) and that which was revealed before thee and are certain of the 'Hereafter'. (3:4).*

(6) *'And who forsaketh the religion of Abraham save him who befooleth himself? Verily We choose him in the world and Lo! in the 'Hereafter he is among the righteous'. (21:130).*

(7) *'And call not those who are slain in the way of Allah 'dead', Nay, they are living, only ye perceive not'. (25:154).*

(8) *'And of them (also) is he who saith: Our Lord! Give unto us in the world that which is good and in the Hereafter that which is good, and guard us from the doom of Fire'. (II:201).*

(9) *'Beautified for mankind is love of the joys (that come) from women and offspring and stored up heaps of gold and silver and horses, branded (with their mark) and cattle and land. That is comfort of the life of the world. Allah! With him is more excellent abode' (III:14).*

(10) *'(And remember) when the angels said: O Marry! Lo! Allah giveth thee glad tidings of a word from Him, whose name is the Messiah, Jesus, son of Marry, illustrious in the world and the Hereafter and one of those brought near (unto Allah)'. (III:45).*

(11) *'As for those, who disbelieve I shall chastise them with a heavy chastisement in the world and the Hereafter, and they will have no helpers'. (III:56).*

(12) *'And whoso seeketh as religion other than the Surrender (to Allah) it will not be accepted from him and he will be a loser in the 'Hereafter'. (III:85).*

(13) *'No soul can ever die except by Allah's leave and at a term appointed. Whoso desireth the reward of the world, We bestow on him thereof, and whoso desireth the reward of the Hereafter We bestow on him thereof, We shall reward the thankful' (III:145).*

(14) *'So Allah gave them the reward of the world and the good reward of the Hereafter. Allah loveth those whose deeds are good'. (III:148).*

(15) *'Let not their conduct grieve thee, who run easily to disbelief, for Lo! they injure Allah not at all. It is Allah's will to assign them no portion in the Hereafter, and theirs will be an awful doom'. (III:176).*

(16) *'O Ye who believe! what aileth you that when it is said unto you: Go forth in the way of Allah, ye are bowed down to the ground with heaviness? Take Ye pleasure in the life of the world rather then in*

the 'Hereafter'? The comfort of the life of the world is but little in the 'Hereafter' (IX:38).

(17) *'Lo! Allah hath bought from the believers their lives and their wealth because the garden will be theirs. They shall fight in the way of Allah and Shall slay and be slain. It is a promise which is binding on Him in the Torah and the Gospel and the Quran. Who fulfilleth the convenant better than Allah? Rejoice then in your bargain that ye have made for that is the Supreme Triumph'. (9:111).*

(18) *'Theirs are good tidings in the life of the world and in the Hereafter — There is no changing the Words of Allah — that is the Supreme triumph'. (10:64).*

(19) *'Lo! herein verily there is a portent for those who fear the doom of the Hereafter. That is a day unto which mankind will be gathered; and that is a day that will be witnessed'. (11:103).*

(20) *'Allah enlargeth livelihood for whom He will, and straiteneth (if for whom He will); and they rejoice in the life of the world, whereas the life of the world is but brief comfort as compared with the Hereafter'. (13:26).*

(21) *'Those who love the life of the world more than the Hereafter, and debar (men) from the Way of Allah and would have it crooked: Such are for astray'. (14:3).*

(22) *'Your God is one God. But as for those who believe not in the Hereafter their hearts refuse to know, for they are proud'. (16:22).*

(23) *'And it is said unto those who ward off (evil); what hath your Lord revealed: They say: Good for those who do good in the world there is a good (reward) and the home of the Hereafter will be better. Pleasant indeed will be the home of those who ward off (evil). (16:30).*

(24) *'But ye prefer the life of the world'. (88:16).*

(25) *'Although the Hereafter is better and more lasting'. (88:17).*

(26) *'That We may transfigure you and make you what ye know not'. (56:61).*

(27) *'We are your protecting friends in the life of the world and in the Hereafter. There ye will have (all) that your souls desire and there ye will have (all) for which ye pray'. (41:31).*

(28) *'A gift of welcome from the Forgiving, the Merciful'. (41:32).*

(29) *'O my People Lo! this life of the world is but a passing comfort and Lo! the Hereafter, that is the enduring home'. (40:39).*

(30) *'This life of the World is but a pastime and a game. Lo! the home of the Hereafter — that is life, if they but know'. (29:64).*

(31) *'And when thou recitest the Quran, We place between thee and those*

who believe not in the Hereafter a hidden barrier'. (17:45).

(32) *'And We place upon their hearts veils lest they should understand it, and in their ears a deafness; and when thou makest mention of thy Lord alone in the Quran, they turn their backs in aversion'. (17:46).*

From the revelations of the Holy Quranic verses, it is more than clear that there is an end to the universe and to all living and non-living things including mankind. The end is the 'Doomsday' as the Quran reveals or the Catastrophic collapse of the universe as the Science of Astrophysics and Cosmology explain. After the Doom or the gravitational collapse of the universe, mankind shall be Resurrected and shall find themselves in the 'Hereafter', which is a pleasant, eternal world full of comforts and full of everything. The Hereafter is a gift of Welcome from the Forgiving and the Merciful Lord. One will get everything there for which his soul desires or for which he prays. That is the enduring home for mankind and that is real life which man with good deeds shall enjoy for ever. Man shall stay immortal in the Hereafter.

Part VI

HUMAN NATURE, THE LOVE OF GOD FOR MAN, CONSUMMATION OF EARLIER DIVINE MESSAGES IN THE LAST MESSAGE OF THE QURAN. ISLAM PERFECTED AS RELIGION AND THEN CHOSEN BY GOD FOR MAN.

MAN'S WORSHIP IS ONLY FOR ALLAH; THE DOCTRINES OF SOCIAL SERVICE IN ISLAM; THE NEED FOR FRESH EXEGESIS OF THE HOLY QURAN TO CONVEY PROPERLY THE SENSE AND SUBSTANCE OF THE HOLY QURAN:

CHAPTER XV

(i) Quran on the Frail and Faltering Human Nature—A mirror reflection of Man of the present time.

(ii) The Love of God for man and the Consummation of Earlier messages of God in the Holy Quran The Last Message of God for man.

(iii) Quran the Absolute Guide for human race on earth.

(iv) Islam perfected as religion and then chosen for mankind by Allah.

(v) Man's Worship is only for Allah the Creator of man and of all things and not to the Sun or the Moon or to stars or the Tree or to the Fire, or to Statues or some other Creations or Creatures.

CHAPTER XVI

The Doctrines of Social Service in Islam taught by the Holy Quran.

CHAPTER XVII — Need for the fresh Exegesis of the Holy Quran by choosing befitting language and Corresponding Words for the Arabic language and to grasp properly the substance of the Quran.

Chapter 15

QURAN ON THE FRAIL AND FALTERING HUMAN NATURE A MIRROR REFLECTION OF MAN

The Holy Quran is centrally concerned with man and is a guide for human race. The Holy Quran reveals that Allah ranked man and preferred him above many of those whom He created with a marked preferment. Allah gifted man with conscience of what is right for him and what is wrong for him. He is given the choice to choose the path of conduct and thus he is responsible being and stands answerable and accountable for his deeds and doings to Allah. The Holy Quran reiterates that all nature has been made subservient to man: nothing in all creation has been made without a purpose and man himself has not been created 'in sport', his purpose being service and obedience to God's Will. The Holy Quran reveals that man is inspired with conscience which enables him to distinguish between the right direction or path or the wrong one. (XCI:8). Despite of this lofty station, the Holy Quran describes human nature as frail and faltering. In this respect, many of the verses of the Holy Quran on human nature and behaviour revealed 1400 years ago, have been found to stand amazingly true today as their applicability to the human nature of present-day man, is miraculously to the point as he takes the plea of one thing but does quite the opposite of it by making mischief, lying and sinfully behaving. He plays mischief in the garb of a peacemaker and add fuel to the fire least realizing that it involves destruction of human race. This is how man plans self destruction and becomes ungrateful to his Lord inspite of his high station among all the creatures and for all the bounties and good things which Allah has provided to mankind on earth.

Following are the Holy Quranic verses on faltering human nature:-

(1) *'And when it is said to them: Make not mischief on the earth, they say: We are Peacemakers only'. (II:11).*
(2) *'Are not they indeed the mischief-makers? But they perceive not'. (II:12).*
(3) *'The lying, sinful fore-lock'. (XCVII:16).*
(4) *'Nay, but verily man is rebellious'. (XCVII:6).*
(5) *'That he thinks himself independent'. (XCVII:7).*
(6) *'Then We reduce him to the lowest of the low'. (XCIV:5).*
(7) *'Lo! man is an ingrate unto his Lord'. (C:16).*
(8) *'Lo! man was created anxious'. (LXX:19).*
(9) *'Man is self destroyed: How ungrateful'. (80:17).*
(10) *'(Self) destroyed is he, how he planned!' (74:19).*
(11) *'Again (Self) destroyed is he, how he planned'. (74:20).*
(12) *'Fretful when evil befalleth him'. (70:20).*
(13) *'And when good befalleth him, grudging'. (70:21).*

The sense contained in the above Quranic verses is very clear, direct and gives perfect and true analysis of the faltering human behaviour which we find today at the individual level, at the national level and at the international level of man on earth.

In the context of the above Holy verses of the Quran, the present self destroyed behaviour of mankind with horrible nuclear and chemical weaponary may be watched, which is violently destructive, cruel, sinful, inhuman and beastly. The ruthless leaders, the conflict-crazy politicians and heads of the powerful nations in the world are at logger-head with one another and against the poor and weak nations of the world. The Holy Quran miraculously reveals that man plans his self-destruction and that how ungrateful he is! The revelations in the Holy Quran quoted above are amazingly true when one finds that powerful nations play mischief with weak nations, attack them and kill them and capture their territories, but declare and argue that they are only peace makers and do all this for the sake of peace.

Similarly powerful nations equipped with nuclear weapons and other deadly weapons constantly threaten one another with annihilation which is man's self-destruction on earth. The Holy Quran declares man to be ungrateful to his Lord for his planned self destruction on earth although Allah provided all good things for man on earth.

Mankind as a nation or community or as a group or class or as an individual frequently get involved in mischief mongering, hypocracy, tyranny, malice, meanness, dishonesty, enmity, prejudice and anger. Man becomes pitiless and adopts prideful attitude which is a cardinal sin of man and adopts rebellious attitude declaring independence from God arrogating to himself the attributes of self-sufficiency and becomes fearless of God and go on committing all sorts of sinful acts. The gift of conscience from God to man and the creation of man as the best community is thus misused for petty worldly gains which man is able to overcome by the gift of the built-in inspired conscience of man if he chooses to do so and thereby avoids all sins. Allah never speaks to mankind directly except through His Chosen Prophets on whom Allah makes revelations by inspiration. The heavenly Quran is a guide and the word of God for mankind to obey and the Holy Quran guides man to avoid all such sins, cruelties and excesses on man, as Allah loves His mankind. Allah makes revelations on Prophets to whom He sends angel messengers or make them hear a voice. In this respect the Holy Quran says:-

> *'And it was not (vouchsafed) to any mortal, that Allah should speak to him unless (it be) by revelations'. (42:51).*

It is very obvious that a mortal can never withstand the direct presence of Allah Who is 'light upon light' and is 'light of the heavens and the earth' and is of Infinite attributes and dimensions and each dimension is Infinity raise to the power of Infinity.

Prophets are the messengers of God and they reveal on mankind what is inspired to them by Allah. The Holy Quran is the Last Message of Allah to mankind and it is for mankind to ponder over it, grasp its sense and obey its teachings and have faith in it as it is the absolute reality from Allah.

Dr. Maurice Bucaille, a French Surgeon, in his book "The Bible, The Quran and Science" has established that of all the Heavenly Books, the Quran alone is untampered. He has also shown that the Quran spans the entire universe and whatever it disclosed 1400 years ago has been upheld by the latest discoveries of science. Unfortunately most of the mankind is ignorant of Islam and the Holy Quran and of the miracles which the divine document contains in its allegorial and direct verses. It is the greatest Message of Allah for mankind and it is for man to ponder over the message which is for the good of mankind on earth and in the Hereafter.

God has created man as His viceroy on earth. Adam's race must therefore behave worthy of the high station and honour and spend life as per the Word of God in the Holy Quran and obey his Creator Who appointed him as viceroy on earth and provided all good things for him.

The Love of God for Man and the Consummation of Earlier Messages of God in the Holy Quran — The Last Message

Muhammad (PBUH) is the last of the Prophets and its greatest member, for in him all the messages of earlier prophets were consummated. Prophet Muhammad (PBUH) revealed the Holy Quran, the like of which no human can produce (11:23).

The Holy Quran categorically states that :-

> *'It is a heavenly Book and is not from any earthly source, for in that case it would be liable to manifold doubts and oscillations'.*

After the revelation of the Holy Quran, 'good and evil have become distinct', so that one may follow whichever one may prefer. Waging war for the sake of acquiring worldly glory, power and rule is strictly prohibited. Allah loves His mankind and the obedience to the Will of Allah is reflected in the mutual love and respect of man by man and the love and obedience by man to his Creator Allah, which is part of the worship to Allah.

The Holy Quran reveals :-

> *'He who slays one human being, it is as if he had slain all mankind: He who saves one human being, it is as if he had saved all mankind'. (5—35).*

What a great lover of human being is the Creator Allah! Distinction and privileges based on tribal rank or race or colour are repudiated in the Holy Quran. Prophet Muhammad (PBUH) declared all men to be 'equal children of Adam', and the only distinction recognized in the sight of Allah is to be based on piety and good acts.

So, it is for mankind to prepare for the 'Day of Judgement' which is absolutely sure and certain.

The Holy Quran reveals :-

(1) *'O Mankind! Lo! We have created you male and female and have made you nations and tribes that ye may know one another. Lo! the noblest of you, in the sight of Allah, is the best in conduct'. (44:13).*

(2) *'He said: The knowledge is with Allah only. I convey unto you that wherewith I have been sent, but I see you are a folk that know not'. (46:23).*

(3) *'Thus Allah the Mighty, the Knower inspireth thee (Muhammad) as (He inspired) those before thee'. (42:3).*

The Holy Quran reveals that the noblest in the sight of Allah is the best in conduct. It further reveals that one who kills one human being is like killing all mankind and one who saves one human being is as if he has saved all mankind.

Attention of man on earth is drawn to the divine reality that the Holy Quran is the Last Message from Allah. There shall be no more message as the Holy Quran is the final message. Man must ponder, seek guidance and submit to the Will of the Creator Allah Who is All Merciful, All Beneficent.

Quran — The Absolute Guide for Human Race on Earth

Quran is a heavenly Book revealing wisdom, knowledge and informations of the two worlds and is a Divine Book of perfect guidance and teaches man the complete code and principles of life to follow. The Holy Quran teaches mankind peace, good conduct, decency, equality, justice, discipline, brotherhood and complete submission to God. The Holy Quran reveals that God is One and Prophet Muhammad (PBUH) is His Messenger on whom the Quran was revealed for the guidance of all mankind. And that man is accountable for his deeds before God when he is resurrected from the grave with the blow of trumpet on the 'Day of Judgement' in the 'Hereafter'. The Holy Quran, therefore, serves as a warner from Allah to guide mankind and teaches to submit to the Will of Allah and to worship Him.

A study and deep contemplation of the following Quranic verses shall clearly reveal more wisdom, **knowledge**, guidance and informations to mankind about the truthful Scripture the Holy Quran, as the Word of Allah and a divine guide for human race in the physical world.

The Holy Quranic verses are :-

(1) *'(This is) a Scripture that We have revealed unto thee, full of blessing that they may ponder its revelations, and that men of understanding may reflect'. (38:29).*

(2) *'And say! Praise be to Allah Who will show you His portents so that ye shall know them. And thy Lord is not unaware of what ye (Mortals) do'. (28:93).*

(3) *'And there is nothing hidden in the heaven or the earth but it is in a clear record'. (27:75).*

(4) *'Nay, but thou dost marvel when they mock'. (37:12).*

(5) *'And seek to scoff when they behold a portent'. (37:14).*

(6) *'Had We sent down unto thee (Muhammad) (actual) writing upon parchment, so that they could feel it with their hands, those who disbelieve would have said: This is naught else than mere magic'. (6:7).*

(7) *'And when the word is fulfilled concerning them. We shall bring forth a beast of the earth to speak unto them because mankind had not faith in our revelations'. (27:82).*

(8) *'And (remind them of) the Day when the trumpet will be blown and all who are in the heavens and the earth will start in fear, save him whom Allah willeth. And all come unto Him, humbled'. (27:87).*

(9) *'And the Trumpet is blown and Lo! from the graves they hie unto their Lord'. (36:51).*

(10) *'Crying: Woe upon us! Who hath raised us from the place of sleep? This is that which the beneficent did promise, and the messengers spoke truth'. (36:52).*

(11) *'There is but one Shout and Lo! they behold'. (37:19).*

(12) *'And say! Ah woe for us! This is the Day of Judgement'. (37:20).*

The above Quranic verses make it absolutely clear that the Holy Quran is full of blessings and guidance for mankind and invites mankind to ponder over its revelations and over the portents from

Allah. Men of understanding if contemplate on the verses of the Holy Quran, would find wisdom, knowledge and information about the physical and the metaphysical worlds. It is necessary that mankind pay heed and study the Holy verses which are expounded in Arabic for people who have knowledge and belief in Allah's revelations. Men having knowledge when argue believe in One Allah and in the Holy Quran as His Word and in Prophet Muhammad (PBUH) as His Messenger, but those who argue about matters of which they have no knowledge would never know, whereas, Allah knows all things. Mankind who have no faith in Allah's revelations revealed on the Prophet Muhammad (PBUH) and disbelieve in the revelations, then when the word is fulfilled concerning them, Allah shall bring forth a beast of the earth who would speak to mankind, because, mankind had no faith in the revelation made through human prophets among which Prophet Muhammad (PBUH) is the Last and the greatest of the Prophets and with him the prophethood ends. The bringing forth of a beast of the earth by Allah would be a very freak and bewildering portent for men to hear the animal speak to mankind which would be surprising, shocking and humiliating and a warner at the same time because people did not believe in Allah's revelations revealed through Human Prophets. This would happen because mankind had no faith in the verses of the Holy Quran revealed by Allah for the guidance and benefit of mankind through His Prophet Muhammad (PBUH), the Last of the Prophets.

On the 'Doomsday', a trumpet or a high frequency divine sound will be blown, when all living creatures in the heavens and on earth will be gathered to resume their original form (may be at the electronic, atomic and molecular level) by the order of Allah through His appointed angels and all dead will be resurrected and revived back to life with the sound of trumpet and will rise up from the place of their sleep i.e. the graves and when they see, they will at once know that this is the 'Day of Judgement' as promised by Allah and His Messengers spoke the truth. The blow of trumpet mentioned in the Holy Verse is some divine sound of high frequency with miraculous consequences of resurrecting mankind from the graves. They will all be gathered and will come in multitudes to their Lord.

Some of the Quranic verses which are allegorial and others which are clear, reveal truth, wisdom, guidance and information to mankind who contemplate over the sense contained in them and have sound knowledge and faith to understand and believe in the invisible and in the metaphysical events of the 'Hereafter'. Faith in the Holy Quran is the force of conviction and the source to know the ultimate reality. Faith in divine matters which are the absolute truth and faith in truth which is beyond the comprehension of man is a must to understand realities of the physical and metaphysical worlds i.e. the visible, the invisible, the hidden and the unseen.

The Holy Quran reveals :-

(1) *'And in the earth are portents for those whose faith is sure'. (51:20).*

(2) *'And (also) in yourself. Can ye then not see?' (51:21).*

(3) *'And by the Lord of the heavens and the earth, it is the truth even as (it is true) that Ye speak'. (LI:23).*

(4) *'A revelation from the Beneficent, the Merciful'. (41:2).*

(5) *'A Scripture whereof the verses are expounded, a Lecture, in Arabic for people who have knowledge'. (41:3).*

(6) *'He it is Who hath revealed unto thee (Muhammad) the Scripture wherein are clear revelations — They are the substance of the Book — and other (which are) allegorial. But those in whose heart is doubt pursue, foresooth, that which is allegorial seeking (to cause) dissension by seeking to explain it. None knoweth its explanation save Allah. And those who are of sound instructions say: We believe therein; the whole is from our Lord; but only men of understanding really heed'. (III:7).*

(7) *'Lo! Ye are those who argue about that whereof ye have some knowledge; Why then argue ye concerning that whereof ye have no knowledge? Allah knoweth. Ye know not'. (III:66).*

(8) *'Race one with another for forgiveness from your Lord and a Garden whereof the breadth is as the breadth of the heavens and the earth, which is in store for those who believe in Allah and His Messengers. Such is the bounty of Allah, which He bestoweth upon whom He will and Allah is of Infinite Bounty'. (LVII:21).*

(9) *'And vie one with another for forgiveness from your Lord, and for a Paradise as wide as are the heavens and the earth, prepared for those who ward off (evil)'. (III:133).*

(10) *'Know that the life of this world is only play and idle talk and pageantry and boasting among you, and rivalry in respect of wealth and children as the likeness of vegetation after rain, whereof the growth is pleasing to the husbandman but afterward it drieth up and thou seest it turning yellow, then it becometh straw. And in the*

Hereafter there is grieves punishment and (also) forgiveness from Allah and His good pleasure, whereas the life of the world is but matter of illusion'. (LVII:20).

The sense contained in the above Holy Quranic verses is explained as follows:-

The Holy Quran reveals verses which are absolute reality, and whose meanings are clear and understandable. Other verses of the Holy Quran are allegorial but persons with doubtful mind disagree in their interpretation and in their correct grasp. The fact is that nobody knows their interpretation and the meanings of allegorial verses except Allah. However, those who are of sound knowledge and information feel and believe in the verses to be Divine revelations from Allah. Only men of understanding really heed, as they have inside wisdom to understand the Quranic verses and their meanings.

Men may argue about matters of which they have some knowledge but to argue concerning matters of which they have absolutely no knowledge, is illogical, and do not make any sense and as such, their arguments are of no value and are irrelevant and are not right. It is Allah Who is the Creator and Who knows everything, and not those men who have no knowledge of such matters. Thus, arguments or discussions on a matter without having any knowledge about it are senseless and useless.

Keeping in view the Quranic truth and guidance, mankind must obey Allah, and compete one with another for forgiveness from Allah for a Paradise and ward off all kinds of evils so that the record of man observed by Allah is found to be of the righteous on his 'Resurrection', at the time of 'Accountability' on the Day of Judgement in the Hereafter. Allah is All Merciful and after accountability the faithful would enter the paradise, which is as wide as the heavens and the earth. This means the Paradise is as wide as seven heavens. Those among the mankind whose faith is sure, find portents of Allah on the earth. Man himself is a universe in miniature and is a clear portent of Allah if he ponders and examines the functions of his body, mind and conscience. Man is a living matter created out of non-living matter and is an assembly of atoms and molecules infused with life and this is as true as truth itself. The Quran guides mankind to submit completely before Allah and worship Allah as the Holy Quran teaches so as to qualify in this world for entering into the Paradise in the 'Hereafter'.

The life of this world is only a temporary phase and is just like a play and idle talk and pageantry and boasting among the mankind. It is nothing but rivalry in respect of wealth and children among the mankind. All this is as pleasing as the growth of vegetation after rain to the husbandman. But afterwards the vegetation turn yellow and dry up and become straw. This Quranic verse is revealed in allegory and gives example accordingly. Man has to taste death and the universe has to collapse on the Appointed 'Doomsday'. Mankind (who is mortal) has to pass through the mortal stage of this world for entry to become immortal into the next stage of the immortal world. In the 'Hereafter', there is severe punishment and a forgiveness from Allah when He pleases. However, the life of this world is nothing but a matter of illusion and is like a play in comparison to the life in the 'Hereafter' which is eternal and pleasant.

Allah created mankind in this world to worship Him. In reality man is on a trial. And if man's actions and deeds and his conduct is humane and decent and is in accordance with Quranic teachings and guidance, then all such deeds and actions of man are a part of worship to Allah and are recorded to help man on his resurrection and at the time of his Accountability on the Day of Judgement in the 'Hereafter' for entering into Paradise, which is the eternal abode for the faithful and obedient and for those who are of good conduct and behaviour.

Hence, the purpose of the creation of man by Allah is to worship Him and as such, Allah made mankind accountable for his conduct and behaviour during his tenure of life-span on earth. In order to guide mankind, Allah sent His Messenger Prophet Muhammad (PBUH) on whom the Holy Quran was revealed for the guidance of mankind. Therefore mankind should believe in the Divine Scripture of Allah and act accordingly. The Holy Quran is a perfect guidance in all respects. Man, after his accountability on the basis of his record, on the Day of Judgement, in the 'Hereafter', if found faithful and of good conduct would enter the Paradise, which is as wide as the heavens and the earth and is an immortal world of eternal happiness. It is for the eternal good of mankind to behave decently and act according to the Quranic teachings and guidance which amounts to worship of God and that is ultimately in man's own eternal interest.

In short, man's actions and intentions, and the signals and impulses transmitted and received by his organs are minutely observed and recorded by Allah through His visible, invisible, hidden and unseen forces and Messengers. Man's own system and his vital organs, such as skin, nervous system, brain, ears, eyes are the witnesses of Allah appointed on him to watch and record and have self transmitting and recording properties. The angels appointed to take note of each man's doings observe complete record of the righteous and of the vile. Thus, it leaves nothing unnoticed or unrecorded for the purpose of accountability. The skin as a tactile and the most sensitive organ plays very important role in communicating the deeds and doings and the feelings of man as the Quranic verses reveal. The skin plays a miraculous part in the process of man's accountability as is indicated by the Quranic verses and perform an invisible watch on man, through the invisible forces due to the impulses from the external nervous system of the skin and the impulses from the brain. The behaviour of the skin vis-a-vis man's accountability has been discussed in Chapter 14.

Islam Perfected as Religion and Chosen for Mankind by Allah

As already discussed the Holy Quran reveals that the religion of Islam is perfected and chosen by Allah for all mankind to follow it. Moreover, all the previous divine messages revealed on the earlier Prophets of Allah are finally consummated in the message of Quran. Islam is therefore the perfect religion for mankind to follow as it is the Chosen Religion of God for man. The prophethood, therefore, finishes with the Last Prophet Muhammad (PBUH). Muhammad (PBUH) is the seal of the prophets and there shall be no prophets in future.

The Message of Quran stands for all times. It is centrally for man and encompasses the knowledge of the universe and describes its reality to man as tokens of Allah. It is the infallible word of Allah. It can contain no mistake. It cannot be superseded by any new discovery. The Holy Quran is a Divine message and cannot be initiated by man. The Quran itself is a complete apperception of Allah. The Quran contains wisdom, knowledge, information and guidance either in the form of allegory or in the form of direct verses in Arabic language. The reader who has faith feels while reading and grasping the sense of the Holy Quran that it is the word of God and is a great divine message for mankind. The allegorial verses, contain great wisdom and knowledge about all that which it describes. With the attainment of more and more knowledge and wisdom, the sense contained in the Holy verses become more and more understandable and clearly indicates that the Quranic verses are from the Creator Allah. The Holy Quran is not man-made and cannot be man-made, as it contains unique informations and guidance full of great wisdom and knowledge about 'Creation' of all types and about many other things 1400 years ago when there was no knowledge worth the name. The Holy Quranic verses are revealed in allegory because the Holy Quran is not a text-book of science. It contains principles and conclusions of realities which are described in allegory and are understandable in the context of science which reveals knowledge of creation of all things and grows more and more with the passage of time.

Man's Worship is only for Allah the Creator of all things and not to the sun or the moon or the tree or to the snake or the fire or to statues or some other creations

The Holy Quran reveals :-

(1) *'And of His portents are the night and the day and the sun and the moon. Adore not the sun or the moon; but adore Allah who created them, if it is truth in Him Whom ye worship'. (41:37).*

(2) *'And if We had appointed in a Lecture in a foreign tongue they would assuredly have said: If only its verses were expounded (so that We might understand)? What! A foreign tongue and an Arab? Say unto them (O Muhammad): For those who believe it is a guidance and a healing; and as for those who disbelieve, there is deafness in their ears and it is blindness for them. Such are called to from a far'. (41:44).*

The sense contained in the above verses is that man is to worship Allah only Who created him and Who created all things and not the sun and the moon and other celestial bodies in the universe created by Allah and which are among the portents of Allah including the earth and man and the formation of the day and the night. Man is not created to worship fire or trees or snakes, or statues except Allah the Creator of all things. The Holy Quran reveals that those who believe in the message of Allah, they will find in it, a guidance and a healing but those who do not believe they are deaf and blind to catch the message of the Creator, which is in

Arabic. If the message would have been in a foreign language, i.e. other than Arabic language, then they (Arabs) would have surely said that if the message would have been in Arabic, we would have been able to understand and follow it. In reality, it is not the language that counts to know Allah and to know His Messenger and the Message and to understand and follow it. This Quran is for all mankind. The language of the Scripture is immaterial. It is the Will of Allah to choose any language. He chose Muhammad (PBUH) as the Last Messenger and the Holy Quran as His Last Message in Arabic revealed on mankind. We have to meet Allah on the Doomsday in the Hereafter. It is the faith and the belief in the Scripture and in Allah which matters. Allah has created infinite portents and tokens for man in the universe and has described in the Quran some of his portents as the visible, the invisible and the unseen and the hidden of the heavens and the earth. Allah is the Creator of the universe. He sustains mankind and the universe and all things in the universe. Allah creates what He will. Allah obliterates what He will. He is the Doer of what He will. Mankind is created only to worship Allah and nothing else.

Chapter 16

THE DOCTRINES OF SOCIAL SERVICE IN ISLAM TAUGHT BY THE HOLY QURAN

The Holy Quran reveals :-

(1) *'O Mankind! Lo! We have created you male and female and have made you nations and tribes that ye may know one another. Lo! the noblest of you, in the sight of Allah is the best in conduct: Lo! Allah is Knower, Aware'. (49:13).*

(2) *'Ye are the best community that hath been raised up for mankind. Ye enjoin right conduct and forbid indecency and ye believe in Allah'. (68:110).*

(3) *'There is no compulsion in religion. The right direction is henceforth distinct from error. And he who rejecteth false deities and believe in Allah hath grasped a firm hand hold which will never break. Allah is Hearer, Knower'.*

(4) *'He it is Who createth you, but one of you is a disbeliever and one of you is a believer, and Allah is Seer of what ye do'. (64:2).*

(5) *'He it is Who hath sent among the unlettered ones a Messenger of their own, to recite unto them. His revelations and to make them grow and to teach them the scripture and wisdom, though heretofore they were indeed in error manifest'. (62:2).*

Because the purpose of the existence of man, as of every other creature is submission and obedience to the Divine Will, God's role in relation to man or the creature is that of the Creator. Whereas, the rest of nature obeys God automatically, man alone is given the conscience and possesses the choice to obey or disobey. The Holy Quran reveals that there is no compulsion in religion as the right direction is distinct from error and he who believes in Allah shall never fail. With the deep seated belief in Satan's existence, man's fundamental role becomes one of moral struggle, which constitutes the essence of the human endeavour.

The doctrine of social service, in terms of alleviating sufferings and helping the needy, constitutes an integral part of the Islamic teachings. Pray to God and other religious acts are deemed to be a pure facade in the absence of active welfare service to the needy and to pay Zakat to the poor. In regard to this matter, the Quranic criticisms of human nature becomes very sharp. Man is by nature timid; when evil befalls him, he panics, but when good things come to him he prevents them from reaching others. The moral struggle primarily consists in freeing oneself of narrowness of mind and smallness of heart. One must expend one's possessions for the sake of others. It is Satan who whispers into man's ears that by spending for others, he will become poor. God on the contrary, promises prosperity in exchange for such expenditure, which constituted a credit with God and grows much more than the money people invest in usury. Hoarding of wealth without recognizing the rights of the poor is threatened with the direct punishment in the 'Hereafter' and is declared to be one of the main causes of the decay of societies in this world. The practice of usury in Islam is forbidden.

The moral, social, spiritual, religious and the socio-economic doctrines of Islam teaches all mankind to be brothers unto each other and to believe in Allah Who is the Creator of mankind and of all things. Allah created mankind as male and female and then made different nations and tribes among the mankind. These nations and tribes are Adam's race whether the colour of their skin is white, black, brown or yellow. Islam teaches that Muslims are all a single brotherhood and that they may know each other. There is no difference between them. The noblests among them in the sight of Allah are those who are the best in conduct and who forbid indecency and believe in Allah Who is the Creator of mankind. Allah has sent Prophet Muhammad (PBUH), the unlettered Prophet as His Messenger and revealed on him the Holy Quran which is the Book of Wisdom and teaches wisdom to mankind. There is no compulsion in the religion of Islam as the right direction is distinct from the wrong one and it is for man to choose the path of his conduct and those who believe in Allah have grasped a firm handhold which will never break. Allah is Hearer and Knower. Among the mankind, there are some who are disbelievers and some who are believers and Allah is Seer of what mankind do. And Allah is the Creator of mankind. It is therefore, incumbent on man to know his Creator, believe in Him and follow the teachings of His Message in the Quran revealed on Prophet Muhammad (PBUH) for the guidance of mankind.

Chapter 17

NEED FOR THE FRESH TRANSLATION AND EXEGESIS OF THE HOLY QURAN BY CHOOSING BEFITTING LANGUAGE AND CORRESPONDING WORDS FOR THE ARABIC LANGUAGE AND TO GRASP PROPERLY THE SUBSTANCE OF THE QURAN

There is a great need for the appropriate translation and exegesis of the Holy Quran by choosing befitting language and corresponding words for its Arabic Script. With the advancement in man's knowledge, and with the interpretation in events taking place, there is a better grasp and understanding of the Holy Quran which necessitates a translation as near to the sense of the Holy Quran as possible. The existing translations by a linguist are one man's efforts and are not clear enough to convey adequate sense behind the literal words of Arabic language of the Quran as it involves highly diversified knowledge of science.

Though sound knowledge of Arabic language is very essential for grasping and understanding the meanings of the Holy Quran. Yet knowledge of science in all branches is of the utmost importance to know the sense and substance of the Quran. Such diversified and specialized knowledge of physical sciences is vital for the accurate translation by choosing appropriate language and words and for the correct explanation of the sense of each word and each verse of the Holy Quran. Fresh translation is therefore essential for a better and more clear understanding of the meanings of the Holy Quran including the allegorial sense of the Holy verses. For centuries, commentators on the Holy Quran have inevitably made errors of interpretation in case of certain verses whose exact meanings could not possibly have been grasped. It is now possible to translate and interpret correctly as more knowledge and information is available.

The Message of Allah from beyond the seven heavens for mankind in Arabic language must become the object of the numerous branches of learning so as to grasp the correct sense of the substance contained in each Holy verse for a befitting and appropriate translation and exegesis or TAFSEER of the Holy Quran. For this purpose efforts must be made to use all kinds of possible resources in order to properly understand the meanings of each Quranic verse in the context of the highly specialized knowledge in all the concerned branches of sciences and the knowledge of Arabic language. The most vital aspect of translation is to correctly grasp and understand the real substance of the allegorial verses of the Holy Quran. A study and explanation of the Holy Quran such as the present one embraces many disciplines. It is found that all established laws of science are in complete similarity with the Holy Quran describing the universe and man right from their creation, evolution, sustenance, and to their ultimate collapse. The study of Quran in such a sense is highly encyclopaedic. It is therefore, vital to have all round knowledge of the physical universe and its objects, man and of all living things so that renowned groups of Exegesists, Religious Scholars, Researchers, Scientists and Intellectuals in all fields and other specialists should collaborate in the study of the Holy Quran subject-wise, ponder over it and analyse its meanings word by word and verse by verse to grasp the sense and the substance of the allegorial and symbolic verses of the heavenly message of Allah beyond space before translating the Quran in many languages spoken by mankind the world over. For this objective, initiative must be taken by all nations of the world and the entire resources specially of the Islamic World must be pooled up to understand the message of God by all mankind on earth and pay heed to the guidance from the Creator to His mankind.

The need is for fresh translation of the Holy Quran and its exegesis with the best possible understanding of its meanings in Urdu, English, French, German, Chinese, Japanese, Russian, Spanish, Italian and in many other important languages spoken all over the world. Proper translation may be undertaken by a specially selected Committee of Expert Exegesists, Scientists, Intellectuals and Religious Scholars. They must include specialists and experts in all the relevant fields so as to translate the Holy Quran and its allegorial verses as best as possible. The Holy Quran cannot be translated to choose befitting language and corresponding words in other languages so as to take the place of the Holy Quran in Arabic as the Glorious Quran is in inimitable symphony. The translation in any other language can never take the place of the Holy Quran in Arabic due to many factors like, correct grasp of allegorial sense, all-round knowledge of physical sciences and knowledge in all other fields, befitting language, corresponding words, vocabulary problems etc., etc. However, its correct sense can be grasped by appropriate translation with the best possible efforts. A beginning can be made with Urdu and English translations of the Holy Quran.

A translator, even an expert, is liable to make mistakes in the translation of scientific verses, unless he happens to be a specialist in the discipline in question. There is a great importance of an association between linguists and scientists so as to understand the scientific sense and knowledge under revelations.

The present translation, specially in Urdu is not appropriately worded. It is not adequately sense-conveying and clear enough. It is confusing because of the lack of vocabulary, the lack of all-round knowledge of the exegesists on scientific subject-matters which the Holy verses reveal, the lack of understanding the allegorial sense of the verses by the exegesists for revealing the hidden and the arcane meanings in the verses about the science of creation, evolution and the catastrophic end of the physical universe and the creation of life and the creation and reproduction of man and other metaphysical events. It is more than evident that an appropriate translation of the Holy Quran cannot be the one man's job. This implies that a thorough linguistic knowledge is not, in itself sufficient to understand these verses from the Holy Quran. It needs the most closest attention of many teams of experts and all-round sound knowledge for better understanding and for suitable translation of the text of each verse.

We are therefore not paying due justice and adequate attention to understand the wisdom in the message of God—the Holy Quran and in proper understanding the religion of Islam as perfected by Allah and chosen by Allah for man to follow. The understanding of the wisdom, information and knowledge of the Holy Quran from the translation made only by one man, who has inadequate knowledge of the modern sciences in respect of the universe and man and of so many other things, is not fair and just to understand the divine document which is full of miracles, wisdom and knowledge, and which provides proof in its verses that the Holy Quran is not man-made and cannot be man-made. In order to understand the substance of the message of Allah in full and in true sense, it is necessary to possess and to pool all-round knowledge by many exegesists. A very large portion of the Holy Quran makes revelations about universe and man which are highly scientific. It cannot be one man's job to grasp the unlimited wisdom and knowledge contained in the allegorial verses of the Glorious Quran which reveals many things on many subjects. However, to study and understand a special subject or matter revealed by the Holy Quran, it would be advisable to collect the concerned Holy verses subject-wise for study in the context of all natural sciences. The Quranic verses on each individual subject are interspersed throughout the text of the Holy Quran. This would give greater understanding of the subject or matter and the sense contained will be more clear and understandable. Thorough knowledge of the Arabic language and thorough knowledge of the subject-matter which the Holy Quranic verses reveal is necessary for proper understanding the Quranic sense contained in each word and each verse before its translation in any language is attempted with appropriate, corresponding and equivalent words for its Arabic script. It is therefore, obligatory on the exegesists to convey as far as possible the original sense of the Quranic verses while attempting exegesis or translation, interpretation and explanation of the Holy Quran.

The Quranic exegesis is gaining great significance with the number of discoveries and inventions in the field of modern science. The Quran is the inspired word of Allah, in which there can be nothing false or antiquated. It teaches the divine truth, which is the absolute truth. The sense of many modern discoveries about Cosmogony, Cosmology, Astrophysics, Astronomy, Quantum, Mechanics, Relativity, Chemical Kineties, Chemistry, Physics, Biology, Genetics, Anatomy,Embryology, Exogiology, Eschetology and many other sciences are already present in the Holy verses of the Holy Quran. The right approach to understand the message is to first of all correctly grasp the sense of the substance contained in the Holy verses in the context of modern knowledge of sciences and then carry out sound and proper translation of the Holy Quran in Urdu and in English and in all other major languages of the world.

The Author who by profession is a Civil Engineer with his limited knowledge and a humble level of understanding has attempted to explain the great sense encompassed in only a few of the Holy Quranic verses which reveal wisdom, knowledge and information about the universe and about life and man, and about the visible, the invisible, the hidden and the unseen matters including the doctrines of Eschatology which the Holy Quran contains either in allegory or in direct form.

Men of wisdom, knowledge, understanding and faith would be astonished and surprised to find miracles of the predated facts and realities already present and beautiful encompassed in the allegorial, symbolic and direct words of the Holy Quranic verses. Is it not miraculous that most modern facts of science and facts which are yet to be discovered are present in the Holy Quran revealed on Prophet Muhammad (PBUH) in Seventh Century A.D.?

The need of the present times is the better understanding of the scientific text of the Holy Quran and its correct translation in the light of higher level of understanding of the modern sciences to understand and grasp the Quranic sense of each word and each passage. This is very necessary for the total understanding and grasp of the substance and sense of the Holy Quran. Accurate and appropriate Quranic translation of the description of physical objects in the universe and their realities revealed by the Quran, are highly necessary, so that, as an inference of such realities, men of knowledge and faith lead to the unflinching belief and to the absolute reality of the metaphysics of Quran and to the firm belief that the Holy Quran is the word of God spanning the knowledge of physical and metaphysical worlds and is for the guidance of mankind. Scientists the world over must take a leap of faith to understand the metaphysics of the Quran.

Unfortunately, the verses from the Holy Quran, specially those concerning scientific matters, are not adequately understood, interpreted, explained and translated with the result that such translations do not convey the real sense which the Holy verses contain and which leads man to believe in the wonders and miracles of the Holy Quran and to the unflinching faith that the Holy Quran is a heavenly Book and is not man-made and cannot be man-made. It is, therefore, imperative that the Holy Quran must appropriately be translated afresh and in a befitting manner so that it conveys exactly the sense which it contains. Accurate translation of the Holy Quran is obligatory on the world of Islam and their religious duty is to inform the rest of mankind. Quranic translation specially in Urdu and in other languages must clearly be understandable in the context of the modern knowledge of sciences. It therefore needs updating and revision in the sense that it should be more clear, appropriately worded, to convey the real and the proper meanings of the Holy Quran and grasp its sense and be correctly understandable by all. The allegorial and the conclusive form of verses revealing the main principles and concepts of sciences need proper explanation. In the past it may not have been possible to do so and to grasp the sense and knowledge contained in the verses, but due to the advancement in knowledge and a better understanding of the universe and man, it is now possible to do so. It is therefore necessary to have more clear and better sense conveying translation of the Holy Quran in Urdu, English and in other languages. Such translation is necessary specially for the verses relating to the science of creation, evolution, sustenance and catastrophic collapse of the universe and for the verses concerning the creation and reproduction of man. Equally vital is the sense contained in the Holy verses about the invisible, the hidden and the unseen creations of the universe and of the metaphysical events in the Hereafter.

The Author, therefore, strongly invites the attention of Learned men, the Research Organizations conducting research on the Holy Quran, and of the entire Islamic World and of all Islamic Governments to undertake specific studies of the Holy Quran for its translation on scientific, systematic and at expert level so that its allegorial and conclusive type of sense be correctly interpreted and wisely decoded. It is obligatory on all the Islamic world, to understand the correct sense of the message of God, ponder over all that which it contains and all that which it teaches and guides mankind in all spheres of life.

It must be clear that the Holy Quran is the message of God for all mankind on earth. It is therefore equally obligatory on all men and women of all the countries of the world irrespective of their religious belief, colour and creed to know what the Holy Quran says. The Holy Quran is the message of God for human beings. All human beings must know the message and those who already know, they in turn must let others know it with proper translation of the original message of God.

In addition to the translation of the Holy Quran, there is a tremendous need for the preparation of an 'Encyclopaedia the Holy Quran'. This is necessary to explain the allegorial sense of the verses and most specially the portion of the Quran which deals with the universe and man. Each word and each verse need proper understanding and thorough grasp of the allegorial and direct sense contained therein, which needs explanation in the context of modern sciences. With the passage of time and with the advancement in man's knowledge and with greater and better understanding, the 'Encyclopaedia the Holy Quran' will also be made more and more near to the real sense encompassed in the Holy Quran and shall need revision and more elaboration from time to time on achieving further knowledge. The wisdom of Quran is for all times. It is unending. Its understanding will go on with more and more discoveries and inventions of the universe and man. This aspect of the Holy Quran is miraculous and proves that the Holy Quran is a divine message and is not man-made and cannot be man-made.

Translation of the Holy Quran in English by Muhammad Marmaduke Pickthal

The translation of the Holy Quran in English rendered by Muhammad Marmaduke Pickthal, published first in 1930 and then in 1935 is an incredible work. Pickthal had gained mastery over the diction and niceties of the Quranic language. He was a devoted Muslim. 'The Glorious Kuran", is the first English translation by an English Muslim, who is an Arabic Scholar, which is rendered almost literally in a most befitting language. Pickthal conducted word by word scrutiny and revision of his momentous translation at Al-Azhar under the advice of the Nizam of Hyderabad Deccan. The translation was finalized with the help and guidance of Shaikh-ul-Azhar Mustafa-al-Maraghi, one of the greatest authorities on the Quran. Rabita-al-Alam Al Islami has selected 'The Glorious Kuran" as one of the authentic English Translations for distribution during pilgrimage. The Holy Quran is untranslatable. One can only convey the sense. A translation, however, good, cannot and will not take the place of the Arabic text. Pickthal's translation is the best attempt to convey the Arabic sense of the Holy verses. His translation is nearest to the original but, with the attainment of more scientific knowledge during the last more than 50 years, and with better understanding of the Holy verses revealing scientific matters and with the interpretation in events taking place and with new discoveries and inventions taking place, the Quranic verses have become more clear and understandable, therefore, it becomes necessary to update translation by selecting befitting scientific words and use relevant terminology to convey better and proper sense of the Arabic substance encompassed in the Holy verses.. Improvement on Pickthal's translation where necessary may be undertaken in the light of modern scientific knowledge

However, in case of Urdu translations of the Holy Quran, momentous efforts are required to update it by clearly understanding and interpretting the sense of the Holy verses and by selecting appropriate and befitting words and its equivalent in Urdu. More efforts are needed for the Urdu-interpretation and translation of the Holy verses concerning the science of creation of the universe and of man and of earth. The existing Urdu translation by linguists revealing scientific matters encompassed in the holy verses is somewhat confusing, unclear and inappropriate. This needs to be updated in the light of greater understanding of the Holy Quran after the attainment of greater scientific knowledge and understanding. The association of scientists with the linguists in the translation of the Holy Quran in any language is a MUST. With the attainment of knowledge and with greater understanding of the Holy Quran, its translation needs improvement and updating from time to time.

Conclusion

A careful study of the Holy Quran reveals that there is an amazing similarity of science in all its disciplines with the Holy Quran. The agreement of most modern science with the Quran which was revealed 1400 years ago is simply bewildering for men of learning. The Holy Quran reveals physical facts about the creation of Adam the First man, or human being in perfect human form and then the reproduction of man, who is sown broadcast in earth and is caused to grow as a growth from the earth. The Holy Quran further gives details of various stages how human life begins. The Holy Quran reveals about the beginning of life in the womb of mother at the level of molecular biology, cell biology, the DNA, genetic, engineering and chromosomes and reveals something much more beyond the molecular biology. It reveals the resurrection of man and reveals about the Creator Allah and His mysterious and wonderful physical universe and His wonderful eternal world of the 'Hereafter', the ultimate abode for mankind on the gravitational collapse of the physical universe.

Also, the Holy Quran reveals about the creation of the universe at the level of particle physics. The Holy Quran gives hints about the creation, evolution and obliteration of the universe at the level of sub-atomic or sub-nuclear particles and at the level of black holes, singularity and zero volume. The Holy Quran contains hints with regard to the working of the universe, as a whole, and includes knowledge in allegories concerning general relativity, special relativity, Quantum Mechanics, uncertainty principle and the interaction of all the four (now three) fundamental forces. It reveals knowledge hinting towards the gravitational collapse of the universe to a point of singularity and zero volume and its obliteration to 'nothing' or 'naught' and to something much more beyond that. It reveals all about from the Big Bang to the Big Crunch and reveals beyond the Big Crunch — the re-emergence of a universe like the present universe and the present earth. It further reveals about the Resurrection of man in the Hereafter. 'One of the most amazing things is that the Universe should be so close to the dividing line between collapsing and expanding' says Stephen Hawking: This finding is also in similarity with the Holy Quran, which reveals:

> *'And Unto Allah belongeth, the unseen of the heavens and the earth and the matter of the Hour (of Doom) is but as a twinkling of the eye, or it is nearer still. Lo! Allah is able to do all things'. (16:77).*

If the universe is closed as is indicated, it could perhaps keep bouncing back and forth in a cycle of different universes. If that is the case, the universe that we inhabit would be just one of many. In this respect the Holy Quran reveals:-

(1) *'The day when We shall roll up the heavens as a recorder rolleth up a written scroll. As We began the first creation, We shall repeat it. (It is) a promise (binding) upon us. Lo! We are to perform it'. (21:104).*

(2) *'On the Day when the earth will be changed to other than this earth and heavens (also will be changed) and they will come-forth unto Allah, the One, the Almighty'. (14:48).*

(3) *'Have they not seen that Allah Who created the heavens and the earth Able to create the like of them and hath appointed for them an end whereof there is no doubt? But the Wrong doers refuse aught save disbelief'. (17:99).*

(4) *'Is not He Who created the heavens and the earth Able to create the like of them? Aye, that He is! for He is All Wise Creator'. (36:81).*

(5) *'Then He ordained them seven heavens in two days and inspired in each heaven its mandate: and We decked the nether heaven with lamps and rendered it inviolable. This is the measuring of the Mighty, the Knower'. (41:12).*

(6) *'Abiding there so long as the heavens and the earth endure save for that which thy Lord willeth: Lo! thy Lord is Doer of what He will'. (11:107).*

(7) *'Allah effaceth what He will and established (what He will) and with Him is source of Ordinance'. (13:39).*

In addition to the above verses the reader may refer to the Holy verses (24:45), (16:40), (II:117), (36:82), (19:35), (6:73), (22:70) on page 179.

It is surprising that this highly scientific aspect of the Quran, which is of tremendous consequences to know Allah, to Know His Messenger and to know His Message of the Holy Quran has not been properly understood and grasped for its tremendous sense and substance encompassed in the Holy verses which is of great importance and clearly shows that the Holy Quran is the message of God for man and is a divine reality in its absolute form. It clearly shows that it is the Message from the Creator to mankind. The Holy Quran is centrally concerned with man and reveals the realities of the physical universe to man as God's tokens or signs or his portents so that man knows God through these tokens. The Holy Quran reveals to man about the doctrines of Eschatology i.e. Death, Resurrection, Accountability, Judgement and Immortality. It reveals about the Hereafter and about man's 'resurrection' on the Doomsday or the gravitational collapse of the universe. The 'Hereafter' is an eternal world for which man is on a transit journey and is on trial for the obedience of God's will in the light of the teachings of the Holy Quran for the period of his life-span in the physical world.

The divine reality of the Holy Quran was revealed by Allah on His Last Messenger, Prophet Muhammad (PBUH) in a span of about 23 years for the mercy and guidance of all mankind 1400 years ago. Prophet Muhammad (PBUH) himself was unlettered. The revelations from God were conveyed to Prophet Muhammad (PBUH) by inspiration through Angel Gibriel who used to come in the likeness of a man. The words of revelations remained as if inscribed upon his heart. These were recited by Prophet Muhammad (PBUH) and many Muslims and committed the whole Quran to memory. The Holy Quran had been recorded in writing before the Prophet's death. The Holy Quran, the Message of God was thus revealed on Prophet Muhammad (PBUH) in this manner for the guidance of all mankind. The Holy Quran is an infallible divine word of God collected in Book Form, literally meaning 'Reading'. The Reading of the man who knew not how to read.

Scientific description in the Holy Quran about the physical realities of universe and man, their creation and sustenance and the ultimate gravitational collapse or the Doom of the universe and the all round similarity of science with the Quran on all such fundamental and vital aspects are clear cut portents of Allah for mankind so that man may know that the Quran is a Heavenly Book of perfect reality from Allah who is the Creator of Universe and man and Who knows the visible, the invisible and the hidden things in the universe. These include visible and invisible living creatures in different form and different environment and non-living matter and energy.

Modern scientific knowledge enables us to understand certain verses of the Holy Quran which until now, it has been impossible to interpret, as man could not compass it in knowledge as the interpretation (in events) has not yet come. It is simply amazing and most stunning that such knowledge was revealed by Prophet Muhammad (PBUH) 1400 years ago. How is it possible that an unlettered man (Prophet) could reveal perfect and real knowledge about the mysterious universe and wonderful man 1400 years ago? All this is Divine Revelations from Allah! It is the Message of the Creator (Allah) through His Messenger Prophet Muhammad (PBUH) for the guidance of all mankind.

All this knowledge and wisdom encompassed in the Holy Quran prove that the Quran is not man-made and cannot be man-made. Numerous proofs of such realities and their descriptions lie in the text of the Holy Quran either in allegory or in direct form as is explained in this study. All those who have sound knowledge if thoroughly ponder over the substance of the Quran and over the text and script of the Quran shall find that the Holy Quran cannot be man-made and is not man-made.

It is highly imperative that Scientists specialized in all disciplines of physical sciences read the verses of the Holy Quran concerning the universe and man, analyse the allegorial and direct verses, ponder over them and they will find to their utter amazement and surprise that most modern scientific facts about the physical realities in all branches of science regarding the wonderful and mysterious universe and man, are already present in the Holy Quran which was revealed on Prophet Muhammad (PBUH) 1400 years ago.

The miracles of similarity, the miracles of agreement, and the miracles of complete concord of established sciences in all branches with the Holy Quran are bewildering and directly prove that the Holy Quran is not man-made and cannot be man-made for all that perfect Wisdom, perfect Knowledge and perfect Information that it contains.

The Holy Quran is definitely the word of Allah Who is the One God, the Creator of man and of all things. Allah is the Alive, the Aware, the Subtile, the Seer, the Eternal, the Shaper out of naught, the Fashioner, the Omniscient, the Omnipresent, the Omnipotent and the Omnific.

The Holy Quran embraces knowledge in all the diversified fields and in all disciplines of Sciences. Indeed, no Scientific discipline is left which is unmentioned by the Holy Quran. The Quran contains and indicates knowledge about living and non-living matter and energy (in visible and in invisible form), right from molecular biology and particle physics to all other fields of science at various levels and thus encompasses the universe and man in knowledge either in allegory or in direct form. The Holy Quran not only discusses life at the level of molecular biology but much beyond and similarly describes the universe at the level of particle physics and much beyond. It discusses metaphysical matters like the resurrection of man, his accountability and about the eternal world of the 'Hereafter' and the re-emergence of the universe after its catastrophic collapse or Doom. These matters are beyond the understanding power of man. And faith with the help of knowledge is the means to understand its absolute reality, which the Holy Quran teaches. In addition, the Holy Quran also reveals about the invisible, the hidden and the unseen of the heavens and of the earth. It reveals about the jinn, an invisible creation created out of smokeless fire or essential fire, parallel to man. It also reveals about the extra-terrestrial life in space. The Holy Quran reveals about the invisible 'Black holes', the DNA, the Spirit and about the unseen world of the 'Hereafter'. The Holy Quran reveals about space travel and about the inviolability of the universe.

Prophet Muhammad (PBUH) was unlettered. He could not reveal all these miracles of Wisdom and of knowledge about the physical universe and man, and about the world of the Hereafter of hispown accord. Moreover, modern knowledge of all the physical sciences present in the Holy Quran was not known at that time (1400 years ago). In addition to above, the most important aspect is that the substance and the sense encompassed in the Holy Quran proves beyond all doubts that the Quran is divine revelation and cannot be man-made. In the seventh Century A.D., there was absolutely no knowledge about the universe and man and of the type which the Holy Quran reveals i.e. about the creation, evolution and the catastrophic collapse of the universe and about the creation and reproduction of man. It is pointed out that the knowledge of physical sciences has its first beginning hardly 500 years ago. This is evident from the fact that Galileo was condemned by the Inquisition in 1633, because he maintained that the earth rotates and revolves. This shows that about 350 years back man never new that the earth rotates! This was man's level of knowledge in the year 1633. The reader may then well imagine the level of knowledge and the understanding power of man nearly a thousand years even before the period of Galileo. Moreover, modern physical sciences has hardly a beginning of less than one hundred years. But the presence of the allegorial hints about the upto-date and recent inventions and discoveries in the Holy Quran, like the Black holes, the DNA, Francis Crick's Concepts like 'Pan Spermia' similar to the broadcast of (human) Adam's spores or seed in earth as revealed by the Holy Quran and to grow as a growth in earth, are simply amazing.

The gravitational collapse of the universe and its obliteration to the state of singularity and zero volume or to 'nothing' or 'naught', and the re-emergence of a similar universe and a similar earth out of naught, the colossal power packed in the structure of atom as Einstein defines in his special theory of Relativity E Mc^2 and the expansion of universe as per Hubble's Law, the working of the universe as a whole as per Einstein's General Relativity, the apocalypse of the universe, i.e. from the Big Bang to the Big Crunch as Dr. Wheeler states, and man's probe in space by overcoming force of gravity of the earth i.e. the indication of space travel and Professor Hawking's concept of uniting Quantum Mechanics which describes matter at atomic level, with General Relativity which explains the working of the universe as a whole, Max Planck's Quantum Theory, Neils Bohr's uncertainty principle, Professor Stephen Hawking's concept of the very close dividing line between collapsing and expanding of the universe etc. and the presence of all such knowledge in the Holy Quran at the level of molecular biology and at the level of particle physics indicate something beyond miracles. It directly indicates the Revelations as the act of Divine Power and shows the existence of the 'Unimaginable Supreme Being', the Creator of the Universe and man, Who is Allah, the One God and the Holy Quran as His Message and Prophet Muhammad (PBUH) as His Last Messenger on Whom the Holy Quran was revealed for the guidance of all mankind.

How is it possible that the Holy Quran contains every modern knowledge about the universe and man and that which is recently discovered concerning the creation, evolution and the catastrophic collapse of the universe or the Doom of the universe and the first Creation of Adam in human form i.e. man and the sowing and broadcast of his seed (sperm) on earth for reproduction on earth. The Wisdom and knowledge encompassed in the Holy Quran explaining the working of the universe as a whole, is in such form and is at such a level that it clearly indicates that only the Creator would know all such things and would reveal such knowledge of such matters and who encompassed it in such a form and revealed the Quran as a documentary miracle 1400 years ago for man to know God and to seek guidance from it.

All facts of agreement between science and the Holy Quran are miracles. These are amazing portents of Allah and very clearly indicate that the Holy Quran is undoubtedly a Heavenly Book and is the word of God and was revealed on Muhammad (PBUH) the Last Messenger (Prophet) of God for the guidance of all mankind.

The proof of the Holy Quran that it is not man-made lie in the realities and in the knowledge and wisdom which the Quran reveals. It gives open invitation to all mankind, specially to men of learning, the scientists, the intellectuals to read it, ponder over it so that they thoroughly understand it and feel it that the Holy Quran is the word of God. And if they try they shall never be able to produce a Surah (Chapter) like the Holy Quran.

The Holy Quran gives an open challenge to all mankind to produce a 'Sura' or Chapter, the like of one in the Holy Quran if they can! Man cannot do so and will never be able to do so. The Holy Quran is not man-made and cannot be man-made as its substance and script, its wisdom and knowledge reveals. The Holy Quran is the word of God and its sense and substance is full of wisdom, knowledge information and guidance and the script of the Holy Quran is unique and miraculous from all aspects. The Holy Quran is the divine message of Allah for all mankind which spans in knowledge, wisdom and information, the physical universe and man, and the metaphysical world of the Hereafter. The Metaphysical world of the 'Hereafter' which is unseen and invisible lie beyond the power of understanding and comprehension of man. Faith in the Holy Quran, the word of God, is the only means to know it and to understand it. Scientific data are unable to cast any light on a subject that goes beyond human understanding.

'Science' is nothing but 'trained and organized common sense' as wrote the great English Biologist Thomas Huxley.

To understand the Quran and to grasp its sense, science or knowledge in all diversified disciplines is the proper means to catch the allegorial sense of the Holy verses discribing the working of the physical universe as a whole and of man. The Holy Quran is not a text book of science but it is a Book of revelations from God and is written in a different style and form on diversified subjects to inform and guide man, and to show portents to man by giving hints so that man believes in it. The Holy Quran contains general concepts, basic principles and hints and gives indications so that men of knowledge who ponder will know for definite that it is the word of God.

The behaviour of matter and energy in the universe indicates that God exists with Infinite Power, Infinite Knowledge and Infinite Wisdom and His 'Creative Power' has created matter, energy and life out of 'naught', a stage or a period before singularity and zero volume.

In the next stage or period, things were brought to the state of singularity and zero volume. In the third stage the Big Bang occurred and in the fourth stage or period, the expansion of the universe and its evolutionary process is taking place by the interaction of fundamental forces under the physical law, i.e. Quantum Mechanics, General Relativity, Special Relativity, Uncertainty Principle and all the four (now three) fundamental interacting forces that took effect. The formation of the planet earth and the creation of life are probably the remaining stages or periods.

The Holy Quran indicates all these stages or periods with a similitude of 'Day' in the creation and formation of seven heavens including our universe and the earth.

To understand the Holy Quran, one has to go to the level of sub-atomic or sub-nuclear particles and to the level of particle physics in respect of the universe and to the level of molecular biology in respect of life when creation of life and the Resurrection of life are indicated by Allah in the Holy Quran.

Allah's 'Creative Power' at the level of sub-atomic particle or sub-nuclear particle and at the level of atomic and molecular level with the Spirit at His Command does all things as He Likes. So, the creation of universe and its formation and its obliteration, and the creation of life and death and its Resurrection and the creation of eternal world as the 'Hereafter' and the Resurrection of mankind to stay immortal in the Hereafter is an easy matter for Allah, as Allah is Able to do all things. Man would know these things if he achieves sound knowledge and have faith in the Revelations of the Holy Quran.

Furthermore, the Holy Quran reveals something much more important than the knowledge about the physical universe and the creation of life in the form of Adam (the first human being) and his race in the earth. Something more which is eternal is to follow on the gravitational collapse of the universe including man i.e. on the 'Doomsday

God created the universe and man out of prime mercy. God created man so that he may worship Allah and submit to His will as per the guidance of the Holy Quran. So, man is on trial with reference to his performance (deeds and actions) in this physical world and is accountable to God on the 'Day of Judgement'.

As a consequence of the creation of the universe and man and as a consequence of the conduct of man in the light of the Holy Quran, man is accountable to God with reference to his deeds and doings in the physical world, which are thoroughly watched and recorded through visible and invisible sources and through the parts of human body. Mankind is therefore warned for their conduct, and are guided to remain civilized in the present world so that they are ready for accountability of their deeds on the 'Day of Judgement' and on the gravitational collapse of the universe or the 'Doomsday' for the requital of their deeds when they are resurrected to answer in the 'Hereafter' or the 'Life after Death' i.e. existence beyond earthly life in another world which is eternal and is the enduring home for mankind and is real life. The Hereafter is a gift of welcome from the Merciful, the Forgiving, the Lord of the worlds, where the ultimate fate of mankind lie.

The cycle of life or the cycle of creation is to be ultimately completed in the above form. God created the universe and man out of prime mercy. Man is created as the best of creatures and is inspired with Soul and Conscience and is made capable to distinguish between right and wrong and is made able to choose the path of his conduct. The Holy Quran (the Message of God) is revealed on Prophet Muhammad (PBUH), the Last Messenger of God for the guidance of all mankind and for the civilization and for the good conduct of mankind as per guidance of the Holy Quran, the compliance of which is worship to God. The physical universe ends on the 'Appointed Day' with the 'Doom' of the universe but man still remains in transit for the 'Hereafter' where he is resurrected for 'Accountability' and 'Judgement' for the requital of his deeds where he will be awarded Paradise or Hell as the case may be. Man will become immortal in the eternal world of the Hereafter. In this way, God completes His cycle of the creation of first man Adam in the Paradise, then the reproduction of Adam's race in the earth in the physical universe and then the transit of man after his stay in the physical world and on the Doomsday he is in the Hereafter.

On the gravitational collapse of the physical world, the resurrection of man shall take place in the eternal world of the Hereafter. Man's good conduct in the light of the Holy Quran, which spans the two worlds in knowledge, is pivotal for the eternal fate and position of man in the Hereafter. The Hereafter is the world of comforts where man will get all that for which his soul desires and is a very pleasing world.

The Holy Quran therefore guides man that the creation of the universe and man are not in play. It is not something by chance. It is not something by itself. It is all with a purpose. There is a Creator behind all the creations of the Universe and man. All things are in His notice and are on Record and are at His Command. The gravitational collapse of the universe and the death of man are not something 'final', or the end of everything, in the sense that man shall be revived back to life and resurrected on the Doomsday. In reality man is in transit to another world, which is an absolute reality but is beyond the power of understanding and the comprehension of man. The divine Book of the Holy Quran confirms its certainty and its reality. Even as an inference one can draw such conclusions i.e. the certainty of the Hereafter from the study of the physical realities revealed by the Holy Quran. The amazing and miraculous agreement between science and the Holy Quran describing recently known physical realities as back as 1400 years ago enables man to take a leap of faith and believe in the doctrines of Eschatology of the Holy Quran.

The Holy Quran assures mankind that after the gravitational collapse of the universe or the Doom of the Universe, Allah shall re-emerge a universe and an earth, similar to or the like of the present universe and the present earth.

A man with knowledge and faith will understand the revelations of the Holy Quran which spans the realities of the Physical universe and the realities of the 'Hereafter'. Islam is the Chosen religion of God for man. So, man must follow its doctrines in his own interest as it is in the interest of all mankind.

It is obligatory on man who is a creature inspired with conscience to know his Creator and to obey and submit to His Will as revealed in the Holy Quran. The creature must worship his Creator and obey Him in the light of His message. Man is therefore, on constant trial. Man must obey God so that after his accountability he is blessed with Allah's mercy to find a place for himself in the Paradise, the eternal abode for man full of comforts and highly pleasing. Man must avoid the displeasure of God to avoid Hell which is the place for the sinners and for the ungrateful disbelievers.

The need for improved translation of the Holy Quran, using befitting language and corresponding words to convey clear sense as near to the original script as possible.

With the increase in knowledge of physical sciences and with greater understanding of the Holy Quran and with the amazing similarity of sciences with the Quranic revelations, and the interpretation (in events) taking place, it is very necessary to undertake fresh and more appropriate translation of the Holy Quran in coordination with the linguists and specialists in diversified knowledge of physical sciences so as to grasp and understand the correct sense and the substance which the Holy Quran mentions about the knowledge in each field and aspect of the physical universe and man. Accurate and proper sense-conveying translation of the Holy Quran by choosing corresponding words or equivalent and appropriate words by a team of exegesists specializing in all disciplines of science which the Quranic verses reveal shall be of far reaching consequences in properly understanding and in spreading God's message to all mankind, and to enlighten them with proper sense and substance of the revelations so that men may understand and follow the text of the Holy Quran by its proper translation in other languages and follow its sense properly and believe in it in their own interest so that God may have His mercy on them in this world as well as in the world of the 'Hereafter,' which is most certain and which is the eternal abode of mankind.

In reality there is a tremendous need for the preparation of 'Encyclopaedia the Holy Quran' to grasp and explain the text of the Holy verses in the context of science where proper explanation of the Quranic verses can be made for greater understanding by the Specialists and Scientists with the help of linguists in the context of the diversified knowledge of physical sciences. The preparation of an 'Encyclopaedia the Holy Quran' will be a great service to humanity for understanding and enlighting them of God's message and help them in having the faith and the belief in One God the Creator of heavens and the earth and of all that which is in between them and of mankind, and have firm faith in the Holy Quran as His

Message to all mankind and the faith in Prophet Muhammad (PBUH) as His Last Messenger on whom the Holy Qurân was revealed.

The preparation of 'Encyclopaedia the Holy Quran' is highly essential to explain specially the allegorial sense of the Holy verses in the context of the diversified knowledge of all modern sciences revealing the arcane meanings and physical facts at the level of molecular biology and particle physics. The Holy verses revealed by indicating and by giving hints in allegory or in direct form about the concepts and basic principles of all matters and of the Creation of matter and energy and about man. The Holy Quran reveals about the working of the universe as a whole, and about its fate and about the creation, reproduction of man and his ultimate fate in the eternal world of the 'Hereafter.' It is vital for mankind to understand the Holy Message of Quran and as such, a proper 'Encyclopaedia the Holy Quran' containing the explanation of such Holy verses in the context of science is highly essential so as to understand the sense and the meanings behid the literal words of the verses of the Holy Quran as far as man's understanding goes.

The Essence of Conclusion

This is a study of the Holy Quran, in the context of most modern and diversified knowledge of sciences, revealing astounding facts of science in complete agreement with the Holy Quran on the origin of life, universe and man at the level of molecular biology, cell biology, DNA, genetic engineering and chromosomes, and particle physics, black holes, singularity and zero volume.

There is a unique similarity of science with the Holy Quran on the Creation of the Universe, and on its working as a whole and on its expansion and its inviolability and its gravitational collapse and then its re-emergence. The Holy Quranic verses revealed 1400 years ago are so clear that it bewilders scientists and men of learning and prove that the Holy Quran is not man-made and cannot be man-made. This study also shows complete concord of science to an astonishing degree with the Holy Quran on extra-terrestrial life in universe. There is an amazing revelation in the Holy Quran which invites mankind to initiate space travel. Science is surprisingly in agreement with the Holy Quran right from the creation of the first man in human form to his broadcast in earth where man's spores or seed or sperms are sown broadcast in earth to grow as a growth in earth and on the reproduction of man in the womb of mother revealing various stages as how life begins.

This study explains 'time concept' of man in various stages, including while asleep and on death and on Resurrection. It also shows that the 'Life' in man is different than the 'Spirit' in man. This study includes the Quranic description of the Oneness of God the Creator of all things and of the 'Hereafter'. It also explains the doctrines of Eschatology in the context of knowledge, wisdom and faith. This study covers the Quranic description of Jinns an invisible living creation created out of fire and of the Angels and many other mysterious and awe inspiring realities of man and of the divine miracles performed through Prophets and of Universe and of the metaphysical world of the 'Hereafter'. It is a study of the Holy

Message of God for man who is on constant trial for obeying God's will and all this is explained in the context of the knowledge of diversified sciences, conscience and reasons, wisdom and faith. It reveals the fate of the universe and the fate of mankind and reveals the eternal abode of mankind on gravitational Collapse of universe.

Bibliography

MAIN REFERENCE

THE HOLY QURAN: The Divine Revelation, the last Message of God for all mankind in Arabic revealed on the last Prophet Muhammad (PBUH), through Angel Gabriel, at Mount HIRA near MECCA, 1400 years ago in Saudi Arabia.

PREAMBLE TO BIBLIOGRAPHY

The study of the Holy Quran in the context of the knowledge of all sciences and their diversified fields, reveals that whatever physical facts are so far known to man in the shape of latest discoveries, physical laws, theories, hypothesis, processes and phenomena are found to be already present in the Holy Quran wherein the basic concepts in conclusive form are mentioned either in allegory or in direct form. The similarity and agreement of modern science with the Holy Quran revealed 1400 years ago, is most bewildering, amazing and miraculous, as modern knowledge has hardly a beginning of one hundred years. It is surprising to find that the Holy Quran reveals wisdom, knowledge and information about life at the level of molecular biology, cell biology, DNA, genetic engineering, genetic destiny and beyond and about the universe (matter and energy) at the level of particle physics, singularity, zero volume and beyond.

The study of the holy Quran, in the light of science or knowledge, leads to the absolute conclusion that it is the word of God, the Message of Allah for all mankind, Who is the Creator of all things and of mankind and of all creatures and creations.

The stunning similarity of science about creation of universe and man with the Holy Quran, and the understanding of the Quran with sound knowledge of science, leads to the absolute conclusion that the sense encompassed in the Holy Quranic verses is 'Absolute Science', or 'Absolute Truth', as it is the Divine word, the word of Allah, the Creator, Who is the Knower of all His Creations.

The books mentioned in the bibliography and the References given, on the work and concepts of scientists are the scientific efforts on the part of man to know physical facts and is the means to understand the substance and the sense encompassed in the Holy Quran, the word of God, the Book of God for the guidance of all mankind.

LIST OF REFERENCES

1. **The Holy Quran**: English Translation by Pickthal Muhammad Marmaduke and Urdu Translation by Maulana Fateh Mohammad. Published by Taj Company Ltd., Lahore, Karachi, Rawalpindi, 1930, 1935.
2. **Encyclopaedia Britannica**: New York, 1979, (30 Volumes. 1980 and 1981 book of the year).
3. **The Bible, the Quran and Science**: Dr. Morris Bucaille, Paris, 1976.
4. **Reader's Digest Library of Modern Knowledge**: 2nd Edition, London, 1979.
5. **Touching. The Human significance of the skin**: Ashley Montagu, 2nd Edition, London, 1978.
6. **The stages of Human Life**: J. Lionel Taylor, page 157, 1921.
7. **Evolution from space**: Sir Fred Hoyle and Chandra Wickramasinghe. England, 1982.
8. **Life Itself (its origin & nature)**: Dr. Francis Crick, Biologist, (U.S.A.)
9. **'Life Cloud'**: Sir Fred Hoyle and Chandra Wickramasinghe, 1978, London.
10. **The Seeds of Life**: Francis Crick, Discover October, 1981. News Magazine, Los Angeles, California.
11. **Napoleon Bona-Parte-et l' Islam**: Cherfils, Paris
12. **News-week**: Madison Avenue, New York. N.Y., Vol XCIX No. 9 No:11, March 1, and March 15, 1982.
13. **Electronics**: Article titled, 'They're close to deciding THE FATE OF THE UNIVERSE', Australia, Sydney,

Article by Peter Gwynne, Published by Magazine Printers Pty Ltd, Sydney, July, 1981.

14. **Science 81 and Science 82**: American Association for Advancement of Science, Washington, 1981 (Full year) and February, 1982.
15. **Discover**: The News Magazine of Science published by Time Inc, Los Angeles. Full year, 1981 to March, 1982.
16. **The Quran Muhammad's Perpetual Miracle**: Islamic productions, 5937 E Pima Street, Tucsen, Arizona 85712, U.S.A., 1976.
17. **Gray's Anatomy**: 36th Edition, Williams and Warwick, Churchill, Livingstone, London, New York, 1980.
18. **Medical Embryology**: Jan Langman, M.D., Ph.D. Professor of Anatomy, University of Virginia, Charlothesville.
19. **Haper's Review of Biochemistry**: D. W. Martin, P. A. Mayes, V. W. Rodwell, Lange Medical Publications, Los Altos, California.
20. **G. A. Gescheider. 'Cutaneous Sound Localization'**: (Ph.D. diss; University of Verginai, 1964, Dissertation Abstract, Vol: 25 (1964) No: 6, 3701.
21. **'What Causes Aging'**: Article by Ben Patrusky, under Mysteries, Science 82, Volume 3, No. 1, February, 1982, Page 112.
22. **Probing the Mysteries of the Galaxies**: Published by Reader's Digest, August, 1979 by Timothy Ferris.
23. **From Whence We Came**: Barbara Krasnoff publishes in 'Future Life' Magazine, September 1981.
24. **President Ronald Regan's Speech**: On August 22, 1980.
25. **'Exploring the Naked Singularity'**: Paul Davies Physicist, Published by Science Digest May 1982.
26. Dr. Albert Einstein's Speical Theory of Relativity.
27. Dr. Albert Einstein's General Theory of Relativity.
28. Dr. Albert Einstein's Relation.
29. Quantum Mechanics.
30. Quantum Theory of Light.
31. Physical Constancy of the velocity of light.

32. Darwin's Theory of Evolution.
33. Dr. Salam's (with two collegues) Theory of Unification of the fundamental laws.
34. Law of casualty.
35. Newton's Laws of Motion.
36. Dr. Edwin Hubble's Law of Expanding Universe.
37. Laws of Conservation of matter and energy.
38. Laws of Thermodynamics.
39. Law of definite proportion.
40. Quantum theory of Incomprehensibility.
41. Process of anihilation and the process of electron-positron creation.
42. Nuclear fusion and Radio-activity.
43. Conservation of matter and energy.
44. The Process of photosynthesis.
45. The Phenomenan of singularity and zero volume.
46. Dr. Albert Einstein. Physicist.
47. Dr. John Archibald Wheeler, Astro-Physicist, University of Taxas.
48. Dr. Stephen Hawking, British Astrophysicist, Cambridge University, England.
49. Dr. Penrose, Physicist, England.
50. Niels Bohr, Danish Physicist.
51. Max Planck German Physicist.
52. Sir Fred Hoyle British Astrophysicist.
53. Chandra Wickermasinghe, Sri Lanca born Astrophysicist University College, Cardiff, in Wales.
54. Arrhencus Physicist, Swedish.
55. Armand Delesmme Astrophysicist.
56. John L. Wilhelm Astrophysicist.
57. J.B.S. Haldone British Astronomer.
58. Dr. Don Page Physicist U.S.A.
59. Dr. Randall Mckee, Physicist U.S.A.
60. Fitch and (Physicist).
61. Cronin, Physicist.
62. Andrei Sakharov Russian Physicist.
63. Dr. Robert Jestrow Director NASA's. Goddard Institute for Space Studies, Professor of Astronomy and Geology at the Columbia University.
64. Herbert Gursky, Astrophysicist of Harvard Smithsonian Centre for Astrophysics, U.S.A

65. Freeman Dyson, (Physicist) of the Institute for Advance Study, U.S.A.
66. Paul Davies, Theoratical Physicist, University of New Castle-Upon-Tyne
67. Heinz R. Pagels, associate Professor of Physics at Rockefeller University, New York City.
68. Dr. Francis Crick, Simon & Schuster, Biologist U.S.A.
69. Dr. Wayne Moyer Executive Director of the National Association of Biology Teachers, U.S.A.
70. Dr. Miller Biologist (U.S.A.)
71. Jerry Resnick Biologist.
72. Harry Mac William of the University of Massachusetts Medical School.
73. Dr. James Watson of the University of Oregon.
74. Laurie Iten of Purdue University, Biologist.
75. Loius Pasteur Biologist, France.
76. Willium Walker of Dalhousie University Nova Scotia.
77. Billingham, Biologist, U.S.A.
78. J. Lederberg, Biologist, U.S.A.
79. Thomas Huxlay British Biologist.
80. Dr. Francis Crick and Leslie Orgel, Biologist U.S.A.
81. Dr. Andren Conway, Physiologist, U.S.A.
82. Professor Dr. Glenn Clark, Biologist.
83. Richard Cannif, Biologist, U.S.A.
84. John Hartung, Biologist, U.S.A.
85. Stephen Jay Gould, Biologist, U.S.A.

THE STUDY AND KNOWLEDGE ABOUT:

Human Life as Living matter and (the inner man)

- The incredible DNA the Chemical Code as the basic matter of life, the molecule that tells cells how to function and how they should reproduce.
- The molecular biology, cell biology and genetic engineering in the reproduction of man in the womb of mother.

INDEX